W9-CKI-561

Brassey's Defence Yearbook 1999

Edited by

The Centre for Defence Studies,
King's College London

109th Year of Publication

BRASSEY'S
London • Washington

Editorial

First English Edition 1999

UK editorial offices: Brassey's, 583 Fulham Road, London SW6 5BY
Email: info@batsford.com Web: http://www.batsford.com
UK orders: Bailey Distribution Ltd, Unit 1, Learoyd Road, New Romney, Kent TN28 8XU

North American orders: Brassey's Inc., PO Box 960, Herndon, VA 22070, USA

Library of Congress Cataloging in Publication Data
available

British Library Cataloguing in Publication Data
A catalogue record for this book is available from the British Library

ISBN 1 85753 297 X Hardcover

Typset by Hedgehog
Printed in Great Britain by
Polestar Wheatons Ltd, Exeter

Centre for Defence Studies

KING'S COLLEGE, STRAND, LONDON WC2R 2LS

Honorary Director

Professor Lawrence Freedman, formerly head of Policy Studies at the Royal Institute of International Affairs, has been Professor at the Department of War Studies, King's College London and is now Chairman of the Board of War Studies. In 1996 he was appointed CBE and in 1997 became the Official Historian of the Falklands Conflict.

Executive Director

Professor Michael Clarke, formerly a lecturer in International Relations at the University of Manchester and the University of Newcastle-upon-Tyne, has been a Guest Fellow at the Brookings Institution in the United States and an Associate Fellow of the Royal Institute of International Affairs. He has been Specialist Advisor to the House of Commons Foreign Affairs Committee, the House of Commons Defence Committee and the Commission of the European Union.

THE CENTRE FOR DEFENCE STUDIES was established in October 1990 at the University of London with a grant from the Ministry of Defence. It is an Associate Member of the School of Advanced Studies at the University of London and is supported in particular by the expertise of the Department of War Studies at King's College London and the Department of International Relations at the London School of Economics. The purpose of the Centre is to act as a focus for research on a wide range of defence and security issues, which it does by conducting its own research, by commissioning research from outside and by organising working groups, conferences and seminars to draw together the work of academic and policy specialists on a wide range of subjects.

The CDS runs six broad research programmes on: British Defence Policy; European Security; Technology and Arms Control; Perspectives on Security; Comparative International Security; and North / South Defence and Security. It organises 40–50 meetings and seminars each year and pursues an active publications programme.

PUBLICATIONS

Among a wide range of publications the CDS produces:

Special Discussion Papers

United Kingdom Defence Policy in the 1990s, 1992, A4, 38pp, £5.00.
Russia: A State of Emergency? 1993, A4, 60pp, £5.00.
A Common Foreign and Security Policy for Europe: The Inter-Governmental Conference of 1996, 1995, A4, 53pp, £5.50.

Britain's Defence and Security to the Year 2000, 1998, A4, 60pp, £7.50.

The London Defence Studies: an annual package of six expertly researched papers plus occasional Briefing Papers; available on subscription at £79 per annum from Turpin Distribution Services Ltd., Blackhorse Road, Letchworth, Herts, SG6 1HN, UK. Individual copies may be obtained at £14.00 each. Titles to date are:

1 *The Gulf Crisis I:* Susan Willett
2 *The Gulf Crisis II:* James Gow, Efraim Karsh, Julian Thompson, Martin Navias
3 *The Crisis in Soviet Military Reform:* Elaine Holoboff
4 *The Prospects for British and European Space Programmes:* Bhupendra Jasani
5 *Yugoslav Endgames: Civil Strife and Inter-State Conflicts:* James Gow
6 *Saddam's Scud War and Ballistic Missile Proliferation:* Martin Navias
7 *The Soviet Military Withdrawal from Central Europe:* Henry Plater-Zyberk
8 *Nuclear Weapons and the Future of European Security:* Beatrice Heuser, Robert O'Neill, Lawrence Freedman, David Yost, Catherine Kelleher
9 *The Politics of Global Warming:* Norman Moss
10 *The Balkan Agenda: Security and Regionalism in the New Europe:* Spyros Economides
11 *Peace-Making, Peace-Keeping: European Security and the Yugoslav Wars:* James Gow and James Smith
12 *Russia: The New Foreign Policy and Security Agenda:* Sergei Karaganov
13 *Arms Control Today:* Sir Hugh Beach
14 *Security Issues of the Ex-Soviet Central Asian Republics:* Maxim Shashenkov
15 *The British Army and NATO's Rapid Reaction Corps:* Colin McInnes
16 *The Western European Union: Pillar of NATO or Defence Arm of*

the EC?: Julia A. Myers
17 *The Defence Select Committee 1979–92:* Oonagh McDonald
18 *Germany and the Future of European Security:* Christoph Bluth
19 *African Conflicts: The Future Without the Cold War*: Abiodun Alao
20 *The Diffusion of Small Arms and Light Weapon in Pakistan and Northern India:* Chris Smith
21 *Peace Conference on Former Yugoslavia: The Politico-Military Interface:* Graham Messervy-Whiting
22 *NATO and Mediterranean Security The New Central Region:* Mark Stenhouse and Bruce George
23 *Eurofighter 2000:* Susan Willett, Philip Gummett and Michael Clarke
24 *The Ambivalence of the US to United Nations Peacekeeping Operations:* Paul Mansell
25 *Crime in Russia: The International Implications:* Anton Surikov
26 *The Future for the Defence Estate: Changing Demands for Army Training:* James Savage
27 *Ballistic Missile Defence: A British Perspective:* Neville Brown
28 *The Evolution of NATO: The Brussels Summit and Beyond:* MJJ de Weger
29 *Crisis for Estonia? Russia, Estonia and a Post-Chechen Cold War:* Graeme Herd with Ene Rôngelep and Anton Surikov
30/31 *The Framework of United Kingdom Defence Policy:* Malcolm Rifkind
32 *Embracing the Octopus: The Integration of European Naval Forces:* Michael Codner
33 *Post-Mortem on UNPROFOR:* Richard Caplan
34 *Sub-Strategic Trident: a Slow Burning Fuse:* Paul Rogers
35 *Arms Control and Proliferation: Russia and International Security After the Cold War:* Christoph Bluth
36 *France's Defence Reforms: The 'Challenge of Empiricism':* Edwina Campbell
37 *NATO Expansion and European Security:* Michael MccGwire
38 *British Intelligence Towards the Millennium: Issues and Opportunities:* Michael Herman
39 *The Military and Social Change: A Personnel Strategy for the British Armed Forces:* Christopher Dandeker and Fiona Patten
40 *Security and Democracy: Civil Military Relations in Central and Eastern Europe:* James Gow and Carole Birch
41 *British Maritime Power: Historical, Security and Military Perspectives:* Christopher Coker, Michael Clarke and Colin McInnes

Contents

Preface to the 109th Edition

The 109th Edition of *Brassey's Defence Yearbook* retains some of the features of previous years and opens up new areas in its mission to provide commentary and analysis on current and emerging themes in defence and security issues. In keeping with previous years, the intention is not to offer a chronicle of events, nor a comprehensive overview of developments throughout the field. This approach is amply covered in and by other yearbooks in the field of security studies, which provide an admirable survey of regional or sectoral developments in ways which are unnecessary to attempt to duplicate here. The aim of the Centre for Defence Studies (CDS) remains what it has been since it assumed responsibility for editing the *Yearbook* in 1992: namely, to distil a number of the new and continuing trends and perspectives which have brought their influence to bear on contemporary defence and security studies. Perhaps more than in previous years, the attempt to incorporate new areas of thinking within the multiple and inter-related areas which impinge on military, defence and security studies is reflected in this year's selection and division of topics. The intention is nevertheless to maintain the distinguished tradition of the Brassey's *Yearbook*, which achieved such a unique place in the field of military studies, defence policy and security studies over more than a century. As a product now of the CDS, and in reflection of the interests and expertise of the publishers, Brassey's, the volume has evolved to encompass our own emphasis on current policy issues, building upon the original research we and our colleagues in the field conduct.

The division of the *Yearbook* into major sections reflects most, if not all, of our evolving research areas. As an institution currently establishing and consolidating new programmes and areas of research, it was felt appropriate this year that the CDS should focus particularly on what is most innovative in our work in 1998-99. The areas that come most immediately to mind are the Complex Emergencies Unit and the Security Sector Reform Unit, the latter arising out of the existing North-South Programme. It is here that the greatest challenges to evolving definitions of the scope of defence and security policy have arisen in a conceptual as well as empirical sense. This is one reason why each section is preceded by a conceptual outline of relevance to the issues detailed in the chapters that follow. Other more established areas of research do not, however, escape the logic of a conceptual re-evaluation as we move closer towards the end of the twentieth century. In the field of British Defence policy, for example, new possibilities for research and reflection have arisen following the UK's 1998 Strategic defence Review, the emergence of an agenda for peace following the Good Friday Agreement in Northern Ireland, and the prospects for greater British activism and leadership in European defence initiatives. The scope for research into European and regional security issues has been broadened by recent and on-going developments in Russia, the celebration of NATO's fiftieth anniversary in April 1999 and by the continuing demands for policy responses to the demands of states and regions on Europe's periphery. These include the Mediterranean and Middle East to the south and the Balkans to the south-east, where CDS enjoys existing expertise and is expanding its practical and conceptual research. Our global focus, however, continues apace in an era in which – as the Asian economic meltdown has demonstrated – events in one part of the world cannot be studied in isolation from their impacts on another. It is no accident that CDS's new areas of research are not geopolitically defined, nor constrained by boundaries, whether of region or even discipline. The meeting points between humanitarian assistance, peace support operations, development issues and broader defence and security agendas have now been firmly established in ways which lend new credence to a growing sense that only cross-sectoral and strategically integrated approaches will rise to the challenges currently facing policy-makers across the globe. Perhaps this is nowhere more evident than in the sphere of arms control where developments in 1998 in the sphere of nuclear testing and chemical and biological weapons proliferation have made cooperative efforts towards negotiated – and verifiable – regimes all the more pertinent.

In commissioning these chapters, we ask our authors to focus on the trends and developments in their spheres of research and practical experience which have, in their view, most bearing on the future of the challenges and questions under examination. In this way, we hope to stimulate reflection on areas which may require sustained attention over the coming months, as well as pointing out, from a London base, what we consider to be the directions in which defence and security agendas are heading. Over a number of years, the contributions to successive editions of the *Yearbook* have sought to capture some of the flavour of an era of turbulent international change. Readers will be able to judge for themselves the success of this endeavour, especially fraught with risks in 1999 due to the absence on a brief sabbatical of the *Yearbook's* General Editor-in-chief, Professor Michael Clarke. Standing in for his extremely competent direction has of necessity required a team effort, without which the volume would have languished further into 1999. My personal thanks are therefore extended to Jen Smith, Lucy Leach, David Martin Jones, Mike Smith and Ken Aldred for their invaluable editorial assistance at crucial moments in its production.

Claire Spencer
General Editor

BRITISH AND EUROPEAN SECURITY

1
Forces of Change in European Security

MICHAEL CLARKE

Executive Director, Centre for Defence Studies, King's College London

The end of the Cold War was less significant for Europe than is commonly assumed. The removal of the Berlin Wall in 1989 and the demise of the Soviet Union at the end of 1991 were the culmination of five years of astonishment as the massive psychological edifice of the Cold War rapidly collapsed during the second half of the 1980s. The fact that communist Europe was dismantled so easily – from the inside – in a generally bloodless political revolution that embraced nine European countries of almost 400 million people provides a strong clue that other powerful forces were almost certainly at work in such a historic turnaround. As we struggle to understand contemporary Europe we should realise that the Cold War did not end only because one of the collective protagonists collapsed; our interest should centre more on the causes of that collapse and the broader trends that undermined the dynamics of the Cold War and have set the main directions of evolution for the whole of contemporary Europe.

Of course, the formal termination of the Cold War was not a trivial occurrence, since it dramatised the process of change, increased the velocity of domestic upheavals, and pointed to the need (not so far adequately met) for new political thinking about security across Europe. But the Cold War had, for some 20 years before 1989, been a conceptual security template across the continent that bore steadily less relation to the substance of defence policies of most European countries. We must look elsewhere, therefore, for the forces and trends which changed the underlying reality of European security and which, since 1991, we have inherited as the conditions of the continent's contemporary security.

The most general condition of our security must be counted as the growth of deep international interdependence and the steady emergence of the global marketplace after three generations of managed international trade and finance. This has had a major effect on world politics during the last quarter century; no more so than in Europe, where interdependence is at its deepest and most intense. It is deep because the economies of Western Europe are mutually penetrated to a low level by manufacturing and service industries that operate internationally both in Europe and globally; and it is at an intense level since there is a cluster of 16 wealthy countries (excluding statelets) inside little more than half of the smallest of the continents – densely populated, very diverse but also highly institutionalised.[1] This concentration of wealth, with a combined GDP of $8,359 billion in 1997,[2] and organisation across so many contiguous countries has produced an intensity of interdependence that has no historical parallel.[3]

Such interdependence may be regarded as a general and pervasive condition of modern European security. Unfortunately, 'interdependence' is more a description or a shorthand for a number of interlocking trends rather than a discernible force in itself. Nor does interdependence develop in a consistent way, as some of the earlier analysts assumed it might.[4] The effects of international interdependence on global and national society are patchy. Some economic sectors (such as finance, energy, traditional manufacturing) are more obviously interdependent than others (such as legal services, non-oil extractive industries, major national utilities[5]). And though interdependence poses management problems in an international way, it does not necessarily promote similarly international solutions. Where problems become so complex as to defeat the imagination of politicians, governments frequently dash for partial and inadequate national solutions that they *can* understand rather than trust their fate to a complex international regime that they cannot.

So the acceptance of the force of interdependence and of the undoubted power of the global marketplace does not get us very far in understanding the specifics of contemporary European security, since the phenomena they refer to apply to all aspects of European politics; and in highly differential ways from sector to sector. Because they constitute a general condition of existence in contemporary Europe, they tell us everything and nothing. To grasp the long-standing causes of structural change in European security, it is more illuminating to examine some of the second-order effects (and in some cases, causes) of the highly interdependent global marketplace.

THE CHANGING ROLE OF THE SUPERPOWERS IN EUROPE

The first long-term factor that suggests itself as a derivative of the interdependence phenomenon is the changing role of each of the two superpowers. The USA is Europe's political superpower; the Soviet Union, and now Russia, is Europe's geographical one. Both they, and the Europeans, find these roles inescapable. In the modern world the USA does not have a realistic isolationist option, partly because of the growth of interdependence, and partly because its only true period of isolationism – in the nineteenth century – was facilitated by a British security umbrella, for which the US will not find another counterpart in the twenty-first. US interests and involvement in Europe may not remain pre-eminent on Washington's agenda, but they will always be highly significant. The other side of the equation, Russia, cannot alter the facts of geography or demography. For a country of 147 million people, 81% of whom are Russian, and the majority of whom live in the west of the country, a major impact on the European continent is unavoidable. Whether the policy in Moscow is cooperative, hostile, or Asian-orientated, the fact is that most Russians live closest to the markets and attractions of Scandinavia and central Europe, and if their economic activity does not eventually have a significant impact on their western neighbours, then their social problems almost certainly will.

Nevertheless, both superpowers are now playing different roles in relation to Europe. The United States is faced with a not very united – but increasingly economically successful – Europe that provides both sustenance and competition for US corporations. Despite Congressional reservations about the implications of European monetary union and the national competition that it implies with North America, the fact remains that US companies have a strong interest in the success of this venture, promising as it does to lower their costs and further develop a sophisticated market of over 400 million consumers. Europe's economic success also changes fundamentally, in the post-Cold War environment, the basic assumption upon which the transatlantic security relationship was always firmly based – that west Europeans alone are not capable of meeting their own security needs. Even wealthy west Europeans would not have been capable of dealing with a concerted Warsaw Pact attack 15 years ago. Now, however, 'the Europeans' are not merely the west Europeans; and their security problems do not revolve around resisting a major assault from the east. The Europeans, self-evidently, should now be capable of handling security challenges within their own region.

As a result of this intuitive sense of transformation in the terms of the transatlantic relationship, the United States tends to view contemporary European security concerns as three concentric circles: one covering the territory of the members of NATO – the 'Article 5 circle'; a second covering the wider Europe outside NATO, and including south-eastern Europe, the Baltic states, Ukraine, Belarus, and western Russia; and the third covering the Middle East, the Gulf and the Transcaucasus.[6] US interests in the Middle East and the Gulf are longstanding and need little explanation, but the recent interest in the Transcaucasus has added a new dimension to this third Eurasian circle. It revolves around American concerns to diversify its energy supplies. The route that new pipelines from the Caspian Sea take will be critical; either cheaply through Russia or Iran, or at twice the cost ($4 billion) through Azerbaijan, Georgia and Turkey. In November 1998 energy secretary Bill Richardson made clear that pipeline routes were a matter of security for the US. 'We are trying to move these newly-independent countries [Azerbaijan, Georgia and Armenia] towards the west,' he said, '...we've made a substantial political investment in the Caspian and its very important to us that both the pipeline map and the politics come out right'.[7] It is a moot point how much the Europeans would share such concerns.

Nevertheless, alliance politics within the first circle remains in good shape; they are highly institutionalised, well-understood and able to cope with new military missions and the evolution of NATO. Security within the second circle matters most to the Europeans, while that in the third, looms largest – and increasingly so – in US eyes. Though it has little faith in its allies collectively to deliver on an indigenous security policy, Washington expects the Europeans to be capable of dealing with their own 'second circle' security challenges; and where they are not, regards US help within this circle as a *quid pro quo* for European support in matters falling under the third circle. During the second Clinton Administration it has been made abundantly clear that European support for US leadership in matters of common interest outside the first and second 'security circles' is regarded as the only meaningful test of allied burden-sharing that Washington is prepared to recognise.[8] It also includes some functional concerns such as support for US counter-proliferation initiatives in the face of more diverse weapons of mass destruction and for more assertive approaches to anti-terrorism. These trends of thought have been clear in recent years, but the fact that the first circle has remained in such good order, and that since 1995 the Europeans have lined up behind the Dayton Accords on Bosnia, has tended to obscure the longer term importance of them.[9]

The role of Russia in Europe is also changing, though much more radically and in ways that were never, and are still not, well-understood in the west. The end of the Cold War did not change Russia so much as the long-term crisis of government and economy that had become manifest from the mid-1970s in the USSR made the Cold War an insupportable pursuit, and the Soviet Union itself, an unsustainable political community. This has left Russia with unenviable political and economic legacies, the most important of which currently is that Russian policy suffers more from a lack of coherence than an excess of antagonism towards the external world. From around 1995 the government in Moscow has been increasingly preoccupied with coping mechanisms to weather the successive and deepening economic crises, with the social distress, criminality and economic loss of control that goes with them. Since the presidential elections of 1996, political power has become rapidly concentrated within an oligarchy around the President; an oligarchy dominated by concentrated financial and industrial interests, who cannot be divorced from the 'black economy'.[10] It is difficult to discern any particular view of the world, still less a security policy strategy, within this oligarchy. In 1991-92 more formal Russian decision-makers thought they were developing a strategic partnership with the US and NATO-Europe, but despite the Founding Act and the Euro-Atlantic Partnership Council, there is little substance, and even less sense, of partnership now among the less formal oligarchs who make policy in Moscow. Meanwhile, Russian military leaders remain very suspicious of events in Transcaucasia and regard unilateral US, or even NATO, action, without the authority of the UN or any other organisation as a growing possibility. Certainly, US/British air action against Iraq strengthens such suspicions within military circles. This general malaise does not mean that Russian policy is without any rationale in a given case; for example, in taking economic stakes in Ukrainian extractive industries, in pursuing arms exports, or in manoeuvring for position in the expectation of another major Transcaucasian crisis in 1999. But beyond reactive policy, it is presently impossible to second-guess how Russia collectively either perceives its interests in European politics, or by what means it will pursue them.

A further variable is the effect that 'economic meltdown' within Russia will have on its role in Europe. The direct economic impact is likely to be small, since Russian GDP at an optimistic maximum of $1,100 billion (1997) scarcely constitutes 12% of the European total. Its ability to raise taxes has been in severe decline since 1993, its large-scale privatisations left the economy vulnerable to speculative shocks and capital flight, and when the rouble collapsed and oil prices tumbled in August 1998 as a result of the economic crises in East Asia, the Russian economy effectively imploded. There were no structurally important economic links between Russia and most other European countries to be broken by this crisis. But apart from reinforcing the stagnation that has beset attempts at wider political reform, the importance of the current crisis is the effect it may have on weakening the power of the Russian Federation to hold its constituent parts together, and the knock-on effects of that on any instabilities within the Russian littoral states. This presents the Europeans with the prospect of a double-bind; Russian instability, economic distress and criminality exacerbating crises mainly within what the US defines as the 'second circle' of European security – the circle in which the US is least inclined to become involved – coupled with a real loss of control in Moscow. The Europeans may find themselves with no effective authority in Russia to which to appeal, or to whom to offer help, in a specific regional case. Further, a Moscow leadership that feels let down in its expectations of a 'strategic partnership' and generally alienated from the mainstream of European politics is likely to be unreceptive to appeals to common security approaches to European problems and may be completely unsympathetic to a western security agenda.[11]

It may be pointed out that in times of economic crisis the economic leverage of the external world is very high – massive loans to stabilise currencies tend to come with a heavy economic and political price; but in times of economic *meltdown* (the most acute form of modern economic crisis) and in conditions of interdependence, the external world may feel a greater need to give the aid than the recipient has to accept it, particularly where central government may have become incoherent and relatively powerless in relation to the wider national economy. Meltdown does not prevent wealthy oligarchies from maintaining their power and wealth – and their escape routes – so even the imperatives of national economic salvation may not elicit a coherent response.

POLITICAL DIFFUSION

Another general condition of long-term change in Europe has been what might be termed 'political diffusion', which has taken different forms across the continent. Four European states went out of business in the 1990s – the USSR, the GDR, Czechoslovakia and Yugoslavia – which resulted in the creation of more than 20 new or reconstituted ones, if we include all the Commonwealth of Independent States. This is both cause and effect of a process of political diffusion, and in some cases fragmentation, which has created a severe interface between hard and soft security issues across the whole continent. The south and east faces fragmentation in the form of nineteenth century-style nationalisms which have proved, in Bosnia, Albania and the Kosovo province of Yugoslavia to be remarkably antagonistic.

The states most affected by the collapse of former Yugoslavia are Albania, Bosnia, Croatia, Macedonia and the present Federal Republic of Yugoslavia (Serbia/Montenegro). While Europe and the US have taken some considerable trouble over their instabilities since 1991, the fact remains that these states are the small, economic basket cases of Europe. Their combined GDP is less than half of 1% of the European total and they have no realistic prospects of integration into any of the important European institutions that would encourage growth.[12] Having always been part of someone's empire, they are comfortable in slipping into someone's sphere of influence. But in the current absence of a self-conscious – and willing – security guarantor for the whole area, antagonisms are not easily contained and have taken on a momentum which the outside world has not had the political will to halt. Despite some indications to the contrary in Croatia and Macedonia, the general inability of these five states to be both sustainable within themselves and to cohere within a viable sub-region, has created a dependency culture in both economic and security terms that appears to go deep into their domestic political structures. It remains an open question whether, and to what extent, this might also prove to be the case in the four countries (two of which are neighbours to former Yugoslavia) bordering the Black Sea – Bulgaria, Rumania, Moldova and Ukraine, or indeed within an increasingly troubled Turkey.

The importance of recognising these pressures is that there are very few systemic forces in Europe working against them – few self-correcting mechanisms that galvanise action when crises threaten to get out of hand – mainly because the five 'Yugoslav' states and at least two of the others, command no structural place in Europe's economy or politics. They are net sources of weakness: conduits for terrorism, illegal arms, crime and black holes for the political initiatives of comfortable nations whose involvement need only ever be indirect.[13] The effects of these developments are manifested in the growth of complex emergencies and our reactions to them as 'complex emergencies'. This is reflected in an unwillingness to become completely involved in what are governmental and economic collapses as much as security vacuums as well as attempts to facilitate indigenous reconstruction with a little 'pump-priming' from the outside, where, in reality, there is little solid to reconstruct and an international environment that is anyway unfavourable to sustained political and economic development. Complex emergencies have also induced a growing awareness of the changes that this implies for the use of armed forces. The political cost-exchange ratio of force is declining (i.e. more force has to be put 'in' to get a relatively modest political result 'out') yet the economic and social alternatives in terms of crisis alleviation or even prevention are expensive in absolute terms – if not ultimately in relative terms – and very difficult to activate among democracies who are beset with other challenges on a number of fronts. It is unlikely that European states will respond to any further crises of fragmentation with more effective instruments than have been deployed so far.

Aside from the separate issue of the future of Russia, the north and west of Europe faces political diffusion in more subtle, but no less important, ways. Here, political power is not being fragmented or lost, so much as devolved to sub-state actors in the form of regionalisation within countries, and economic diffusion from central economic managers to private firms and groups, whilst sovereign authority is being rapidly shared, and in some cases clearly diminished, by integration processes throughout the rich states of the European Union. It has become a condition of contemporary European politics that there are few economic, foreign or security issues on which any one government alone has sufficient competence to act effectively. Political power has to be diffused and sovereignty shared as a coping mechanism to meet the challenges. Though the rhetoric of many past and present European politicians would seek to deny it, modern European governments have to shed important areas of their centralised powers to survive.

EUROPEAN INSTITUTIONAL EVOLUTION

One of the most important effects of deep and pervasive interdependence in the global market is the way in which it promotes increasing institutionalisation among nations. Some forms of institutionalisation are more enlightened than others. As was pointed out above, interdependence does not *automatically* promote international responses, and the number of international meetings is not an indicator of the strength of international action that will flow from them. Governments frequently enter multinational forums only to promote narrowly national agendas. Nevertheless, one of the distinguishing features of modern Europe is the intensity and extent of the institutional web which developed among the west Europeans and is now being extended throughout central and eastern Europe. This web takes two general forms. One is the rapid growth of European-based international regimes in a number of economic and social sectors, such as automobile production, aerospace manufacturing, oil distribution, civil air traffic control, and increasingly in European policing. The greatest of all in this category is the attempt to build European Monetary Union, which from this year takes the form of what could be called a grand regime. Such constructs are certainly not exclusive – American and Japanese companies are deeply embedded in automobile and aerospace production, for example – but they are based around European capacities and can reasonably be described as European, as opposed to global, regimes. Such regimes affect the security calculus in Europe: they institutionalise the facts of interdependence and make challenges to any aspect of European security inescapable.

Regardless of what European politicians addressed in their high policy councils in NATO or the EU after 1991, for example, the crisis occasioned by the collapse of Yugoslavia, came automatically onto the agendas of the OSCE, the Council of Europe, the European Investment Bank, the International Air Traffic Control Authority, the European Transport Association, and the Danube Commission, to name but a few; in the same way that the implications of reunification for the German economy remains automatically on the agendas of the OECD, the Group of Seven, the UNECE and so on.[14]

The other form that the thickening European institutional web takes is through the more obvious processes of NATO and EU enlargement, and the functional evolution of both organisations in direct response to their new membership. NATO enlargement has attracted far more attention in security circles, partly because it is happening more quickly, is more feasible, and only involves, so far, three new members; the Czech Republic, Hungary and Poland. But EU enlargement will almost certainly emerge as the more important process to European security, involving as it now does the start of accession negotiations with six new members, with another six – of variable prospects – standing hopefully in the wings.[15] Such negotiations concern a wider range of issues and a longer and more ambitious timescale. Not least, the inter-relationship between the two processes of enlargement has received very little attention and is likely to become a far more interactive business as new memberships, hard and soft security problems, and regimes and formal institutions tend to converge on new issues and crises as they arise.

Certainly, the movement of the European Union towards a greater and more independent security role, as foreshadowed by Prime Minister Tony Blair in late 1998[16] is likely to affect European security equations in a number of ways. It will undermine the stance of the four neutral members of the EU and make NATO membership a more logical step for them. Leading politicians in Austria, Sweden and Finland (though not Ireland) are already openly campaigning for NATO membership, which they anyway see as inevitable with EU enlargement to encompass new NATO entrants.[17] Further, the dual enlargement of NATO and the EU and the convergence of some security functions would, in the words of Karsten Voight, 'complete Germany's multilateral integration, already carried out in the West'.[18]

For Germany, this would represent the culmination of a process of security retrenchment, but Germany's partners, especially the United States, would have to accept the steep change in influence this would give Germany over the security future of the whole continent. Not least, such convergence would put security more explicitly on a number of other domestic agendas within the EU, whilst institutionalising 'soft security' issues within NATO. These may all be regarded as major changes in the European arena which would not come about were it not that both the EU and NATO are enlarging at the same time, albeit in different ways and for rather different reasons.

The effects of these – mutually reinforcing – forms of institutionalisation on European security are curious. The web of institutions is, itself, a symptom of stability, wealth and growing harmonisation among a range of states. It acts as a magnet to other European countries who are anxious to be included in such a wealthy security community, and already, the prospect of NATO membership can be seen to have had some beneficial effects on the security policies of aspirant members such as Rumania and Bulgaria who are keen to meet the criteria for membership as soon as possible. In addition, the web of institutions makes it more difficult for the security of any one part of the continent to be divorced from that of any other. As individual nations, the Scandinavian states may feel very differently to the Mediterranean states of Europe on a number of important issues. But their politicians, bureaucrats and economic élites have to sit down in common fora all over the continent, listen to each other and trade off their differential interests in package deals that their institution can sustain. On the other hand, this degree of institutionalism can also exacerbate the opposite response and stimulate complete sclerosis in the face of complex, interdependent security problems, providing a legitimising cover for a re-nationalisation of security policy among European states. This can happen where the institutions of Europe continue to meet, issue statements, and provide all the appearances of activity where, in practice, agreement has broken down between their members, or where the political will to co-ordinate action is simply lacking. Action is therefore either not forthcoming at all, or else is unilateral. The reality of European security politics in such cases is that it again comes to resemble the exercise of multiple balances of power.

NATO grapples with this problem in acknowledging the need

to be prepared to back 'coalitions of the willing', but this only scratches the surface of the issue.[19] For if European security swings back towards the immediate, national preferences of the key military powers (the US, Britain, France and Russia) the key economic powers (the US, Germany and the Scandinavian countries) or those major powers simply closest to the problem (France in North Africa, Italy in the Balkans, or Turkey in the Transcaucasus) it may become very difficult indeed to maintain *effective*, collective approaches. Policy, as a result, will be unduly influenced by unaccountable actors – such as multinational companies – or informal ones – such as criminal syndicates trading in contraband resources, weapons, narcotics or refugees. In other words, the security benefits of deep institutionalism are great, but so are the penalties of failure. If the sophisticated institutionalism of modern Europe is unable to promote collective approaches to European security, the alternative – re-nationalisation – is likely to be more volatile, and almost certainly more dangerous, than anything Europe saw during the Cold War.

THE IMPERATIVES OF THE GLOBAL MARKETPLACE

The greater penalties of failure that interdependence puts on European institutions to perform effectively and collectively is paralleled by the imperatives of the global marketplace that have emerged in the last two decades. European institutions are faced with the prospects of meeting the new challenges or failing completely – falling back to the patterns of achievement of 20 years ago is not possible – and the task of European economic management reinforces this trend. European governments are faced not only with the need to respond to the global marketplace in order not to forfeit its benefits, but also with the need to avoid significant market failure across the continent, defined as the inability to sustain high quantitative growth through market integration.[20]

This arises because the globalised market has diminished the powers of even powerful governments, de-politicised – at least from national party politics – a number of economic management mechanisms, and dramatically increased the impact of private corporations and financial institutions on the lives of all European citizens. To some extent, the role of government in economic management has been transformed from one of regulation and promotion of domestic and foreign investment to be that of a mere facilitator and attractor of it. Nor is this a matter of national choice. According to many analyses of interdependence in Europe, modern capital and manufacturing investment is so knowledge-based and mobile, so attuned to disaggregated operations across different countries to benefit from the greatest efficiencies in production costs, taxation and geography, that, in effect, it demands that governments provide an attractive, *collective* framework for investment, which involves tighter and more harmonised qualitative frameworks of public policy in political, legal, social and ecological sectors.[21] The Multilateral Agreement on Investment, concluded through the OECD early in 1998 was precisely such an instrument which was aimed to provide a more consistent arena in which investment could take place even though it was clear it would override a number of individual national regulations.[22] It might have suited the old-fashioned multinational giants of 30 years ago to play off one government against another for the best tax breaks, but as production itself has internationalised with its ability to deliver previously undreamed-of efficiencies, the game for a far greater number of modern multinationals is now altogether different.[23] The multinationals operating in Europe support monetary union for precisely these reasons; if it succeeds it will provide an inter-governmental regime among the major economies which manages key aspects of the economic interdependence among them – in interest rates, monetary policy, synchronised growth strategies, etc. – so providing a lower cost, attractive regional economic environment in which they can operate more efficiently.[24]

A more immediate imperative demonstrated by the globalised marketplace in 1998 was how contagious, and systemic, market failure can be. The 'meltdowns' of the last year and the teetering global recession raises the question as to whether we are now witnessing the end of a 40-year bull market. Is the meltdown phenomenon the first, most dramatic change in a prevailing mood that will slow growth rates throughout Europe, create more social distress and at the same time diminish the resources and willpower to address the economic problems that will be created – and the security problems that will be exacerbated – by it? If so, then all the challenges outlined above will be harder to address successfully and we might witness in very stark terms how intense interdependence has the power to induce complete political sclerosis.

CONCLUSION

Within these four particular trends – the changing role of the superpowers, the diffusion of political authority in Europe, the growth of institutionalism and the imperatives of the global marketplace – the ways in which interdependence has affected European security can be more accurately discerned. The analyses which follow develop in more detail some of the themes outlined here: the contrasts between political processes in the NATO/EU debates and those surrounding Kosovo, the attempts to make some sort of Russian-Western and European-Mediterranean security partnership meaningful, and the struggle to define new attitudes to the use of force from the level of independent nuclear forces to political responses to terrorism.

One other general trend derived from this analysis is likely to overlay these issues, however. It is that as Europe emerges from the security perceptions that were dominated by the template of the Cold War, it is increasingly obvious that the major European powers do not have a closely shared vision of the role that the continent should play in the future. The US shows every sign of being assertive in the world – unilaterally if it cannot persuade its allies to join it.[25] Ironically, it is France which comes nearest to the US view that a more united Europe can play a global defence and security role on behalf of western democracy and liberal capitalism. Germany, which finds it so difficult not to agree with the US in all its public pronouncements, would also develop a more cohesive European security role, but with the explicit purpose of exercising it only within Europe. Germany is in no sense a globalist power. As Edwina Campbell points out, if the US had not been so used to German rhetoric that tuned into what it wanted to hear, and Bonn had not been able to delude itself so easily that it meant what it said, the difference in American and German conceptions of what European security was all about – and what it should now be for – would have been startlingly obvious. A French model of a European future would come much nearer to what the US would eventually like to see than a German one, though it still seems paradoxical to say so. Nevertheless, all the indications from this general analysis would tend towards the conclusion that a German version of Europe's security future is likely to predominate as the next two decades unfold.

This sets the British approach in a delicate context. The British see the future of transatlantic security relations very much as the US would want it to: that a European future be built on the continuing vitality and relevance of NATO; and that European nations should not be frightened to support the US in 'third circle' politics wherever possible and appropriate. This could provide the basis for some reconciliation between London, Paris and Bonn of the competing visions of Europe's security future. But Britain can only play this role from a position more committed to European integration. In the first two years of the present Labour Government, there is a good deal of circumstantial evidence that this point has been made inside Whitehall and the Cabinet; from the tone of the Strategic Defence Review to the statements of the Prime Minister at the Edinburgh summit in the autumn of 1998, and of the Chancellor in October in relation to membership of the EMU.[26] Nevertheless, it is still unclear how firmly committed the government might be to playing such a role, or how easily it might be blown off track. Not least, it is still an open question whether the British public would be prepared to make the broader political sacrifices – as opposed to the defence policy sacrifices it has frequently proved itself prepared to make – to see such a long-term policy through.

Notes

1. The core, generally contiguous, list of 16 consists of Austria, Belgium, Denmark, Finland, France, Germany, Ireland, Italy, Luxembourg, Netherlands, Norway, Portugal, Spain, Sweden, Switzerland and the United Kingdom. Greece and Turkey have less of a case for inclusion on both economic and geographical grounds, though Slovenia, the Czech Republic, Hungary and perhaps Poland might have a sustainable place in such a list.
2. In 1997 the core 16 accounted for $8,359 billion in their combined GDP, while the other 26 states of Europe (including Russia and excluding Iceland) accounted for just under $1,864 billion. By comparison, the US figure in 1997 was $8100 billion.
3. Pierre Jacquet, 'EMU: A Worthwhile Gamble', *International Affairs* 74(1) 1998, p.70.
4. See, for example, the interesting essays in, R.O. Keohane and J.S. Nye, eds., *Transnational Relations and World Politics* Cambridge, MA., Harvard U.P., 1971.

[5] Privatised national utilities are increasingly owned by foreign companies in many European states, but they do not generally feature internationalised production or standardised marketing; they remain as national assets, usually within a framework of government regulation.

[6] This perspective is derived from a series of interviews with US officials and observers.

[7] Quoted in *The New York Times*, 8 November 1998, p.A8.

[8] A view distilled from interviews.

[9] See, M. Brenner, *Terms of Engagement: The United States and the European Security Identity*, Westport, Ct., Praeger, 1998, Ch.3.

[10] G. Herd, *Russia in Crisis: The Disintegration of the Federation?*, London Defence Studies 47, London, Brassey's/Centre for Defence Studies, 1998.

[11] See, for example, a trenchant analysis by Sergo A. Mikoyan, 'Russia, the United States and Regional Conflict in Eurasia', *Survival* 40(3), 1998, pp.123-4.

[12] Even if the three larger states in the region – Slovakia, Rumania and Bulgaria – are added, the combined GDP in 1997 is still barely above 1% of the European total.

[13] F/n 13: see, for example, M. Milivojevic *The Balkan Medellion* in *Jane's Intelligence Review* 7(2), February 1995, p.68; or Mark Galeotti 'The Drug Threat from Eastern Europe' *Jane's Intelligence Review* 7(ii), November 1995, p.486.

[14] Organisation of Economic Cooperation and Development; the United Nations Economic Commission for Europe; the Group of Seven is one example of the many international banking forums.

[15] The first six are Cyprus, the Czech Republic, Estonia, Hungary, Poland and Slovenia. The hopeful six are Slovakia, Latvia, Lithuania, Bulgaria, Rumania and Turkey. This takes no account of any further prospects for the troubled states of south eastern Europe.

[16] Tony Blair, 'It's Time to Repay America', *The New York Times*, 13 Nov. 1998, p.A29.

[17] *The Guardian*, 27 October, 1998, Analysis, p.4.

[18] Quoted in J. Haslam, 'Russia's Seat at the Table: A Place Denied or a Place Delayed?' *International Affairs*, 74(1) 1998, p.121.

[19] In the words of Beatrice Heuser, 'At the heart of this issue is the future of European integration'. *Transatlantic Relations: Sharing Ideals and Costs*, London, Pinter/RIIA, 1996, p.112.

[20] See, W. H. Reinicke, 'Transatlantic Economic Relations and the Globalization of the World Economy', in CeSPI, *Globalization in the Economy, Regionalization in Security?*, Rome, Centro di Studi de Politica Internazionale, 1997.

[21] This general point is finding its way into the more theoretical literature on politics and globalisation, as, for example, in, Buzan, *et.al., Security: A New Framework for Analysis*, London, Lynne Reiner Publishers, 1998, p.105-106; D. Armstrong,

'Globalization and the Social State', *Review of International Studies* 24(4), p.477.

22 'Meet the New World Government', *The Guardian*, 13 Feb. 1998.

23 'Meet the Global Factory' *The Economist*, 20 June 1998, Special report. In 1996 it was discovered that the total time required to put a can of cola on a Tesco supermarket shelf, from a bauxite mine in Australia where the aluminium was produced, to the point where the item was ready for sale, was 319 days. The can was more expensive than the cola, and only 3 hours within that 319 days was spent in activities that added value to the product. More than 14 different storage sites were involved. The scope for manufacturing efficiencies remains immense. *ibid.*, p.11.

24 Jacquet, *op. cit.*, p.58-9.

25 S. Sloan, 'The US Role in the World: Indispensable Leader or Hegemon?', Congressional Research Service, CRS Report for Congress, 97-1046 F, 10 Dec. 1997.

26 The British 'national changeover plan' for EMU was not due to be published until after the next election, but Chancellor Brown announced that it would be published before the end of January 1999. *New York Times*, 4 November 1998, p.C2.

2
Northern Ireland

CONOR A. GEARTY

Professor of Human Rights Law at King's College London

The Good Friday Agreement, concluded in Belfast on 10 April 1998, represents the most significant attempt to solve the Irish problem since the treaty agreed between the British government and the forces of Irish nationalism in December 1921. Like that treaty, it is bound profoundly to influence political developments in Britain and Ireland for decades ahead. This will be regardless of whether or not it succeeds in its aims: whatever its consequences the Agreement has profoundly transfigured political relations on these islands. At best a solution to the centuries old British-Irish problem has now been found and the historical boil that has produced so much subversive violence over so many centuries has been effectively lanced. At worst, the Agreement has changed entirely the way in which politics will be practised in the province, and in particular has made the ideas of partnership and consensus so integral to its process of self-government that a return to the Manichaean absolutism of the past now seems inherently unlikely. Some uncertainty remains over the disruptive potential of rejectionist violence, but the signs are that the conditions which precipitated such unprecedented levels of inter-communal fighting in the 1970s and 1980s are no longer present. In any event, the political process of which the Agreement has been the high point has so far managed to avoid tying its fate to ambient levels of violence, and its leadership is unlikely to permit itself to be steered in such a fatal direction.

Great uncertainty remains over the wrecking potential of the insistence by the Unionist party, one of the main parties to the Agreement, that substantive progress on its terms should depend on the decommissioning of paramilitary weapons by organisations which were not themselves parties to the Agreement but which are closely associated with others that were. Though the issue is a complex one, and provides within itself various potential solutions over a variety of time-scales, the fact remains that if the Agreement proves politically impossible to deliver for the mainstream Unionists and their leader David Trimble, it will be through an uncompromising approach to decommissioning that such a failure will be announced. There are elements to the Agreement which can be expected to survive any such collapse, however, and it is this that gives the accords their special force. The political thinking that underpins the Agreement is larger than the details on which it appears at times to depend. It is an awareness of this underlying fact that made the Good Friday breakthrough possible in the first place and it can also be expected to sustain it in good times as well as bad.

This chapter will be divided into three parts. In the first, we will set out the background to the Agreement and explain why such a pivotal achievement should have proved possible now, after so many years of seemingly inevitable failure. In the second section, we will analyse the content of the Agreement and consider the ways in which it has managed successfully to reconcile the various elements on these islands whose divisions seemed until the very last to be unbridgeable. In the third part, we will consider the prospects for the future and analyse the various ways in which the Agreement might work or not work and what the consequences in each case would be.

THE BACKGROUND TO THE AGREEMENT[1]

There is both a deep and a more immediate political background to the Good Friday Agreement. The first of these relates to the general rejection of violence as a political tool which occurred in Northern Ireland sometime during the 1990s. It is impossible to be precise about exactly how and why this occurred, but the evidence of such a trend is there, across the two communities in the province and – equally significantly – among the police and military forces charged with keeping the peace. Turning first to the republican side, it would be going too far to say that at the time the nationalist supporters of separatist violence disapproved of such quasi-military actions as the Deal barracks bombing which killed 11 in 1989 or the assassination of the Conservative MP Ian Gow the following year. But a growing sense of futility had by then begun to dilute the triumphalism with which such actions had previously been greeted, with the emphasis subsequently being less on how such violence moved politics along than on how it showed only that the IRA was still around. Even if this was enough to justify attacks on 'legitimate' targets, proof of the existence of such durable competence was hardly a sufficient reason for IRA 'mistakes', and it was in respect of the civilian casualties of the late 1980s and early 1990s that the shift away from violence became most apparent. Pivotal in this regard was the killing of 11 people at a remembrance service in Enniskillen in 1987. The IRA bombs in Warrington in March 1993 which caused the deaths of two young boys were also a sharp reminder that even the hitherto widely supported 'mainland campaign' against property targets[2] carried risks that were by now widely felt to be disproportionate to the results they produced.

Allied to this growing sense of disillusionment with violence, and deepening it further, was the emergence of a viable political alternative to the IRA in the form of Sinn Fein. The party had emerged greatly strengthened from the hunger strikes crisis of the early 1980s and had built a highly effective political machine which was strategically but not emotionally separated from the IRA. As its leadership found itself more and more successful in ordinary politics, so the violence that had earlier been their spur to success grew into an obstacle, holding the party back from even greater gains. In an important document published in 1991, *Towards a lasting peace*, the Sinn Fein leadership signalled its availability to the idea of a peace process to move the problem of Northern Ireland beyond violence. This was a project that was then enthusiastically taken up by John Hume MP, leader of the constitutional nationalist party the SDLP, and after an intense period of secret talks which intertwined with contacts that were also ongoing between the British government and the IRA, the joint Downing Street Declaration was agreed on 15 December 1993.[3] This in turn paved the way for the IRA's announcement on 31 August 1994 of a complete cessation of violence, a development that was greeted with as much relieved joy in nationalist Northern Ireland as it was in the rest of Britain and Ireland.

The extent to which the loyalist communities were also by this time prepared to contemplate an end to subversive violence only became apparent after that first IRA ceasefire was declared. The announcement of a cessation of violence, made by the Combined

Loyalist Military Command (representing the leadership of the Ulster Freedom Fighters, the Ulster Volunteer Force and Red Hand Command) on 13 October 1994, was perhaps the most remarkable and was certainly the most liberating of the movements away from violent subversion that occurred at this time. Without such a ceasefire, it was hard to credit that the IRA's self-imposed pacificism would have been long maintained; with it the political vistas unlocked by the new situation were rich and varied. The final piece in the non-violent jigsaw that came together at this time was supplied by the forces of law and order. It had been the use of unjustifiable violence by the army and the police that had over the years been as responsible as anything else for the nationalist perception that their community was an unwelcome stranger within an alien political body. The mark left by such catastrophes as internment, 'Bloody Sunday' and the 'shoot to kill' controversy of the mid-1980s had left successive generations of nationalists deeply estranged from their own state institutions. In contrast, the decade since the last and most dramatic of these events – the shooting dead of three IRA members in Gibraltar in March 1988[4] – has been mercifully free of this kind of counter-productive state violence, and the momentum for peace described above has therefore been relatively unhindered by the need to be seen to respond to official violence. Neither is it the case that the RUC and the army have not been put under strain during the same period; indeed the policing of Orange marches which has been the 'law and order' issue of the 1990s has sometimes produced tensions to rival any seen in the previous 30 years. But it is undoubtedly true that the official forces responsible for the enforcement of the law have managed to deal with disorder without at the same time provocatively adding to it. In ways, barely publicly acknowledged by any of the parties to the resolution of the Northern Ireland conflict, this has been one of the main reasons why a space for the Good Friday Agreement was found to be possible.

This broad background to the Belfast accords suggests that progress should have been made far earlier than April 1998. While this is certainly true, it fails to take account of the more immediate political context, which is the second of the two backgrounds to the Agreement to which we earlier referred and to which we now turn. It is very clear that accompanying the slow rejection of political violence at the turn of the decade was a growth in political opportunity that included but went beyond the movement of Sinn

Fein away from irredentist isolationism towards the peace process which has been described above. The Anglo-Irish Agreement in 1985 had established conclusively that the British government was interested in a political accommodation in Northern Ireland which embraced constitutional nationalist as well as unionist opinion.[5] Building on this initiative, in June 1991 the then Secretary of State for Northern Ireland, Peter Brooke, initiated the three-stranded talks process which was to form the basis of much of what eventually appeared in the Good Friday Agreement. During 1991-94, however, this was a process in which the only participants were the Northern Ireland political parties which were unconnected with paramilitary organisations. Still contaminated in official circles by their association with ongoing IRA violence, Sinn Fein were emphatically excluded from it, as were the smaller loyalist parties associated with Sinn Fein's rivals on the other side of the sectarian divide. This 'political process' was the relic of Britain's long-standing determination to achieve a solution to the Northern Ireland problem which was rooted in the non-violent centre of the province's political life and which did not need to bend its knee to the subversive extremes on either side. Moral and logical though the policy may have been, its fatal weakness was the way in which it could be undermined by tactical violence from either of the two excluded paramilitary groupings, and this is in fact what had regularly occurred since its first and most ambitious product, the Sunningdale Agreement, had been ingloriously destroyed in exactly this way in 1973-74.[6]

After the IRA and loyalist ceasefires of 1994, the way should have been clear to link the mainstream 'political process' to the 'peace process' in which John Hume, the two governments, the IRA and Sinn Fein had in various ways been involved. The momentum was however badly affected at this point by political instability in Westminster. The weakness of the Major government made imaginative movement difficult, particularly insofar as this would necessarily have involved at this juncture public negotiation with political actors who had long been stigmatised as 'terrorists'. The Unionist party was particularly disinclined to allow the political process to be swamped by a peace process of which it was deeply suspicious, and it was also more than willing to use its disproportionate power at Westminster to keep the two processes separate as long as was politically possible. The result was very slow progress, with the first meeting between ministers and Sinn Fein not taking place until 10 May 1995, and with the prior decommissioning of paramilitary weapons being increasingly insisted upon in government and unionist circles as a prerequisite for further political progress, notwithstanding the comparative solidity of the republican ceasefire. When on 22 January 1996 the British government refused to accept in full the findings of George Mitchell's international commission[7] designed to solve the decommissioning impasse, offering instead elections to a new Northern Ireland forum, it seemed only a matter of time before the IRA ceasefire would end. On 9 February, the IRA duly exploded a huge bomb at Canary Wharf, London, killing two and injuring 100, and in the process causing millions of pounds worth of damage. The Major government played out its last days with little new to offer on Ireland and was forced to endure sporadic IRA violence, much of it targeted within Britain and involving extensive destruction of property with some loss of civilian life.[8]

The election of a Labour government on 1 May 1997 clearly offered a fresh opportunity to rekindle the political momentum in Northern Ireland, but no one was prepared for the remarkable engagement with the issue shown by the incoming Prime Minister Tony Blair. Just eight days after his election victory, Blair held talks with his Irish counterpart John Bruton and four days later he found the time to meet with the leaders of the province's three main parties, John Hume of the SDLP, David Trimble of the Unionist party and Ian Paisley, leader of the DUP. On 16 May, Blair made his first trip to Northern Ireland as Prime Minister, deftly combining a public declaration of his commitment to the union with a decision to authorise talks with Sinn Fein in advance of a new ceasefire. Four days later, the transfer of two IRA prisoners from England to Northern Ireland gave a tangible indication that here was a government with an entirely fresh perspective on the province's ancient quarrel. Perhaps Blair's most decisive act of statesmanship was his failure to allow the cold-blooded killing of two police officers in Lurgan on 16 June to derail the process he had so energetically sprung back into life. Here was the clearest statement in 30 years that the 'politics of the last atrocity' were loosening their grip on Northern Ireland.

On 25 June the Prime Minister oversaw the ussuing of a joint British and Irish paper on decommissioning, telling the Commons that substantive talks on the political future of the province would begin in September and that the 'settlement train [was] leaving with or without Sinn Fein'. This intelligent gamble got its reward in the form of a second IRA cessation on 20 July and an affirmation by Sinn Fein on 9 September of its commitment to the Mitchell principles of democracy and non-violence. With David Trimble prepared to commit his party to these talks, only Ian Paisley's DUP and a fringe unionist element were missing when they finally began on 7 October. Under the astute guidance of their chairman George Mitchell, and with Blair's energetic Secretary of State Mo Mowlam in constant attendance, this talks process weathered sporadic violence designed to destroy it, the temporary expulsion of certain of its participants, and many public rows, to emerge on 10 April 1998 with an overall settlement to which all the major participants felt they could subscribe. The Agreement then secured the backing of over 70% of those who voted in the subsequent referendum in Northern Ireland, as well as an overwhelming majority of those who voted on the issue on the same day in the Republic of Ireland. For the first time since the partition of the island, the whole of Ireland had spoken with one voice, albeit in two jurisdictions, and it was to express clear support for what had been achieved in Belfast. With parliamentary support also being achieved, each of the 'triple locks' of parliament, parties and people, devised by Blair's predecessor John Major as a means of guaranteeing the legitimacy of any agreement, had been triumphantly negotiated.

THE GOOD FRIDAY AGREEMENT [9]

The core of the Agreement reflects the three-stranded approach first delineated by Peter Brooke's political process some seven years before. Strand one is entitled 'Democratic Institutions in Northern Ireland'. It provides for 'a democratically elected Assembly ... which is inclusive in its membership, capable of exercising executive and legislative authority, and subject to safeguards to protect the rights and interests of all sides of the community.'[10] This assembly is to be made up of 108 members, elected by PR (Single Transferrable Vote) from existing Westminster constituencies, and with 'full legislative and executive authority'[11] in respect of those matters which are currently within the remit of the six Northern Ireland government departments. All members will need to designate themselves as of 'nationalist, unionist or other'[12] identity. This is because key assembly decisions will be required to be taken on a 'cross-community basis', defined in the Agreement as '*either* parallel consent, i.e. a majority of those members present and voting, including a majority of the unionist and nationalist designations present and voting; *or* a weighted majority (60%) of members present and voting, including at least 40% of each of the nationalist and unionist designations present and voting.'[13] The Agreement provides that key decisions requiring this cross-community support will include election of the chair of the assembly, the making of standing orders and decisions on budget allocations.[14] In addition any decision which is the subject of 'a petition of concern brought by a significant minority of Assembly members (30/108)'[15] shall be subjected to the procedure, and if such a petition should arise the question whether to allow the matter to proceed shall be determined on a cross-community basis.[16] The effect of these various rules is to give both communities a veto over legislation and other matters. It is intended that this system of mutual vetos will stimulate political horsetrading across the community divide so markedly set in stone by the Assembly's imposition of a sectarian label on its members.

Executive authority in the new Assembly shall be discharged by 'a First Minister and Deputy First Minister and up to ten Ministers with Departmental responsibilities'.[17] The first two of these posts must be jointly filled on a cross-community basis in accordance with the procedure described above, with the other posts being allocated in a way which reflects party strength in the Assembly following the d'Hondt system.[18] A critical provision is paragraph 25 of strand one:

> An individual may be removed from office following a decision of the Assembly taken on a cross-community basis, if (s)he loses the confidence of the Assembly, voting on a cross-community basis, for failure to meet his or her responsibilities including, inter alia, those set out in the Pledge of Office.[19] Those who hold office should use only democratic, non-violent means, and those who do not should be excluded or removed from office under these provisions.

A civic forum is also envisaged by strand one, which will 'comprise representatives of the business, trade union and voluntary sectors, and such other sectors as agreed by the First Minister and the Deputy First Minister'.[20] Its function will be to 'act as a consultative mechanism on social, economic and cultural issues'. Over time the Agreement envisages the Northern Ireland Assembly securing increased power from Westminster over sensitive matters that will for the time being remain in the hands of the Secretary of State, whose office will remain after the Agreement comes into operation.[21]

Turning now to strand two, its most prominent feature is the establishment of a 'North/South Ministerial Council.' The function of the new body is 'to bring together those with executive responsibilities in Northern Ireland and the Irish Government, to develop consultation, co-operation and action within the island of Ireland – including through implementation on an all-island and cross-border basis – on matters of mutual interest within the competence of the Administrations, North and South.'[22] The complex language here betrays the senstivity with which this issue was approached by all participants to the negotiations, with some expressing suspicion of the very concept of such bodies and others seeking to achieve through them a prototype of the united Ireland to which they remained committed. The Council will meet in plenary session twice a year but also 'in specific sectoral formats on a regular and frequent basis'[23] to deal with those issues that have been passed over to it. Participation will be a duty of service for ministers in the Northern Ireland administration, so it will not be possible for such persons to debilitate the body by their refusal to attend.[24] The Agreement envisaged the identification by 31 October 1998 of at least 12 subject areas 'where co-operation and implementation for mutual benefit will take place,'[25] with an annex to strand two setting out a selection of non-prescriptive possibilities, such as agriculture, education, transport, environment, tourism, inland fisheries, and health. A particularly important feature of the Agreement is its interlocking nature, and in this regard paragraph 13 of strand two is of particular relevance:

It is understood that the North/South Ministerial Council and the Northern Ireland Assembly are mutually interdependent, and that one cannot successfully function without the other. Strand three is the least widely noticed aspect of the Agreement but it is the one with perhaps the greatest potential for dynamic development in the future. It envisages the establishment of a British-Irish Council (BIC) 'to promote the harmonious and mutually beneficial development of the totality of relationships among the peoples of these islands.'[26] Membership is to consist of 'representatives of the British and Irish

Governments, devolved institutions in Northern Ireland, Scotland and Wales, when established, and, if appropriate, elsewhere in the United Kingdom, together with representatives of the Isle of Man and the Channel Islands.'[27] The body is to meet at summit level twice per year and in specific sectoral formats on a regular basis.[28] What it will do precisely is left slightly vague, its main task being to 'exchange information, discuss, consult and use best endeavours to reach agreement on co-operation on matters of mutual interest within the competence of the relevant Administrations.'[29] It seems that what is anticipated here is discussion of such matters as transport links, and agricultural, environmental, cultural and health issues. It may be that one possible remit, 'approaches to EU issues',[30] will come over time to dominate. Members of BIC will also be able to develop bilateral or multilateral arrangements between them which will be without prejudice to BIC's wider ambitions.[31] The structure can therefore deepen, wither away completely, or throw out new more narrowly-defined roots. The success of the body will depend on whether the perceived need for it at the time of the accords is proved over time to have been well-judged. A more familiar British-Irish body will be the intergovernmental conference which is intended to supersede the framework established by the Anglo-Irish Agreement of 1985. This will allow the Irish government to retain a say on matters related to Northern Ireland which have not been devolved to the Belfast assembly. The accords also throw out the possibility of a deepening of the inter-parliamentary links between the various new elected assemblies of the various parts of the United Kingdom and Ireland, 'perhaps building on the British-Irish Interparliamentary Body'.[32]

The elements to the Agreement discussed above reflect the three-stranded nature of the 'political process' that had been maturing in Northern Ireland since the Brooke initiative first commenced in 1991. On its own, it would not have been enough to have secured the support of the parties linked to paramilitary organisations whose ceasefires had won them places at the negotiating table. It was the bundle of concessions that were made to keep these organisations onside during the days leading up to Good Friday that has given the Agreement what has proved to be its most controversial edge. In retrospect this is not surprising: the greatest difficulty was always bound to be at the intersection of the political and the peace processes. Least problematic in this regard are those provisions relating to 'rights, safeguards and equality of opportunity', set out at length in a separate section of the Agreement. Included here are such initiatives as new human rights guarantees,[33] a wide-ranging equality commission,[34] greater recognition of the suffering of the victims of violence,[35] and official recognition of the need to act on a variety of economic, social and cultural issues.[36] Much more controversial are the Agreement's various formulae on decommissioning, the reform of the Royal Ulster Constabulary (RUC) and the release of paramilitary prisoners.

As far as the first of these is concerned, the Agreement does not require prior decommissioning as a precondition for participation in the structures that it establishes. Instead, its signatories specifically draw attention to previous progress on the subject, particularly by the independent international commission on decommissioning, and 'accordingly reaffirm their commitment to the total disarmament of all paramilitary organisations.'[37] This critical passage continues:

> They also confirm their intention to continue to work constructively and in good faith with the Independent Commission, and to use any influence they may have, to achieve the decommissioning of all paramilitary arms within two years following endorsement in referendums North and South of the agreement and in the context of the implementation of the overall settlement.[38]

This paragraph goes as far as was judged possible in requiring participants to influence their paramilitary associates, but it came as an inevitable disappointment to the Unionist party which had, as we have seen, become recklessly accustomed to insisting on prior decommissioning as a precondition of political progress. Also deeply dissatisfying to that party is the Agreement's recognition that its terms provide 'the opportunity for a new beginning to policing in Northern Ireland with a police service capable of attracting and sustaining support from the community as a whole.'[39] To this end an independent commission – with terms of reference fairly precisely delineated in the Agreement[40] – is envisaged by the accords and required to report no later than summer 1999.

The most difficult aspect of the Agreement for many of its participants, not just for unionists but also to some extent across the political divide, relates to prison releases. Here the demands of the representatives of the paramilitaries, reflected in the Agreement, were at their most unpalatable to those who had worked hard in the pre-existing talks' process. Both governments promise in the Agreement to 'put in place mechanisms to provide for an accelerated programme for the release of prisoners'[41] associated with organisations whose ceasefires are judged 'complete and unequivocal'.[42] The governments go on to make clear their joint intention, 'should the circumstances allow it', that all such prisoners would be free by the end of two years after the commencement of any such early release scheme.[43] The combined effect of these three initiatives, on decommissioning, the RUC and on prisoners, was such that, as far at least as the unionist community was concerned, much of the early gloss was taken off the Agreement's headline achievements. Certain of David Trimble's colleagues on the unionist negotiating team felt unable on this basis to lend their support to the accords and those of his own party who afterwards opposed him tended to focus on these rather than on other issues. Thus, it emerged that the elements which it was thought would be the most difficult of all both to negotiate and to sell, relating to North-South bodies and power-sharing in the new Assembly in particular, turned out to be far less problematic than had been expected. To some extent, the seven years of preparation in the – at times – seemingly endless three-strands talks' process had done an effective job of preparation. It was the necessary but not nearly so well anticipated overlay of 'peace process' concerns that has proved to be the Agreement's hardest selling point.

PROSPECTS FOR THE FUTURE

The power of the Agreement and its potential durability lie in the fact that it gives every party to it some tangible achievements while also providing them with the opportunity in the future to win all that each might want. Thus every party can claim partial victory now, but also point to the chance to secure total victory in the future. In an important sense, therefore, the Agreement is less a compromise about ends than it is a reorganisation (and it is hoped a pacification) of the way in which those ends are pursued. This is clearest of all in relation to the nationalist parties, including for these purposes both the SDLP and Sinn Fein. The former has secured the power-sharing and 'Irish dimension' to the government of Northern Ireland that have been its chief immediate goals since its inception. Sinn Fein is also able to point to an extensive human rights and equality agenda in the Agreement, issues on which the party astutely focused in the run up to Good Friday and with which it has since then distracted attention from its failure to realise its more historic political goal. Unlikely though it might be thought to be, however, the Agreement by no means rules out a united Ireland. On the contrary, if it should prove to be the will of the Irish people north and south to achieve such an end, then 'it will be a binding obligation on both Governments to introduce and support in their respective Parliaments legislation to give effect to that wish.'[44] The Agreement provides for the holding of a poll in Northern Ireland to test opinion on the issue, not more frequently than once every seven years, if it 'appears likely'[45] to the Secretary of State that 'a majority of those voting would express' such a wish. The proposed changes to the Republic of Ireland's constitution likewise do not remove that jurisdiction's aspiration to territorial unity so much as modify the vehemence with which it has been expressed.[46]

Preoccupied by their concerns over decommissioning, the unionist signatories to the Agreement have been less than emphatic in identifying their short-term achievements. The union with the United Kingdom has been preserved and strengthened in the short-to-medium and perhaps also the long-term. Even if unity with the Republic of Ireland were effected, the nature of that unified body will have been profoundly affected by the Agreement. Dealing with constitutional issues, the Agreement affirms:

> that whatever choice is freely exercised by a majority of the people of Northern Ireland, the power of the sovereign government with jurisdiction there shall be exercised with rigorous impartiality on behalf of all the people in the diversity of their identities and traditions and shall be founded on the principles of full respect for, and equality of, civil, political, social and cultural rights, of freedom from discrimination for all citizens, and of parity of esteem and of just and equal treatment for the identity, ethos, and aspirations of both communities.

This is a far stronger set of substantive safeguards, even if they eventually come to be applied within an expanded Republic, than the conditional guarantee of UK membership to be found in earlier Westminster legislation, and which is now superseded by the Agreement.

There is a more profound way in which the Agreement may eventually change the way in which these islands view each other and themselves. In just a few years, it is highly likely that there will be a common currency within, as well as a common travel area between, Britain and Ireland. There will be governments of sorts in Dublin, Belfast, London, Edinburgh, Cardiff and possibly also the English regions, all connected in various ways with each other at executive and legislative levels. All these jurisdictions will be subject to a common code of law, rooted in the European Union but also in the European Convention on Human Rights. If unity with the Republic were eventually to occur, it is unlikely that the cross-border bodies laboriously created out of strand two would be casually jettisoned. The 'parity of esteem' between cultures and traditions that permeates the Agreement would be highly likely to survive any territorial transfer under its aegis. In a very real sense, therefore, it would be hard to see what Irish unity would mean were it to be eventually achieved. The genius of the Agreement may lie in the way that it preserves all the options for the future while setting in train a sequence of events that drains these goals of the debilitating negativity with which they have always been perceived by those who have not shared them.

We are left with the threat that, at the time of writing, decommissioning continues to pose for the integrity of the process as a whole. This has already delayed the identification of areas of cross-border co-operation which, as we have seen, the Agreement stated should have reached by 31 October 1998. It may be merely political ineptitude that has ballooned this essentially peripheral matter into one that has the capacity to destroy the Agreement, but this fact does not diminish its current negative importance. The two year time frame 'to achieve the decommissioning of all paramilitary arms ... in the context of the implementation of the overall settlement'[47] may not bind the subversive organisations themselves, but this does not mean that the pressure to deliver in the spirit of these words would not be overwhelming if everything else were seen to be falling into place. In some ways therefore the only true deadline in the Agreement is this one; if nothing happens on weapons despite movement on everything else, then it would be hard to resist the conclusion that those holding these arms are not serious about a permanent peace. If the Agreement collapses before then on account of decommissioning, however, it will probably have been because the Unionist party did not have the political strength to make it work. Even some months after the popular endorsement of the accords, and despite the Nobel prize it has won for its leader, it is not at all obvious that the Unionist party has the strength in depth to back its leadership on the compromises that the Agreement requires, and to which David Trimble has signed up on its behalf.

If the Agreement were to fail in a way for which the unionists were unable to deny responsibility, then it is probable that what we would see would be a fresh disentanglement of the political process from the peace process, and a new inter-governmental emphasis on the latter to the exclusion of the former. Though it is asserted that the Agreement stands or falls in its entirety, it would be improbable that the UK and Irish governments would not persevere with those parts of the Agreement which reflect the success of the peace process in having achieved a massive de-escalation in subversive violence in Britain and Ireland. In the months after the Agreement, there has been substantial progress on this agenda. Many prisoners have been released, the scale of British military activity in Northern Ireland has been markedly scaled down and the Patten Commission on the RUC has been appointed and begun work. It would be eccentric indeed not to continue with the justice and equality agenda merely because a party which was never very keen about any of these matters chose to precipitate a collapse on a separate issue entirely.[48] In an atmosphere of relative peace, with the ceasefires of the main paramilitaries being broadly adhered to, a failure of the Agreement would not lead to any hardening-up of the official position on decommissioning. In fact the reverse would be likely to occur. The pressure now on the formerly violent subversive groups would be likely to ease as the desire to placate the unionists diminished.

The negative power of the unionists lies therefore in their capacity to destroy the political aspects of the Agreement, in the form of the three strands. While this is undoubtedly true, it is not obvious what the party would gain from such an eventuality. The strand three links follow, broadly speaking, a unionist vision of these islands. While strand two is disliked by unionists, at least it allows the hated Anglo-Irish Agreement to be wound down, something that would not happen if the Good Friday accords disappeared. Strand one gives the party back its devolved assembly after a gap of over a quarter century, in a form, moreover, whose necessity for which almost all unionists now recognise to be neccessary. Rational analysis suggests that the unionists have to make the Agreement work or face political impotence while the even more despised Anglo-Irish

Agreement enjoys a new lease of life and the portions of the Good Friday accords most unattractive to them are fully promulgated over their heads. Rationality is not, however, the only precipitator of political action in Northern Ireland, or indeed anywhere else. Nor is it ever wise to dismiss out of hand the disruptive power of truly terrible political violence. The deaths caused by rejectionist IRA violence in Omagh on 15 August 1998 were a terrible reminder both of what Northern Ireland is trying to escape from and of the dangers that lurk along the way.

Notes

1. For a good general background, see Maillie, Eamon and McKittrick, David, *The Fight for Peace*, Heinemann, London, (1996).
2. The IRA bomb outside the Baltic Exchange on 10 April 1992 had claimed three victims without causing the same negative reaction to political violence.
3. Joint Declaration by the Prime Minister, Rt Hon John Major MP and the Taoiseach, Mr Albert Reynolds TD on 15 December 1993.
4. On which see *McCann v United Kingdom* (1995) 21 *European Human Rights Law Reports* 97.
5. Pl 3634 (Republic of Ireland); Cmnd 9690 (United Kingdom). See Hadden, Tom and Boyle, Kevin, *The Anglo-Irish Agreement. Commentary, Text and Official Review*, Sweet and Maxwell, London (1989).
6. See Wilson, Tom, *Ulster Conflict & Consent*, Basil Blackwell, Oxford (1989), ch. 17. A good general account is Arthur, Paul and Jeffrey, Keith, *Northern Ireland since 1968*, Basil Blackwell, Oxford (1988).
7. Report of the International Body (Senator G J Mitchell (Chairman), General John de Chastelain, Mr Harri Holkeri).
8. In particular the bomb which wrecked the Arndale Centre in Manchester on 15 June 1996.
9. Set out in Command Paper 3883. The citations that follow are taken from the text of the Agreement as agreed in Belfast in the form in which it was presented to the public on that day.
10. Strand 1, para. 1.
11. Strand 1, para. 3.
12. Strand 1, para. 6.
13. Strand 1, para. 5(d).
14. *ibid.*
15. *ibid.*
16. Strand 1, para. 13.

[17] Strand 1, para. 14.
[18] Strand 1, para. 16.
[19] Set out as Annex A to Strand 1, this includes *inter alia* a 'commitment to non-violence and exclusively peaceful and democratic means'.
[20] Strand 1, para. 34.
[21] Strand 1, para. 32.
[22] Strand 2, para. 1.
[23] Strand 2, para. 3 (ii).
[24] Strand 2, para. 2.
[25] Strand 2, para. 8.
[26] Strand 3, para. 1.
[27] Strand 3, para. 2.
[28] Strand 3, para. 3.
[29] Strand 3, para. 5.
[30] *ibid.*
[31] Strand 3, para. 10.
[32] Strand 3, para. 11.
[33] Rights, safeguards and equality of opportunity: human rights, paras. 1-10.
[34] Rights, safeguards and equality of opportunity: human rights, para. 3.
[35] Rights, safeguards and equality of opportunity: human rights, paras. 11-13.
[36] Rights, safeguards and equality of opportunity: economic, social and cultural issues, paras. 1-5.
[37] Decommissioning, para. 3.
[38] *ibid.*
[39] Policing and Justice, para. 1.
[40] In annex A: Commission on Policing for Northern Ireland.
[41] Prisoners, para. 1.
[42] At least this is implied to the extent that groups which are not maintaining such ceasefires are automatically excluded from such schemes: Prisoners, para. 2.
[43] Prisoners, para. 3.
[44] Constitutional Issues, para. 1(iv).
[45] Constitutional Issues, Annex A, schedule 1, para. 2.
[46] Constitutional Issues, para. 1(v).
[47] Decommissioning, para. 3.
[48] See Police (Northern Ireland) Act 1998; Public Processions (Northern Ireland) Act 1998.

3
Europe And The Mediterranean: Regional or Sub-Regional Security Approaches?

CLAIRE SPENCER

Deputy Director, Centre for Defence Studies, King's College London

INTRODUCTION

The Mediterranean as a focus of the attentions of policy-makers and policy analysts has undoubtedly increased in importance since the 1980s. This is partly as a result of the expansion of the European Community (EC) and the North Atlantic Treaty Organisation (NATO) southwards to include Spain (admitted to NATO in 1982 and the EC in 1986) and Greece and Portugal (admitted to the EC in 1981 and 1986 respectively). It is also a function of the search by NATO and the Western European Union (WEU) for a role to play in the regions to the south, as well as to the east, in Europe's security planning and institutional enlargement.

Because the challenges identified as originating in the Mediterranean are vague, largely human, and not focused on state-state conflicts or even military menace (unless Libya's renewed chemical and biological weapons build-up is to be fully substantiated[1]), the Mediterranean security agenda has encapsulated a series of general and hypothetical, rather than specific, security concerns. One main consequence of this vagueness of threat perception is that the Mediterranean continues to play a subsidiary role in European defence and security planning, both on the part of European security institutions themselves (including NATO) and of states and actors in the Mediterranean itself.

This chapter will look more deeply into the question of why it is that the Mediterranean continues to play a subsidiary role in Europe's security planning, in order to assess the effects this situation has had on regional and sub-regional security planning in the Mediterranean Basin. The latter may not be just a question of cause and effect, insofar as states and actors within what might be termed the non-European Mediterranean Basin have been slow to organise themselves into alliances to deal specifically, or even tangentially, with security issues, whether under external pressure to do so or not. It has, in fact, become commonplace to observe that there are no security organisations to parallel either NATO or the WEU along the southern and eastern shores of the Mediterranean.

Underlying this observation, at least from the European side, is the expectation that at some stage in the not too distant future, there perhaps ought to be organisational groupings with which NATO, the WEU and the EU could have some meaningful dialogue over areas of mutual concern. Until now, however, such arrangements as exist have largely been externally imposed, or at very least, encouraged through the setting up by NATO, the WEU and the EU of various dialogues (bilateral in the case of NATO and the WEU) or fora (multilateral in the case of the EU's Euro-Mediterranean Partnership initiative launched in 1995). Where the non-European, non-NATO states of the region have organised themselves – in the five-member Arab Maghreb Union, for example – the purpose of that organisation has rarely been for explicitly security purposes, and falls a long way short of the kind of collective defence arrangements envisaged by NATO, or the new security functions (the 'Petersberg' tasks) drawn up by the WEU.

In short, nearly ten years after the end of the Cold War, none of these initiatives has given rise to institutional or organisational co-operation of any magnitude within the region, or between the region and European security arrangements. This is in stark contrast to the evolving process of incorporating former Warsaw Pact member states into closer security relationships with Europe and the west, whether through NATO's Partnership for Peace (PfP) initiative, incorporation within the NATO or EU enlargement processes or a combination of both. Where initiatives have arisen within the region, such as the Egyptian-led Mediterranean Forum set up in 1991 to increase security co-operation among North African states and their southern European neighbours, the process has made little mileage beyond preliminary exchanges of information on issues of mutual interest.

Active security co-operation, as in the participation of Egyptian, Moroccan and Jordanian military contingents in the IFOR and SFOR missions in Bosnia, has taken place at the invitation of, and under the auspices of northern alliances, in this case NATO.

Earlier attempts to create regional security identities, such as the Hispano-Italian proposal to create a Conference on Security and Co-operation in the Mediterranean (CSCM) in 1990, to parallel the CSCE (later OSCE) for a wider Europe, were stillborn, above all because of disagreements over which states and actors within and beyond the Mediterranean should be included in the process. It was then, and still is, inconceivable that states as disparate as Israel, Syria, and Libya sit at the same table to discuss substantive issues of security co-operation. Why this was and remains the case, as well as the prospects for the evolution of this situation will form the main focus of this chapter.

THE MEDITERRANEAN: WHOSE REGION, WHOSE CONCERNS?

There are several layers, or levels, to an argument as to why security co-operation within the Mediterranean has remained in its infancy, while other sub-regions, such as the Black Sea and the Baltic Sea regions have begun to make strides in this direction. From the outset, however, it should be noted that attempts have indeed been made in the Mediterranean to create security processes. The success of these can only be judged, as in the Black Sea and Baltic Sea regions, on an on-going basis, and relative to the paucity of the arrangements and the evolution of the underlying philosophies which existed before these processes were embarked upon. Nevertheless, the Mediterranean as a 'unit of currency' in the evolving debate about security structures raises a number of issues which the other regions face to a lesser degree, and which this chapter will argue may well require a slightly modified or differentiated model for future progress to be made.

The first level of argument is the simplest, and also the hardest to pin-down. This is: what exactly is meant by the Mediterranean and does the region actually exist independently of a European (and American, which may be differently conceived) desire to group a series of issues together under a convenient security umbrella? Most debates on the subject insist that such an entity as the Mediterranean does exist, to which, *inter alia*, Fernand Braudel's extensive histories of the cultural, economic and political genesis (and eclipse) of the region attest and are frequently cited.[2] In modern geopolitical terms, however, the fragmentation and dual focus of much of the region is evident, most notably in the increasingly European-integrationist, and hence northern-focused, vocations of the states and societies of 'Mediterranean' Europe: Italy, Spain, Greece and Portugal, if one overlooks Portugal's lack of a Mediterranean sea border. In turn, even though its Mediterranean role is significant, it is not primarily as a Mediterranean state that one thinks of France, nor indeed as France thinks of itself, but rather as an actor at the heart of integrating the richness and diversity of Europe's political and cultural identity. France's quintessential encapsulation of the northern and southern aspects of this identity in fact overshadows Italian attempts to argue a similar vocation.

What this means for the states and societies on the southern and eastern shores of the Mediterranean forms the hard part of the question. It goes without saying in much of the debate on the subject that they are not part of Europe. Even here, there are grey areas giving rise to issues still to be openly tackled or fully resolved: Morocco applied for EC membership in 1987 and received a trenchant rejection; Israel is part of the European Song Contest community, but no other; Cyprus is considered European enough to have had its wish to join the EU accepted in the first tranche of new applicant members in 1997, while the issue of Turkey's Europeanness simmers on unresolved since its first steps towards EC membership were planted in 1963.

Any parallels to be drawn with the variable geometry unfolding in other regions on the outskirts of Europe – to the east, north- and south-east – nevertheless stop here. While Bulgaria or Lithuania, for example, may reasonably expect to find themselves engaged in one European security project or another, in a future even closer than they think themselves ('stuck' as Lithuania may feel itself to be as a mere Associate Partner of the WEU), the reality for most of the southern Mediterranean states is that they are set firmly outside any integrative projects envisaged by European institutions. Association Agreements have been offered to 12 partners of the EU (from west to east: Morocco, Algeria, Tunisia, Malta, Egypt, Cyprus, Israel, the Palestinian Authority, Lebanon, Syria, Turkey and Jordan), but these are economic, and like the Customs Agreement with

Turkey, inter-regional in conception, rather than a stepping-stone towards intra-regional integration. Whatever the conceptual arguments about the perceived preparatory role of the PfP for eventual NATO membership, or the relative merits of seeking EU, rather than NATO membership, the European vocations of most of Europe's eastern and northern neighbourhoods is neither questioned nor denied.

For the southern Mediterranean, however, the ghost at the European feast is Islam. Regardless of Braudel's depictions of the cultural, social and economic entanglements to have arisen over centuries of Mediterranean history, or of Salvador de Madariaga's descriptions of the glories of Muslim Spain, the modern European image of Islam is one that sets Islam and Islamic cultural influences firmly outside the history of Europe, and therefore beyond the borders of the modern European project. Partly as a result of this, but also as an extension of the fillip given to modern Islamic identities by Europe's colonial history in North Africa and the Levant, this image of external 'otherness' to Europe is often mirrored in the Muslim states and societies of the Mediterranean. In terms of security co-operation, where the eastern, north- and south-eastern states of Europe have been clamouring for some kind of affiliation to the EU, NATO or even WEU (supposing, now, that the latter much survives the turn of the century), the states of North Africa and the Levant – with the exception of Morocco – have expressed no interest in joining the queue of would-be member states. This may, of course, be due to anticipated responses, as evinced by the ill-fated experience of Morocco and the EC. Even at the time of Morocco's thwarted 'European' ambition, however, it was generally accepted that the application was made not in any expectation of a favourable response, but to underscore a different point, namely, that the region could not remain a backwater of European interest forever.

MEDITERRANEAN SECURITY PERSPECTIVES FROM OUTSIDE EUROPE

This in turn raises questions about what the expectations of the non-European (mainly Arab, Islamic) Mediterranean states might be should they seek closer affiliation and co-operation with the states and security institutions of Europe. It has not gone unnoticed, for example, that to qualify for NATO, EU or WEU associate or full-membership, certain basic criteria – not least in terms of internal governance, military and political restructuring – have to be fulfilled. In states still wary of being drawn back in to the spheres and governance structures of their erstwhile colonial overseers, there remain levels of reticence, for both good and bad reasons, to becoming subject to external scrutiny and terms of conditionality in processes over which, at best, they would exercise only a very limited control. Where they have accepted forms of conditionality in the economic sphere – to which most have already become reluctantly accustomed in their dealings with the IMF and external creditors over debt repayments from the late 1970s onwards – they are extremely reluctant to accept similar levels of intervention in their political and security affairs.

There might be room for greater co-operation over security interests, if there were clearly defined areas in which this were to prove of mutual benefit to Europe and the Mediterranean states in question. The discovery of these mutual interests, ranging from encouraging greater familiarity with Europe's security instruments and military planning and practice, to the setting of mutually agreed standards of information-sharing and the establishment of channels for dialogue to foster conflict prevention for example, have formed the basis for what has in fact been achieved (through NATO, EU and the WEU) since the end of the Cold War. Future possibilities for trans-Mediterranean co-operation have also been raised over what might be referred to as the 'shopping list' of 'soft' or 'semi-soft' security threats/risks/challenges in the region (namely, drug trafficking, organised crime, illegal migration), the main problem being to define what these menaces are to the mutual satisfaction of all potential participants in their prevention or cure. What has been missing in the process, however, are sufficient mutual interests or incentives for the measures already elaborated – particularly 'confidence-building measures' applied loosely to the Mediterranean context – either to result in greater sub-regional organisation towards security goals (so-called 'south-south' co-operation) or in addressing existing sources of conflict in the Mediterranean region.

There are several reasons for this, which moves the argument on to a second level. While the Mediterranean might function as a recognisable, and even coherent, regional umbrella for security co-operation, all developments in this inclusive direction have stumbled across the hurdle of the need to keep discussions at a fairly general level, and as content-free as possible. This requirement for generalities is a function of sustaining the region's inclusiveness. In other words, if all parties to discussions at the Mediterranean security table are to be kept there, and indeed, encouraged to come back for more, then the details of individual, bilateral or sub-regional sources of tensions have to be kept in check. Overcoming this difficulty, is, in fact, a dilemma faced by the other regional groupings mentioned above, in the Baltic and Black Sea areas. The key challenge for the Baltics, as for the Mediterranean is, as Olav Knudsen writes:

> How does one create a new regional security-community where none existed before? How can one make the leap from confrontational alliances to co-operative arrangements between states used to regarding each other as actual enemies or possible opponents?[3]

The essence of this challenge is to find ways of encouraging individuals, states, politicians, minority/majority populations to co-operate over issues of common interest rather than concentrating to detrimental effect on their differences.

In the Mediterranean, the kind of inter-state tensions which exist have rarely led to war, except in the earlier days of the Middle East conflict which pitted Arab states and communities against the nascent state of Israel, founded in 1948. Since 1979, and the Camp David accords between Egypt and Israel, Arab-Israeli tensions have persisted, but considerably fewer possibilities exist for this situation to lead to another large-scale Arab-Israeli war. This is not least because the Arab states have been severely weakened, politically, militarily and economically by their successive defeats. Their internal unity as a bloc has been mortally damaged by this and their own inter-regional frictions, set in stark relief in the 1990-91 Gulf War. Because of a dependence on Europe for their markets and economic assistance, and the US for financial aid (Egypt and Israel), natural resource investment (Algeria), debt forgiveness (Syria) and strategic backing (Turkey), the non-European Mediterranean states are fragmented along a number of faultlines, which sets them more in competition than in direct conflict with one another.

What prevents the Arab states, at least, from seeking greater cohesion in terms of ensuring their collective defence and security is that external threats are not real enough to warrant greater organisational structures than already exist in the region. In essence, these organisations are the Arab League, which stretches beyond the Mediterranean to the Gulf with an almost non-existent capacity to address defence and security issues, and the Arab Maghreb Union across North Africa, in which Egypt has sought observer and loose associate status. What security means for most of the states in the region is internal, and generally equated more directly with regime security than with the security of the populations of each state, as has become increasingly evident in the high, and continuing civilian death toll in Algeria. From this perspective, what needs defending is the sovereignty of each regime within the confines of individual state borders, free from any kind of external interference, as outlined above. Security co-operation is thus usually only of interest over issues such as terrorism (rarely defined) or environmental degradation, which affect a group of states to an equal or similar degree.

The only bilateral conflict that threatens to erupt from time to time – usually only verbally, or symbolically – is that between Greece and Turkey in the eastern Mediterranean. Because this concerns a EU member state in one context, and two NATO members in another, states external to these organisations express no competence in intervening or facilitating the emergence of the kind of confidence-building measures (CBMs) often proposed by NATO and the EU to resolve their own more limited differences or to combat the misunderstandings which may arise in their relations with Europe. It is one of the paradoxes of the Mediterranean security debate that CBMs are more often invoked for others than those who actually need them. In the case of Israel, as will be seen, a separate process (that is, not one included under a 'Mediterranean security' umbrella) exists to address confidence-building and conflict resolution issues, which pending a satisfactory settlement for the Palestinians serves to preclude the foreseeable emergence of a regionally-generated Mediterranean Forum which would include both Arab states and Israel. This has not, however, stood in the way of the emergence of limited Israeli-Turkish defence and security co-operation, of increasing concern to their Arab neighbours, engaged, as is Syria, in disputes (over water and land) with both.

To this extent, the 'participant inclusive', relatively content-free Mediterranean security agenda conceived by the Europeans concurs with a predisposition in the non-European Mediterranean not to delve too far into actual sources of conflict in the region. In most cases, because these are to be found at the sub-state, internal political or societal level, the key to European pressure on individual governments to do more to resolve internal conflicts hinges on these conflicts' external or regional effects. Where these are limited to and within the Mediterranean, or have few or no overspill effects into Europe, European governments and collective security organisations have shown themselves to be extremely reluctant to interfere or intervene. To parallel this, the limited regional organisations referred to (the Arab League and AMU) have also been extremely reluctant to assist in resolving the internal or domestic problems of member states any more than those which exist between them. This is clearly because inter- or intra-member conflict resolution is neither their purpose, nor within their capacities or competence. This is in fact similar to the way in which NATO can plan and prepare against external threats, but not against those posed mutually to and by Turkey and Greece within the NATO fold.

A third level of argument, or rather examination, is whether there is any room for advancing the Mediterranean security agenda, beyond the listing of instruments, such as the human rights treaties, or arms control conventions adhered to by individual states within the region. This is a dilemma currently facing the EU's Euro-Mediterranean Partnership (EMP) initiative, which, with 27 members (the EU 15 plus 12 Mediterranean partners) encompasses the largest security process in the region. In the Political and Security chapter of its three areas of focus for 'partnership building' (the others being financial and Economic Co-operation, and Human, Social and Cultural Resources), the EMP is seeking to develop a Euro-Mediterranean Charter for Peace and Stability. Not only what is to be on the agenda, but also what form this charter is to take has preoccupied discussions in the follow-up meetings to the EMP's founding Barcelona Conference of November 1995. The reality is that unless ways can be found to find a compromise between the overriding requirement that all 27 participants meet at the table, but have little of immediate substance to discuss, then little progress at the 'Mediterranean umbrella' level is likely to be made. At the outset, it should be said that few participants on the European side have much enthusiasm for a greater institutionalisation of a process, which at the level of exchanging general views on security concerns and environmental damage limitation, has a certain, but increasingly limited utility.

In terms of exchanging or sharing information about institutional and military practice, the WEU and NATO bilateral dialogues with a more restricted group of Mediterranean states have already largely covered the ground.[4] In the case of the WEU dialogues, the process of continually summoning up the requisite WEU representation in Brussels to meet with Mediterranean ambassadors one at a time is beginning to show strains in terms of bureaucratic time and focus, as well as in the content of such meetings.[5] With the possibility that these meetings might in future take the form of round-table discussions with all dialogue partners present at once, the process runs the risk of running foul of the law of diminishing returns or of a replication of the exchanges taking place under the EMP's 'political and security' umbrella. In this connection, and having already partially examined what motivates – or fails to motivate – the southern states of the Mediterranean, the real objectives of Europe in the region require closer examination.

WHAT CAN, OR DOES EUROPE EXPECT?

A final level of argument, and a largely unspoken reality of the Mediterranean security agenda for Europe, as well as for the US, is that it is essentially constituted of what is left over after the important issues of security have been dealt with elsewhere. The Balkans, for example, are rarely cited as states and societies in or of the Mediterranean, despite the Balkan peninsula's prominent position in the eastern Mediterranean. Falling within the logic of the 'European project', the Balkans are more significant for their attachment to the European mainland, and are approached as such in European security terms. Cyprus, in turn, is of and in the Mediterranean, but is European – despite ambivalence over the Turkish factor therein – and thus falls under a similar 'European mainland plus' security focus. The Middle East, which is definitely separate from Europe, is managed under a different security logic, which projects the Arab-Israeli conflict beyond the limitations of the Mediterranean Basin into the much more significant geopolitical hinterland of the Gulf, with its western-allied oil reserves overshadowed by the 'dually-contained' 'rogue states' of Iraq and Iran. The complexities and importance of this region warrant more security muscle than Europe can ever provide alone, and thus is firmly under the security guidance and controlling hand of the US,

Russia being kept increasingly in the background. Even the Western Saharan conflict, which despite a long-standing military stalemate continues to bedevil Morocco-Algerian relations, is dealt with as a UN (MINURSO and Secretary-General-led) issue, rather than as a direct concern of Mediterranean security. The conflict in Algeria, meanwhile, where it is addressed or dealt with at all outside Algeria, is not a polite topic to bring to the Mediterranean security table.

The result of this is that in many ways, the *laissez-faire* approach adopted by the non-European states to existing conflicts and violence in the Mediterranean is shared by their European neighbours. This is not to assert that nothing is said about human rights abuses in Algeria or the Western Sahara, violence on the Green Line in Cyprus, or the continuing arms build-up in the Middle East. What is relevant is that these are not issues dealt with explicitly or in any detail within what is understood to be an evolving Mediterranean security agenda. The corollary is that if an issue is deemed to be important enough, or requiring of more concentrated or focused attention, it leaves the Mediterranean agenda to find its place elsewhere. If the outcome of this upgrading is greater peace and enhanced stability in the Mediterranean, then this is self-evidently not a cause for criticism or complaint. The danger, however, arises when crises which simmer under the surface, or are kept from closer scrutiny, are not identified in time for the kind of regional and inter-regional processes currently envisaged to react or respond to them constructively. The case of Algeria, again, illustrates the kind of security neglect which has arisen in a situation where upwards of 100,000 people have died since 1992, with little regional or European understanding of how this has come to pass, nor of how to forestall future loss of life. This state of affairs would be inconceivable, for example, in the Balkans.

A further, and perhaps harsher, reality of European security approaches to the Mediterranean is that the overriding concern is to ensure stability in the region. In a number of ways, this diverges from promoting Mediterranean security insofar as the wider, and longer-term dimensions of a dynamic stability – based on respect for the rule of law, democratisation, the peaceful settlement of conflicts at the domestic as well as external level, respect for individual rights – are largely subjugated to the short-term goal of maintaining the status quo. Efforts towards establishing co-operative security arrangements with these objectives in mind have suffered when it has become clear that European policy-makers will tolerate a number of infractions in pursuit of regime stability at the state level, and predictable and well-managed inter-state relations at the regional level. The promotion of a regionwide respect for human rights has been a particular casualty of this prioritisation, where states such as Israel, Egypt and Algeria have been allowed to cite the menace of terrorism in defence of the systematic – and in the case of Israel, legally recognised – use of torture on detainees.

Again, what is significant here is not that individual European governments do not speak out against human rights abuses, but that these concerns are silenced beyond generalised aspirations for longer-term improvements in this sphere once they feature on the Mediterranean security agenda. This is true of other issues placed loosely under the banner of CBMs; the question of establishing a regional arms control regime, for example, has necessarily been placed in abeyance by the fluctuations of the Middle East peace process. Arab states are swift to cite Israel's nuclear capability to justify their own conventional (and less conventional) arms build-ups, but it is also the case that Israel's non-adhesion to the Non-Proliferation Treaty is passed over in almost total silence by European policy-makers. Other areas where regional security co-operation might be sought have, in fact, been continually overshadowed by the vicissitudes of issues dealt with elsewhere, having a direct bearing on the shaping of perceptions and the very processes of confidence building to which the EMP, at least, attaches considerable importance.

To cite but a few examples: it is a widely-held, if erroneous view, in the Arab world that 'the west', and above all Europe, failed to come to the aid of Bosnian Muslims, because they were Muslims; the sanctions regime against Iraq is perceived as an infliction of suffering on ordinary Iraqi citizens, for whom little concern is expressed in Europe; UN Security Council resolutions apply with vigour to Iraq and Libya, but not to Israel; Israel in turn suspects Europe of indifference towards its own internal security concerns in favour of the establishment of a Palestinian state at all costs. Last but not least, Europe's economic and migration policies towards the Mediterranean impinge directly on security considerations, where for many North Africans, keeping people and agricultural exports, if not their less competitive industrial products, out of the EU forms the very *raison d'être* for Europe having embarked on security co-operation in the Mediterranean in the first place.

IMPLICATIONS FOR REGIONAL SECURITY CO-OPERATION

The above discussion paints a fairly gloomy picture for the future of Mediterranean regional security co-operation. There is nevertheless room for progress if some of the issues currently obscured, and the expectations raised, by the current processes are broken down into more manageable parts. The first of these is to acknowledge that the Mediterranean is not, nor likely to become, an arena for European security co-operation of the same magnitude or depth as that envisaged on the current eastern and northern borders of Europe. At very least, Mediterranean security goals lack the shared European and integrationist vision implicit in the fora and networks being built up (their shortcomings included) to the east and north of Europe. The second is to recognise that while a 'Mediterranean umbrella' of 27 or more participants may provide an occasionally useful global overview of developments in the region, it can achieve only so much without being subject to the limitations described above. Attempts to adapt a CSCE/OSCE model to the Mediterranean have invariably failed, on the one hand because of the absence of erstwhile superpower engagement in the project(s), and on the other because of the lack of a common 'European cement' to meld its different components together within a shared whole.[6] Where there are concrete objectives to be addressed – such as the restoration of peace in Algeria, or in promoting less volatile Turkish-Greek relations – then smaller, more focused sub-regional fora, or negotiating processes, are more likely to achieve these objectives.

Even without concrete objectives, much could be learnt from a comparative study of the experiences of sub-regional security co-operation elsewhere, as described in the book recently edited by Dr Andrew Cottey.[7] In examining the terms, style and content of approaches to CBMs, for example, in the Baltic and Black Sea areas, the Mediterranean would at least be able to build on the strengths of existing approaches, as well as finding itself on a similar footing to nascent security communities elsewhere.[8] For this to work, however, the Mediterranean may need to be sub-divided between an eastern and a western regional focus, where the dominance of the Middle

East peace process in the east, for example, has hitherto overshadowed an altogether different set of issues (drugs, migration, the Western Sahara) in the western Mediterranean and across the Straits of Gibraltar. The 'Mediterranean umbrella' could continue to work in the direction of overall regional integration, but not so evidently, as at present, at the expense of seeking to resolve existing conflicts and tensions. Smaller sub-regional fora might equally only include those European states directly represented in the area in question, rather than *de rigueur* (and quite often, reluctant) representatives of the entire EU-15, WEU or NATO. An example of what might be envisaged is a western Mediterranean military cooperation forum, in which the states contributing to the WEU's rapid deployment call-up forces EUROFOR and EUROMARFOR (France, Spain, Portugal and Italy) could undertake joint training exercises with rapid reaction forces drawn from the North African states, not only for mutual familiarisation and operational purposes, but also with the ultimate goal of prompting domestic security sector reform in the partner states in question.

In smaller fora, Mediterranean states could also be encouraged to seek regional commonalities with as much vigour as they cite injustices and long-standing grievances against one another and against Israel in particular. The sticking point for much of the Arab world has always been the progress made, or not made, by Israel in the normalisation of its relations with the Palestinian Authority. However, Israel has also played the convenient role of regional scapegoat, where other aspects of regional co-operation or the peaceful settlement of conflicts have not been dependent on Israeli behaviour, words or actions at all. Recognising that this scapegoating, from which Israel draws protective benefits itself, has actually served the purposes of states as reluctant to engage in regional integration processes as they are to undertake domestic political reform is one of a number of factors that need to be taken into consideration. The establishment of sub-regional security fora will require the creation of incentives, as well as potential penalties, to change long-standing habits of avoiding precisely the kind of constructive co-operation deemed to be of benefit to states in other peripheral regions of Europe.

There is also a problem of what might be termed the selectivity of silences, in which Europeans have been almost as wanting as non-European Mediterranean states. The Egyptian government, in conjunction with a Saudi and an Iranian delegation,[9] recently deployed its not inconsiderable diplomatic skills to diffusing tensions between Turkey and Syria over the Kurdish issue and a long-standing water dispute related to Turkey's damming of the Euphrates River upstream from Syria. Where less is said or done, however, is where violence, or the threat of violence, pertains not so much to inter-state conflicts, but to the internal affairs of a single state. Here, one suspects, the silence maintained in the Arab world over the situation in Algeria, with the notable exception of a thwarted Lebanese initiative to convene a regional conference to investigate the massacre of villagers in late 1997, has been largely to protect the principle of the sovereign inviolability of state governments and state borders. It remains the case, however, that if Europe did indeed do little to save Bosnian lives, the Islamic world did little too, and continues to do very little to save Algerian Muslim lives.

Incentives also need to be found to encourage greater regional activism in support of the goals – of democracy, human rights and arms control – to which all the EU's Euro-Mediterranean Partners have subscribed, in order to move away from an entrenched acceptance (by Europe, as much by the rest of the Mediterranean), that progress in these directions will necessarily be slow, or subject to the prior resolution of the Middle East peace process. An encouraging shift in approach has been witnessed in Europe's challenge to the sovereign right of the Serbian government to 'contain' their Kosovar minorities through violent means. Although the 'verifiers' may have arrived late in the day, the principle of the sovereign inviolability of state borders has been shaken on the grounds of the protection of human rights. The same approach might profitably be applied by Europeans to a number of states in the Mediterranean, not to justify or engage in any form of military intervention, but to establish the principle that the requirement of governments to live up to their undertakings is as pertinent outside as it is within Europe.

For this to take root, however, Europe's political and security institutions will need to act with a little more consequence towards regions situated, like the Mediterranean, outside its broader European vision. The Arab world's accusations of European double standards in respect of the application of their own democratic, legal and moral standards are not entirely without foundation, where on a number of occasions, the lives of Arabs and Africans appear to count for considerably less than those of Europeans, however 'new' or distant they may be from the western capitals of Europe. The Mediterranean is on Europe's doorstep, and in the case of Morocco, only 14 km away from the southern shores of the EU. Democratic progress in states such as Morocco should be recognised and rewarded, just as undifferentiated references to 'terrorist problems', without any due process of law or substantiation should be questioned and discouraged. The irony is, however, that without continual references to Islamists, terrorists and hordes of illegal migrants bearing drugs and guns, it is unlikely that Europe would have a Mediterranean security agenda at all.

Notes

1 See Joshua Sinai 'Ghaddafi's Libya: the patient proliferator' in *Jane's Intelligence Review* Vol. 10, No. 12, December 1998, pp.27-30.

2 For the weightiest tomes see: Fernand Braudel *The Mediterranean and the Mediterranean World in the Age of Philip II* Vols I & II, London, Fontana Press (5th edition), 1987.

3 Olav F. Knudsen *Cooperative Security in the Baltic Sea Region,* Chaillot Papers, No. 33; Paris, Western European Union Institute for Security Studies, November 1998, p.4.

4 The WEU has conducted bilateral dialogues with Morocco, Algeria, Tunisia, Israel and Egypt, since 1992 with the first three and 1993 with the last two; NATO's dialogue under the Mediterranean Initiative of 1995 is with Morocco, Tunisia, Israel, Mauritania, Egypt and Jordan.

5 See Arnaud Jacomet *La coopération européenne en matière de securité et la Mediterranée: La dialogue mediterranéene de l'UEO* (Seminaire d'information à l'intention des officiers militaires mediterranéens, WEU Institute for Security Studies, Paris, 28-29 September 1998).

6 The CSCE originally encompassed a Mediterranean 'volet', continued under the OSCE, but this has always skirted round hard security issues in favour of cooperation over natural disaster relief and environmental hazards: a not insignificant goal in itself, but not what first comes to mind in discussing security cooperation.

7 Andrew Cottey (ed.) *Sub-Regional Co-operation in the New Europe – Building Security, Prosperity and Solidarity from the Barents to the Black Sea,* London, Macmillan.

8 Turkey is, of course, already a participant in the Black Sea Cooperation Council, but unlikely to be able to translate this experience directly in building cooperation

with wary Arab neighbours. The latter could however, adapt and learn from the model.

[9] See Al Venter 'Turmoil in the Mediterranean' *Pointer*, December 1998, p.4-5.

4

The EU and NATO Enlargement Debates in Comparative Perspective: Building a Pan-European Security Order?[1]

DR GRAHAM TIMMINS

Head of Polical History, University of Huddersfield

DR MARTIN A. SMITH

Senior Lecturer, Royal Military Academy Sandhurst

INTRODUCTION

It is now just a little over a decade since Hungary and Poland took their first tentative steps towards economic reform and, in doing so, provoked a series of events that led to the collapse of Soviet Communism. Few, if any, observers at the time could have envisaged either state entertaining realistic hopes of joining the European Union and NATO in the near future. That this is now the case underlines the immensity of the changes that have taken place in such a relatively short period of time. Since the end of 1997 the broad parameters concerning preparations for both EU and NATO enlargement have become much clearer. The Luxembourg European Council summit on 12-13 December 1997 provided further elaboration on the decision taken at the Amsterdam Summit in June 1997 to commence accession negotiations with the Czech Republic, Estonia, Hungary, Poland, Slovenia and also Cyprus. As part of the Presidency Conclusions, it was announced that:

> The task confronting the European Union would be to prepare both the applicant states and itself for enlargement and that enlargement would be via a staged

> process allowing applicant states to accede at their own pace and according to the level of preparation... As a prerequisite for enlargement of the Union, the operation of the institutions must be strengthened and improved in keeping with the institutional provisions of the Amsterdam Treaty'... The accession talks would be conducted via a 'European Conference' that would comprise the European Union and all 'European States' aspiring towards accession. All states would be required to share a common commitment to peace, security and good neighbourliness, respect for other countries' sovereignty, the principles upon which the European Union is founded, the integrity and inviolability of external borders and the principles of international law and a commitment to the settlement of territorial disputes by peaceful means, in particular through the jurisdiction of the International Court of Justice in the Hague.[2]

At their ministerial meeting on 16 December 1997, NATO member states concluded protocols of accession with the Czech Republic, Hungary and Poland following the Madrid Declaration on Euro-Atlantic Security and Cooperation signed in July 1997.

> Today, we invite the Czech Republic, Hungary and Poland to begin accession talks with NATO. Our goal is to sign the Protocol of Accession at the time of the Ministerial meetings in December 1997 and to see the ratification process completed in time for membership to become effective by the 50th anniversary of the Washington Treaty in April 1999. During the period leading to accession, the Alliance will involve invited countries, to the greatest extent possible and where appropriate, in Alliance activities, to ensure that they are best prepared to undertake the responsibilities and obligations of membership in an enlarged Alliance. We direct the Council in Permanent Session to develop appropriate arrangements for this purpose ... Admitting new members will entail resource implications for the Alliance. It will involve the Alliance providing the resources which enlargement will necessarily require. We direct the Council in Permanent Session to bring to an early conclusion the concrete analysis of the resource implications of the forthcoming enlargement, drawing on the continuing work on military implications. We are confident that, in line with the security environment of the Europe of today, Alliance costs associated with the integration of new members will be manageable and that the resources necessary to meet those costs will be provided.[3]

This is by no means the end of the story for either the EU or NATO. Key debates about the management of enlargement are only now getting underway in earnest. One of the most important challenges facing both the EU and NATO is what the authors here term the '*acquis* factor', which affects each institution in different ways.

WHAT KIND OF EUROPEAN UNION?

All new entrants accepted into the European Union are required to conform with all existing principles, policies, laws, practices, obligations and objectives or, as it is commonly referred to, the *acquis communautaire*. In short, the European Commission's central concern is that new entrants will be prepared and willing to meet the full obligations of the internal market. This requirement can be interpreted as being more than a set of rules and can be viewed as an important structuring factor in assisting and encouraging the applicant states to develop compatible systems with those already in existence in the EU.

The White Paper published by the European Commission in May 1995 was specifically aimed at this issue but the Commission was nevertheless faced with a dilemma when formulating its opinions on the applications received from the East-Central European (ECE) applicant states. If the basis of the opinions were to be the current situation, then none of the applicant states would be able to meet the *acquis communautaire*. However, if the future situation were to be applied, the response would more than likely be affirmative. The Commission opted for the medium-term future, which was understood as in five year's time.[4] The Commission has concentrated on the administrative capacities of the applicant states, particularly where their judicial systems are concerned. It has long been recognised that there is a time lag between the overt processes of democratisation i.e. the establishment of political parties, the holding of elections and constitutional change and the less apparent process of personnel turnover. With this issue in mind, the Commission has refrained from making conclusions in the majority of cases but has been critical where it has identified sources for concern, e.g. in the case of the Slovenian civil service, which the Commission has described as being understaffed in key departments and lacking in appropriately qualified civil servants.[5] In raising the *acquis* factor, the Commission provokes debate surrounding the potential tensions between the political cultures of the existing member states and the ECE applicants. There has so far been very little discussion of what kind of members the ECE states will become, namely, whether they would be generally compliant with the broad range of EU legislation or not. Just as important, there is the unresolved question of how enlargement into East-Central Europe will affect the very nature of the European Union itself.

Although the Amsterdam Treaty first introduced the concept of 'flexibility' into the public domain, variations on this theme have a long history stretching back to the Treaty of Rome in 1957 and it was central to the Tindemans Report in 1975.[6] But it was the Schäuble-Lamers paper published in 1994 that has exercised most influence on the current debate on flexible or differentiated integration. In September 1994, Karl Lamers, the then Foreign Affairs Spokesman for the German Christian Democratic Union (CDU) parliamentary faction presented a paper to the German Parliament which was co-authored by Wolfgang Schäuble, who it was anticipated would be Helmut Kohl's successor as leader of the CDU. Entitled, *Reflections on European Policy*, its contents were designed to reconcile the growing conflict between the objectives of deepening and widening. The paper began by acknowledging the limitations of the 1992 Treaty on European Union in terms of movement towards the construction of a new European political order and highlighted the importance of enlargement for the Union's future global role:

> For the present members of the EU, eastward expansion constitutes both a challenge and a test not only in terms of the material contribution they are able and willing to make but also in terms of their moral and spiritual self-conception. The Union's response will show whether it is able and willing to become the main pillar of continental order, alongside a democratised and once again stable Russia and in alliance with the USA.[7]

The means of achieving these objectives would be an increase in the democratic and federal characteristics of the EU's structures and practices, including the passing of a 'quasi-constitutional document' which would include a restriction on veto rights. Finally, by way of 'variable geometry', member states would be able to choose the level of integration with which they felt most comfortable, a proposal that reflected the growing frustration of Germany towards those nations that have been reluctant to endorse the Maastricht agenda. 'It is essential that no country should be allowed to use its right of veto to block the efforts of other countries more able and willing to intensify their co-operation and deepen integration.'[8] It was stressed that the 'hard core', built around the Franco-German alliance with the inclusion of the Benelux states, would not be a divisive mechanism. 'The foundation of a core group of countries is not an end in itself but a means of reconciling the two ostensibly conflicting goals of widening and deepening the EU.'[9] Moreover, by establishing a 'multi-speed Europe', the above mechanisms, it was suggested, would facilitate the accession of the ECE states and enhance the prospects of success in the transformation process:

> Poland, the Czech and Slovak Republics, Hungary (and Slovenia) should become Members of the European Union around the year 2000. Their accession should depend on the implementation of the measures outlined above and also be their objective. The certain prospect of EU membership, and membership itself even more so, is likely to promote the political and economic development of these countries more than any form of external assistance. Apart from the clear political and psychological advantages, accession at that time would, however, impose such a serious economic strain on members old and new that it will only be possible through a combination of measures. These include not only the approximation of laws in the acceding countries, already provided for in the Europe Agreements, but also changes in various fields of EU policy, above all with regard to agriculture. In addition, to allow for economic adjustment there must be a case for the application of the concept of 'variable geometry'. The result must be that the costs for both sides are no higher than would be the case if accession were to take place at a later date. It must be borne in mind that the later accession takes place, the higher the costs are likely to be.[10]

As Alexander Stubb explains, the debate on flexibility encompasses the three sub-categories of a multi-speed Europe, variable geometry and a *Europe à la carte*. Whereas a multi-speed Europe envisages the movement towards common objectives, both variable geometry and a *Europe à la carte* present the opportunity for a multi-track Europe to emerge, whereby not all member states are expected to move towards the same objectives. The difference between the latter two sub-categories is that variable geometry presumes the separation of a hard core of states from the remainder which wish to push ahead with a specific integrative mechanism such as the Western European Union (WEU), European Monetary System or the Schengen border agreement outside of the main treaty framework.

The *Europe à la carte* model differs in that member states are given the choice to opt out of treaty conditions such as the social chapter (as the UK did prior to 1997), economic and monetary union (UK, Denmark and Sweden) and citizenship (Denmark).[11] The debate has, moreover, been made more complicated by the semantic differences that have emerged. The suggestion of a 'hard core' using variable geometry in the Schäuble-Lamers paper provoked considerable controversy, not least between the German and Italian Governments regarding the single European currency. Theo Waigel, the then German Finance Minister, argued that Italy would be in no position to form part of the core as its chances of qualifying for Economic and Monetary Union as part of the first wave were slim given its economic circumstances. With the hard core notion seen as too politically insensitive, 'differentiated integration' became an increasingly common substitute whilst the European Council in Turin in 1996 adopted 'flexible integration' before settling on flexibility in the Amsterdam Treaty. Stubb's suggestion is that 'enhanced co-operation' is the most politically correct version and was the term employed at the European Council summits in Turin and Florence in 1996.[12]

The assumption often made is that the *acquis* is a set of fixed rules with which all member states are expected to comply. In fact, as with any constitutional arrangement, the *acquis* is a dynamic entity that develops over time. In the case of enlargement, the influx of new member states will have an unavoidable impact upon the institutions and working practices of the European Union, not least in the area of security. The Common Foreign and Security Policy (CFSP), which emerged out of the Intergovernmental Conference (IGC) on Political Union was intended to represent an effective partnership with the Western European Union (WEU) and provides the main EU security instrument. Article J.1 of the Treaty on European Union envisages the creation of a CFSP that will:

> safeguard the common values, fundamental interests and independence of the Union; strengthen the security of the Union and its Member States in all ways; preserve peace and international security in accordance with the principles of the United Nations Charter as well as the principles of the Helsinki Final Act and the objectives of the Paris Charter; to promote international co-operation; and to develop and consolidate democracy and the rule of law and respect for human rights and fundamental freedoms.[13]

But in stating such bold and ambitious objectives, the CFSP's weakness in practice lay in that it remains essentially an intergovernmental mechanism. Article J.2 stipulates that 'wherever it deems it necessary, the Council shall define a common position. Member States shall ensure that their national policies conform to the common positions'.[14] In other words, the formulation and implementation of a common position would rely entirely upon the creation and maintenance of a working consensus amongst the member states. Furthermore, Article J.4, binds member states to nothing other than a symbolic gesture to consider 'the eventual framing of a common defence policy, which might in time lead to a common defence'.[15] It would, on one level, be possible to discuss any future European security order purely in terms of the CFSP. An alternative view is that whilst the CFSP has an important contribution to make to the theoretical discussion of a European security order, its practical relevance has so far been extremely limited. It remains the case then that the EU and NATO will be required to develop a closer *modus vivendi* in the future as a means of realising a genuine security order.

NATO AND UNDERLAPPING SECURITY GUARANTEES

Although the whole matter of institutional *acquis* is usually referred to and discussed in the EU context, it is of great relevance for NATO too. Former NATO Secretary-General Manfred Wörner was fond, in the early 1990s, of referring to NATO's own *acquis atlantique*. He saw this as having become embedded in the long-standing habits and practices of military co-ordination and co-operation developed and practised by member states within the NATO institutional framework. Fundamental to all of this has been the joint security guarantee, which forms the basis of the North Atlantic Treaty.[16] Given the relative power and invulnerability of the United States, this is in effect an American guarantee of the security of NATO's European member states.

A hitherto firm principle amongst NATO member states has been that nothing should be permitted to dilute the guarantee. In this context concern has emerged over what US officials sometimes call the threat of 'underlapping security guarantees' being created by the enlargement of the EU and, specifically, the WEU. Under the terms of the Maastricht Treaty, new members of the EU are entitled to apply for membership of the WEU as well, giving them access to the WEU's own security guarantee which is contained in the 1948 Brussels Treaty. Many American officials have been concerned that new EU/WEU members may assume that they have *de facto* coverage by the US/NATO guarantee as well, even though they may not have joined and accepted the responsibilities of NATO membership. There are two particular issues of concern connected to this. One is that the United States might find itself sucked into wars and conflicts in which it has no wish to become involved on behalf of countries with which it is not formally allied. The second is that NATO's institutional viability might be progressively undermined if ECE states felt that they could gain effective access to its security guarantee without having to apply, and risk being turned down, for actual NATO membership.

For some NATO supporters this concern has provided a strong rationale for instituting overt linkage between the NATO and EU enlargement processes of a kind which would involve general acceptance that new members be expected to join both institutions and also, perhaps, that current EU members be actively encouraged to join NATO too if they are not members already.[17] Presumably if this approach were adopted the European NATO members not also in the EU would have to be invited to join the latter in turn.

The risk of 'underlapping' security guarantees emerging in the manner described above has been something which West European as well as American leaders have taken pains to guard against. This effort in fact predates the recent debates on EU and NATO enlargement and can be traced back to at least 1987. In that year Alfred Cahen, the then Secretary-General of the WEU, elaborated a number of principles for states aspiring to membership of the WEU. These countries should, he argued, be either a member of, or a serious applicant to, the then European Community and also an existing member of NATO.[18] Cahen's principles were developed against the background of applications by Spain and Portugal to join the WEU; this was the first time the organisation had been invited to enlarge its membership since being established in its present form in 1954-55. Both the Iberian states concerned were in fact well qualified according to the Cahen principles as they were members of both the then EC and NATO. Thus, a problem did not arise.

Such is not, of course, the case with all five of the ECE states which opened accession negotiations with the EU during 1998.

Unless something goes seriously wrong in their individual negotiations, or the EU enlargement process moves forward at a glacial pace overall, Estonia and Slovenia are likely to join the EU, and be eligible for membership of the WEU, in advance of any future membership in NATO assuming that they join at all. To date NATO and EU members have adhered to the Cahen principles and the view that no new members of the EU should be admitted as full members of the WEU unless they are or become NATO members also. This was set out clearly in the 1995 NATO *Study on NATO Enlargement* which had been drafted in the months immediately following the accession to the EU of Austria, Sweden and Finland in January of that year. These three states were all, of course, neutral and non-aligned during the Cold War and none have expressed a firm interest in joining NATO. The relevant passage in the September 1995 NATO study might, therefore, be read as a diplomatic warning to them not to rock the boat by applying for full membership of the WEU. It read:

> All full members of the WEU are also members of NATO. Because of the cumulative effect of the security safeguards of Article V of the modified Brussels Treaty and of Article 5 of the Washington Treaty, *the maintenance of this linkage is essential* ... An eventual broad congruence of European membership in NATO, EU and WEU would have positive effects on European security. The Alliance should at an appropriate time give particular consideration to countries with a perspective of EU membership, and which have already shown an interest in joining NATO, in order to consider ... how they can contribute to transatlantic security within the Washington Treaty and to determine whether to invite them to join NATO (emphasis added).[19]

To date the three new EU members have, notwithstanding indications from time-to-time that they are interested in the WEU, tacitly abided by the existing norm and contented themselves with WEU observer status.[20] This situation could of course change in the future. Speaking in the spring of 1997, Cahen himself suggested that his decade-old principles should now be changed. He asked rhetorically whether:

> You have instantly to be a member of the [NATO] Alliance to become a member of the European Union or is it sufficient, if you are applying for NATO membership, to be a member of a reinforced Partnership for Peace? I would be inclined to think that any applicant who belongs to a reinforced Partnership for

> Peace and is a member of the European Union is also entitled to full membership of our [WEU] organisation.[21]

This idea, if adopted, would in fact represent an important redefinition of the established principles governing the enlargement of WEU that Cahen himself had set out in the late 1980s. Whereas his previous position was that new WEU members *must* be in NATO and *might* be in the then EC at the time they joined, the position being suggested by Cahen in 1997 changed these priorities around. There will almost certainly be scope for discord if serious moves are made to amend the understanding codified officially in the 1995 NATO enlargement study that new WEU members must already be members of NATO. Such discord could arise not only between the US and West European governments, but also amongst EU and WEU members who may take different perspectives along Atlanticist and Europeanist lines. This possibility has been foreseen by members of the WEU's own parliamentary assembly.[22] It will be made more likely if those who suggest modification of the established norm link this to support for the view that the European Union should over time effectively absorb the WEU. This view was expressed by Alfred Cahen in his 1997 remarks referred to above. The British government is likely to be the major dissenter from such an approach within Western Europe. Notwithstanding the change of government in May 1997 the British approach to the future of the WEU has been consistent. The UK, under both Conservative and Labour governments, has been opposed to suggestions for an EU-WEU merger. The continuity of this policy was reflected at the EU's Amsterdam summit in June 1997 when Prime Minister Blair hastened to assure the world's press that the UK would not consent under his government to a merger, even though such an option had been formally written-in to the newly-agreed Treaty of Amsterdam.[23]

UNDERSTANDING CONCEPTS OF PAN-EUROPEAN SECURITY

In 1997 William Wallace asserted that 'implicit in the discussion of Eastern enlargement of both the EU and NATO is the suggestion that some notion of solidarity is required to make either or both feasible or sustainable'.[24] By this Wallace means the compatibility of basic value systems underlying the western European-transatlantic relationship which was set within a Cold War context up until 1990. As Timothy Garton-Ash points out, the Cold War prompted US support for European reconstruction through the Marshall Plan and integration for geopolitical reasons whilst the Soviet Union acted as a catalyst for the reconciliation of traditional Western European rivalries. Moreover, the 'Iron Curtain' provided the scope for integration between a relatively small number of western, liberal democracies enjoying a high degree of socio-economic homogeneity. It is, therefore, 'only after the Cold War [that we are] discovering just how much European integration owed to it'.[25] The inference in Wallace's analysis is that the EU and NATO, therefore, now find themselves compelled to redefine the basis of solidarity on a pan-European level if enlargement is to succeed, and succeed it must if it is accepted that the status quo, namely, non-enlargement is not a viable alternative. Clive Archer draws a similar conclusion in defining security within the context of a triangle of peace, freedom and stability. He suggests that *peace* normally refers to the 'absence of war or violence' but may equally be equated with 'a state of harmony between people or groups, freedom from strife or law and order within a state'. *Freedom* is taken to mean 'autonomy, self-government, or independence' for a state or its peoples but can also highlight 'the sense of enjoying personal or civil liberties or of being free from something unpleasant or bad'. Finally, *stability*, refers to 'steadiness, firmness or being lasting or permanent'. Taking these notions together, Archer refers to the interaction of peace (as the absence of war and violence) and freedom as the *'security of surviving'* whereas the interaction between peace (as a state of harmony) and stability is viewed as the *'security of thriving'*.[26]

Traditional concepts of security during the Cold War stressed the 'security of surviving' with the Soviet Union clearly labelled as the potential aggressor. However, the Conference on Security and Co-operation in Europe (CSCE) and Conventional Forces in Europe (CFE) agreements went some way to fostering a 'security of thriving' mentality through the creation of a security regime involving 'principles, rules, and norms that permit nations to be restrained in their behavior in the belief that others will reciprocate'.[27] With the end of the Cold War the emphasis has switched to a 'security of thriving' and, as a result, the 'traditional' roles of both NATO and the EU have been called into question. Whilst the Western European integration process in the post-war period was clearly a 'peace and stability project' and had the specific function of reconciling Franco-German relations, it also contributed to the creation of a Deutschian security community among the member states.[28] However, what the Western European integration process could not do was address the external security context provoked by the Cold War or the 'security of surviving' agenda, which depended upon US military support through NATO. Although the enlargement of the EU into East-Central Europe is viewed as the extension of the 'peace and stability project' and the EU has been explicit in inviting applications from all 'European' states, there is little possibility of Russia being invited to join.

The alternative remains a security regime and the creation of such a mechanism seems more probable through the EU and the CFSP than NATO given Russia's hostility to NATO enlargement into East-Central Europe yet relative disinterest in the EU enlargement process. Of significance here is that the concept of a security regime in contrast to a security community does not require inclusive membership. As Wallace suggests, the prospect is of a European core based around those EU member states signing up for EMU and political initiatives such as CFSP and Justice and Home Affairs (JHA) co-operation, a middle circle comprising of the remainder of the EU member states together with the 'first wave' ECE states which are unable or unwilling to sign up for the core policy components and an outer circle of all other 'European' states having looser forms of economic and political co-operation with the EU.[29] However, the creation of such a security regime assumes reference to the concepts of co-operative and comprehensive rather than collective security. Collective security is based on military defence capability and was well suited to NATO's role of resisting Soviet aggression.[30] Co-operative security, on the other hand, stresses common security threats such as nuclear annihilation and co-operation between security institutions whilst comprehensive security stretches the agenda beyond military considerations to environmental, economic and social dimensions. The EU is undoubtedly in a position to exercise a leading role in co-operative and comprehensive security given sufficient political will but this is less the case where collective security is concerned. Archer's conclusion is not surprisingly that 'it is recognised that the institutions of the EU – and even the WEU – are a poor substitution for the more developed infra-structure of NATO in the case of collective security'.[31]

This analysis leads towards the conclusion that the development of a pan-European security order in the short to medium term will be based on both NATO's 'hard security' or military role and the EU's 'soft security' or economic role. There are two consequences arising from this view. First, the 'Russian Question' is unlikely to be further addressed in the near future and will remain the Achilles heel of a Pan-European Security Order. Second, the EU and NATO are incapable of achieving a Pan-European Security Order independently from each other and will be compelled to co-ordinate their policies towards East-Central Europe more deeply as the enlargement process progresses.

CONCLUSION

There is an obvious difference in the EU and NATO enlargement debates which is their different starting points. The EU found itself exposed to growing internal and external pressures to recommence the historic mission of integration following the end of the Cold War. As such, it has been the moral imperative to enlarge the EU that has been most predominant in driving on developments.[32] In stark contrast, NATO found its very existence endangered by the end of the Cold War and the Clinton administration turned to enlargement as a pragmatic response to this predicament. It was only by enlarging and taking on the role of 'an agent of change' that NATO was able to justify its presence in the building of a New World Order. The Treaty on European Union went some way to establishing an institutional framework for the formal interaction between the EU and NATO on security affairs but any co-ordination of enlargement policy has been on an informal and seemingly *ad hoc* basis. In fact, the two enlargement debates have become increasingly interwoven, not least in the minds of the candidate states, and this has led to an incremental linkage of the two processes.[33] The suggestion here is that the phenomenon of incremental linkage will become more extensive the nearer the two institutions get to realising enlargement. In the case of NATO this will be in 1999 whilst EU enlargement will take place sometime around 2006.[34] This still leaves the issue of the so-called 'pre-ins': those EU candidate states that have not been selected for a first wave of entry and those states aspiring to NATO membership mentioned in the 1997 Madrid Declaration.[35] In addition, there remains the thorny issue of Russia and, to a lesser extent, Turkey which are unlikely to be seriously considered for membership in the near to medium future (in the case of Turkey, this refers to the EU of course). To be more specific, a pan-European security order will be less than orderly if it fails to take account of Russian security concerns and socio-economic developments. In this sense, a pan-European security regime which would address both hard and soft security issues is essential. Such a regime would need to embrace not only current and future members of the EU and NATO but also those states that have no real prospect of joining one or the other, or even either. In this context structures which include Russia are especially important and the Council of Europe and Organisation for Security and Co-operation in Europe (OSCE) are examples of this. Also important are specific EU and NATO based structures and programmes which include Russia such as the EU's TACIS (Technical Assistance to the Commonwealth of Independent States) programme and the NATO-Russia Permanent Joint Council.

If a pan-European integration process is to continue successfully, it is doubtful whether this can be achieved by muddling through on an incremental basis or by reacting to crises. Rather, as Vaclav Havel stated in a speech to the Council of Europe in October 1993, the 'New Europe' of today must rekindle some of the vision that the post-war leaders had in attempting to build their New Europe if a stable political order for the continent as a whole is to be generated.

> Are we really so incorrigible? Twice in the twentieth century the whole of Europe has paid a tragic price for the narrow-mindedness and lack of imagination of its democracies. These democracies first failed when confronted with Nazism; they retreated and refused to resist the embryonic form of this evil, only to have to pay a million times more in the struggle against Nazism in its more developed form. The second time, they allowed Stalin to swallow up one half of our continent and bring history there to a halt. Today, this failure is coming back tragically to haunt not only those who have recently escaped from Soviet tyranny, but everyone. There is a saying, 'Everything good and evil comes in threes'. Democratic Europe cannot afford a third failure.[36]

Europe now finds itself on the eve of a historic step in the development of the European integration process. A bigger Europe there will most certainly be but whether this becomes a better Europe is less clear.

Notes

[1] This paper is based on a project that the authors are currently completing. See Smith, Martin and Timmins, Graham, *Building a Bigger Europe: The EU and NATO Enlargement Processes in Comparative Perspective'*, Ashgate, London (1999) and Smith, Martin and Timmins, Graham, 'The EU and NATO Enlargement Processes in Comparative Perspective: A Case of Incremental Linkage?', *West European Politics*, (1999 forthcoming).

[2] *Presidency Conclusions,* Luxembourg European Council 12/13 December 1997, European Commission, Brussels (1997).

[3] *Madrid Declaration on Euro-Atlantic Security and Co-operation* M-1(97)81, NATO Press Service, Brussels (1997).

[4] Avery, Graham and Cameron, Fraser, *The Enlargement of the European Union*, p.40, University Press, Sheffield (1998).

[5] Avery and Cameron, *ibid,* pp.50-51.

[6] C-G.Stubb, Alexander 'The 1996 Intergovernmental Conference and the Management of Flexible Integration', *Journal of European Public Policy*, 4(1), p.41, (1997).

[7] Lamers, Karl, *A German Agenda for the European Union*, p.12, Federal Trust for Education and Research/Konrad Adenauer Foundation, London (1994).

[8] Lamers, *ibid*, p16.

[9] Lamers, *ibid*, p18.

[10] Lamers, *ibid,* p23.

[11] Stubb, *ibid*, (1997). p.39. See also Alexander C-G.Stubb, 'A Categorisation of Differentiated Integration', *Journal of Common Market Studies,* 2(2) (1996).

[12] Stubb, *ibid,* (1997), p.39.

[13] *Treaty on European Union*, Title V, Article J.1 (section 2), European Commission, Brussels (1992).

[14] *ibid*, Title V, Article J.2 (section 2).

[15] *ibid,* Title V, Article J.4 (section 1).

[16] Article V of the treaty famously states that: 'The Parties agree that an armed attack against one or more of them in Europe or North America shall be considered an attack against them all and consequently they agree that, if such an armed attack occurs, each of them, in exercise of the right of individual or collective self-defence recognised by Article 51 of the Charter of the United Nations, will assist the Party or Parties so attacked by taking forthwith, individually and in concert with the other Parties, such action as it deems necessary, including the use of armed force, to restore and maintain the security of the North Atlantic area'.

[17] This is a key concern in Rühle, Michael and Williams, Nicholas, 'NATO Enlargement and the European Union', *The World Today*, 51(5), pp.84-8 (1995).

See also Asmus, Ronald and Larrabee, Stephen, 'NATO and the Have-Nots: Reassurance after Enlargement', *Foreign Affairs*, 75(6), pp.14-15 (1996).

[18] Cahen, Alfred *The Western European Union and NATO,* pp.51-2, Brassey's, London (1989).

[19] *Study on NATO Enlargement*, p.8, NATO Information Service, Brussels (1995).

[20] Wallace, William, *Opening the door: the enlargement of NATO and the European Union*, p.15, Centre for European Reform, London (1996).

[21] *Enlarged Security: The Security Problems Posed by the Enlargement of NATO and the European Institutions*, Assembly of the Western European Union, Paris (1997). The Partnership for Peace initiative launched in January 1994 provides opportunities for ECE states to develop military co-operation programmes with NATO and participation is also widely seen as being an essential precursor to full NATO membership for those ECE states aspiring to join.

[22] *The Consequences of the Madrid NATO Summit for the Development of WEU's Relations with the Central and Eastern European Countries and Russia*, Assembly of the Western European Union, Paris (1997).

[23] During the autumn of 1998 indications were that a change in the UK position on an EU-WEU merger might be under consideration by the Blair government.

[24] Helen Wallace's article from 1997, 'Pan-European Integration: A Real or Imagined Community', *Government and Opposition*, 32(2) is in many ways a path-breaking article in this area, particularly so as it highlights discussion surrounding the Deutschian concept of a 'security community'. Deutsch, according to Wallace, argues that genuine security integration requires 'compatible values, a distinctive way of life, expectations of economic ties or gains, and some points of economic growth, enhanced political capabilities to manage shared policies; unbroken lines of social communication, a broadening political élite; mobility of persons; and, multiple ranges of communication and transaction in social and cultural spheres as well as economic and political, (p.219).

[25] Ash, Timothy Garton, Europe's Endangered Liberal Order', *Foreign Affairs*, 77(2), p.54 (1998).

[26] Archer, Clive, 'The European Union, Security and the Baltic Region', paper delivered at the *European Consortium for Political Research, Standing Group on International Relations/International Studies Association Conference,* Vienna, pp.1-3 (1998).

[27] Jervis, Robert, 'Security Regimes', *International Organisation*, 36(2), p.357 (1982).

[28] Deutsch *et al,* Karl, *Political Community and the North Atlantic Area*, University Press, Princeton (1957).

[29] Wallace (1997), *op.cit.,* p.216.

[30] Although it is possible to challenge the assumption that NATO can be regarded as a collective security institution on the grounds of its limited membership.

[31] Archer (1998), *op.cit.,* p.15.

[32] Timmins, Graham 'European Union Policy towards East-Central Europe: The Prospects for Enlargement', *Contemporary Politics*, 3(1) (1997).

[33] See Smith and Timmins (1999) *op.cit.* for a further discussion of the incremental linkage debate. For a brief discussion of the US role, see Smith, Martin, 'The NATO Factor: A Spanner in the Works of EU and WEU Enlargement?' in Karen Henderson (ed.), *Back to Europe: Central and Eastern Europe and the European Union*, UCL Press, London (1999).

[34] The assumption made at the Amsterdam European Council summit was that entry would take place in 2002. This was, however, an indicative date and most recent estimates suggest that 2006 could be the earliest date of entry. See *The Economist*, 'Widening the European Union – but not too fast' 349(8093) (1998) and Timmins (1997), *op. cit.* for further discussion of the political debate surrounding enlargement.

[35] In terms of EU 'pre-ins' this refers to Bulgaria, Latvia, Lithuania, Romania and Slovakia. In the case of NATO, the Madrid Declaration mentioned specifically the Baltic States, Romania and Slovenia.

[36] Havel, Vaclav, *Address to the General Assembly of the Council of Europe*, Vienna, 8 October 1993.

5

Russia's Economic Security

GRAEME P. HERD

Deputy Director, Scottish Centre for International Security, University of Aberdeen

INTRODUCTION

The government of Prime Minister Yevgeni Primakov is currently struggling to cope with the worst crisis to beset Russia since the collapse of the Soviet Union in 1991. The most obvious sign of meltdown is in the financial and economic sphere, where we are witnessing the start of stagflation – economic stagnation and hyperinflation. The Russian Central Bank has begun to print roubles to inject cash into the economy and this will exacerbate the devaluation of the rouble, which looks set to continue under the Chairmanship of Viktor Gerashchenko. Inflation in August 1998 was 15%. Payments of back wages were worth only a third of their value and barely two weeks after devaluation, food prices were up 20% (imported goods at 80% dearer). The banking system has begun to collapse, on the verge of liquidation as well as consolidation through mergers with the former likely to triumph in the context of an incipient global recession. The Ministry of Internal Affairs stated that the annual flight of capital from Russia was 'comparable to the International Monetary Fund stabilisation loans'.[1] The external flow of capital into Russia has been drying up, and 50% of the current budget is now servicing debt repayment, on current projections moving to 70% in two years time.[2]

As a result, the prospect of Russian economic resurgence in the near or medium future is highly unlikely, given the current state of public and private finances compounded by the inability of the state to collect taxes. Whilst the export branches of the economy (oil, gas, and natural resources) are productive and known reserves are massive, other sectors are in disarray – particularly the manufacturing and agricultural sectors. Few external loans or investments appear forthcoming in the context of hyperinflation and a global recession. Moreover, over 60% of Russian natural resources formerly under state control have been privatised, passing strategic and profitable industries under private oligarchic control. This may also include enterprises within the military-industrial sector.[3]

This economic meltdown, the culmination of six years of attempted systemic transformation, has serious implications for Russia's ability to consolidate its 'market-democratic' transition. Indeed, disintegration, stagnation and recession currently appear more viable concepts through which to interpret Russia's modernisation project than the notion that democratic transition will be followed by democratic consolidation. The fusion of oligarchic economic power with political influence has created a critical distortion of the transition process. This threatens Russia's ability to sustain its independent arms production capability, it entrenches social polarisation as 'losers' in the transition process vastly outnumber the 'winners', and it blurs the margins between the white and black economies, between legal and criminal activity.[4] These economic insecurities could potentially undermine the very fabric of Russia's fragile post-Soviet state building project, and so the continued viability of the Federation itself as a coherent entity.

AN ANATOMY OF OLIGARCHIC POWER

In a move, which caught the political élite in Moscow unaware, on 23 March 1998 Boris Yeltsin dismissed the government of Victor Chernomyrdin for its failure to advance economic reform. Boris Berezovsky, a leading Russian financier, flew into Moscow on the 22 March and gave a televised interview in which he assessed the electability of potential candidates for the 2000 presidential election. He surmised that current politicians were either personally incapable, or effective but unelectable and that: 'the authorities have immense opportunities to bring forward new people' to ensure 'a succession of power'.

In August 1998, just before the government of Sergei Kiriyenko (March- August 1998) collapsed, it attempted to push through tough new taxation measures aimed at tightening tax collection or taking control of the large private monopolies and to wind up banks which had declared themselves technically bankrupt. Again Berezovsky was alleged to have brought pressure to bear on the President and on 23 August, after only five months in office, Kiriyenko's government fell.[5] Both the timing and effectiveness of this intervention threw into sharp relief the link between financial industrial groups (FIGs) and political power, raising the pertinent question: 'Who governs the Russian Federation?'

On November 1 1998 the question did receive an answer: oligarchic and nomenklatura-bureaucratic capitalism. In a *Financial Times* interview, Boris Berezovsky, also Deputy-Secretary of the influential Russian Security Council, boasted that seven Russian financiers now controlled 50% of Russian natural resources.[6] This 'Group of Seven' or 'Big Seven' ('*semibankirshchina*') consisted of Vladimir Gusinsky's Most Group (Media Most, Most Investment, Most Development), Bank Menatep's Mikhail Khodorkovsky, Mikhail Fridman and Pytor Aven (former Russian Minister of Foreign Economic Relations) of Alfa Group, Alexander Smolensky of SBS-Agro Bank, Vladimir Vinogradov's Inkombank, Boris Berezovsky's LogoVaz and Uneximbank's Vladimir Potanin.[7] This admission raised a series of related questions – not least, whether it was true or a triumph of public relations. How, then, were oligarchic FIGs created? What are their defining characteristics? To what extent do they influence government policy-making in the economic sector and what are the implications for our understanding of post-Soviet governance within the Russian Federation?

Although these dominant financial groupings share several fundamental characteristics, the most apparent is their strongly entrenched economic power base centred upon Russia's productive raw material exporting potential.[8] FIGs have also secured a dominant control of Russia's print and broadcast media, providing them with 'information power'. Their political influence is extended through their contacts at the highest levels within the government and private sector power structures, illustrated by their ability to conclude strategic partnerships with global multinational companies. The final key characteristic lies in the nature of their relationship to regional governors within the Russian Federation and influence over policy-making related to the strategic development of economic assets within former Soviet space. FIGs, then, can best be characterised as 'vertically integrated corporate structures in which a large financial institution with close ties to the state anchors an array of trading companies and industrial enterprises.'[9]

Boris Berezovsky, for example, trained as a mathematician, but entered the business community as a financial agent through his contacts with Vladimir Kadannikov, Chairman of AvtoVaz, who appointed him director-general of LogoVaz in 1989. Between 1989 and 1992 Berezovsky moved into the finance and export sectors. By 1994 LogoVaz had accrued huge debts, but through mobilising contacts in Moscow, Berezovsky avoided bankruptcy. As a financial agent for the Soviet élite, Berezovsky received government funds with which to invest.[10] How, though, did Berezovsky proceed from car-salesman to super-capitalist, with half of Russia's natural resources at his feet? The answer lies in his ability to harness his role as financial agent to the business community to Yeltsin's precarious political position in early 1996.

In late 1995, the Communist Party of the Russian Federation had romped home in the parliamentary elections as the largest party. In January 1996 opinion polls placed Yeltsin's popularity at 6%, rendering him the weakest of candidates in the June 1996 presidential elections. His inner circle of advisers had suffered a loss of faith in their ability to engineer Yeltsin's re-election. The Chechen war (December 1994 - November 1996) was deeply unpopular with the electorate and dominated the political agenda, the social and psychological cost of reforms was mounting and communist parties had swept to power in almost all second round elections throughout Eastern Europe. These factors all contributed to FIG fears that their empires would be dissolved in the wake of a communist comeback.

Despite this gloomy backdrop, Berezovsky successfully galvanised the election campaign in early 1996 by opening negotiations with key bankers (the 'Group of Seven') and persuading them to finance the election campaign in return for holding shares and management positions as collateral in key state industries still to be privatised. The implications of this support were profound. As one analyst noted: 'the loans-for-shares' scheme thus translated into a 'loyalty-for-shares' scheme (those closest to the government were duly rewarded for their partisanship) and a 'loans-for-patronage' scheme (in exchange for bank loans, the government offered not merely blocks of industrial shares, but also tax and custom breaks and other privileges).'[11]

The 'Group of Seven' met weekly to co-ordinate the re-election strategy, utilising their control of print and broadcast media, as well as ready supplies of cash, to this end. As Berezovsky commented at the time: 'The Communists expected to see weak willed democrats, whom they hoped to defeat hands down – only to be confronted with capitalism's bared fangs.'[12] Essentially, just as Berlusconi had done in the Italian elections of 1994, the 'Group of Seven' was able to run an American-style campaign in Russia exacerbated by the absence of any of the checks and balances usually associated with the democratic political process. Presidential gratitude ensured political promotion, with Berezovsky appointed to Deputy-Secretary of the influential Security Council by Presidential edict in October 1996. He focused on implementing the peace settlement in Chechnya, and was considered to be the architect of the Chernomyrdin-Mashkadov agreement signed in Moscow in November 1996.

From within government until his dismissal on 5 November 1997, Berezovsky began to exploit the newly acquired dominance of FIGs secured through the loans-for-shares scheme. He was also able quietly to recruit key personnel from within the former KGB's 6th Directorate, the economic counter-intelligence structure, to this end. In the Soviet period it fulfilled two functions: it possessed accurate information on the economy of the Soviet oil and gas industry (the key to maintaining the Soviet Union's hard currency reserves), and controlled the shadow economy (especially prevalent in the Caucasus, Central Asia and Ukraine). This role provided it with excellent contacts within the old Soviet oil and gas energy *nomenclature* which could be utilised to influence privatisation projects within the emergent post-Soviet energy sector. As a result, Berezovsky's business empire has allied itself with the oil and gas monopolies Gazprom and LUKoil, and a number of high profile energy sector companies.

Through late 1996 and into 1997 companies whose shares had been offered as collateral against loans to the government were privatised, and on every occasion the banks holding their shares as collateral were winners in the supposedly open auctions.[13] Over a period of 18 months, key strategic industries, financial and media assets were privatised amidst allegations of insider dealings, corruption and favouritism. In this short period, key FIGs managed the process through which they secured controlling interest in the bulk of Russia's profitable economy – the raw material export sector, financial and media assets.

Controlling interest of Russia's leading magnates

Organisation	Financial	Commercial	Media
Moscow Government Yuri Luzhkov	Moscow Bank	Various city and rural enterprises Real estate	Centre TV, *Obshaya Gazeta* (w), *vechernaya Moskva* (n); subsidies for *Moskovsky Komsomolets* (n)
Gazprom[1] Rem Vyakhirev	Bank Imperial Gazprom Bank National Reserve Bank	Gazprom (oil and gas)	*Trudm Rabochaya Tribuna* (n), 30% share in NTV
Uneximbank Vladimir Potanin	Uneximbank MKF Renaissance	Sidanco (oil) Norilsk Nickel (metals) Svyazinvest (telecom)	*Komsomolskaya Pravda Russky Telegraf, Izvestia* (n) Radioa Europa Plus
Berezovsky Group Boris Berezovsky	Obyedinyony Bank	Yuksi (oil) Logovaz (car manufacturing and trading)	ORT (tv), TV-6 *Nezavisimaya Gazeta, Novy Izvestia* (n) *Ogonyok* (m)
LUKoil Vagit Alekperov	Bank Imperial (shared with Gazprom)	LUKoil (oil)	*Izvestia* (shared with Uneximbank)
Menatep	Menatep Bank	Rosprom (45% share in Yukos) and Vostochny (oil) import-export, trading firms	Several provincial newspapers, *Literaturnaya Gazeta* (w) television stations, shares in ORT
Most Group Vladimir Gusinsky	Most Bank		NTV; Ekho Moskvy r); *Segodnya* (n), *Itogi* (m), various newspapers, television stations
Alfa Group Mikhail Fridman Pytor Aven	Alfa Bank	Tyumen Oil import-export, trading firms	Several provincial newspapers, television stations, shares in ORT

Key m=magazine • n=newspaper • r =radio • w=weekly

[1]Majority state-owned companies, but effectively independent

With kind permission:
'Russia's magnates: competing for influence, *Strategic Comments*, IISS, 4 (3), April 1998

Both Berezovsky and Potanin had themselves been employed in government service, allowing direct personal access to both bureaucrats and influence within the political élite. Potanin established a strong relationship with the MoD, particularly Chief of the General Staff (General Anatoly Kvashnin), and Head of the GRU (General Valentin Korabelnikov). The former Deputy Prime Minister, Anatoly Chubais, was also considered to be a Potanin ally and the relationship between the two was brought into focus with the sale of Svayzinvest in July 1997. Gusinsky, for example, stated: 'For me, Anatoly Borisovitch [Chubais] is not Deputy Prime Minister; he is rather one of my competitors ... He represents one of my competitors – Uneximbank.'[14] The Privatisation Minister Alfred Kokh was directly accused of favouring Potanin with 'insider' information and this resulted in his forced resignation in August 1997.

During the second phase privatisations of 1996-97, Berezovsky's political allies included Victor Chernomyrdin, the former Russian Prime Minister (December 1992-March 1998) and former Soviet Gas Industry Minister and head of Gazprom (the post-Soviet gas monopoly). Berezovsky has enjoyed direct influence within the presidential family, through Yeltsin's daughter Tatiana Dyachenko and the Presidential Head of Administration Valentin Yumashev, who effectively control Yeltsin's access to information. These contacts at the highest level of government are complemented by support within power ministries, particularly Anatoly Kulikov, the former Minister of the Interior (MVD), who controlled 250,000 MVD troops whose nucleus was the former Dzerzhinsky 'Iron' Division, located in Moscow.

These trends, evident in late 1997, were intensified in early 1998 with a rash of mergers within the energy sector. The looser tactical alliances or 'marriages-of-convenience' created in 1997 were now set to be consolidated and institutionalised through mergers and take-overs. The largest and sixth largest oil companies, LUKoil and Sidanko, entered discussions on the possibility of a defensive merger to form Russia's largest oil company in terms of output. The second and sixth largest producers, Yukos and Sibneft, have merged to form the Yuksi holding company – a company with the greatest production capacity and refining capability. Business analysts speculated that Yuksi could then expand again to incorporate Eastern Oil Company and the Eastern Siberian Oil and Gas Company, so forming a fuel monster on the scale of Shell or BP.

How might the inter-relationship between the exercise of political power and the accumulation of economic dominance during 1996 to 1998 be understood? It appears that a Faustian bargain was struck in early 1996. In order to engineer Yeltsin's democratic re-election in June 1996 and so preserve capitalism, the governing élite prepared to sacrifice the western-style free-market path of economic modernisation. In late 1996 and early 1997 this allowed a tactical alliance of *nomenklatura*-bureaucrats and oligarchs to dominate and control the heartbeat of Russia's economy, the privatisation programme. By mid-1997 the loosely affiliated semi-homogenous 'Group of Seven' which oversaw Yeltsin's re-election in 1996, had fragmented into two antagonistic financial groupings, one headed by Boris Berezovsky and the other by Vladimir Potanin. The split was fuelled by fierce competition for the rich former strategic state industries. Each of these oligarchic groups have emerged with two main objectives – to consolidate their control over their post-Soviet business empires, and to fulfil the strategic imperative of achieving outright economic hegemony within former Soviet space.[15]

FIGS AND THE STATE: TROJAN HORSES OR PRAETORIAN GUARDS?

In examining the relationship between FIGs and executive power it appears that their role in shaping policy-making and influencing key appointments is increasing at the expense of both state independence and the viability of Russian federal structures. This interpretation of politics generally supports the contention that Russia is bereft of opposition, the *Duma* as an institution is ineffective and irrelevant and that parties are empty shells, lacking ideological coherence and embracing only the politics of personal gain. With centralising and pan-Federative structures enfeebled, this interpretation supports the contention that the Russian Federation is undergoing a slow and controlled process of disintegration, where the only coherent and consistently articulated strategies involve economic growth by companies who have achieved a dominant financial position within the Federation.

The role of oligarchic groups in politics became more apparent and visible during 1998, partly due to the poor performance of the Russian economy. 1997 represented a bittersweet year for the Russian economy. It began with high expectations that the 'young reformers', the two Deputy Prime Ministers Anatoly Chubais (responsible for the Finance Ministry) and Boris Nemtsov (Fuel and Energy Ministry) would kick-start the Russian economy. It ended with a series of much publicised crises amid underlying indicators of economic growth. The key economic failure was perceived to be the continued poor tax revenue collection and the government's inability to formulate a new tax code or ensure that employees would receive back pay by January 1 1998. Although the value of the rouble slipped in response to the Asian meltdown, this was more positively indicative of the growing integration of the Russian economy into global markets. Macro-economic indicators were a cause of celebration. For the first time since 1991 the World Bank reported that Russian GDP grew by 0.4%, and inflation at 11% represented the lowest level since 1990 and the Russian stock market basked in the glow of an over 100% increase in the value of stocks.[16]

However, these end of year assessments proved too optimistic. In the first six months of 1998 Russian stocks shed 58% of their market value, precipitating the collapse of the Chernomyrdin government in March and a month long paralysis whilst Yeltsin sought to appoint a new prime minister and government and the *Duma* attempted to resist his choice. By June 1998 interest rates had increased from 24% to a 150% peak, and Russia, as the weakest emerging market outside Asia, was considered especially susceptible to the Asian financial contagion which broke out in Thailand in July 1997: 'it could, however, hit Russian tax revenues as falling demand in Asia cut world prices for key Russian exports such as oil and metals.'[17] This economic down-turn provided the economic backdrop for a government-led attempt to curtail the power of oligarchs and assert government independence in policy-making. This attempt failed – evidenced most notably by the collapse of the government. It did, however, raise an interesting public debate about the essential nature of Russia's post-Soviet modernisation paradigm.

In February 1998, First Deputy Prime Minister Boris Nemtsov, one of the young reformers who oversaw Russia's second phase privatisation project during Yeltsin's second term Presidency, reported to the anti-monopolies committee. He stated that the failure to get rid of Russia's monopolies had resulted in 'a dictatorship of oligarchical groupings with interests across industry, finance and information'.[18] Nemtsov argued that between 1991 and 1995, Russia faced a choice between communism and capitalism. With the election of Yeltsin as President in 1996, capitalism had finally consolidated its hold over the Russian economy. As Chubais argued, Communists would never be able to nationalise private property because 'in a country where private enterprise put out 75 per cent of GDP, nationalisation is impossible.'[19]

Which amongst the competing paths to the market economy would Russia now choose? Nemtsov outlined three options. First, *nomenklatura*-bureaucratic capitalism, where power, property and money are held by the old Soviet bureaucracy. Second, the 'Indonesian or Asian model' of oligarchic capitalism, where power, property and money belong to a small circle of businessmen who own most of the national wealth, the media, and hire and fire ministers. Last, the west European model of popular capitalism, in which administrative power is held by elected officials and property and money is widely distributed throughout society. In Russia a 'near-crystallised' bureaucratic-oligarchic system is developing in which oligarchic businessmen control 'privatised' governmental bureaucrats and owe their success through capitalising upon their 'informal relations with the authorities'.[20] Nemtsov described the current political system in the country as an 'oligarchy' and a 'monster' and warned of the rise of an 'authoritarian, semi-military' regime. Just as the choice in 1996 was between 'vulgar communism and vulgar capitalism – Zyuganov and Yeltsin – in the year 2000 the choice will be between a bastard oligarchy and a people's democracy.'[21] Nemtsov somewhat provocatively argued that the power of the metropolitan oligarchs was not yet hegemonic: 'Their position is quite shaky. Their financial empires might fall to dust overnight.'[22]

The role and significance of FIGs and oligarchs as political and economic actors within the Russian Federation are nevertheless hotly debated. Two parallel but contradictory views have emerged, each of which focuses on the social impact of oligarchic capitalism. One view holds that FIG-led or 'forced insider privatisation' produces unemployed workers who are socially dependent upon the newly privatised former state companies. This raises the danger that privatisation might lead to asset stripping and that the collapse of companies would create mass unemployment. Such unemployment would require a strengthening of authoritarianism in Russia and an imposition of censorship. In this reading, oligarchic economic systems are perceived to presuppose the imposition of authoritarian political regimes.

Before his dismissal First Deputy Prime Minister Anatoly Chubais, for example, stated that a government should run Russia, rather than a 'group of tycoons' who are not publicly accountable. He argued that a 'struggle for power which draws on all means, possible and impossible, admissible and inadmissible' was underway in Russia. He warned that the Russian Federation faced a 'choice between normal, democratic authority, a strong state authority, one which is accountable to the people, and shadow structures which pull the strings and run the show from behind the scenes.'[23]

Yegor Gaidar, architect of Russia's first phase privatisation project, holds an opposing view. He argues that the American experience of capitalist development provides a model that indicates the likely path of Russian economic development. He looks to America at the end of the nineteenth century, a period characterised by the rise of robber-barons – the Morgans, Carnegies, Rockerfellers, Du Ponts, Vanderbilts – who constructed a network of railways and factories, a banking system, modern chemical, metallurgy and petroleum production and refining industries, creating the foundations for modern mass-scale industrial production. Predatory, unbridled capitalists act as 'agents of progress', create employment, nurture a thriving middle class and reduce poverty. Russia's privatisation strategy was based on the contention 'as much as possible as quickly as possible' to entrench capitalism and make it irreversible. The presence of oligarchic capitalists, it follows, is merely a characteristic of the early stages of Russia's post-Soviet marketisation programme.

In February and March of 1998 key state officials attempted a failed state-led fight-back to curtail the power of the FIGs. Chubais stressed the need for the state to control oligarchs through tax collection, regulating monopolies, fighting corruption and strengthening the independence of the judiciary.[24] In mid-February Nemtsov tried to change Russian oil and gas policy, announcing that the government would not support mergers between oil companies that leave them with a market share of more than 30%.[25] However, companies were able to circumvent state measures. On 24 February LUKoil and Tatneft signed an agreement on 'strategic partnership', that is a merger in all but name, despite the company's protestations that: 'the agreement does not provide for the two oil giants merging into one company.'[26]

AUTUMN MELTDOWN AND ECONOMIC CRISIS IN LATE '98

By mid-1998 the political role of oligarchs became more public as the fragility of what has been termed 'Potemkin capitalism' became more transparent. Beneath the surface veneer of Russian capitalism

– the vibrant securities markets, a handful of world-class corporations, and a few hundred thousand quasi-middle class professionals in Moscow, St. Petersburg and Nizhni-Novgorod – lies the great majority of citizens, living 'almost entirely outside the cash economy, trapped in dying factories that seldom or never pay wages. Most find subsistence by growing their own food, sharing within extended families, bartering, and by evading taxes and cash obligations.'[27] Arbitrary pricing, the reliance on a barter system, the absence of mass bankruptcies and the accumulation of inter-enterprise debts disguises the reality of a Russian 'virtual economy' – that is an economy in which Soviet-era enterprises can still 'subtract value from inputs rather than adding it. This means the value of a Russian fridge is still lower than that of the metal, plastic and other raw materials used to make it.'[28]

Amidst the formulation of anti-crisis (or 'stabilisation') plans based on slashing public spending and increasing the effectiveness of tax collection, the debate over the role of oligarchic groupings in shaping Russian modernisation has been brought into sharp focus. The financial gain of these companies is perceived to have arisen at the expense of the consolidation of a democratic transition and the entrenchment of popular marketisation. Informed external bodies and respected internal Russian reports and analyses have advanced this assessment, though in much harsher and more colourful language. At a special hearing of the US Congress in October 1997, the ruling regime in Russia was described as a 'criminal syndicate'. In the same month, the Washington Centre for Strategic and International Studies characterised the Russian government as a 'crime syndicate', with gangsters controlling two thirds of the economy. Transparency International, a Berlin based-think tank, rates Russia as the world's fourth most corrupt country, after Nigeria, Bolivia and Colombia.[29] Even Jeffrey Sachs, an adviser on economic reform to the Russian government who resigned in January 1994, has stated that the reform process was 'wilful, glib and a deliberate act of a massive redistribution of wealth to a narrow circle of people'.[30] By August 1998, one commentator noted: 'Russia's credit rating is below Indonesia's. The size of its economy is smaller than Switzerland's. And its stock market is worth less than the UK water industry.'[31]

These critical external reports have been balanced by a growing awareness in Russia of the role of the economy and economic security for the continued stability of the Federation. The *Russian National Security Blueprint* of 26 December 1997 of openly stressed that 'the fusion of executive and legislative branches with criminal structures and their penetration into the sphere of management of the banking business, major production facilities, trade organisations and commodity networks' are a result of mistakes made in implementing systemic transformation.[32] In a weighty report published in 1997 the Russian Academy of Sciences estimated that capital investment in 1995 was 25% of the 1989 level, and in 1998 it stands at 8%; whilst Russia's GDP fell by 83%, industrial output by 81% and real unemployment rose by 10-fold to 13 million people.[33] The former Russian Minister of Internal Affairs, Anatoly Kulikov, reported that 60 million Russians are in one way or another linked to the 'shadow economy', 40,000 companies have come under 'criminal influence' and that 45% of the economy (representing $100 billion or three times Russian capital investments in the economy in 1995) is illegal.[34]

These fundamental distortions of the Russian economy have exacerbated the impact of what one analyst has labelled a 'global, systemic, virulent financial crisis that's shaking markets around the world.'[35] The financial crisis hitting Russia, following the crash of Asian markets and the depression of oil prices, has highlighted the role of the oligarchs in Russian politics and policy-making.[36] The Kiriyenko government ostensibly relied on oligarchs as it lacked the political 'weight' or *gravitas* and a macro-economic strategy with which to prevent a budget collapse. The inherent weakness of the coalition government led by Primakov should not mask the differing interests of FIGs from that of the state. Whilst FIGs proved (at a price) reliable partners for the incumbent political élite in 1996, it can be argued that in 1998 it is in the interests of some of the oligarchic groupings to undermine the very position they are ostensibly attempting to buttress. In fact, rouble devaluation would 'weaken the Central Bank as a pillar of one of Russia's largest financial industrial groups: Gasprom-Central Bank-Sberbank-Vneshtorgbank.'[37]

On 17 August 1998 the government finally devalued the rouble under the euphemism of a 'floating rouble' policy (6 – 9.5 roubles to the dollar). This heralded the collapse of both the Russian national currency and the Kiriyenko government on 23 August. Currency stabilisation had allowed for price stability and low inflation and it represented the Yeltsin Project's main (and many have argued only) economic achievement. Once out of office Kiriyenko outlined a number of factors that contributed to the rouble devaluation: oil and gas supplies Russia with foreign income and a positive balance of payments, but the prices were depressed; a decline in Russia's gold currency reserves; foreign capital flight; and, a crisis of confidence in state foreign and domestic securities. The government and Central Bank proposed a package of measures to stabilise the economic situation, including the restructuring of domestic debts, and a freezing of the state debt market. A 90-day moratorium on the payment of obligations to international financial organisations by Russian commercial banks and companies has been put in place. Primakov's government battled to create an economic policy that could address the economic crisis.[38]

'Crony capitalism' and 'forced-privatisation' is not the prime cause of economic instability in Russia; instability is an inherent feature of emergent markets. It is likely, however, that FIGs, with their powerful political connections, will ensure that the government's response to the economic crisis is in line with their immediate goals, rather than the long-term stability of the Russian economy. To this extent they will distort Russia's ability to respond to the crisis. For example, SBS-Agro and Inkombank were to benefit from massive Central Bank credits days before the rouble devaluation, and the consequent decision to default on state debt once the 'floating rouble' policy had been adopted benefited the banks. Such protectionism is set to continue: 'the political forces behind the new government – a malign mixture of populist politicians and plutocrats – are opposed to improving tax collection and tax reform.'[39]

CONCLUSIONS

The power of the FIGs to operate within informal 'clan'-type alliance networks, which include control over media, politicians, parties and armed security forces – in essence their ability to suborn state structures to private ends, to privatise power – makes it impossible for single government ministers to curtail their growing dominance. Alliances between differing FIGs are based on tactical and short-term considerations, rather than ideological allegiance. Their power is based around informal personal relations amongst the FIG decision-making élites and buttressed by both the relative stability of this élite and its fusion with political structures. Indeed, their power seems set to increase with involvement in 'Near Abroad' privatisation programmes and the exploitation of FSU energy resources. With the collapse of the Kiriyenko government in August 1998 it was clear that because there was no consolidated government anti-monopoly 'war' initiated against the FIGs, Russia's systemic transformation towards 'market-democracy' had been derailed. This has rendered political and economic developments in Russia – including the presidential elections in 2000 and the continued viability of a federal system of government – more dependent upon the struggle between business groupings than upon the democratic process.[40]

Indeed, on the evidence presented, it is not at all clear that 'Russia' is in a democratic transition, let alone the start of its consolidation. Some of the constituent parts of the Federation have begun this process – certain regions and parties – but others are either ungovernable or have resorted to highly authoritarian modes of behaviour. In post-Soviet Russia democratic norms are still weakly assimilated by the élite, and large sections of the electorate have yet to be assimilated into civic society. The exercise of political and economic power within Russia on the eve of the twenty-first century continues to raise the fundamental question: 'can the Russian Federation remain united and democratic?'

On this interpretation of Russian political and economic development, it is clear that the maintenance of Federal unity is incompatible with the implementation of a consistently applied and coherently articulated state-led democratisation project. It is more likely that, barring total systemic collapse, the Federation will retain its patch-work 'unity' through the haphazard observance of provincialism, regional diversity and an acceptance of the centre's limited ability to govern effectively throughout the Federation. Stagnation, disintegration and democratisation processes will hopefully continue to co-exist, but it is likely that no one ingredient will provide a definitive flavour to Russia's political system in the short or medium term.

Notes

[1] 'Capital flight from Russia said equivalent to IMF loans', BBC Summary of World Broadcasts (SWB), SU/3319 B/9, 31 August 1998 – *RIA news agency*, Moscow, 27 August 1998.

[2] Although IMF aid has provided external legitimisation to the Yeltsin regime, the consequence of the policies have led to a weakening of internal support for the Federation and have discredited 'market-democracy'. The EU represents Russia's largest trading partner, credited with 50% of Russia's foreign trade and 70% of foreign investments in the Russian economy; it is highly unlikely the EU will continue to inject funds into a fundamentally unsustainable Russian quasi-market economic system.

[3] 'More sell-offs planned under new strategy', SWB, SUW/0548 WA/6, 31 July 1998 – *ITAR-TASS news agency*, Moscow, 23 July 1998.

[4] Lilia Shevtsova, *Yeltsin's Russia: Challenges and Restraints* (Carnegie Moscow Centre, Moscow 1997), pp.10-11. For competing definitions of economic security, see: Barry Buzan, Ole Weaver & Jaap de Wilde, *Security: A New Framework for Analysis* (Lynne Rienner Publishers, London and Boulder, 1998), pp.95-118.

[5] 'Former Deputy Premier Nemtsov sees tycoon Berezovskiy as 'unstoppable'', SWB, SU/3318 B/10, 29 August 1998 – *Kommersant Daily*, Moscow, 27 August 1998.

[6] Chrystia Freeland, John Thornhill & Andrew Gowers, 'Moscow's Group of Seven', *Financial Times*, 1 November 1996.

[7] For an analysis of the rise and composition of the post-Soviet Russian economic élite, see: O. Kryshanovskaya & S. White, 'From Soviet Nomenklatura to Russian Élite', *Europe-Asia Studies*, Vol. 48, no. 5, pp.711-733; D. Kotz, *Revolution From Above*, (Routledge, London, 1997); and, J.R. Blasi, M. Kroumova & D. Kruse, *Kremlin Capitalism*, (Cornell University Press, Ithaca & London, 1998).

[8] Juliet Johnson, 'Russia's Emerging Financial Industrial Groups', *Post Soviet Affairs*, 13 (14), 1997, p.p.333-365 and Michael McFaul, 'State Power, Institutional Change, and the Politics of Privatization in Russia', *World Politics*, 47, (2), 1995, pp.210-243.

[9] Michael McFaul, 'Russia's Privatized State as an Impediment to Democratic Consolidation, Part II', *Security Dialogue*, 29 (2), September 1998, pp.315 -332. See also 'Part I', *Security Dialogue*, 29 (2), June 1998, pp.191-199.

[10] 'Character Reference – Vladimir Berezovsky', *Russia Briefing*, 4 (9), 5 October 1996, p.11; I. Starodubrovskaya, 'Financial-Industrial Groups: Illusions and Reality', *Communist Economies and Economic Transformation*, 7 (1), 1995, pp.5-19; J.E. Prokop, 'Industrial Conglomerates, Risk Spreading and the Transition in Russia', *Communist Economies and Economic Transformation*, 7 (1), 1995, pp.35-50; L. Gorbatova, 'Formation of Connections between Finance and Industry in Russia:

Basic Stages and Forms', *Communist Economies and Economic Transformation*, 7 (1), 1995, pp.21-33.

[11] Natalia Dinello, 'Bankers' Wars in Russia', *CSIS Post-Soviet Prospects*, 6 (1), February 1998. For an engaging contemporary analysis of campaign strategies during the 1996 Russian Presidential elections, see: Jack F. Matlock, Jr., 'The Struggle for the Kremlin', *The New York Review of Books*, XLIII (13), 8 August 1996, pp.28-34.

[12] Yuriy Ryazkskiy, 'Berezovskiy's Brains', *Moskovskiy Komsomolets*, 24 January 1998, p.4. See also: Oleg Yuryev, 'The Business Cocktail: A Mixture of Petroleum, Engine Oil, and Crime', *Moskovskiy Komsomolets*, 31 October 1996.

[13] Yelena Babak, 'Capitalist Bridge', *Dyelovoi Mir*, 10-14 November 1996.

[14] Christian Lowe, 'MOST-Group Mogul Slams Chubais', *The Moscow Times*, February 5 1998.

[15] For recent summaries of FIG power and development, see: Graham P. Herd, 'Robbing Russia?' *The World Today*, Vol. 54, No. 4, April 1998, pp.93-94 and 'Russia's magnates competing for influence', *Strategic Comments*, 4 (3), April 1998.

[16] Jeanne Whalen, 'Turnaround Year?' *The Moscow Times*, Business Extra, 13 January 1998.

[17] Mark Whitehouse, 'Asia's Second Wave', *The Moscow Times*, Business Extra, June 23 1998.

[18] 'Nemtsov laments 'dictatorship' of economic monopolies', SWB, SU/3157 B/2, 21 February 1998 – *ITAR-TASS news agency*, Moscow, 20 February 1998.

[19] 'Deputy premier rules out the return of communism even if left wins elections in 2000', SWB, SU/3182 B/2, 23 March 1998 – *Interfax news agency*, Moscow, 22 March 1998.

[20] *Moscow Moskovskiye Novosti*, no. 6, 15-22 February 1998.

[21] 'First Deputy Premier Nemtsov warns of 'authoritarian' and 'semi-military' future', SWB, SU/3180 B/1, 20 March 1998 – '*Argumenti i Fakty*', Moscow, 17 March 1998.

[22] 'First Deputy Premier Nemtsov asserts independence of financial circles', SWB, SU/3181 B/2, 21 March 1998 – *Interfax news agency*, Moscow, 20 March 1998.

[23] 'First Deputy Premier Chubais rejects Russia's oligarchic capitalism', SWB, SU/3170 B/1, 9 March 1998 – *NTV*, Moscow, 6 March 1998.

[24] John Thornhill, 'Chubais warns against 'cronyism'', *Financial Times*, 6 March 1998.

[25] 'First deputy premier outlines oil and gas policy', SUW/0526 WA/9, 27 February 1998 – *Interfax news agency*, Moscow, 24 February 1998.

[26] 'Oil companies to co-operate but not to merge', SUW/0526 WA/9, 27 February 1998 – *Interfax news agency*, Moscow, 24 February 1998.

[27] Fred Weir, 'Veneer of Capitalism Obscured Growing Crisis', *The St. Petersburg Times*, June 19 1998, p.8. 'Potemkin privatisation' has also been referred to as

prikhvatizatsiya ('the great grab'). See: Steve Stolnick, *Stealing the State: Control and Collapse in Soviet Institutions* (Cambridge, MA: Harvard University Press, 1998).

[28] John Thornhill, 'Magic Realist Economy', *The Financial Times*, August 1 -2, 1998, p.7; Clifford Gaddy & Barry Ickes, 'Russia's Virtual Economy', *Foreign Affairs*, 77 (5), September/October 1998, pp.53-67; Barry Ickes, Peter Murrell & Randi Ryterman, 'End of the Tunnel? The Effects of Financial Stabilization in Russia', *Post-Soviet Affairs*, 13 (2), April-June 1997, pp.105-133.

[29] Vasily Safronchuk, 'The Russia We Lost, and Berezovskiy, Gusinsky, Potanin, and Company Acquired', *Moscow Sovietskaya Rossiya*, 25 December 1997, p.5 – FIBIS-SOV-98-002.

[30] Jeffrey Sachs, 'The Not-immaculate Conception of Russian Capitalism in Russia', *New York Times*, June 1998, p.41.

[31] John Thornhill, 'Who lost Russia?', *Financial Times*, August 28 1998, p.14.

[32] 'National Security Blueprint of the Russian Federation', SWB, SU/3114 S2/1, 1 January 1998 – '*Rossiskaya Gazeta*', Moscow, 26 December 1997.

[33] Cited by Fred Weir, 'Veneer of Capitalism Obscured Growing Crisis', *The St. Petersburg Times*, June 19 1998, p.8.

[34] 'Ex-interior minister assesses shadow economy', SWB, SUW/0549 WA/4, 7 August 1998 – *Interfax news agency*, Moscow, 30 July 1998.

[35] Thomas Fuller, 'Asian Crisis: More Than Just Crony Capitalism', *International Herald Tribune*, August 14, 1998, p.p.1 & 7.

[36] Andrei Piontkovsky, 'Oligarchy Has Ministers at Its Beck and Call', *The Moscow Times*, June 25 1998.

[37] Yulia Latynina, 'Two Different Sides of the Rouble', *The Moscow Times*, No. 1484, June 30 1998, p.10.

[38] William Tompson, 'The Future of the Russian Banking System: Liquidation or Mergers?', Russia in Crisis, *CSRC Occasional Series Papers* (1999).

[39] Martin Wolf, John Thornhill & Stephen Filder, 'Meltdown', *The Financial Times*, August 28 1998, p.15.

[40] Anatol Lieven, *Chechnya: Tombstone of Russian Power* (Yale, University Press, 1998), Chapter 4: 'The Masque of Democracy', pp.150- 184.

6

'NATO plus' CJTFs for Eurasia: is cooperation possible?

IRINA ISAKOVA[1]

Research Associate, Centre for Defence Studies, King's College London

Current developments in European and Eurasian security institutions demonstrate the possibility of Combined Joint Task Forces (CJTFs) becoming significant blocks in the European/ Eurasian security architecture as well as a vehicle for limited and controlled involvement of states in potential areas of conflict outside their national territories. Conflict management of this kind could become the dominant trend in the post-NATO enlargement period.

Initially, the CJTF concept was introduced in western, and primarily American, approaches as a response to the necessity of restructuring the armed forces and increasing their compatibility, effectiveness and efficiency. Since the NATO decision of 1994, the CJTF became the officially recognised structural unit for the new European operational tactical security structures.[2] The CJTF could be described as a multinational, multiservice, task-tailored force consisting of NATO, and possibly non-NATO, forces capable of rapid deployment with a view to conducting limited duration peacekeeping/peace-enforcement missions, under the integrated military structure of NATO or the Western European Union.[3] Briefly, the CJTF is envisaged as a temporary force for rapid crisis response, executed by 'highly trained multinational forces, backed by pre-established political terms of reference, standardised procedures, regular exercises and in-place infrastructure'.[4] The uniqueness of the NATO CJTF initiative is in the permanent institutionalisation of the multinational task-force concept, which was previously a temporary 'command and control' arrangement employed by ad hoc coalitions. In fact, CJTFs became associated with the political decisions to view them as a training mechanism for new potential allies that would be capable of assisting NATO states in crisis management operations.

Western military planners envisaged three CJTF employment scenarios: a 'NATO-only' CJTF (for Art. V missions or 'inner core missions' under the Washington Treaty[5]); a 'NATO-plus' CJTF (including some non-NATO states); and a WEU-led CJTF.[6] The second option - 'NATO-plus'- is considered particularly desirable within the CJTF initiative and is accorded high priority by NATO's Partnership for Peace (PfP) planners as part of a burden-sharing tendency involving PfP partners in out-of-area operations. The participating states are given functions and share a certain level of integration with the NATO member states, depending on the possibility of their joining the alliance as full members, or of 'hosting' NATO/WEU CJTFs in case of crises. 'NATO-plus' CJTFs not only differ, theoretically, from other scenarios through their choice of participants and potential areas of deployment, but by the functions and types of missions they have to perform. 'NATO-plus' missions have to be prepared and deployed to execute Military Operations Other Than War (MOOTW)[7].

Presently only the IFOR/ SFOR and Kosovo missions could be named as being CJTFs[8] in practice. There are nevertheless formidable problems to be solved before the minimum requirements of the CJTF concept could be met and become an effective operational reality. However, extended bilateral training programmes and the 'enhanced PfP' are aimed at closing the gap between NATO and non-NATO states in 'command and control' (C^2) procedures, information connectivity and assistance in air power and air lift operations. Thus, in preparing the potential participants for 'NATO plus' missions, it was considered essential for non-NATO participants in the CJTF to be motivated to take part in 'out-of-area' missions if they were to deal with emergencies that might affect the stability of their own regions.

'NATO PLUS' CJTFS 'WITH' AND 'FOR' EURASIA

In accordance with NATO and WEU analysis, the Caucasus and Central Asia are becoming an increasing focus of interest of the western powers and security institutions.[9] Factors in this region's importance for the West are energy and natural resources as well as US long-term policy objectives[10]. Taken together with the oil reserves in the Middle East, the Caucasus represents 71% of the world's oil reserves. One third of the world's total natural gas reserves are in the Caucasus-Caspian basin alone. The region has also rich resources of water and gold, which could increase western interests in the region by 35-40% by the year 2010.[11] Equally, Russian dependence on the natural reserves (especially oil, gas, ferrous and non-ferrous metals) of its neighbouring states in Eurasia is likely to increase by 2002-2005. Access to the natural resources, transportation and communication networks of the Commonwealth of Independent States (CIS) is considered by Russia vitally important for its economic survival and security considerations.

At the same time it is proving to be a very volatile area. For instance, the Caucasus has been the most troubled 'hot spot' in the CIS. Four out of six conflicts within the CIS were located in the area (Nagornyi Karabakh, Abkhazia, South Osetia and Chechnya). There are several other potential conflicts in the region, such as those around Ajaria or the Armenian enclave in Georgia, or Russia's Muslim autonomous republics of Transcaucasus. These developments will unavoidably affect the transportation of the Caspian oil to western Europe and Turkey. Thus, stability in the Caucasus is becoming important for the implementation of western energy security. Conflicts in Central Asia might stimulate the involvement of Russia, Iran, Turkey, and China in regional affairs, and potentially destabilise the situation in Southwest Asia, Central Eurasia, and South Asia. Both the Caucasus and Central Asia are experiencing high-density drug and arms trafficking in multiple directions; Islamic extremism and fractional conflict, ethnic tensions; environmental degradation and the possibility of becoming a transit area for weapons of mass destruction-associated materiel and technology proliferation.

All the former Soviet Republics take part in NATO's PfP initiative. Ukraine, Uzbekistan, Georgia and Azerbaijan have become selected CIS states in the 'enhanced PfP'. Ukraine, Uzbekistan and most recently Georgia and Azerbaijan have chosen a kind of 'self defence support policy' for their national military strategies. While NATO provides logistics and helps improve national forces for these states, the latter remain largely self-sufficient. But they retain the possibility of upgrading NATO military assistance to 'air power projection' and/or 'joint power projection', which could be implemented in CJTFs, and 'forward presence' as the last resort in a chain of escalation crises.

The practical realisation of 'NATO-plus' humanitarian and peace support operations presupposes:

- A functioning international network of situation centres for early warning and political consultations through evolutionary prototyping, with national situation centres as the principle sources of information;
- existing rapid reaction forces - CJTFs - prepared for deployment and execution of MOOTW

The Network of Ethnological Monitoring and Early Warning of Conflict (EAWARN) could be considered as one of the prototypes of the early warning systems for Eurasia.[12] The network was designed to collect and process information for early detection of potential ethnic and political conflicts. However, since 1994-1995 the main activities in early warning monitoring have been transferred to the national ministries for emergency situations and the national security councils of the former Soviet states. The monitoring activities of the national ministries for emergency situations were designed primarily for collecting data on natural and technological catastrophes and have been expanded to cover other areas. Within the framework of PfP, the Eurasian states, including Russia, have been receiving and installing equipment for early warning monitoring and rapid reaction capabilities that is compatible with US/NATO standards.[13]

The international early warning system (under the NATO umbrella) was established with the creation of the Euro-Atlantic Disaster Response Coordination Centre at NATO HQ, Brussels, in June 1997. Institutionally it linked national early warning centres, NATO and the UN Office for the Coordination of Humanitarian Assistance. It brought about the introduction of common indicators for crisis monitoring and management as well as the standardisation of the decision-making process for granting assistance in any crisis (ethnic, technological or other) within the Euro-Atlantic Partnership Council (EAPC) area of responsibility. Consequently, international assistance programmes will be adopted in future in line with the analysis done by international disaster assessment teams. The data provided by international early warning networks will be especially important in cases of potential humanitarian intervention in the distress areas. The Centre is to provide the operational link between disaster assistance units (the Euro-Atlantic Disaster Response Unit) and rapid reaction forces for MOOTW in the case of requests from UN or EAPC member-states.[14]

The training for NATO/WEU-led CJTFs is undertaken through bilateral and multilateral exercises within the PfP. The composition of the multinational task-force is usually tailored to the requirements of the specific mission. However, current developments in MOOTW dictate interoperability at least in C^2I, logistics and air support operations. The call for specialisation for national units assigned to the CJTFs has been applied most recently to the Eurasian states and priority has been given to:

- civil-emergency planning and crisis management exercises (CMX 98);
- the tactical/operational level of peace support operations (Exercises Peaceshield 97 and 98);
- developing mutual understanding in the areas of close air support, forward air control and combat search and rescue (Exercise Co-operative Zenith 1998);
- interoperability of air defence and air control procedures (within the framework of the Regional Airspace Initiative, aimed at establishing NATO-compatible Air Sovereignty capability, a common and safe air traffic control system and a NATO-compatible airspace management architecture);
- adapting new aircraft radio navigation systems to comply with international standards;
- deploying and testing of a CJTF HQ communications infrastructure (e.g. Exercise Cooperative Guard 1997);
- cooperation on frequency management, including the introduction of NATO standardised equipment, with common tuning ranges and technical characteristics, and common radio frequencies, as well as providing mobile communication systems to the PfP partners.

One of the goals of the PfP programme is also to assist the former Soviet states to develop their own defence capabilities, thus allowing them options other than reliance upon Moscow in their security policy. Assistance in promoting regional and sub-regional military cooperation was one of the main political objectives of the PfP and bilateral programmes. In this context, the modernisation of transport infrastructure and telecommunications is seen as essential for the military and economic development of the countries, for regional and cross-regional cooperation and for preparing conditions for 'hosting' international humanitarian aid operations and potential CJTFs. Despite the fact that, usually, CJTFs have to rely fully on their own communication systems, adequate civil telecommunications are important for out-of-area Peace Support Operations, when close interaction with local government and non-governmental organisations are added to the more traditional military chain of command.[15] Thus, establishing communication networks for the Eurasian states that bypass Russia is becoming important for economic and military purposes. In this respect, the construction of the Trans-Asia-Europe fibre-optic communications line and the introduction of direct digital communication systems should be considered essential.[16] While renovation of the aviation infrastructure is essential for 'NATO plus' deployment, modernisation and construction of transportation networks is considered important for regional coalition building and promoting the mobility of the local armed forces. Thus, integration of the TRANCECA transportation system[17] with the Cretean Corridors, Baltic-Pontic routes and the Euro-Asian Corridor[18] has economic, political and military significance for the Eurasian region.

All the "enhanced PfP" Eurasian states so far mentioned - Ukraine, Uzbekistan, Georgia and Azerbaijan - are going through different stages of military reform. All are planning to develop new force structures that are not based on the old Soviet model. Ukraine and Uzbekistan, being at a more advanced stage of reforming their armed forces, began to reconfigure their ground forces into a corps-brigade-battalion structure for greater flexibility. By the end of the year 2000 the second stage of reforms for both militaries should be completed with the transition to a new staff organisational structure, new systems of training, personnel recruiting and operational, logistical and technical support. These changes are viewed as being consistent with the preparation of the forces, command and control systems necessary for multinational operations.

PARADOXES OF EURASIA

Ukraine, Uzbekistan, Georgia and Azerbaijan, as the 'enhanced PfP' participants and most likely candidates for 'NATO-plus' CJTFs, have been viewed as the 'mall anchor store(s)'[19] in the sub-regional groupings in the post-Soviet era. The interest in security arrangements on the sub-regional level is progressively increasing, not least amongst NATO and western states. Presently there are few regional groupings that have established, or are planning to establish, multinational peacekeeping units that are trained and organised as CJTFs. In Eurasia the groups that have a special relationship with NATO and western security institutions are the Central Asian Union (CAU, founded as an economic association in 1993), with CENTRAZBAT (a joint Uzbekistan-Kyrgyzstan-Kazakhstan peacekeeping unit that has operated since 1995)[20] and GUAM.

GUAM as its acronym suggests was established by Georgia, Ukraine, Azerbaijan and Moldova as an informal alliance for the coordination of foreign and economic policies in October 1997. According to the organisation's protocol, signed by deputy foreign ministers in November 1997, its objectives are: cooperation on international level, resistance to 'separatism', mutual support regarding the settlement of regional conflicts, a common approach to peacekeeping operations, the development of transit routes and preparations for eventual accession to western European and Transatlantic institutions.[21] In December 1997, the creation of a joint battalion by Azerbaijan, Georgia and Ukraine was announced. Moldova failed to provide a military contingent due to unresolved issues with Transdniestria and the stationing of Russian forces in the vicinity. However, with the September 1998 decision of Uzbekistan to join the GUAM group, the political and military coordination of these sub-regional groupings will unavoidably increase. Both the CAU and GUAM have expressed interest in promoting political and military consultations with NATO on regional security. Defence and security units are about to be established within the South Eastern Cooperation Initiative (SECI) and the Black Sea Economic Cooperation Council (BSEC). The states of Eurasia are now members of several overlapping sub-regional arrangements and such regional groupings are increasingly viewed as potential joint recipients of US and western assistance and as collective participants in 'out-of-area' missions.

The Caucasus and Central Asia have long been considered by Russia to be in its zone of influence and the increased rate of PfP activity and CJTF training throughout 1994-1997 led to the Russian government's reacting with unease[22]. However, such a reaction did not prevent Russia from seeking to extend relations with NATO, or from stopping NATO's expansion of activity in the region. The answer to this paradox is quite simple. Since 1995 Russia has recognised the necessity of acknowledging the realities of increasing regionalisation in Eurasia. The preservation of the Commonwealth of Independent States (CIS) and the Treaty of Collective Security depend on Russia's ability to adjust to the existing tendency of a regionalisation of security space within it. Regional groupings, such as CAU, or potential sub-regional cooperation in the Caucasus overlap with regional demarcation zones of the CIS security system. Strengthening the capabilities of the coalition group of forces (or multinational operational forces (MOS) - the Russian version of the CJTF in the demarcation zones is considered to be an advantage for regional stability. More than that, some of the requirements that were applied to the coalition of Eurasian states (in accordance with the CIS Collective Security Treaty) were identical to the requirements for CJTFs.[23] The situation is different with the GUAM security arrangement, as this grouping tore apart the boundaries of the CIS security demarcation zones.

While encouraging regional and sub-regional cooperation and unavoidably accepting their increased defence capabilities, Russia is not interested in withdrawal from the Caucasus or Central Asia. However, in order to deal with military reform and the modernisation of its own forces under extremely difficult financial conditions, the Russian military has planned to shift the financial burden to the local communities and make the newly independent states (NIS) pay for their own security. At the same time the focus has been on the preservation of the joint Operational Commands, subordinated to the Russian General Staff, and liaison teams in the local Ministries of Defence and General Staffs for coordination of military activities among the states. Such arrangements, according to Russian military planners, are supposed to ease the financial burden for Russia while preserving a unified security space by leaving the possibilities for upgrading the Russian presence in case of escalating conflicts in the territories of her neighbouring states.

Another paradox in military developments in Eurasia is to be found in the similarities in the reorganised structures of the ground forces in the countries that have recently rejected any idea of establishing unified regional security arrangements with Russia (e.g. Ukraine and Uzbekistan). Military reforms in Russia, Ukraine and Uzbekistan are developing in parallel, presenting similar approaches to restructuring the military. As a result, assistance to national forces or regional multinational multiservice task forces could arrive both from Moscow and from NATO depending on political developments in the Eurasian states and the regional balance of power. Thus, the upgrading of local multinational task forces in situations of crisis will become a critical issue in relations between NATO and Russia, especially since direct confrontation is possible between Russia and the West over the CIS states. At the same time, existing similarities in operational planning and common interests and shared concerns over soft security issues, arms control, uncontrolled drug trafficking and terrorism create possibilities for cooperation.

RUSSIA: A FRIEND OR FOE?

Eurasia is considered to be an extremely sensitive area for Russia, the NIS and the West. Threat assessments undertaken by the Russian General Staff show that there are possibilities for a series of local conflicts in the Caucasus, Central Asia (within 5-7 years) and along the borders of the Russian Federation[24]. The situation could be aggravated due to the following factors: a) both Russia and the US/NATO have stated that they have interests and responsibilities in the Caucasus and Central Asia; b) both Russia and the US have proclaimed a policy of 'intensive geopolitical presence' in the region and both countries rely on nuclear deterrence and 'forward deployment' in the region in case of crisis escalation.

The new stage of preparations for 'NATO plus' CJTFs with the Eurasian states was marked by NATO and US regional commands assuming responsibility for the region. For NATO, the responsibility of AFSOUTH has expanded to cover Azerbaijan, Georgia, Armenia, Kazakhstan, Turkmenistan and the Caspian Sea Region. One of the challenges this presents is the necessity to establish the proper formalised relationships with Russia and Ukraine.[25] In preparation for potential CJTFs with PfP partners, the Eurasian region (with exception of Russia) was divided by US defence planners among US regional commands in early 1998. US European Command, which had overseen the PfP programme, assumed military responsibility for the Caucasus and US Central Command, already covering the Middle East, assumed responsibility for Central Asia.[26] The challenges for the Southern region dictated the necessity of this proactive policy for NATO and the WEU - a policy of 'forward presence and forward engagement.' This has not been welcomed by Russian military planners. As Sergei Larionov says:

'Our military no longer point to a map and say, "Here it is, our main enemy." Indeed, how can it say this when its Supreme Commander said, for the whole world to hear, that Russia doesn't want to fight anyone. And yet, our military knows who they may have to fight. It is hardly a secret that NATO is the number one potential enemy for the Russian General Staff.'[27]

The situation is getting increasingly complicated due to the fact that both US/NATO and Russia view the same areas of 'middle Europe'[28], Transcaucasus and Central Asia as areas of applied 'intensive' geopolitical and geoeconomical competition. In justifying their policies, both Russia and US appeal to a modified deterrence concept and state their right to preserve the possibilities for 'forward presence' in the Eurasian region. The US policy of 'regional deterrence' suggests that the United States adopt a national military strategy based on the ability to deny the opponent's political/military objectives, either by basing US forces within the region in times of crisis or by convincing the adversary that they can be forward deployed rapidly if the need arises.[29] Similarly, Russia has introduced the strategy of 'realistic deterrence'. This concept signals acceptance by Russia of its limited financial resources and force capabilities that prevent its continued and permanent military presence in the CIS while at the same time introducing a new type of Russian presence in the region (through Operational Commands and a established liaison missions in the ministries of defence of the former republics). The concept officially proclaims the lowering of the threshold for using nuclear weapons in regional conflicts.[30] The new version of the Russian Military Doctrine (to be in operation until the year 2005) states that:

'Russia would consider as a direct military threat any deployment of the foreign troops on the territories of the adjacent states as well as concentration of forces near its borders.'[31]

This is the only statement that directly addresses the future deployment of CJTFs in Eurasia. Otherwise there are no public international agreements between the CIS states (with exemption of Russian-Belarusian agreements) that address the issues of deployment of the Western states on the territories of the CIS countries.

At the same time Russia and NATO have areas of mutual interest. Since 1995, Russia has conducted joint emergency relief exercises as part of PfP, taken part in an extensive exchange programme with US and European border guard services, installed elements of early warning systems as part of an agreement signed between NATO and Ministry of Emergency Situations and Civil Defence, and expressed interest in cooperation between Ministry of Interior and NATO. Although rejecting participation in CJTF exercises, Russia has conducted exercises between the different services and force ministries that are considered to be integral parts of the operational task forces (JTF) and MOS. The SFOR experience of cooperation between Russian and NATO peacekeepers demonstrated the absence of any transparency at operational or tactical-operational levels. Any joint commands at the level of regiments or battalions still function under dual chain of command, with the areas of responsibility are divided. A need for definition of joint or unified doctrine for peacekeeping and possibly for combat performance at later stages of co-operation was seen as a precondition for establishing any CJTF.

However, Russia has its own vision of multinational, multiservice and multifunctional task forces. At the core of the Russian military reform is the introduction of joint and combined doctrine for the Russian territorial defence. From 1997, the Russian military planners moved away from focusing on mobile forces as a key major structural block and concentrated their efforts on the multi-functional units.[32] However, the Russian versions of CJTFs are usually formed by neighbouring states and are linked to specific geo-strategic sub-regions. Another key difference is that while the main issue for the CJTF is adjustment of the military to the revolution in military technology and military affairs, the MOS has to face mostly the task of preservation of its combat capabilities in the situation of collapsed or non-properly functioning armies.

GETTING INVOLVED

There are several legitimate ways for mandating and conducting multinational missions: traditional UN peacekeeping operations; rapid re-deployments of a UN-led force made up of member states capable of providing resources on relatively short notice; UN-mandated operations led by one nation and made up of a coalition of willing and able participants (ALBA operation/Italy); and a UN or OSCE-operation conducted by regional organizations.

According to the CIS Military Co-operation Cell (which coordinates peacekeeping activities in the CIS), the decision on the involvement of the Multinational Operational Force in any type of crisis should be based on the following:

- a complex analysis of the crisis situation. This could be done either by the international or CIS crisis analysis center, or by individual member-states (using a compatible and agreed methodology) and presented to the international institution for consideration.
- a defined mandate and structure for the implementation force. It is expected (by the Russians) that such recommendations could be monitored by the centres / regional centres set up by the regional organization that was nominated for the implementation of the mission and decides the composition of forces, C3I and infrastructure use.

Russian opposition to the use of force in Kosovo (1998) was mainly motivated by the perceived threat of creating a precedent in mandating the use of force in a conflict area on appeal from a neighbouring state outside of the established international institutional frameworks (UN or OSCE). Russia was concerned that this precedent could be used within the CIS area or even in the Russian separatist regions (e.g. Chechnya, Dagestan). They perceived such a possibility arising if the neighbouring PfP member-states considered developments in the adjacent regions to be endangering their national security. For instance, the risks of potential escalation of regional conflict or mis-interpretation of Russian actions and intentions in the neighboring states might trigger them to appeal for the security guarantees under the PfP framework and explore the idea of the necessity of international humanitarian intervention in the conflict area. In practice the debate on establishing a proper mandate to use force in Kosovo helped at least to clarify the framework under which the EAPC institution might be used in future. It seems that appeals for humanitarian assistance and security guarantees for the PfP states[33] would get a more favorable response from the NATO member-states, if such requests came from the legitimate authority of the state where the assistance is to be implemented.

There are several possible channels for the international

community to get involved in the CIS area in cases of conflict. The most probable option that the Western states would be asked to get involved in the potential conflict by the individual member state. However, the most secure way of getting into the area without triggering a massive response from Russia would be to use the regional groupings and institutions, thus spreading 'collective' responsibility for the political decision. The other possibility for the Western states to get involved in Eurasia is by being 'dragged' into the peacekeeping or peace enforcement mission in region. The Eurasian states have an extended programme of co-operation and assistance within PfP in cases of natural and technocratic disasters. In 1997-98 there was a drastic increase in number of such catastrophes in the Eurasian states with a potential damaging effect to the environment. This tendency is bound to continue due to the aging of equipment and machinery, non-implementation of the maintenance procedures and limited possibilities to address potential emergency situations (or technological breakdowns) due to the financial shortages. As a result, all post-Soviet states are bound to appeal to international community for assistance, especially to NATO within the PfP framework. However, the majority of the crises in the CIS should be considered as complex emergency situations, accompanied by necessity to deal with an intensification of criminal activity and possible ethnic unrest, with refugees and uncontrolled migration, famine, or even interstate and cross border hostilities. There would be an increased number of situations when the local authorities, in order to safeguard the possibility of receiving financial, medical and food assistance from international institutions, would have to 'share the responsibility' with the Western nations in dealing with the escalating crises. By inviting Western participation at the early stages of the complex emergency, the aim would be to provide conditions for Western support for assured humanitarian assistance. However, there might be a difference in Russian (and some Eurasian states) and Western approaches to the type and levels of expected and preferred international involvement in such situations. Thus, the most difficult time in an escalating crisis for the states participating in the CJTF in Eurasia will be the time of decision for upgrading forces and the probability or 'sliding to peacekeeping/ peace-enforcement operations from missions of humanitarian assistance.

Nevertheless, such missions are possible. For effective 'NATO-plus' missions, obstacles such as language and cultural differences and doctrinal discrepancies need to be overcome. In the short term priority might be given to equipment incompatibility. Eurasian states might address this issue either by opening their procurement markets to imported equipment, or, when possible, by providing and stimulating the possibilities for joint ventures between the Western and local military complexes for production of weapons and communication systems to NATO standards. For peace-enforcement operations, the standardization and interoperability of command and control, communication and logistics (especially in fuel and ammunition) is becoming essential. The PfP training of commanders and staff to conduct multinational peacekeeping operations with differently equipped, organized, and doctrinally oriented counterparts proved that such difficulties could be overcome. Whether crises in Eurasia will be managed by a cooperative or confrontational approach from the parties involved, and especially NATO and Russia, depends to a large extent on political developments in the Eurasian states and Russia.

Notes

1 This research has been undertaken with the support of a John D. and Catherine T. MacArthur Foundation Post-Doctoral 'Regional Security in a Global Context' Fellowship at the Department of War Studies, King's College, London.

2 'Declaration of the Heads of State and Government participating in the meeting of the North Atlantic Council held at NATO Headquarters, Brussels, on 10-11 January 1994, NATO Review 42 (1);30-3;

'Ministerial Meeting of the North Atlantic Council in Berlin, 3 June 1996, Final communiqué, Press Communiqué M-NAC-1 (96) 63, NATO, Brussels.

3 CJTF - A Lifeline for a European Defence Policy? Ed. by Edward Foster and Gordon Wilson, RUSI Whitehall Paper Series 1997, p.7, 13, 80; Franco-British summit- Joint declaration on European defence, 4.12.98,- http://www.ambafrancee.org.uk/db.phtml?id=1950

4 Charles Barry. Combined Joint Task Forces in Theory and Practice, In: *NATO's Transformation. The Changing Shape of the Atlantic Alliance,* Ed. by Philip H. Gordon, 1997, p.204.

5 The terminology 'inner' (for Art. 5 missions) and 'outer core' (for non-Article 5) missions was introduced in the Report of Senator William V. Roth, Jr., President of NAA 'NATO in the 21st Century', 2 October 1998. - http://www.naa.be/docu/1998/ar5gen-e.html

6 Charles Barry, *op. cit.* p.213.

7 Robert Banker. Failed-state operational environment concept, *Military Review,* October 1997.

8 Leaving aside the debates about how representative they are for the CJTF concept, they do represent a hybrid of coalition forces and standing headquarters under NATO.

9 Adm. T. Joseph Lopez, Commander-in Chief, AFSOUTH. Colloquy on the European Security and Defence Identity, Madrid, May 5, 1998.

10 Sources of Conflict in the 21st Century. Regional Futures and U.S. Strategy, Ed. By Zalman Khalilzad, Ian O. Lesser, RAND, 1998, pp.336

11 Glen E. Howard. NATO and the Caucasus: the Caspian axis. In: NATO after enlargement: New challenges, new missions, new forces. Ed. by Stephen. J. Blank, c,sis. US Army War college, September 1988, p.175.

12 The network was established within the framework of international project 'Ethnic Conflict Management in the Former USSR' in 1993. The project was coordinated by the Institute of Ethnology and Anthropology, Russian Academy of Sciences, and Conflict Management Group, Harvard Law School, in cooperation with the International Laboratory of Mass Communications (VEGA). The project was funded by the Carnegie Corporation, New York. - Tishkov, V., Ustinova, M., Early Warning: The Case of the Former Soviet Union, In: *Synergy in Early Warning. Conference Proceedings,* Ed. by Sussanne Schmidt and Howard Adelman, 15-18 March 1997, Toronto, Canada, p.77-83.

13 The computer support systems and space-based communications systems are being introduced within PfP, thus, helping the states to reach technological requirements for joint crisis management and prevention. - NATO enlargement to the East and Russian National Security. Debates at the Federation Council, 13 May 1997, *Rossia i mir: politicheskie realii i perspectivy,* Independent Experts' Council on Strategic analysis of Foreign and Domestic policy of the Federation Council, Russian Federation, May 1998, p.201; RIA-Novosti, Hotline, 8 June 1998, Issue 032.- http:/ /www.ria-novosti.com/products/hotline/1998/06/08-032.htm

14 Francesco Palmeri, A Euro-Atlantic disaster response capability, *NATO Review,* No 3, Autumn 1998, pp. 24-28.

15 Ragnar Dag Wik, A CJTF HQ Communications Infrastructure Based on COTS Equipment, 1997.

16 *Delovaya Nedelya* (Almaty, in Russian), 6 September 1996, p.12; Fakhrutdinova N.A. *The Legal Base of Information Security in Uzbekistan.* Paper presented at the International Conference 'Information Technologies, Security and Conflict Resolution', 28-30 April, 1998, Moscow.

17 TRANCECA was launched in April 1993 in Brussels by the European Union and eight post-Soviet states: Azerbaijan, Armenia, Georgia, Kyrgyzstan, Uzbekistan, Kazakhstan, Tajikistan, and Turkmenistan. Ukraine joined the project in October 1996.

18 In December 1996 Ukraine, Azerbaijan and Georgia signed an agreement on creation a transnational transport corridor between Ilichivsk (near Odessa, Ukraine) to Baku (Azerbaijan) via Georgia's Pontic port Poti and Tbilisi. This segment of the transportation corridors was considered as pivotal in linking Europe to Asia.

19 Dianne L. Smith, *Breaking away from the Bear*, SSI, US Army War College, 3 August 1998, p.41.

20 PfP exercises that took place with CENTRAZBAT tested the coordination of command, control and logistics of national units in a UN-authorized, NATO-led CJTF in Central Asia.

21 *Jamestown Monitor*, 26 November 1997.

22 In 1994 there were no exercises in the region, in 1995 - 6 exercises, in 1996 - 11, in 1997 - 19. - In: Rachel Bronson. NATO's Expanding Presence in the Caucasus and Central Asia, *NATO After Enlargement: New Challenges, New Missions, New Forces*, ed. by Stephen J. Blank, CSIS and US Army War College, September 1998, p.235-236.

23 *Osnovy formirovaniya Sistemy Collectivnoi bezopasnosti gosudarstv-uchastnikov SNG,* Nauchno-Teoreticheskie materialy, Chast' 1, Moscow 1998, p.93-98.

24 S. Larionov. The feeble Forces of the Russian Federation, *Moskovskyi Komsomolets,* 12 May, 1998.

25 Glen E. Howard. NATO and the Caucasus: the Caspian Axis, In: *NATO after enlargement: New Challenges, New Missions, New Forces,* Ed. by Stephen j. Blank, CSIS & US Army War College, September 1998, p.209

26 *Defence News*, 2-8 March, 1998, p.2

27 Sergei Larionov, 'The Feeble Forces of the Russian Federation', RIA-Novosti, Daily Review, 12 May 1998. K. Watman, D. Wilkening, J. Arquilla, B. Nichiporuk *US Regional Deterrence Strategies*. 1995.

28 The term 'middle zone between Russia and NATO' was recently been introduces in addressing three states of the former Soviet Republics - Belarus, Moldova and Ukraine. - Sherman W. Garnett and Rachel Lebenson, 'The Middle Zone and Post-Enlargement Europe'. IN: *NATO After Enlargement: New Challenges, New Missions, New Forces,* Stephen J. Blank, (CSIS & US Army War College, September 1998), pp.73-94.

29 K. Watman, D. Wilkening, J. Arquilla, B. Nichiporuk *US Regional Deterrence Strategies*. 1995.

- This report assesses the requirements of a deterrence strategy for application to potential regional adversaries. The US military problem of regional deterrence in this instance focuses on two factors: how the United States can make its deterrent threats highly credible; and what military capabilities are required for credible denial and punishment threats.

30 *Nezavisimoye Voennoye Obozrenie*, No 7, 1998, p.5.

31 Makchmut Gareev. Military Doctrine of Russia. *Nezavisimoye voennoe obozrenie*, No 29, 9-15 August 1997, p.4.

32 National Interests and security policy goals of Russian in the CIS region in the light of the RF participation in the peacekeeping missions. IN: A. Nikitin. O. Chklestov, Y. Fedorov, A. Demurenko. *Peacekeeping in the CIS: the issues of international law, politics and logistics. Report Series*. Center for Political and International Studies and Moscow Office of the Public Science Foundation, Moscow: 1998, p.80.

33 in accordance to the articles on security guaranties in the PfP agreement between the state and NATO.

7

The Impact of the Kosovo Crisis on Albania and Macedonia

DOMITILLA SAGRAMOSO

Research Associate, Centre for Defence Studies
King's College London

The three wars endured by the peoples of the former Yugoslavia in Croatia, Bosnia and Kosovo have brought to light the high inter-linkage among all the main players and entities in this area of the Balkans. All three questions have been handled separately by the international community, as a result of which, efforts to put an end to violence in one area have opened the door to further eruptions of violence elsewhere. The unconditional recognition of Croatia in January 1992 allowed for an end to violence in that country but left the Serbian minority in Krajina unprotected, and resulted in an outbreak of war in neighbouring Bosnia. Similarly, the Dayton Peace Accords which put an end to the Bosnian War only partially solved the question of Bosnian unity. Moreover, by neglecting to handle the Kosovo question and by rewarding, to all intents and purposes, the use of force, it allowed for Kosovo's violent struggle for independence. Similarly, the hasty Kosovo deal that American Special Envoy Richard Holbrooke extracted from Yugoslav President Slobodan Milosevic in October 1998, remained full of short-comings. Not only was the future status of Kosovo left unresolved, but other regional aspects directly related to the crisis were totally ignored, in particular, the fate of Albanian minorities in Macedonia and Albania's domestic instability. The international community seemed again to have forgotten about the regional repercussions of such a war, and the negative implications that a partial settlement could have on regional stability. Although the outbreak of a general

Balkan war seems highly unlikely, the chances that regional instabilities and simmering conflicts will persist remains high. If all these issues remain unresolved, any attempt at solving the Kosovo crisis will eventually fail.

The current chapter examines the underlying instabilities in Albania and Macedonia in view of the outbreak of violence in Kosovo. Albania's state fragility and border insecurity, and Macedonia's delicate ethno-political balance have been severely affected by developments in Kosovo. Close ethnic ties, geographical proximities, and a common historical past have transformed domestic problems into regional issues. In order to minimise the damage already caused by the war in Kosovo and avoid a constant over-spilling of violence, negotiations on Kosovo's future should ideally be part of an all-encompassing attempt aimed at reaching a long-term solution to the most pressing conflicts of the region. The international community seems unable and unwilling to handle such an overwhelming task. However, attempts to resolve individual problems should be handled as part of an effort to reach a full regional solution.

ALBANIA'S DOMESTIC INSTABILITY AND BORDER INSECURITY

The outbreak of violence in Kosovo placed Albania at the forefront of the crisis. The close ethnic ties that link both communities together – 90% of Kosovo's inhabitants are ethnic Albanians – as well as the chronic domestic instability affecting Albania resulted in the latter playing a much greater role in the outbreak of the Kosovo crisis than its government actually intended. The sympathies among Albanian citizens, particularly in the north of Albania, for the Kosovar cause, was reflected in a vast amount of Albanian and foreign weapons finding their way into Kosovo after the collapse of the Albanian state, contributing, to a great extent, to the escalation of violence in that region. In turn, the outbreak of war in Kosovo severely affected Albania's fragile domestic stability by boosting the illegal arms trade, hampering Tirana's efforts to restore control over the northern areas of the country, and placing additional strains on Albania's already weak and highly criminalised economy. Kosovars found in northern Albania an unchecked source of weapons and a sort of 'safe haven', from whence to conduct operations. In other words, events in Kosovo and Albania had reciprocal repercussions and both areas seemed to be feeding each other's insecurity and instability. The current section will examine the impact of the Kosovo crisis on Albania's main underlying problems: chronic domestic instability, open borders and weapons smuggling, and criminalisation of the economy.

ALBANIA'S DOMESTIC INSTABILITY

In the spring of 1997, Albania witnessed a major state collapse when the crash of fraudulent 'pyramid' investment schemes brought the Albanian population on to the streets in violent protest against the government. The inability of the Albanian army and police force to stop the uprising resulted in many areas of the country, especially the south, falling under the control of rebel groups or local criminal bands. During the upheaval, military bases, barracks and police stations were attacked and up to a million light weapons looted, together with 1.5 billion pieces of ammunition, to be used not only for personal protection but for criminal purposes as well. Open insurrection was brought to an end by the arrival of an Italian-led Multilateral Protection Force and the replacement of President Sali Berisha by a new Socialist government headed by Prime Minister Fatos Nano. However, law and order were never totally restored. As the government lost the monopoly of force, control over the southern areas of the country fell into the hands of criminal bands involved in drug-trafficking and smuggling of illegal immigrants. In the north, clan-based factions, supportive of Berisha, and organised crime syndicates linked to their Croatian and Montenegrin counterparts took control.[1] By the end of 1998, the government had proved unable to restore control beyond Tirana and the surrounding countryside.

Restoration of public order and efforts to confiscate weapons

Restoration of public order became an overwhelming task given the high number of weapons distributed among the population. In spite of the efforts conducted by the Albanian authorities very few of the light weapons were ever recovered.[2] Albanians remained reluctant to hand in weapons as long as the security situation in the country stayed highly volatile. The upheavals of 1997 resulted in a mounting death toll from criminal incidents and politically motivated killings. Criminal gangs and political rivals resorted to violence as the most effective way to settle their scores, as theft and looting became a constant feature of Albanian life.[3] A low level of constant simmering insecurity took root. In view of these developments, the international community placed emphasis on retraining and re-equipping Albania's security forces as the best means of restoring order. To that intent, the Western European Unions' Multinational Advisory Police Element (MAPE) was established, which provided a group of 70 advisers involved in police training and equipment support. In close collaboration with MAPE, an Italian programme of consultancy, training and assistance for the Albanian police forces, border troops and armed forces was also set up. However the limited number of personnel placed at the disposal of these operations and its restrained mandate (police advisers were not to be involved in the restoration of public order nor in the recovery of weapons) resulted in a low rate of success. Serious underlying problems, such as the low pay of Albanian policemen, high levels of corruption among officers, as well as the overall criminalisation of society, made the government's task extremely difficult.

The restoration of law and order inside Albania might ultimately lie in the introduction of a substantial international police force, similar to the SFOR operation in Bosnia. However, the chances of such a high commitment by the international community remain very slim. The decision by the IMF to make its $300 million loan for 1998-2001 conditional upon the government restoring civil order is a step in the right direction, provided that funding for an efficient police force is also granted.[4] However, domestic political difficulties linked to the ill-functioning of democracy and the collapse of state institutions make the task even more difficult.

Institution-building

The upheavals of 1997 resulted in the almost total disintegration of state structures. The looting of state assets, the disruption of economic activities, the collapse of border posts and customs units resulted in a major institutional vacuum which remains. Albania's administrative structures had always been highly inefficient and had been conceived by the various ruling élites as instruments of power as opposed to institutions for public service.[5] Patronage and clientelism flourished under the socialist authoritarian regime of

Enver Hoxha, and became the norm during Berisha's presidency. When he arrived in power, Prime Minister Nano attempted to shake up the administrative machinery and state institutions by engaging in a thorough purge, which included the military, the judiciary, government ministries, local government and universities. He argued that the replacement of politically biased or corrupt officials was aimed at creating a cadre of democratically responsible civil servants and an independent judiciary. However, such moves were interpreted by the opposition as serving the interests of the governing Socialist Party, reflected by the ruling coalition parties' insistence upon a large share of posts being distributed among their members. Aware of the difficult tasks ahead, the Council of Europe, and in particular the Italian government, launched an 'institution building' project which entailed financial support and government expertise for the rebuilding of Albania's public administration. The project devoted particular attention to the improvement of the judiciary, health and education systems.

However, the difficulties of rebuilding state institutions were exacerbated by the malfunctioning of Albanian democracy. The lack of co-operation between the main opposition party, the Democratic Party, and the smaller parties allied to it, in drawing up the constitution, undermined the whole process of building a healthy democracy. Moreover, Berisha's refusal to recognise the electoral victory of the Socialist Party and his decision to boycott parliamentary sessions during most of Prime Minister Nano's tenure further undermined the strengthening of democracy. The frequent scenes of violence in parliament added to the gloomy picture. Berisha's decision to resort to violence in September 1998 in order to overthrow the government by force failed, but it brought to light the underlying instability of the Albanian state. The adoption of a new Constitution in November 1998 seemed to provide new hope. However, Berisha's decision to refuse to abide by it, arguing that the referendum on its approval, held on 22 November 1998, did not get the necessary support, again complicated matters. The decision by the aid donors' conference on 22 October 1997 to offer Albania around $600 million, on condition that progress was made in the establishment of a functioning democracy and the introduction of a new Constitution may prove helpful.[6] However, the willingness of the opposition to collaborate in such a task remains dubious given that it would not get the credit for any successful economic or political recovery. The opposition remains committed to overthrowing the government, and the outbreak of violence in Kosovo has provided it with an additional area of confrontation.

Pressure for involvement in Kosovo

The escalation of violence in Kosovo during the summer of 1998 placed an additional strain on the already fragile domestic situation. The Socialist government found itself under increasing pressure from the opposition to display open support for the plight of neighbouring Kosovar Albanians. The Nano government, in line with the requests of the international community, had maintained a moderate policy towards Kosovo throughout the spring of 1998. It refrained from recognising Kosovo's independence and demanded a solution to the conflict within the internationally recognised borders of the Federal Republic of Yugoslavia. However, domestic pressure for some kind of intervention grew in the summer and autumn of 1998 as the situation on the ground became more acute. Belgrade's full-scale military operation against Albanian Kosovars resulted in hundreds of deaths and over 230,000 refugees and displaced persons. The Albanian government's tone sharpened as it condemned the military operations of the Serbian forces calling them 'ethnic cleansing and genocide'.[7] However, recognition of Kosovo as an independent state was avoided and the involvement of Albania's military forces in support of Kosovar Albanians was ruled out. Intervention by NATO was demanded instead. The Socialist government's restrained policy brought into question its nationalist credentials, as the opposition Democratic party, which had historically sympathised with Kosovar aspirations and provided the Kosovo Liberation Army (KLA) with cover military support, demanded the recognition of Kosovo as an independent state and assistance to the KLA.[8]

The chances of Albania getting directly involved in the fighting seem particularly slim, given Albania's own limited capabilities, its dependence on Western economic support and its desire to join Euro-Atlantic security structures. However, if a satisfactory solution is not found in the medium term, and the plight of the Kosovars increases, as does the flow of refugees into Albania, support by the government cannot be ruled out completely, especially if there is a change of government in Tirana.

OPEN BORDER AND WEAPONS SMUGGLING INTO KOSOVO

The widespread lawlessness and rampant corruption which followed the spring 1997 crisis, led to a major flow of Albanian and European weapons into Kosovo. Although intensive terrorist actions by the KLA did not begin until the winter of 1997-98, a significant number of weapons had reached the area several months earlier when the Albanian state collapsed and all controls along the Kosovo-Albanian border were removed. Lucrative profits involved in the smuggling and local sympathies for the Kosovar cause accounted for the flow. Widespread support amongst northern Albanians for the Kosovars is based primarily upon close ethnic ties – both belong to the Gheg branch of the Albanian people – and on personal links between former President Sali Berisha and the Kosovar Albanians' organisations. Berisha's open support for Kosovar independence, allowed him to obtain substantial financial support from the Albanian émigré communities in Switzerland and Germany for his 1992 election campaign.[9] In return, Berisha's supporters shipped the KLA large quantities of weapons and ammunition across the Kosovar-Albanian border and via the port of Durres during 1997.[10]

The outbreak of open hostilities in Kosovo in February 1998 led to an increase in the demand for and flow of weapons along the Kosovo-Albanian border. Systematic attacks by KLA supporters on arms depots in northern Albania coupled with the flourishing of open markets for weapons in towns close to the border such as Tropoje, Kukes and Bajram Curri, transformed this area into a region where lawlessness and corruption dominated.[11] The inability of the authorities in Tirana to restore control over the northern areas resulted in the KLA slowly filling the vacuum of power in co-operation with local clans supportive of Berisha. By the summer of 1998, the KLA had succeeded in extending its area of activities well beyond the Kosovo region to inside the Albanian northern districts, where its members and supporters operated freely, buying weapons, establishing ammunition depots and apparently even setting up training camps. This resulted in Serbian forces conducting operations beyond the border well into Albanian territory. Regular shootings, airspace violations, and cross-border bush fires, were reported by OSCE and other independent observers.[12] Although the Albanian government refrained from taking military action against Serbia, the chances of Albania being dragged into direct military confrontation with Serbia significantly increased. [13] NATO's Partnership for Peace exercise 'Co-operative Assembly' in August 1998 was aimed at sending a signal to Milosevic. However, this was only partially successful. Although a major confrontation was averted, regular Serb violations of Albanian territory continued.

Tirana's efforts to seal the Kosovar-Albanian border and stop the smuggling activities also proved ineffective. Attempts to strengthen the border were hampered by Tirana's weak control over the northern regions of the country, the lack of adequate infrastructure and communication equipment, the difficult nature of the terrain, and the sympathies among local Albanians for the Kosovar cause.[14] In the summer of 1998, at the height of the Kosovo campaign, only 67 poorly-equipped police border guards were responsible for patrolling the entire border. The international community limited its response to the dispatch of a small number of OSCE and EU monitors to the border areas. Their presence did not provide a sufficient deterrent to prevent KLA supporters and smugglers crossing the border. The detection of mule tracks over the remote Albanian highlands by ill-equipped observers remained virtually impossible.[15] The deployment of an UNPREDEP-type[16] or NATO force along Kosovo's border with Albania designed to stabilise neighbouring countries, control the smuggling, and deter cross-border attacks by Serbian forces would certainly provide a more credible alternative. However, such a deployment would face serious logistical difficulties, in view of the absence of the necessary infrastructure. Electricity supplies are meagre, roads sometimes impassable, water supplies erratic, and telephone communications limited and unreliable. Lack of adequate security in Albania's lawless northern regions makes it difficult to envisage NATO supplying the necessary infrastructure, especially given the high chances of the most valuable items being immediately stolen.[17] Moreover, on its own, such a move would actually help Yugoslav President Milosevic by cutting off arms supplies to the KLA and containing the rebellion within Kosovo's borders. The response to the problem again lies in finding a solution to the restoration of public order and control over the northern borders by the Albanian forces themselves. This should come hand-in-hand with an upgrading of basic infrastructures in the northern areas (roads, communications, electricity) and, last but not least, the rebuilding of the Albanian armed forces. NATO's efforts, within the Partnership for Peace framework, to assist Albania in the restoration of its armed forces are a step in the right direction. However, the difficulties of rebuilding the shattered armed forces to adequate levels is likely to prove a daunting task.

DETERIORATION OF THE ECONOMIC SITUATION AND CRIMINALISATION OF THE ECONOMY

The wars in former Yugoslavia and the collapse of state authority in Albania during 1997 resulted in the flourishing of criminal activities involved in the violation of the Yugoslav economic and arms embargo and in the highly profitable traffic of drugs and illegal immigrants into Europe. With the break-up of Yugoslavia, Albania and Macedonia became the main entry points of all narcotics originating in Asia destined for Western European consumers. The same well-established smuggling routes used by violators of the Yugoslav embargo during 1992-95 and running through Kosovo-Montenegro-Bosnia-Croatia, were also used for drug trafficking.[18] But the 1997 crisis and the instability that ensued led to the flourishing of another important drug smuggling route under the control of Albanian and Italian criminal groups: from the Albanian ports of Vlores and Durres to the southern Italian harbours of Brindisi, Bari and Otranto. Albania, moreover, developed into a relatively important local production area for marihuana and hashish of excellent quality. Heroin originating from Turkey apparently also became transformed into morphine in Albanian clandestine laboratories.[19]

The drugs trade became closely linked with the traffic of illegal immigrants, as young Albanians paid their transport fees by carrying drugs over to Italy. The crisis of 1997 resulted in a major flow of migrants across the Adriatic, creating serious concerns among the Italian authorities. During March and June 1997, a total of 16,000 Albanians entered Italy. Most of these slipped out of officially provided accommodation and became illegal immigrants often involved in illicit activities such as prostitution and drug smuggling. Italy decided to put a stop to new arrivals, and in April 1997 agreed with the Albanian authorities to jointly patrol the Albanian sea coast in order to contain the flow of immigrants. Although these measures reduced the large-scale flows, Albanians still tried to reach Europe through Italy. Criminal organisations on both sides of the Adriatic collaborated in the traffic of illegal immigrants across the Adriatic Sea.

The economic difficulties of Albania were also exacerbated by the arrival of over 15,000 Kosovo refugees, as the country was ill-prepared and ill-equipped to deal with such a substantial influx of newcomers. The small progress achieved by the government in terms of macro-economic stabilisation and economic growth was dashed by the outbreak of hostilities in Kosovo. Although Albania continued to receive important financial support from the international community, in particular from the EU and the IMF, foreign investment was put on hold. Moreover, the rigorous measures prescribed by the IMF and strictly abided to by the Nano government harshly hit the impoverished population.[20]

IS THERE A WAY OUT?

The collapse of the Albanian state in 1997 represented a major threat to regional stability. The outflow of weapons into the unstable neighbouring regions of Kosovo and Macedonia, as well as the flow of refugees and drugs into Greece and Italy, demanded an urgent solution. The first responses of the international community initially seemed quite adequate. *Operation Alba* restored a semblance of order and allowed for the holding of elections and the arrival of a new government. However, the shortcomings of the operation soon became apparent and *Operation Alba* in fact remained quite limited and low key. Although the main communication roads were opened there was no attempt to venture into risky areas and to disarm the population. Later efforts by the international community did not bring about the necessary changes either. Although international actors successfully singled out the main problems which needed to be addressed in order to bring Albania back to normality, the necessary commitment seemed to be lacking. Limited resources, restricted mandates and reduced personnel explain the meagre successes of many of the initiatives in the areas of institution building and security sector reform. The war in Kosovo brought to light the risks of the existence of such an unstable country in the highly volatile southern Balkan region. However, the international community appears to attach much more importance to preventing Bosnia's disintegration than to avoiding Albania's state collapse. Ultimately, however, the answer to the country's troubles lies in the willingness of the Albanians themselves to change, and in the capacity of the international community to push them in the right direction.

FORMER YUGOSLAV REPUBLIC OF MACEDONIA'S FRAGILE INTER-ETHNIC RELATIONS IN AN UNSTABLE REGIONAL ENVIRONMENT

As the only former Yugoslav republic which managed to reach independence in a peaceful way and keep itself out of the wars of Yugoslav dissolution, the FYR of Macedonia appeared to outsiders to be the only beacon of hope in the Balkans. Despite initial difficulties, Macedonia managed to hold together as a country. However, serious doubts as to its long-term viability remain. The presence of a large Albanian ethnic minority in the western areas of the country represents a potential source of domestic instability. Relations with its closest neighbours show clear signs of improvement but many issues still remain unresolved. When Macedonia obtained independence in 1992, almost everything about the country, from its borders, to its language, flag, name and ethnic composition remained controversial. The outbreak of violence in Kosovo created fears that the conflict might further destabilise this already fragile domestic balance, through a radicalisation of the ethnic Albanian population and increased pressure for greater autonomy. Moreover, the increased arms smuggling activities through Macedonia, and the risks of a potential military and humanitarian spill-over created additional strains.

THE ETHNIC ALBANIAN MINORITY

The fragile inter-ethnic relations between the Albanian minority, which composes 23% of the population, and the titular Macedonian population continue to represent the greatest threat to the country's internal stability. Although relations between ethnic Albanians and Macedonians significantly improved with the advent of independence and democracy, as repression eased and opportunities for ethnic Albanians increased, the Albanians claimed that they lacked a series of fundamental rights.[21]

First, Albanians objected to the minority status conferred upon them by the preamble of the Macedonian constitution, which specified that Macedonia was constituted as the national state of the Macedonian people. Other minorities such as Albanians, Turks, and Roma were granted full civil equality.[22] The Albanians argued that such a status did not correspond to their numerical importance, and demanded to be considered a constituent nation of the Macedonian state. Moreover, the Macedonian constitution considered Macedonian as the sole official language and the Macedonian Orthodox Church as the official creed.

Second, Albanians insisted that although they were allowed to participate actively in the country's political life, they were still discriminated against and under-represented in local government institutions, the public administration and state enterprises, the police and the military, and that they were regularly subjected to police brutality.[23] In other words, they demanded a sort of 'affirmative action' policy which would allow them to participate actively in the country's political institutions.

Third, the Macedonian constitution guaranteed primary and secondary Albanian-language education to the Albanian minority, but no such rights were extended to higher education. Albanians demanded the recognition and accreditation of the Albanian-language university set up by the Albanian community in Tetovo in 1994, and an increase of Albanian-language courses at the faculty of Skopje. They also asked for an increased use of the Albanian language in central and local government. Finally, Albanians demanded the decentralisation of central government and the transfer of greater power to local government enabling municipalities to manage their own affairs.[24]

Aware of the above claims, the government in Skopje adopted various measures aimed at further integrating Albanians and other minorities into the political life of the country. Although many of the measures did not directly address the demands of ethnic Albanians, they attested to an effort towards building ethnic harmony. Albanians benefited from primary and secondary education in their own language, were allowed to set up their own political parties and to regularly participate in elections. Moreover, the 1994-98 Crvenkovski coalition government offered the moderate ethnic Albanian political party, the Party of Democratic Prosperity for Albania (PDPA), five ministerial posts, despite the fact that the ruling coalition (the Alliance for Macedonia) already had a sufficient number of seats to form a government. Similarly, the winning coalition of the October 1998 parliamentary elections, formed by the Internal Macedonian Revolutionary Organisation (VMRO-DPMNE) led by Ljubco Georgievski and the Democratic Alternative headed by Vasil Tupurkovski offered Arben Xhaferi's Democratic Party of the Albanians five seats in the new government. In an additional gesture of goodwill towards ethnic minorities, in June 1998, the government adopted a new electoral system which combined majority and proportional representation. 85 of the parliamentary seats were selected on a constituency basis whereas the remaining 35 were chosen on the basis of proportional representation, in order to guarantee minority parties a higher parliamentary representation.

In spite of these efforts, inter-ethnic relations remained tense. A series of incidents between the Albanian minority and the Macedonian authorities during 1995-97 reduced the sense of loyalty of Albanians to the state, revived anti-Albanian slogans and widened the distance between the two communities even further. Of particular relevance was the controversy linked to the opening of the Albanian-language university in Tetovo by the Albanian community in late 1994. Macedonian authorities interpreted such a move as an attempt to set up 'parallel' structures, that could eventually lead to a 'Kosovar model' of unofficial state institutions. Skopje refused officially to recognise the university and in an exaggerated display of force sent in the police to raid the premises in December 1994.[25] Although the university continued to function, the dispute remained unresolved despite attempts by the OSCE to defuse the issue. OSCE official Max van der Stoel called for an end to the parallel Albanian education system and suggested instead the introduction of an ethnic quota system for university entrants and the re-opening of the Faculty of Pedagogy, with a new programme of classes in the Albanian language. These proposals failed to get the support of the Albanian community.

Tension again erupted in July 1997 when an attempt to display the Albanian flag on the town hall of the ethnically Albanian city of Gostivar met with a sharp response from the Ministry of the Interior police units. Violent clashes resulted in four deaths and some 250 wounded. Moreover, the mayor was given a harsh prison sentence of 13 years (later reduced to seven). During subsequent demonstrations in protest against the sentence the police showed restraint and open clashes were avoided. However, relations among

Albanians and the Macedonian police remained tense.[26] This somewhat violent reaction attested to the lack of experience of the Macedonian élite, which resulted in responses far exceeding the standard norm. The EU decision to place as a precondition for associate membership the respect for individual human rights and minorities is probably a step in the right direction, as was the decision to prolong the presence of the UN Preventive Deployment Force (UNPREDEP) until tension in the region cooled down. The international community, particularly NATO and the EU has a major role to play in this respect, given the willingness of Macedonia to become fully integrated into European and Atlantic institutions.

The escalation of violence in Kosovo and the Kosovar Albanian demands for independence exacerbated relations further. The Kosovo conflict quickly divided the Macedonian population along ethnic lines, with Albanians overwhelmingly supporting their kin in Kosovo, and ethnic Macedonians identifying with the Serbian side. Ethnic Macedonians drew parallels between Kosovo Albanians' demands for independence and Macedonian Albanian requests for increased political and social rights.[27] The Albanian minority however refrained from demanding outright independence, and restricted its claims to greater autonomy within Macedonia's borders. But the widespread support for territorial autonomy, expressed by the Albanian community in a January 1992 unofficial referendum, in which 75% of the voters provided their support for autonomy, raised fears among the Macedonian authorities, that requests for autonomy might result in eventual demands for independence. Ethnic Macedonians tended to see a dilution of their own Macedonian identity in every measure adopted in favour of the Albanian minority. The struggle of neighbouring Albanians in Kosovo for independence was therefore interpreted as creating a precedent for the Albanian minority in Macedonia. It explained Skopje's demands to find a diplomatic solution to the Kosovo question within the frontiers of Yugoslavia.[28]

SPILL-OVER EFFECT: BORDER PROTECTION AND WEAPONS SMUGGLING

The outbreak of violence in Kosovo in February 1998 led to an upsurge of smuggling activities along the Albanian-Macedonian border, as an alternative transit route to Kosovo. In view of these developments, the Macedonian authorities promptly strengthened their northern and western borders by creating a second line of control, comprising special forces from the army and units from the Ministry of the Interior. These preventive measures together with the additional presence of the UNPREDEP observer force increased the risks to arms traffickers and contributed to the overall stability along the border. However, Macedonian attempts to seal its borders were, to a certain extent, undermined by the inability of the Albanian authorities to properly control their own side of the Albanian-Macedonian border. In view of the lax border controls on the Albanian side, during the spring and summer of 1998, Albanian gangs increased their smuggling activities into Macedonia across the natural passes of the Korab mountains in the north and through the lower hilly terrain in the south along the Debar-Lake Okhird section.[29] Moreover, the plight of the Kosovo Albanians at the hands of the Serb security forces led to a conscious reversal of policy within Macedonia, a trend that became more evident as the Serb forces took firmer control over Albanian border crossing points. Since August 1998, it seemed that the Macedonian security forces had allowed themselves to lose control of arms trafficking due in part to ethnic sympathy but also due to pressure from Macedonia's own ethnic Albanian parties. Border police along the Albanian-Macedonian border tended generally to be supportive of the Kosovo cause.[30] The risk therefore grew of Macedonia becoming a major transit supply route of weapons into Kosovo.

The fear of a direct spill-over of the Kosovo crisis, prompted the Macedonian Defence Ministry to place its military capabilities on alert. However the small Macedonian armed forces remained ill-prepared to handle a frontal attack. The presence of UNPREDEP acted only as a deterrent against Serbian incursions. In a major confrontation with Serbia, Macedonians hoped to rely on NATO for support.[31] The development of close military ties with NATO within the Partnership for Peace framework was seen as a step towards NATO support and eventual membership. NATO's policies in Macedonia were initially aimed at improving the capacity of Macedonian forces to handle the crisis with limited NATO support. The outbreak of violence in Kosovo increased NATO's commitment as the US seemed increasingly keen to transform the Krilovac training centre into an American military base. NATO's presence in Macedonia during the summer of 1998 acted as a major deterrent against a spill-over. But it inadvertently also put regional stability at risk. NATO's exercise *Determined Falcon,* conducted over the airspace of Albania and Macedonia in June 1998, brought Macedonia into direct confrontation with Yugoslavia and exacerbated inter-ethnic tensions. The exercises sent the wrong signal to the KLA, divided Macedonian public opinion along ethnic lines, and resulted in Yugoslavia conducting several air incursions over Macedonia's airspace.[32] Similarly, NATO's request to use Macedonia as a base for its rapid reaction force aimed at rescuing endangered OSCE monitors in Kosovo, irritated authorities in Belgrade. Careful consideration should therefore be given to the regional repercussions, before NATO's operations are conducted directly from countries in the region.

REGIONAL ENVIRONMENT

The challenges posed to Macedonia's very existence by neighbouring Greece, Serbia and Albania when it declared independence, as well as the long-dated claims by Bulgaria on close to kin Macedonia, created serious doubts about Macedonia's long-term viability. Greece represented the greatest threat to the emergence of Macedonia as an independent entity. Immediately after Macedonia declared its independence, an acrimonious dispute developed over Macedonia's state symbols and official name, which resulted in the imposition of an economic blockade in 1993. The controversy was partially solved, once Greece became aware that Macedonia's poor economic performance and limited military potential would not represent a threat to Greek's territorial integrity. On 14 September 1995, an agreement was reached between both states which stipulated Greek recognition of Macedonia, an end to the embargo, the relaunching of negotiations on Macedonia's name and the change of the flag's emblem.[33] Serbia let Macedonia go without a shot, concentrating its efforts on retaining only those parts of Yugoslavia with substantial Serb populations. However, it only officially recognised Macedonia in April 1996 and a pending border dispute complicates mutual relations.

Albania's delayed recognition of Macedonia in 1996 was motivated by support for the status of constituent nation claimed by the Albanian minority. The former government of President Berisha tended to portray itself as a defender of the greater Albanian nation in both Kosovo and Macedonia. However, it was eventually forced to play the role of a moderator. Anxious to obtain political, economic and military support from the West, and aware that Albania's limited economic and military capacities ruled out any significant support for Albanians elsewhere, Berisha opted for a conciliatory policy. Bulgaria recognised Macedonia's independence as early as 1992, but it refused to accept the existence of a separate Macedonian nation. Differences over the definition of the Macedonian language added to the tension, and although an agreement on good-neighbourly relations was reached in March 1997, very little was achieved in terms of strengthening economic, political and cultural ties.[34]

In the past few years, concern over an external threat substantially subsided as a result of the recognition of Macedonia's statehood by all its neighbours. However, the war in Kosovo and an eventual dismemberment of the Former Republic of Yugoslavia has created the spectre of Macedonia splitting along ethnic lines, resulting in a struggle for influence among neighbouring countries. Although the likelihood of a major Balkan war over Macedonia can probably be ruled out, the possibility of simmering tensions and local conflicts persists. Concern for Macedonia's state viability has led the Macedonian authorities to try to establish good relations with its neighbours and to conduct a policy of integration into Atlantic and European institutions such as NATO, the EU, and the WEU, which they believe to be vital for the security and viability of the country.

WILL MACEDONIA REMAIN 'A BEACON OF HOPE IN THE BALKANS'?

The outbreak of war in Kosovo led to an increased destabilisation of the already fragile Macedonian politics. Ethnic tensions thus exacerbated further, the military strained its resources to confront a potential spill-over, and weapons smuggling activities into Kosovo intensified. The international community had already become aware in 1993 of the key strategic importance for the southern Balkan region of a stable and secure Macedonia, to which the UNPREDEP contingent was sent as a peacekeeping force. When hostilities erupted in Kosovo, NATO's members again singled out Macedonia, together with Albania, as the main countries that required additional NATO assistance. However, more could be done to address the underlying instabilities of Macedonia. Probably the greatest role in this domain could be played by organisations such as the OSCE or the Council of Europe which could offer their expertise in handling human and minority rights questions. However much Macedonia is interested in participating in Euro-Atlantic institutions, it will not be ready to do so, if such participation hampers relations with its next-door neighbours. Yugoslavia remains Macedonia's main trading partner which means that Macedonia is forced to balance its regional requirements with those of the international community. Obviously the alternatives for the international community are limited, given the economic and political costs involved in actions which entail high displays of personnel and equipment, and which are difficult to justify to publics far away from the area. The likelihood of Macedonia disintegrating along ethnic lines and the outbreak of a major Balkan war seem distant. However, for Macedonia to remain 'a beacon of hope in the Balkans' its problems will need to be addressed at the same time as the the Kosovo crisis is managed.

Notes

1. Andres de Leonis, 'How Albania's Navy was left high and dry ... and in Italy', *Jane's Intelligence Review*, July 1998, p.8.
2. Albanian government claimed in July 1998 to have recovered 10% of the weapons and about 3% of the bullets and artillery. (Talif Deen, 'UN Helps Albania Retrieve Stolen Weapons', *Jane's Defence Weekly*, vol. 30 no. 2, 22 July 1998).
3. In the southern city of Girokaster a total of 17 bombs exploded between mid-December 1997 and mid-March 1998, they were politically motivated incidents ('Supporting Albania's Long-Haul Recovery,' *ICG Albanian Programme*, International Crisis Group, 18 March 1998, p.6).
4. *Albania EIU Country Report*, The Economist Intelligence Unit, 4th quarter 1997, p.7; *Albania EIU Country Report*, The Economist Intelligence Unit, 2nd quarter 1998, p.7.
5. Sergio Sechi, 'Aiuti all'Albania: Caccia algi errori da non ripetere', *Limes*, 2/98, p.271.
6. *Albania EIU Country Report*, The Economist Intelligence Unit, 4th quarter 1997, p.19, and EIU, *Albania EIU Country Report*, The Economist Intelligence Unit, 1st quarter 1998, p.8.
7. *RFE/RL Newsline*, vol.2, no. 115, part II, 17 June 1998, p.5. He also demanded that Yugoslav President Slobodan Milosevic be investigated for war crimes at the International Tribunal in the Hague. (*RFE/RL Newsline*, vol.2, no. 192, part II , 5 October 1992, p.8).

[8] *RFE/RL Newsline,* vol.2, no. 196, part II, 9 October 1998, p.11.

[9] Berisha's 1990 Democratic Party Manifesto in 1990 endorsed an eventual union of Albania with Kosovo ('The View from Tirana: The Albanian Dimension of the Kosovo Crisis', International Crisis Group, 10 July 1998, p.4).

[10] *ibid.* p.12.

[11] On 11 April 1998, a military weapons cache in the suburbs of Durres was attacked and on the same day, gunmen attacked the Kukes police station where a number of weapons were known to be stored. On 8 June 1998, an arms depot in the northern Albanian district of Mirdita was attacked. Guards exchanged fire with the attackers until gunmen withdrew. *RFE/RL Newsline*, vol. 2, no. 109, part II, 9 June 1998 p.5; 'The View from Tirana: The Albanian Dimension of the Kosovo Crisis', International Crisis Group, 10 July 1998, p.12)

[12] *OSCE Newsletter*, August 1998, vol.5, no. 8, p.3, Andi Bejtja, 'Albania Spins Out of Control', *Transitions*, October 1998, p.46; *RFE/RL Newsline*, vol.2 no. 117, part II, 18 June 1998, p.6; *RFE/ Newsline*, vol.2, no. 197, part II 12 October 1998, p.6; and *RFE/RL Newsline*, vol.2, no. 198, part II, 13 October 1998, p.6.

[13] 'The View from Tirana: The Albanian Dimension of the Kosovo Crisis', International Crisis Group, 10 July 1998, p.8, *RFE/RL Newsline*, vol. 2, no. 195, part II, 8 October 1998, p.6.

[14] In frontier areas of Kukes and Bajram Curri the KLA remained extremely popular, Albanian border patrols trying to apprehend Kosovo Albanians smuggling weapons were regularly subjected to attacks by local inhabitants.

[15] Serbia's military operation along the northern side of the Kosovo-Albanian border during the summer of 1998, which broke KLA supply lines and restored control over the Decani-Dakovica-Prizren axis, did not put an end to the smuggling activities. New arms supply routes quickly emerged inside Albania, the major conduit being the Drini river which links the small town of Koman to Shkodra, northern Albania's largest town close to the Kosovo border.

[16] The United Nations Preventive Deployment Force (UNPREDEP), composed of 750 military observers from the USA and Scandinavian countries, was sent to Macedonia in 1993.

[17] 'The View from Tirana: The Albanian Dimension of the Kosovo Crisis', International Crisis Group, 10 July 1998, p.7.

[18] Zoran Kusovac, 'Another Balkan Bloodbath? Part One', *Jane's Intelligence Review*, 1 February, 1998 p.13.

[19] *Fenomenologia della Criminalita' Albanese in Italia*, Servizio Centrale Operativo della Polizia dello Stato, 31 December 1996.

[20] Andi Bejtja, 'Albania Spins Out of Control', *Transitions*, October 1998, p.48

[21] Under communist rule Macedonia's communist authorities supported and eventually

copied Serbia's crackdown on ethnic Albanians.

[22] 'Macedonia is constituted as the national state of the Macedonian people, in which the integral civil equality and enduring coexistence of the Macedonian people with Albanians, Turks, Valchs, and Roma and other nationalities inhabiting the Republic of Macedonia are protected.' ('The Albanian Question in Macedonia: Implications of the Kosovo Conflict for Inter-Ethnic Relations in Macedonia' International Crisis Group, 11 August 1998, p.5).

[23] 'The Albanian Question in Macedonia: Implications of the Kosovo Conflict for Inter-Ethnic Relations in Macedonia' International Crisis Group, 11 August 1998, pp.5,8.

[24] *ibid.*, p.8, '1998 Elections in Macedonia,' International Crisis Group, 9 October, 1998, p.15.

[25] Gordana Icevska, 'Macedonia's Open Wound,' *Transitions*, 25 August 1995, pp.47-48.

[26] In the autumn of 1998, radicalisation seemed to be growing as attacks on religious buildings, bomb explosions near government buildings and the destruction of graveyards brought to light the underlying tensions among the communities.

[27] Gordana Icevska, Macedonia's Open Wound, *Transitions*, 25 August 1995, p.47.

[28] RFE/RL Newsline, vol.2, no. 192, part II, 5 October 1998, p.7.

[29] Christopher Smith and Domitilla Sagramoso, 'Small Arms trafficking may export Albania's anarchy.' *Jane's Intelligence Review,* vol.11, No.1, January 1999, pp.24-28.

[30] *ibid.* p.9; Gordana Icevska, Macedonia's Open Wound, *Transitions*, 25 August 1995, p.48.

[31] Zoran Kosovac, 'Interview: Lazar Kitanovski, Defence Minister of FYR of Macedonia,' *Jane's Defence Weekly*, 7 October 1998, p.56.

[32] Marc Rogers, 'Air Power Makes its Point in Kosovo,' *Jane's Defence Weekly*, 24 June 1998, p.3.

[33] Sophie Clement, 'Les relations greco-macedoniennes: de l'affrontement au rapprochement', *Politique etrangère*, p.394.

[34] Sophia Clement, 'Conflict Prevention in the Balkans: Case Studies of Kosovo and the FYR of Macedonia,' *Chaillot Papers*, no. 30, December 1997, pp.20-24.

COMPLEX EMERGENCIES

8

Complexities and Uncertainties: Protracted Conflicts and International Security[1]

KARIN VON HIPPEL

Complex Emergencies Programme Centre for Defence Studies King's College London

The term 'complex emergency' inappropriately describes the conflicts subsumed under its umbrella. After all, which conflicts are not complex, and indeed, how many long-term conflicts and civil wars, such as in the Sudan or Somalia, can still technically be called emergencies? Albeit a misnomer, the term has become *de rigueur*, without a comprehensive understanding of what it means nor how to cope with them, particularly for the defence community. Leaving aside the question of semantics, this chapter provides an overview of complex emergencies and the challenges they pose for the security community, while the following chapters delve deeper into certain aspects that have not yet been fully explored, or that demand re-analysis as we enter the new millennium:

- how can the media be harnessed to help resolve long-standing disputes?
- what is the role of the corporate sector in complex emergencies?
- how do the definitional/theoretical issues constrain us on an international level as we attempt to cope with crises?
- and finally, how does one address new dimensions, such as the economic meltdown in Asia?

The following chapters clarify these issues, enabling us to move beyond the now dated 'post-Cold War' analyses.

First, what do we mean by the term, and are there

commonalities manifest in these crises that need to be tackled independently before the 'emergencies' can proceed on the path to recovery? The international community is indeed facing a profound crisis over how to react to the growth of what the United Nations calls 'complex emergencies', most notably in Africa, but increasingly also in other parts of the world. Although the UN, which first coined the term, has never actually defined what comprises a complex emergency, the term has come to represent the compounded, and in many cases protracted, political and military conflicts that have significant humanitarian consequences. These crises have vexed the world since 1989 – although their genesis occurred many years before – in Afghanistan, Albania, Algeria, Angola, Burundi, Cambodia, Central African Republic, Chechnya, Congo-Brazzaville, Democratic Republic of Congo, Georgia, Haiti, Liberia, Mozambique, Namibia, Ngorno-Karabakh, Nigeria, Rwanda, Sierra Leone, Somalia, Sudan, Tajikistan, and all parts of the former Yugoslavia.

The sudden disappearance of the superpower stranglehold and the consequent threat of a Security Council veto, along with the increase in civil conflicts, have allowed (or compelled) the UN to put humanitarian concerns high on the agenda, effectively ignoring state sovereignty when so desired by labelling some of these crises threats to international peace and security.[2] Particularly from April 1991, when safe-havens for the Kurds were established after the Gulf War due to their unforeseen flight to the mountains in large numbers, and the Reagan Doctrine was no longer applicable, international intervention, sanctioned by Chapter VII of the UN Charter and approved by the Security Council, has occurred in cases that would have been considered distinctly domestic during the Cold War – without significant international opposition.[3] As Thomas Weiss explains:

> access to civilians has become a recognized basis for intervention, building logically on precedents established by the actions of developing countries themselves against white minority governments in Rhodesia and South Africa, where violations of human rights were considered not just an affront to civilization but also a threat to international peace and security.[4]

This humanitarian concern is also based on a drastic increase in civilian casualties in conflicts since the Second World War, in which

90% of deaths were military and the rest civilian. Today, the statistics are the exact reverse.[5]

Some cases have thus provoked a military reaction that evolved into a Peace Support Operation (PSO), as in Angola, Bosnia, Cambodia, Liberia, Rwanda, and Somalia. Yet these operations have been problematic, expensive, and most have not been considered successes. The disappointing outcomes have consequently dampened enthusiasm for involvement in other crises – at any level of commitment – especially in parts of the world that do not directly impact on the perceived national interests of western states (e.g. sub-Saharan Africa). In the majority of these conflicts, the world now passively watches the tragedies unfold, with involvement confined to the deployment of human rights observers or investigators, as in the former Zaire in late 1996 to early 1997.

Yet the preponderance of these conflicts requires a more effective response. Unrestrained, they only tend to snowball: they create large numbers of refugees and Internally-Displaced Persons (IDPs), have the potential to destabilise the security of neighbouring states because of the proliferation of light weapons, interfere with international trade, and, in several instances, have contributed to state collapse, as has occurred in the Balkans, East and Central Africa, and much of West Africa. In sharp contrast, political stability, even in places far removed from the major powers, serves the interests of all states for economic, political and security reasons.

Before we can improve our response, however, we need to have a better understanding of the underlying factors that exacerbate these conflicts. The remainder of this chapter discusses seven interrelated, yet distinct, components that need to be addressed before a composite response can resolve these so-called emergencies. These components are externally and internally-driven, since no conflict develops in isolation, while all are of concern to the security community. They are:

- mercenaries and warlords;
- child-soldiers and light weapons;
- refugee flows and hostage populations;
- security for humanitarian space;
- civil-military relations;
- the role of the private sector;
- state collapse and reconstruction.

A comprehensive analysis of the following seven themes is vital if the difficulties encountered by the international community in complex emergencies are to be overcome.

THE PRIVATISATION OF SECURITY AND THE INFLUENCE OF NON-STATE ACTORS

Privatisation of Security

The privatisation of security now occurs in situations where the state no longer maintains its legal monopoly on violence within its territory. Two factors related to privatisation require further analysis. The first is the need for citizens, businesses and Non-Governmental Organisations (NGOs) to provide for their own security in the absence of a competent state authority. At a minimum this may involve 'Neighbourhood Watch' type organisations. Other types of security provision include multi-national corporations hiring sections of the national armed forces (e.g. as British Petroleum has done in Colombia), or the employment of private bodyguards or security firms (the International Committee for the Red Cross, and the US and British embassies in Congo-Kinshasa, for example, have hired the United States Defense Systems Ltd (DSL) for this purpose). The extreme is the employment of mercenaries.

Organisations, such as Executive Outcomes and DSL, have been contracted by governments and private multi-national organisations in many parts of the world, including Angola, Algeria, Bosnia, Liberia, Papua New Guinea, Sierra Leone, and the former Zaire. In certain instances, such as in Angola and twice in Sierra Leone, they have markedly influenced the conflict.[6] Some corporate security companies, such as American Military Professional Resources Incorporated (MPRI), have achieved legitimacy through government contracts: the American government sponsored MPRI to manage the 'train-and-equip' programme for the Croat-Bosniac Federation. Others, such as Executive Outcomes until 1999 and DSL, are expanding into the business of logistical support for peacekeeping operations, and oddly enough, even political reconstruction activities, disarmament and demobilisation. To whom are these organisations accountable? Are they more or less cost-efficient than the deployment of foreign militaries?

The Influence of Non-State Actors

The second side of privatisation is the emergence of non-state actors who take advantage of the state's inability to provide security. When a state collapses, pathological short-termism and fear prevail, while power devolves to villages and streets, where warlords and independent militia groups thrive and terrorise communities exactly because there is no state. Rule is subsequently concentrated within fluid mini-fiefdoms. Because warlords contributed to the collapse, they are then in a position to consolidate their power by controlling strategic resources (e.g. banana plantations or diamond mines) and valuable real estate (e.g. ports and airports), to which they charge heavy access fees for use.

When an external mediator becomes involved in a conflict and selects an 'authority' with whom to negotiate, this choice can have serious repercussions. For example, in Somalia, General Mohamed Farah Aideed was empowered at home and abroad by being demonised by the US government. At the time, there was a plethora of warlords operating throughout Somalia, with no one warlord controlling the entire territory – an important point that the international community misread and continues to do (for example in the 1997 Cairo initiative).[7] Although each faction leader may claim control over large chunks of territory, they are incapable of delivering their promised constituencies since their rule is fluid and dependent on their military strength. Once they lose control of a port or airport (which is inevitable due to the intense competition over strategic territory), they can no longer pay their militias, who subsequently move on to the employ of the next highest bidder.

The easiest option for the international community, and the one that normally transpires, is that of letting these warlords be responsible for establishing a new state, which in fact, is how most European states developed. Charles Tilly argued that European states were formed by analogous warlords who eventually became weary of the day-to-day insecurity that they themselves created. In order to ward off other marauders, they therefore legitimated their position by establishing a central authority.[8] Yet they will only agree to rule in a manner that assures continued control (see final section for more information).

THE CHILD-SOLDIER PHENOMENON AND THE PROLIFERATION OF LIGHT WEAPONS

Child-Soldiers

Children now comprise a significant percentage of rebel groups and the army in most of the world's conflicts. In Liberia and Afghanistan, for example, approximately 10 per cent of the soldiers/rebels in the recent civil wars have been children.[9] Many of these children missed formal education, and only have an understanding of war and guns. While some argue that it is too late for the rehabilitation of these children – many of whom have killed their parents or their neighbours in bizarre initiation rituals – because they are too damaged to re-integrate in civil society, others have demonstrated that they can be rehabilitated.[10] In parts of sub-Saharan Africa, for example, home communities have successfully performed healing rituals for returnee child-soldiers.[11] Re-integration methods need to be compiled and their widespread applicability debated.

The UN Secretary General recently appointed Ambassador Olara Otunnu as a Special Representative to Study the Impact of Armed Conflict in Children. He would like to continue the work of Graça Machel of Mozambique, who in her 1996 study on children in war revealed that the child-soldier problem was far worse than previously imagined.[12] Child-soldiers pose a particular problem for international NGOs because these children have special needs related to the traumas they have experienced. Most NGOs do not have the experience or wherewithal to cope with these needs, nor with children who are still armed.

Light Weapons Proliferation

The child-soldier phenomenon has been exacerbated by the massive proliferation of light weapons throughout Africa, the former Soviet Union, parts of Asia, and even the United States. Light weapons are robust and easy to use, and therefore accessible even to very young children (from seven years old). Supplies of mostly light, foreign-made weapons circulate with greater ease and less accountability than before, because these weapons are now procured either new or second-hand from a range of states. The second-hand ones are inexpensive and flow through black market networks from one conflict area to another. The cheapness and availability of these weapons means that, in some areas, a 'Kalashnikov Culture' dominates and ordinary crime has been militarised.

The weapons – predominantly light – that poor states purchase are responsible for much of the carnage in civil conflicts today, and there are no international protocols to impede this fast-growing and lucrative trade.[13] Boutros Boutros Ghali expressed his concern over the damage caused by these weapons:

> Small arms ... are probably responsible for most of the deaths in current conflicts. The world is awash with them and traffic in them is very difficult to monitor, let alone intercept. The causes are many: the earlier supply of weapons to client States by the parties to the cold war, internal conflicts, competition for commercial markets, criminal activity and the collapse of governmental law and order functions (which both gives free rein to the criminals and creates a legitimate reason for ordinary citizens to acquire weapons for their own defence).[14]

The availability of light weapons threatens the work of relief organisations and foreign militaries in peace support operations (see section five). Another aspect of the proliferation problem is that of landmines. Mines that have been sown in previous conflicts can hamper humanitarian efforts in complex emergencies – as witnessed by the massive movement and misplacement of mines in Afghanistan due to the earthquake, and in Somalia after flooding. Although there has been international action to tackle the production of landmines, existing stocks will cause problems for decades to come.

REFUGEE FLOWS AND HOSTAGE POPULATIONS

Refugee flows, if large enough, can contribute to the collapse of neighbouring states, especially in less-developed states where the majority of people live below the poverty line. For instance, during a drought (often exacerbated by civil conflicts), food-stressed rural dwellers flee to cities – either in their own state or in a neighbouring one – where resources are inadequate to cope with the massive influx. Today, many African 'mega-cities', such as Abidjan in the Ivory Coast, are home to more refugees and IDPs than 'natives'. Looking at the hundreds of thousands of Liberian and Sierra Leonian refugees and IDPs that have fled into each other's territories, and into neighbouring Guinea and Ivory Coast, Robert Kaplan noted that 'the borders dividing these four countries have become largely meaningless'.[15]

The disintegration of social cohesion and civic structures due to clashes of culture and religion, the effects of over-population and insufficient resources is thereby guaranteed. As the situation becomes more tenuous, any small incident could ignite (or re-ignite) a civil war, which, in time, ultimately erodes remaining state structures, often creating severe humanitarian crises in their wake. This has been witnessed throughout the Great Lakes region over the past three years.

Refugee camps can also become hostage to faction leaders who infiltrate them. This occurred in eastern Zaire after the Rwandan Hutus responsible for the genocide in Rwanda fled across the border once the Tutsis re-captured the state. The end-result was that UNHCR effectively fed the militias, who controlled aid distribution within the camps, while also inadvertently allowing them to re-arm. The Genocide Convention was never invoked, nor was there any political will on behalf of the international community to commit troops to provide security to the camps.

During the initial stages of a crisis, most governments cannot easily prevent refugees from arriving, not only because it is difficult and expensive to police borders, but also for humanitarian reasons. Moreover, this situation is often exploited by developing countries. President Aristide used the threat of increased refugee flows from Haiti to America to demand more foreign aid, while King Hassan of Morocco has over the years issued similar warnings in negotiations with Spain. Even without such threats, aid to developing countries, especially those located in the sphere of influence of the major powers, is partially driven by the desire to improve the situation at home so that the inhabitants will not want to leave. The focus should be on strengthening governance and the local economy, as this may be the only way to stop such large flows, while overall policy needs greater clarification to avoid a repeat of the disaster in Zaire.

SECURITY FOR AID WORKERS, RELIEF SUPPLIES AND HUMANITARIAN SPACE

The aforementioned issues have produced unique challenges for humanitarian relief and development, and simultaneously, made it extremely difficult for aid workers to be viewed as neutral. Indeed, recent experience in Burundi, Chechnya, Liberia, Rwanda, Somalia, the former Yugoslavia, and the former Zaire, has demonstrated in a tragic and disturbing manner that foreign aid workers – once considered above the conflict – can become targets. The past decade has witnessed a sharp rise in the confiscation of aid equipment, the kidnapping and even murder of humanitarian relief workers, and the resulting withdrawal of aid in regions deemed too insecure.

Increasingly, interdicted aid is used to arm and feed militias, who are becoming dependent on stolen relief supplies. As mentioned, militias are now holding distressed populations hostage in order to feed their members and re-arm. In extreme cases, these developments cause the international community to intervene militarily to protect relief, as in Bosnia and Somalia. Once the intervention occurs, the fear of attacks on foreign troops, as well as on aid workers, interferes with the smooth running of the operations, as witnessed again by Bosnia and Somalia.

The growth in casualties among the aid community can be deliberate or accidental, but the end-result is the same. These threats ultimately cause aid workers, NGOs and donors to withdraw from conflict zones, as in the former Zaire, parts of Burundi and most of southern Somalia, thereby ensuring that emergency relief is withdrawn. In these regions, distressed communities founder without hope, while militias achieve their objective of starving their enemies. The impartial witnesses to acts of genocide have also, conveniently, been removed.

Accordingly, there is an urgent need to investigate security issues pertaining to humanitarian space so that aid workers can operate without fear and the vulnerable can receive the help they desperately need. The associated levels of risk need to be reduced through more co-ordinated standard operating procedures. If the international community cannot learn how to protect humanitarian aid workers, then donors, NGOs and governments will become increasingly unwilling to commit to the more violent and anarchic conflicts, especially if juxtaposed with a shortfall in resources and negative domestic political opinion. Both conceptual and practical issues need to be properly addressed – notably the 'militarisation of aid', how assistance can be secured for those who risk their lives in order to relieve the destitute victims of natural and man-made disasters, and how added security would affect the nature of operations and the perceived neutrality of aid workers.

CIVIL-MILITARY RELATIONS

Civil-military relations – in peace support operations as well as within the humanitarian response community – have certainly improved during this decade, from Somalia where there was little co-operation, to Haiti, Bosnia, and eastern Slavonia, where both have been involved in the planning and implementation of political reconstruction, albeit the arrangements in the latter have been contrived in an *ad hoc* manner. Even in conflicts with no military presence, security procedures require frequent interaction between civilians and security personnel (normally retired military or police personnel) in order to carry out day-to-day activities. Two fundamental concerns that must be addressed are: improved mechanisms for co-ordination, and greater clarification of tasks and responsibilities for each.

Enhancing Co-ordination

US Secretary of Defense William Cohen recently remarked, 'Smaller-scale contingency operations will .... put a premium on the ability of the US military to work effectively with other US government agencies, non-governmental organisations, private voluntary organisations, and a variety of coalition partners.'[16] This also holds true for European militaries. Yet when it works, co-ordination depends too much on the personalities involved rather than on a prior agreement on standard operating procedures.

In the most extreme cases, which are peace support operations, co-operation is fundamental to the success of the operation. In Somalia, UNOSOM I, UNITAF and UNOSOM II together represented the peace support operation with the worst management problems.[17] There was a conspicuous lack of harmony on all sides and turf wars: between UN Headquarters in New York and the field office in Mogadishu, between civilian and military operators in Somalia, and even between US and foreign militaries. Additionally, while preparing for the intervention, there was no joint planning between the military and the heads of relief organisations. In such a climate, it was hardly surprising that it became extremely difficult to carry out the mandate.

In sharp contrast, the operation that experienced the fewest difficulties in implementation was the Haitian peace support operation that began in September 1994. Under the direction of the Special Representative of the Secretary-General (SRSG), Lakhdar Brahimi, the military, civilian and development agencies were melded in a tight partnership. The development role was integral from the beginning. Civilian and military actors were trained together before deployment, and a civilian directed the entire operation. This does not signify that Haiti will develop a stable democracy, and indeed the country continues to undergo extreme difficulties, but at least a well-co-ordinated initial phase has allowed for the best possible environment in which democratic reforms may take root.

In Bosnia, co-ordination has improved after Carl Bildt's period as High Representative during IFOR, when he was not given any authority over the military and therefore had no means to enforce the Dayton Accords. The military and civilian roles were not linked at all. Meanwhile, UNTAES[18] in eastern Slavonia, which integrated the two, achieved more success in executing its mandate. Recently, the former Transitional Administrator for UNTAES, Jacques Paul Klein, was appointed deputy to Carlos Westendorp, the subsequent High Representative, and he has provided an appropriate mix since he is a former military officer in a civilian post, with a successful record of civil-military integration in the former Yugoslavia.

Greater flexibility can only enhance the operation, but co-ordination and decision-making mechanisms need to be improved. Although lessons have been learned, they have arisen from unique circumstances in some, but not other, operations and they therefore have not yet been fully applied.

Terms of Reference

A second fundamental issue that needs to be addressed is whether the military should remain involved in activities other than the establishment of a secure environment. Civil Affairs, Psychological Operations (PSYOPS) and Special Forces already build roads, bridges and radio stations, and even monitor elections and information activities. Should this type of activity be encouraged or limited? A related consideration is how external financial resources can be allocated in the most appropriate and efficient manner in order to achieve strategic and political objectives. Does this inevitably mean choosing between military and civilian agencies? There are some instances when the military or even the corporate sector could perform a task better and more cheaply than an NGO, even though it may be a job traditionally performed by an NGO (for example, digging a well).

Of future concern are strategies for synthesising civilian and military operations more fully on the ground, and reducing the distrust between the two. This includes considerations such as whether the host state should be included in co-ordinating mechanisms, and whether foreign militaries should continue to use international NGOs to interface with the local population instead of allowing direct contact. Finally, are there circumstances in which the humanitarian agencies could employ local militias for their security or should they always use foreign troops or commercial security firms?

THE ROLE OF THE PRIVATE SECTOR

The private sector, both foreign and local, also plays an indirect – and sometimes direct – role in complex emergencies, one which hitherto has been overlooked. Multinational corporations can exacerbate conflicts, but they can also help in their resolution. Many mining and oil companies, for example, have a large stake in unstable regions and often wield enormous influence with whatever remnant of a government exists, and even in some cases, with rebel groups.

Relevant to the first section above, multinational corporations now hire private security firms in areas where local structures are inadequate. In these areas, warlords also work directly with these companies, as in the banana industry in Somalia, which thereby gives them further legitimacy on an international scale. The end-result is that warlords negotiate with companies, which in turn hire mercenaries to protect their companies from other warlords. In this sense, private corporations can also directly contribute to the conflict. Should they therefore be included in all co-ordination to avoid contradictory activity?

On the positive side, multinationals also provide jobs for the local population and can give the economy a much-needed boost during the post-war reconstruction phase. During the emergency relief operation, they can also often provide services at a lower cost than NGOs or the military. Some large engineering firms already provide logistical support to peace support operations, for example. Should they therefore also be involved in strategic planning? If they are included in planning, how could this be achieved? Should they also be able to compete with NGOs or UN agencies for emergency relief contracts in situations where traditionally they have been excluded?

A Corporate Code of Conduct could be developed that would commit private corporations to adhere to the same rules as followed by the humanitarian agencies, in return for involvement in planning and co-ordination. This code could include guidelines for 'ethical investment'.

The role of the corporate sector is extremely important, as UN Secretary General Kofi Annan recently noted when he said, 'peace and prosperity cannot be achieved without partnerships involving governments, international organisations, the business community and civil society. In today's world, we depend on each other.'[19] A better understanding of corporate involvement in conflicts would also shed light on the role of natural resources in disputes.[20]

STATE COLLAPSE AND RECONSTRUCTION

Finally, the most extreme occurrence that transpires from a combination of any of the above is the collapse of effective government. The western-driven approach to rebuilding collapsed, or partially collapsed, states needs to adapt to the realities of the post-Cold War environment. A fresh approach should consider three fundamental elements: empowering civil society, co-ordinating international efforts, and re-establishing the legitimate monopoly on force. First, a brief discussion of state collapse.

Why States Collapse

A state collapses when public institutions, legitimate authority, law, and political order (including the police and judiciary) disintegrate, and most state assets are either destroyed or stolen. This happens when states are unable to contain the disruptive forces that contribute to the deterioration of central authority, such as corruption, ethnic and territorial disputes, humanitarian disasters, international interference, over-expenditure on defence, and refugee flows.

The recent increase in state collapse has been a by-product of the end of the Cold War. The majority of these states can be found in Africa, where over one-third of the total number of states have experienced collapse or are threatened. Burundi, Central African Republic, Congo-Brazzaville, Liberia, Rwanda, Sierra Leone, Somalia, and the former Zaire have already imploded, while Algeria, Angola, Chad, the Comoros, Guinea-Bissau, Mali, Mozambique, Nigeria, Sudan, and Zambia may be at risk.[21] The only major difference between a collapsed and a collapsing state is that in the latter, the government still controls the capital city, and therefore maintains some control over the economy and security.[22] When the state finally collapses, chaos engulfs the capital city as well, and aid agencies and foreign embassies withdraw.[23]

Something entirely new may need to replace the old order so that the state will not revert to the situation that caused the implosion (and often the foreign intervention) in the first place, as ultimately occurred in Somalia. In Haiti, this worry has caused the UN Security Council to renew the mandate of the peace support operation numerous times, and in Bosnia, SFOR will most probably be extended past the June 1999 mandate. Yet this 'something' may have to take the shape of a 'government' that stretches beyond the state's external frontiers and includes various power-sharing mechanisms – even rudimentary forms of democracy should be flexible enough to be adapted to entities where there is no effective central authority.[24]

Empowering Civil Society

Not only do new forms of government need to be formulated, but external states acting as mediator or intervening party must also realise the influence they possess when deciding with which non-state actors they will negotiate. When more attention is paid to the warlords, this usually occurs at the expense of traditional leaders from civil society. As Kenneth Allard remarked, 'During operations where a government does not exist, peacekeepers must avoid actions that would effectively confer legitimacy on one individual or organisation at the expense of another.'[25] Ignoring the faction leaders is arguably ineffective, since they control the situation on the ground and will need to relinquish their hold if peace is to be realised, as occurred in Haiti, yet they should also not become the focus of attention.

Leaders from civil society should be included in all

negotiations, as they still maintain the respect of their communities, and could be capable of convincing those with weapons to disarm and negotiate, if sufficiently empowered. Special emphasis should also be placed on the inclusion of women, as their role is often enhanced during civil conflicts. Pressure and attention from the international community and NGOs can help to empower members of civil society in these negotiations.

Members of civil society also have a vested interest in promoting democratic reforms to ensure that warlords (or another dictator) do not maintain control. When warlords discuss the composition of a future state, the debate tends to be over who will fill which post in the next government – particularly the positions of president, prime minister and minister of finance – not what type of government should be established. Democracy is not a priority for the faction leaders, who are mainly concerned with sustaining and aggrandising the areas they control. Further, the normal assumption is that the new state will be unitary, because this type of state is easier to dominate. In direct contrast, civil society leaders consider power-sharing mechanisms and decentralisation as fundamental components of a new state.

Civil society leaders should be included in national reconciliation talks, but the international community can also help to strengthen their power base through supporting democratic reforms in a variety of ways, including programmes that strengthen the rule of law, enhance respect for human rights, support international electoral observers, improve financial management and accountability, promote decentralisation, expand civilian control of the military, and improve electoral processes, legislatures, political parties, the media, and education at all levels of society. Each reform is linked to the others, and requires an overall co-ordinating mechanism to ensure adherence.

International Co-ordination

Due to the volatility of crisis environments and the multiplicity of external actors engaged in mediation and assistance efforts, international co-ordination has been increasingly considered a crucial element of involvement in conflict prevention, management and resolution. The five communities that need to be co-ordinated are: non-governmental organisations, donors/governments, multilateral organisations, militaries, and the private sector. Co-ordination of international efforts in conflicts is particularly vital for the following reasons:

- to facilitate the adoption of common policies and responses.
- to prevent overlap of programmes.
- to maximise the effective use of available resources.
- to promote a secure operational environment for aid activities (e.g., against hostage-taking, harassment or extortion).

The Afghanistan Programming Board, the Monitoring and Steering Group in Liberia and the Somalia Aid Co-ordination Body, which were all established on an *ad hoc* basis, are the best examples of such international co-ordinating mechanisms. In May 1997, the Organisation for Economic Co-operation and Development (OECD) issued a policy paper entitled 'Guidelines on Conflict, Peace and Development Co-operation', in which international co-ordination was considered a key principle for successful international involvement in crisis management.

Although agreement has been reached that co-ordination is necessary, attempts to develop common objectives and principles on an international level are cursory at best. A comprehensive analysis of the utility and potential of co-ordination should be undertaken before standard operating procedures are established. A lessons-learned study of co-ordination that examines the impact on conflicts that these co-ordinating bodies have had, including cases when a UN agency, such as UN High Commission for Refugees (UNHCR) or UN Development Programme (UNDP) has acted as lead organisation in co-ordination. The relations between these bodies and non-state actors also need clarification. There is an urgent need to explore the respective attitudes of the private sector, humanitarian agencies, and the donor community in conflict management as well as in post-conflict reconstruction, and to examine where common interests and actions can lead to improved decision-making in order to confront the unique challenges faced in these environments.

Re-establishing Security

In order to implement democratic reforms, the state needs to reestablish a sufficient degree of security. In most developing states, governments are unable to do this. Instead, they are forced to share protection with a number of non-state actors, who may be called warlords, the Mafia, rebels, guerrillas, terrorists, paramilitaries, or even private business interests. The re-establishment and maintenance of governmental control over security is contingent upon police and military reform (the state may also choose to abolish the armed forces entirely and maintain only the police, as in Costa Rica, Haiti, or Panama), as well as on judicial and penal reforms.

Police and military reform training can take place in peace support operations or in instances where the local community or central authority requests it. In many countries where reform has been initiated, a comprehensive change in mindset of the police, the armed forces and the local population is necessary, as previously the police and military had only served to terrify civilians through extortion and torture, instead of providing protection.[26] In most cases, an entirely new force is necessary, one that could ensure public safety and gain the confidence of the local population.

In peace support operations such as those in Haiti, Somalia and Bosnia, the new police force has been trained by international civilian police under the auspices of the UN operation (often referred to as CIVPOL), but individual countries, such as the United Kingdom or India, also send police for training purposes to states that request it. Thus far, the newly-trained forces have inevitably included some members of the old force due to the lack of experienced personnel and the belief that it would take longer to train an entire corps of new officers than to re-train some of the old. Such a policy has not been without controversy, although the method applied in Haiti appears to have garnered more domestic support in phasing out the old force in increments, while simultaneously recruiting and training new troops. Police reform is also important in peace support operations in order to prevent foreign troops from being considered an occupying force.

A permanent CIVPOL unit could be established at UN headquarters to co-ordinate all police reform activities, and similar units could be created for military, judicial and penal reforms. While CIVPOL training, military, judicial and penal reforms have improved over the years, a thorough investigation of all options and ways of standardising procedures would only serve to enhance security on the ground and therefore support democratisation efforts.

CONCLUSIONS: COUNTERING COMPLEX EMERGENCIES

Western-led interventions in complex emergencies need to incorporate appropriate responses to the issues discussed above before doctrine can be applicable and relevant. Once a multi-functional paradigm is developed and broadly accepted by the major agencies in Europe and in the United States, it can be used to develop policy, as well as to guide the planning and conduct of operations and the training of *all* involved agencies, both military and civilian, so that future responses will achieve greater success. This paradigm needs also to include non-military options, since some responses to complex emergencies are, or become, civilian-led. In such a circumstance, the need for effective co-ordination remains inescapable, as is a clearer understanding of the nature of international response in general.

As military institutions seek to evaluate the makeshift peace support operations of the early-1990s, and as peacekeeping doctrines undergo analysis and change, it is important that tacticians and planners look forward as well as backward – and that the development and military communities enhance their own understanding of civil-military co-operation. There is more to the development of peacekeeping practice than learning the lessons of the past, and co-ordination of all communities is key to future success. The very existence of complex political emergencies of necessity brings the civilian and military actors into each others' orbits. Because there are a multitude of causal factors that interact with each other and external actors (humanitarian, military as well as rogue elements), the resulting conflicts are indeed complex. Attempts to resolve, or at the minimum, mitigate their harmful effects must take into account as many of these factors as possible, if their resolution can be sustained. The term 'protracted and compounded conflicts' may be a more apt description, but even more important than changing the term is a full-scale change in response.

Notes

1 The author would like to thank the staff at the Centre for Defence Studies for their considerable assistance in preparing this chapter, particularly Professor Michael Clarke, Dr John Mackinlay, Dr Randolph Kent, Dr Claire Spencer, Dr Joanna Spear, and Dr Chris Smith. Additional assistance was also received from Alexandros Yannis,

Nick Harvey, Alastair Newton, Gordon Adam, Professor Walter Clarke, and Professor Robert Rotberg. All errors in the text, however, can be attributed only to the author.

[2] This is not to say that during the Cold War both superpowers complied with the non-interventionary norm, which they also ignored at whim. Rather, interventionary policy was based on the policy of containment, the prism through which most foreign policy decisions were measured.

[3] See James Mayall, 'Nationalism and International Security After the Cold War,' *Survival*, Spring 1992, pp.19-35.

[4] Thomas G. Weiss, 'Collective Spinelessness: U.N. Actions in the Former Yugoslavia', in Richard H. Ullman, ed., *The World and Yugoslavia's Wars*, the Council on Foreign Relations, 1996, p.62.

[5] This statistic comes from a number of sources, see for example, the International Federation of the Red Cross on the web (www.ifrc.org), or Dan Smith, 'Towards Understanding the Causes of War,' in Ketil Volden and Dan Smith, eds., *Causes of Conflict in the Third World,* Oslo: North/South Coalition and International Peace Research Institute, Oslo, 1997, pp.9-10.

[6] For further information on Executive Outcomes, see William Reno, 'Privatizing War in Sierra Leone', *Current History*, 97:610, May 1997; Herb Howe, 'To Stabilize Tottering African Governments', *Armed Forces Journal International*, November 1996; and Jim Hooper, 'Executive Outcomes', *World Air Power Journal*, 28, Spring 1997.

[7] One of the many recent failed 'peace' deals, signed in Cairo in late 1997, catered once again to the warlords, while leaving out important members of civil society.

[8] Charles Tilly, 'War Making and State Making as Organised Crime', in Peter Evans, ed., *Bringing the State Back In*, Cambridge University Press, 1985. See pp.169-191 for more information.

[9] Mike Wessells, 'Child Soldiers', *The Bulletin of the Atomic Scientists*, 53:6, Nov/Dec 1997, p.34.

[10] See Margaret McCalin, *The Reintegration of Young Ex-Combatants into Civilian Life: A Report to the International Labour Office*, ILO, Geneva, 1995; and Guy Goodwin-Gil and Ilene Cohn, *Child Soldiers: The Role of Children in Armed Conflicts*, Clarendon Press, Oxford, 1994.

[11] See Mike Wessells, 'Child Soldiers', *The Bulletin of the Atomic Scientists*, 53:6, Nov/Dec 1997, for more details.

[12] Report of the Expert to the Secretary-General, Graça Machel, on the 'Impact of Armed Conflict on Children', Doc. A/51/306 Add. 1.

[13] For more information, see Joanna Spear, 'Arms Limitations, Confidence Building Measures, and Internal Conflict' in Michael Brown, ed., *The International Dimensions of Internal Conflict,* MIT Press, 1996.

[14] Supplement to an Agenda for Peace, A/50/60 – S/1995/1, Report of the Secretary-General on the Work of the Organisation: Position Paper of the Secretary-General on the Occasion of the Fiftieth Anniversary of the United Nations, 3 January 1995.

[15] Robert Kaplan, 'The Coming Anarchy', *The Atlantic Monthly*, February 1994.

[16] *Report of the Quadrennial Defense Review*, May 1997 (Section III, Defense Strategy).

[17] UNOSOM stood for United Nations Operations in Somalia, while UNITAF meant Unified Task Force for Somalia, also known as Operation Restore Hope. These operations began in April 1992 and terminated in March 1995.

[18] United Nations Transitional Authority for eastern Slavonia, Baranja and western Sirmium.

[19] UN Press Release, SG/SM/6448, 30 January 1998.

[20] For more information on this area, see recent published material by Dr Charles Alao.

[21] This is not to say that many of these states, such as Mozambique, are not on the road to recovery, but rather that they are evaluated by their current status (early 1998). Nor does it include the Western Sahara, which has not yet been granted recognition and has been mostly usurped within Morocco.

[22] The governments in both Nigeria and Sudan still control territory outside the capital, with networks that extend throughout the state. These two cases thus have not reached the stage that the others listed in the aforementioned group have.

[23] See Karin von Hippel, 'The Proliferation of Collapsed States in the Post-Cold War World', in *Brassey's Defence Yearbook 1997*, Brassey's, London, 1997, for more information.

[24] See Jeffrey Herbst, 'Alternatives to the Current Nation-States in Africa', *International Security*, 21, 3, Winter 1996/7.

[25] Kenneth Allard, *Somalia Operations: Lessons Learned*, Institute for National Strategic Studies, National Defense University Press, 1995, pp.8-9.

[26] See, for example, William Stanley and Charles T. Call, 'Building a New Civilian Police Force in El Salvador', in Krishna Kumar, ed., *Rebuilding Societies After Civil War: Critical Roles for International Assistance*, Lynne Rienner, Boulder, 1997, pp.107-134.

9

Can Tigers Change their Stripes? Strategic Implications of the Financial Meltdown in the Asia-Pacific

DAVID MARTIN JONES

Senior Lecturer, Department of Government
University of Tasmania, Australia

A prepaid electronic 'touch and go' card provides the most effective way of negotiating the toll booths that interrupt travel along the otherwise impressive North-South highway that traverses Malaysia from Johore to the Thai border. By an unintended irony, the title of the card effectively summarises the current state of the Malaysian economy as well as that of the other erstwhile 'tiger' economies of Pacific Asia.

The impact of the financial meltdown that began in Thailand in July 1997, two years after the North-South highway opened, has had a traumatic impact on the economic, social and political arrangements of those East Asian states that modernised in the course of the Cold War through their alliances with and access to the United States and its market. Yet whilst the causes of the crisis have been widely advertised and its economic consequences extensively prognosticated, much less attention has been given to the impact of the meltdown on the security implications of the crisis at both the regional and the state level. Indeed, amidst the almost daily reports of collapsing *chaebol* (conglomerate), gangster-dominated *keiretsu* and Japanese banks with less liquidity than Manhattan during the prohibition era, it is a curious fact that until recently, the dominant orthodoxy in the study of political development and international relations considered East Asian miracle growth and the 'open regional' order it promoted the basis for a borderless world of 'post-modern' multilateral dispensation. What, we might wonder, happened to the uniquely Asian values that sustained the Asian model and what impact will the spectre of financial meltdown currently haunting the political élites of Pacific Asia have upon the domestic and foreign relations of the states of the Pacific littoral? Will it entail an increased emphasis on Asian bonding and 'multi-level regionalism' or something far more uncertain and unstable?[1]

THE NATURE OF THE CRISIS AND THE WEAKNESS OF THE DEVELOPMENTAL STATE

In its now historically curious 1993 study of the 'miracle' economies of South Korea, Taiwan, Hong Kong, Thailand, Malaysia, Singapore and Indonesia, the World Bank attributed the sustained growth achieved over three decades to a bureaucratic capacity for long-term planning. In a classical summary of the central features of the East Asian model, Chalmers Johnson maintained that it consisted of:

> a strong developmental state coalition; state regulated access to and allocation of capital; harmonious labour relations; state bureaucratic autonomy; administrative guidance; and state directed conglomeratisation.[2]

All the East Asian states identified by the World Bank in its 1993 report as participants in the 'East Asian Miracle',[3] but now experiencing the consequences of long-term financial mismanagement shared some, but by no means all, of these features. Indeed, important differences exist between the governed market, conglomerate-based industrialisation that developed relatively early in the Cold War era in Northeast Asia and the more foreign direct investment FDI (corps) friendly, technology-less growth that occurred primarily during the 1980s in Southeast Asia.

Despite this significant comparative difference in the modernisation experience of Northeast and Southeast Asia, their economies, nevertheless, were symbiotically connected and this, in retrospect, accounts in part for their shared and spectacular economic demise. Thus, under the international trading order established at Bretton Woods towards the end of the Second World War, Japan, the progenitor of the most successful form of Asian capitalism, and to a lesser extent, South Korea and Taiwan, moved up the technology ladder by protecting domestic markets and exporting to the relatively open and developed economies of North America and Western

Europe. When, in the early 1980s, both the US and European governments became increasingly alarmed at the state of their balance of trade with Northeast Asia, they induced Japan, South Korea and Taiwan to revalue their 'undervalued' currencies. In the aftermath of the Plaza Agreement and the Louvre Accord of the mid-1980s, Northeast Asian currencies rose, and labour intensive manufacturing moved offshore together with an *endaka*[4] inspired wave of FDI.

After 1985, this liquidity fuelled strong regional growth and disguised poorly regulated and opaque financial systems with an endemic weakness for lending to crony capitalists and shaky *chaebol*. Thus, although Japan entered apparently permanent recession as early as 1990, the strong yen, together with cheap credit fuelled a brief era of rampant property speculation, overbuilding and asset inflation from Seoul to Jakarta. When the credit crunch came, banks across littoral Pacific Asia found themselves sitting on a mountain of non-performing loans. Problematically, the Asian developmental way considered the bank and the stockmarket an extension of state-led administrative guidance. The fatal flaw in the Asian model it would seem was its indifference to financial accountability facilitated by a legal system that ceded power to an omniscient technocracy guided by a largely unaccountable political élite and a patrimonial tax system. The latter channelled savings and FDI to inefficient and increasingly indebted conglomerates like Fuyo in Japan or Kia in South Korea, or to business cronies like Suharto's golf partner, Mohamed 'Bob' Hassan in Indonesia.

THE FEARFUL SYMMETRY OF THE TIGER STATES

As Japan has become politically and economically calcified, those economies that sought to emulate the Japanese model of development, yet remained, paradoxically, dependent upon access to the Japanese market, Japanese investment and higher technology, confront an even bleaker future. Kenneth Courtis, chief economist at Deutsche Bank, Tokyo, observed, 'if Japan continues to contract, then the other countries in the region have no hope of turning their economies around.'[5] The inability of government and bureaucracy to reform the banking sector in Japan makes such a scenario increasingly plausible.[6] Indeed, the formerly strong states of the Asia Pacific littoral, irrespective of their purported transition to democracy, share a fearful symmetry of bureaucratic overload, bad loans, lack of liquidity and evolving political fragility and instability. Since the crisis began, the World Bank's JM Severino calculated that $115 billion has fled Malaysia, South Korea, Thailand, Indonesia and the Philippines. In effect, the equivalent of 18% of GDP has vanished from the Asia Pacific region since July 1997.[7] Significantly, Japan is both the major creditor of the ailing tiger economies and directed 40 percent of its exports to Pacific Asia.[8] Between 15-25% of the exports of the meltdown economies go to deflating Japan. Since the crisis began regional trade has plummeted by 50%. As regional trade accounts for almost a quarter of the total trade of these export-oriented economies, lower consumer demand in each receding tiger affects the export performance of its neighbours.

What seemed like a virtuous Asian circle of high savings, and state-engineered growth ultimately transpired to be vicious. This has engendered a variety of political and social problems at both state and regional level.[9] Thus, South Korea has had to endure the 'national shame' of a $58 billion dollar IMF bailout package, a 6% contraction in GDP, a liquidity crunch, high interest rates and, with unemployment rising to 10% of the workforce, mounting labour unrest. Significantly, the constitutional transition from Kim Young Sam to Kim Dae Jung in December 1997 has done little to address South Korea's failed corporatist, conglomerate-based economic and political model. Despite the amalgamation of a few banks, the South Korean financial sector remains opaque. Kim Dae Jung's promises to reform the power of the big *chaebol* have come to naught. Despite mounting losses and labour unrest, *chaebol*, like Hyundai, continue to stamp their monolithic footprint over the economy and resist foreign access to ownership of domestic companies. Irrespective of political moves to constitutional, as opposed to military rule, the Korean economy and Korean politics continue to be mired in an oppressive culture that views the state as a benign paternalistic guardian and resents the intrusion of foreign goods into the domestic market or foreign takeovers of indigenous economic champions. Notwithstanding IMF blandishments to open the South Korean market, both Microsoft and Ford motors abandoned attempts to take over failed South Korean software and motor manufacturers complaining of dubious political and bureaucratic pressures that rendered their bids unsustainable.[10]

Given the continued appeal of corporatism to the national

psyche and the predilection to see the global market as a threat rather than an opportunity, the prospect for South Korean recovery in the near future looks increasingly bleak. Moreover, official appeals to national unity against the challenge posed to entrenched cultural understandings by liberalising domestic markets and a rule of law based political pluralism does not augur well for any immediate diplomatic resolution to the disaster that is North Korea. Since the era of Park Chung-hee, South Korea, like the other developing states of the Pacific Asian littoral sought to define itself against an external other. Both the global threat of the market and the immediate nuclear threat posed by an imploding North Korea only serve to reinforce the post-war emphasis on the inflexible maintenance of South Korean unity at whatever cost. Moreover, the growing propensity of North Korea to use its nuclear potential as a means of extorting handouts from the US and its immediate Asian neighbours, as demonstrated by the recent testing of ballistic missiles over Japan, only renders a diplomatic solution to the Korean problem increasingly remote.

If the 'state of the state' in Northeast Asia looks grim, the prospects are even bleaker in Southeast Asia. Thailand which triggered the crisis in July 1997, when the Bank of Thailand ineptly tried to maintain the baht peg to the dollar, received an IMF rescue package of $18 billion. The unavoidable restructuring of the economy witnessed the bankruptcy of financial institutions, manufacturing decline, rising interest rates and unemployment rates, and a liquidity crunch. However, although the coalition government tried to implement elements of the IMF package, the continuing opacity concerning the extent of private and public sector debt combined with laws that restrict foreign ownership of Thai property and businesses deters the foreign investment necessary to generate recovery. In Thailand, as in South Korea, democratic leaders show little evidence of making any more than cosmetic adjustments to a political, financial and business culture inured to self-serving clientelism. Moreover, Chuan's unstable six-party coalition has not only failed to implement radical economic reform, it has also laid itself open to charges of widespread corruption. [11]

Similar practices have long characterised the New Economic Policy that the UMNO dominated National Front coalition government carefully nurtured in Malaysia after interethnic riots in May 1969. Malaysia has yet to have recourse to the IMF. But the private sector is nevertheless, 'tied up with debts'. Worryingly,

Malaysia has one of the highest ratios of debt to GDP output in the world. The Economist Intelligence Unit reports that non-performing loans could rise to between 25-30% of all loans by early 1999.[13] If half of these loans went bad, Malaysian banks would face write-offs equivalent to 20% of GDP.[14] Malaysia, then, suffers from the same systemic weaknesses that afflict all the tiger economies: non-performing loans on speculative property investments; conglomerates seeking court protection from creditors;[15] shaky local banks, like Sime Darby and Bank Bumiputera;[16] and a collapsing currency. Yet the dubious policy, promulgated by Prime Minister Mahathir Mohamad's favourite financial adviser, Daim Zainuddin, in August 1998, of reducing interest rates in order to allay recession merely facilitated capital flight to Singapore. The subsequent decision to reimpose currency controls not only led to the resignation of the director of Bank Negara, the Malaysian central bank, it also indefinitely postponed future western investment and the infusion of liquidity necessary to revive growth. Further attempts to stimulate the economy through handouts to failing indigenous conglomerates like Renong and Mirzan Mahathir's *Konsortium Perkapalan* indicate the enduring charms of cronyism. Mahathir's petulant attacks on western finance capital, the removal of his more market-friendly deputy, and putative heir apparent, Anwar Ibrahim for sexual misconduct amounting to treason, together with restrictions on 'negative' reports[17] in the state-controlled press indicates that, unlike elsewhere in the region, the Malay political élite has yet to accept that it even faces impending economic catastrophe. Indeed, the sacking and proposed prosecution of Anwar for high crimes and misdemeanours has turned an economic crisis into a potential political crisis amongst the hitherto unified Malay governing élite.

If Malaysia is still in denial concerning the economic crisis, Indonesia, the most flawed economy in Southeast Asia, is on a life-support machine. Triggered by the baht crisis, the meltdown of the rupiah in August 1997 exposed a 'vast overhang of unhedged short-term private sector debt' conservatively estimated at $80 billion .[18] The collapse of the financial sector and various Chinese and Suharto family-linked conglomerates followed. The economic crisis undermined the authority of President Suharto's New Order and following riots and student demonstrations in May 1998, the ageing President resigned in favour of his Vice-President B J Habibie.

REGIONAL IMPLICATIONS

This economic and political collapse continues to resonate across the ASEAN region and the manner in which it is resolved will profoundly affect international relations in the Asia Pacific. Indonesia was, the PRC apart, both the largest, the croniest and least bureaucratically competent of the emerging Asian economies. The flight of capital, the failure of Indonesian banks, and the collapse of Indonesian business necessitated an IMF bailout package of close to $50 billion. In July, Finance Minister Bambang Subianto calculated conservatively that GDP would contract by 12%, and inflation rise by 60% during 1998. The minister observed that, at the rather optimistic exchange rate of 10,600 rupiah to the greenback, the government required 95 trillion rupiah per annum merely to service its debt repayments.

Throughout Pacific Asia economic dislocation has caused rising unemployment along with rising interest rates. The Asian emphasis upon family values means that there is no safety net for those who have fallen into poverty. Nowhere is the absence of welfare provision more acutely felt than in Indonesia. Drought caused by *El Niño*, coupled with environmental degradation, requires the normally self-sufficient Bulog, the government agency for rice production and distribution, to import at least three million tons of rice this year.

The spectre of five million people facing famine and half the 220 million population falling below the poverty line with no imminent prospect of economic recovery raises the political and economic stakes. The replacement of Suharto by his protegé Habibie has done little either to legitimate or stabilise the post-Suharto order. In fact, President Habibie's suggestion that Indonesians should fast two days a week to overcome food shortages symbolises the bankruptcy of his political style. The period between the resignation of Suharto in May and the convening of a special session of the People's Consultative Assembly in November to agree on the process for a presidential election next year, moreover, witnessed a proliferation of political parties that resembles the *aliran* (political streams) of unstable post-independence Indonesia (1950-57). Thus, Mochtar Pakpahan, recently released from detention, the charismatic President of the Prosperous Labour Union, articulates the radical demands of the organised working class represented in the pre-

Suharto era by the Indonesia Communist Party (PKI). Megawati Sukarnoputri's faction of the *Parti Democrasi Indonesia* (PDI) seeks to revive the nationalist legacy of her father. Abdulrachman Wahid's Nadhlatul *Ulama*, Indonesia's largest Islamic organisation that had previously shunned politics for 14 years, announced its decision to establish a political party in June 1998 to represent the rural Islamic *pesantren* tradition. Meanwhile Amien Rais' *Mummadiyah* reflects the middle-class, reformist, modernising Islamic nationalism represented in the pre-Sukarno era by *Masumi.* It is to this constituency that Habibie also appeals through *Golkar*, the official New Order party of government, which has survived the transition and retains its extensive organisational base. Historically, these various political streams have shown little capacity for compromise.

Political uncertainty and economic turmoil will exercise little appeal for the Indonesian military (ABRI) that still remains ideologically committed to its dual function (*dwi funcsi*) as the source of order and guarantor of the Indonesian status quo. Although, since the events of May and revelations about its capacity to make dissidents 'disappear', the army has kept a low-profile and is internally divided between nationalist (*merah putih*) and Islamic *(hijau)* factions, it is unlikely that either faction could accept the uncertainty of multipartism, the diminution of its authority, or 'special' autonomy for troublesome provinces like Aceh, Irian Jaya and East Timor.

Significantly, the controversial role of army factions in both the riots of 13-20 May and during the special session of the national assembly in November 1998 illustrated both the contradictory forces at work within the army and the uncertain status of the Indonesian Chinese, the traditional scapegoats for political and economic breakdown. The flight of Chinese capital from Indonesia adds a previously quiescent ethnic component to the apparently shared Asian values of the Association of South East Asian Nations (ASEAN) and the ARF.

THE IRRELEVANCE OF THE ASEAN WAY TO THE NEW SECURITY DILEMMAS IN THE ASIA PACIFIC

Largely unremarked in the media coverage of the state they are in, is the fact that the Asian model for internal development was extended in the course of the 1980s to regional diplomacy. Much was made of an Asian way to facilitate what former Malaysian Deputy-Premier, Anwar Ibrahim, termed an Asian Renaissance[19] and to constitute the ideological foundations of a Pacific Asian order appropriate for the eagerly anticipated Pacific century. Part of the problem here was that some of the more enthusiastic proponents of the 'Asian way' also doubled as academic analysts. These scholar-bureaucrats from Canberra to Tokyo considered the Asian values of face-saving and face-giving co-operation, consensus, hierarchy, and harmony and balance the ideological template for a new Pan-Asian order. Western democracies might, with reservations, join the new dispensation. They would have to accept however, that the Asia-Pacific was a 'two way street'.[20] What informed this Asian strategic thinking was a rejection of rule-based and contractually binding approaches to economic and political problems (which smacked of an imperialistic western rationalism)[21] in favour of close bilateral ties founded on good interpersonal relationships, endless rounds of golf, and a vaguely defined consensus without any embarrassing loss of face for non -compliance.

Regional agreements on trade, like the APEC brokered Bogor Declaration (1994), which appeared to presage a new era of economic and political interdependency, assumed shared Asian values in its provision for regional economic development. Expounding its principles in 1994, Indonesian President Suharto explained 'consensus must be broad and flexible, decisions should be made collectively and there can be no quick ... implementation.'[22] APEC agreements were neither enforceable nor binding. Nevertheless this *modus operandi* was enthusiastically embraced by Australian academics in second-track diplomatic fora who claimed it evinced a dynamic, but disturbingly oxymoronic, 'open regionalism'.[23]

Equally insubstantial and even more grandiose in its regionalist pretensions was the rapid expansion of ASEAN. This sole indigenous regional grouping of any note received growing international respect in the post-Cold War era. After 1991, European, North and South American and Australasian diplomats and political economists scrambled to attend its dialogue groups, workshops and multilevel fora. Its many admirers claimed its excursions into multilateralism through arrangements like the ASEAN Free Trade Area (AFTA) and the ASEAN Regional Forum (ARF) constituted the building blocks of the new regionalism. Yet a brief interrogation of ASEAN's development suggests that the organisation's achievements are more rhetorical than real. Significantly, its much vaunted capacity to manage regional problems, through opaque mechanisms of consensus and confidence building, had little impact on the arms race in which all the economies of the Pacific Asian littoral participated. Pacific Asian bonding, somewhat curiously coincided with burgeoning budget expenditure on high-tech weaponry which ranged from Japan's purchase of AWACs and P-3 submarines to Malaysia's Ministry of Defence shopping for cut-price MiG-29s and South African attack helicopters, whilst the Indonesian government with characteristic ineptitude purchased the East German navy.[24] Even during the heady days of the putative Asian Renaissance, the distinctively Asian approach to regional diplomacy had by no means removed intramural tensions. Nor has it begun to address the security problem posed by an increasingly irredentist Greater China, which in the course of the 1990s came to assert its claims to the rebellious province of Taiwan and to regard the South China Sea as a Chinese lake. Given these post-Cold War developments and the deracinating effects of the meltdown, the limited purpose ASEAN had once served, as a Cold War regional club for ailing gerontocrats with a shared opposition to Indo-Chinese communism, has been rendered largely irrelevant. What then, does this imply for security in what will become an increasingly unstable Southeast Asia?

NOT THE WAY TO GO

ASEAN's inauspicious roots lay in a number of abortive regional experiments of the 1960s that attempted to secure the fragile post-colonial regimes in Southeast Asia from an external, communist, threat. In the somewhat vague terms of the Bangkok Declaration (1967) the initial member states[25] agreed to ignore the various ethnic, religious, ideological and territorial rivalries that had sustained the bitter *konfrontasi* between Indonesia and Malaysia from 1963-66. The public philosophy of ASEAN expressed in the Bangkok Declaration commended non-interference in the internal arrangements of member states and the resolution of domestic and regional instability through a recipe of economic growth.[26] In 1976, after a decade of drift, the ASEAN Heads of Government eventually agreed to a Treaty of Amity and Cooperation (TAC).The treaty established a code of conduct for regional interstate relations and established this self-denying ordinance as the basis of regional order. It was, however, in the course of the Cambodian conflict that ASEAN's international reputation grew, but even here the group acted essentially as a convenient proxy for Chinese and US regional interests. Thus, although by the 1990s ASEAN had evolved an identity as a diplomatic community with a collegial style and practice, and had in the aftermath of the Cold War extended its embrace across the region through mechanisms like ARF and AFTA, its actual contribution to regional security and economic integration remained distinctly abstract. Despite its well-honed interpersonal networks and endless preoccupation with confidence-building measures, ASEAN has secured only minimal institutional deepening.

The grouping instead placed its faith in the maintenance of good relationships established over time and the cultivation of bilateral ties rather than any multilateral security structure. Consequently, ASEAN achieved its regional standing through a capacity to manage problems rather than to solve them and this strategy, soothed by the opiate of two decades of untroubled economic growth, had remarkably little impact on the intramural disputes that troubled its formation prior to 1967. Moreover, the practice of non-interference in the domestic affairs of neighbouring states, fostered festering claims to autonomy by disappointed regional minorities. Thus in southern Thailand and Mindanao in the Philippines, Islamic separatism has assumed an increasingly fundamentalist hue. Human rights abuses in East Timor continue to undermine Indonesia's international credibility, whilst ASEAN's 'constructive engagement' with the State Law and Order Council of Myanmar has exacerbated relations with both the US and the EU.

A potent symbol of the inherent weakness of the ASEAN approach is the smog from burning rainforests in Sumatra and Kalimantan that embraces Singapore and Malaysia each August and relinquishes its grip only with the arrival of monsoon rains. In the ASEAN way, the smog was officially redefined as 'haze' and sedulously ignored because of its potential to damage relations with Indonesia and the interests of Suharto cronies like Bob Hassan's powerful Apkindo group. Only when the impact of the haze on the ASEAN economies became so great that it could no longer be ignored did ASEAN leaders reluctantly acknowledge that a regional eco-problem actually existed. In 'ASEAN think', then, all regional difficulties would be resolved through a bizarre mixture of indifference, insouciance and a Panglossian faith in sustained economic growth. Both the ASEAN ministerial meeting in July and the APEC summit in Kuala Lumpur in November demonstrated the inability of regional fora to agree upon a formal response to the crisis. In terms of the financial crisis, regional arrangements have proved inadequate. Moreover, the fact that the crisis has awakened the ethnic and religious tensions hitherto managed, but never fully addressed during the period of benign growth, questions the continuing plausibility of these regional structures.

THE PROBLEMATIC STATUS OF THE OVERSEAS CHINESE (*HUA QIAO*) IN SOUTHEAST ASIA

As the depth and severity of the economic crisis engulfing the export-oriented economies of Indonesia and Malaysia intensified, long-suppressed ethnic tensions have become increasingly visible. Significantly, the severity of the recent economic downturn once again throws into question the role of the overseas Chinese population in the economies of Malaysia and Indonesia in general and the status of Singapore as an island of Chinese 'sojourners' in what Lee Kuan Yew famously termed a 'sea of Malay peoples'. Why, we might wonder, has the economic meltdown so dramatically undermined the consensus that had characterised the region's most significant regional grouping, ASEAN, and its core economies Indonesia, Singapore and Malaysia? And what are the prospects for regional stability premised as it is on continued economic growth, and driven by the official ASEAN ideology of bonding, good interpersonal relations and non-interference in the internal affairs of member states?

The inter-ASEAN difficulties that have recently emerged between Singapore and its neighbours must be cast against a backdrop of the growing popular appeal of a revived Islamic identity to Malay and Indonesian political reformers and the increasingly hostile perception of economically influential, but 'non-indigenous' Chinese minorities. Ethnic and religious suspicion, coupled with economic turmoil and the attractions of a plot mentality make for a heady regional brew. The re-emergence of these long-suppressed communal tensions have additional implications for both regional institutions and economic recovery in Southeast Asia.

A notable feature of economic growth in Southeast Asia in the boom decades after 1969 was both its curiously technology-less character and the disproportionately influential role played by Chinese business. In Indonesia, although the Chinese represent less than 4% of the population, Chinese conglomerates accounted for two thirds of Indonesia's private, urban economy. They dominated the distribution network for food and other essentials[27] and controlled 80% of the assets of the top three hundred conglomerates. In Malaysia, the numerically much larger Chinese population similarly occupied a disproportionately influential role in commercial life. Here, the big Malay-Chinese conglomerates, like Hong Leong and the Robert Kuok group, cultivated close ties with key figures in the ruling ethnically Malay, UMNO (United Malay National Organisation) élite, ensuring that élite business activity occurred beyond the realm of public scrutiny or comment.[28]

This distinctive and opaque relationship between Chinese business and an ethnically dissimilar political élite reflected the contingent historical legacy that marked the emergence of the new states of Southeast Asia after 1945. Both the post-colonial Malaysian and Indonesian states deliberately evolved an official distinction between indigenous and non-indigenous subjects (*bumiputera* and *non-bumiputera* in *Bahasa Melayu* or *bumi* and *non bumi* in *Bahasa Indonesia*). Whilst who precisely constituted the *bumi* remained vague, the prime function of the category was to exclude the Chinese.

The post-war attitude of the People's Republic of China (PRC) and the exiled Nationalist government of China in Taiwan (ROC) further complicated the question of the loyalty of the overseas Chinese to the new states. The *Kuomintang* (KMT) regime that has ruled Taiwan since 1949 followed Qing dynasty practice of regarding all those of Chinese descent living overseas as Chinese nationals. By contrast, Maoist China treated both the new states and the overseas Chinese ambivalently. It was only in 1980 that the PRC introduced a formal nationality law, recognising that 'ethnic Chinese would cease to be Chinese citizens once they had foreign citizenship.'[29] Significantly, perhaps as many as a quarter of Chinese Indonesians remained effectively stateless.[30]

Whilst the terms on which the Chinese communities of Malaysia and Indonesia were incorporated into the emerging nation states remained disturbingly unclear, the ruling indigenous élites evolved policies that excluded them from political participation. In Malaysia, following inter-ethnic riots in 1969, the UMNO dominated *Barisan Nasional* coalition that ruled in the Malay interest introduced a discriminatory New Economic Policy (NEP) designed to enhance *bumiputera* participation in the economy and the professions. In Indonesia, the corporatist character of the New Order strictly controlled the terms of political participation and promoted an official assimilationist policy of national integration. The New Order government curtailed the use of the Chinese language, required Chinese children to attend Indonesian language schools, and prohibited the use of Chinese characters.

Nevertheless, despite their political and cultural marginalisation, Chinese business conglomerates remained central to the rapid growth of these tiger economies after 1970. In Malaysia conglomerates like the Kuok group acted as business proxies for the Malay élite, whilst in Indonesia conglomerates like Lim Sioe Liong's Salim group existed in *cukong* or clientilistic arrangements with Suharto or, in the course of the early 1990s, the conglomerates run by Suharto's sons and daughters.

ECONOMIC DOWNTURN AND CHINESE PARIAHS

The paradox of being economically powerful but politically impotent seemed unimportant when the regional economy boomed. If things went wrong, however, the wealthy Chinese *towkay* stood out as an obvious target for the politically and economically disaffected. And things, of course, have gone spectacularly wrong. The tendency to scapegoat the Chinese community has evident domestic and regional implications. In Malaysia, since his political emergence as a Malay 'ultra' in the aftermath of the 1969 riots, Prime Minister Mahathir has promoted a eugenic vision, outlined in *The Malay Dilemma* (1972). This emphasised the need to forge a modern, dynamic *bumiputera* identity for a new Malaysia Incorporated. A notable feature of Mahathir and the UMNO controlled press's rhetoric in dealing with the current crisis has been to stress the dangers of communalism, the need for Malay unity and to blame either western speculators or Chinese Singapore for bad faith in their financial and commercial dealings with Malaysia. As Mahathir's handling of the economic crisis turned into a political one, Islamic groups supporting deposed Deputy Prime Minister Anwar Ibrahim and demanding *reformasi* intimated the collapse of Malay unity that had sustained UMNO's centralisation of political power since 1969. This collapse by no means presages a new political pluralism. Significantly the Chinese minority that accounts for over 37% of the population, remains politically isolated. Indeed, the inability of the Malay élite to adopt credible structural reforms to address the crisis has ominous implications both for ASEAN, Singapore-Malay relations and Chinese business groups in Malaysia.

More disturbingly still, in Indonesia, the Chinese community, already traumatised by the events in May in which organised groups of *primam* (hooligans) systematically murdered, raped and pillaged their way across the Chinese districts of Glodok, West Jakarta and Solo, East Java, constitute the obvious scapegoat for economic failure. The continuing political uncertainty that induces permanent fear of further racial unrest undermines the ability of Chinese business to function in Indonesia, casts doubt on the capacity for Indonesia to feed itself let alone economically recover, and adds a new and disturbing ethnicist component to regional dynamics. Nevertheless, despite the centrality of Chinese traders to Indonesian food distribution, Habibie has done little to allay the anxiety of those who have fled the country. Their place, he insouciantly observed in July, could be 'taken over by others'.[31] The fact that both popular democratic reformers like Amien Rais and former New Order technocrats like President Habibie (together with Anwar Ibrahim in Malaysia) share a vision of establishing suitably modernised Islamic values at the centre of a reformed polity explains this insouciance.

Although both military and civilian politicians hold the Chinese conglomerates largely responsible for Indonesia's difficulties, the plight of the overseas Chinese has not gone unremarked elsewhere in the region. In July 1998, the Chinese foreign ministry expressed 'concern and sympathy for the ethnic Chinese people' attacked, murdered and raped in the May riots.[32] In August, it more forcefully reiterated the view that the Indonesian authorities should punish those responsible for the racially motivated assaults.[33] Meanwhile, the PRC's remaining rebellious province, Taiwan, suspended rice shipments to Indonesia in the same month in order to demonstrate its concern at the Indonesian government's indifference to the plight of the Indonesian Chinese.[34]

Ethnic tension, coupled with economic decline and the contentious role played by overseas Chinese networks in developing

Southeast Asia's ersatz form of capitalism, has weakened regional consensus. Economic collapse and the re-emergence of old religious and ethnic cleavages in the cultural mosaic that constitutes the ASEAN region has revealed that organisation's incapacity to address these difficulties. Two faultlines have appeared in the arrangement that to many observers prior to 1997 offered the basis for a secure and economically prosperous Pacific Asia.[35] First, spokespersons for ASEAN's more autocratically disposed members, like Indonesian Foreign Minister, Ali Alatas, consider the grouping's central tenet of non -interference "misunderstood" and are unwilling to abandon it , whilst representatives of the more democratically accountable ASEAN countries, like the Thai Foreign Minister, Surin Pitsuwan, maintain the crisis requires the organisation to adopt "flexible engagement on issues that have a negative bearing on others in the region".[36] Across this emerging ideological divide runs a less widely advertised cultural cleavage which isolates the overseas Chinese, whose home base in Southeast Asia is Singapore, from an increasingly Islamised cultural area. Despite a shared regard for the ASEAN ideology of non-interference established in its Treaty of Amity and Cooperation (1975), Singapore's relations with both Malaysia and Indonesia have cooled dramatically since the inception of the crisis. Lee Kuan Yew's accurate, but undiplomatic observation, that Suharto's misguided decision to appoint B J Habibie's appointment as Vice-President would 'disturb' financial markets did little to enhance the good interpersonal relations between regional leaders that provides the capstone of ASEAN-style diplomacy. The recent failure of Singapore to disburse $3 billion in trade credit guarantees promised in April, because Indonesian officials refused to abide by Singapore Ministry of Trade and Industry conditions, prompted President Habibie to describe the city state as a mere 'dot on the map', unresponsive to a 'friend in need.'[37]

At the same time, a number of recession related factors have frayed the always volatile relations between Singapore and Malaysia. Malaysian officials criticise Singapore banks for aiding capital flight out of Malaysia. Adverse Singapore newspaper comment on the new, but vermin infested, Subang airport, together with the decision to move passport control for the city state without sufficiently consulting the Malaysian government have further provoked Malaysian ire. Continuing disagreement over treaties guaranteeing Singapore's water supply into the twenty-first century, and the

Malaysian government's requirement that all exports leave the country from Port Klang rather than Singapore further exacerbate the ever-present anxiety of Singapore's ruling élite. The Malaysian government's recent decision not to participate in Five-Power Defence Arrangement (FPDA) manoeuvres with Singapore, UK, New Zealand and Australia for the first time in 27 years and restrict Singaporean access to Malaysian airspace further demonstrated the fraying of regional bonds.

The banks and state-owned enterprises of the well-run technocratic machine that organises every aspect of Singapore are worryingly exposed to insolvency in the Malay and Indonesian economies in which they are closely integrated. When Malaysia arbitrarily decided to reimpose currency and stock exchange controls in September, Singapore banks had to clear billions of ringgit in transactions made in its foreign exchange market. As one local economist observed, 'in the process of taking control' of its currency, 'the biggest casualty is Singapore'.[38] Yet, the ruling PAP's neurocratic propensity to advertise publicly its concerns over the policies responsible for regional recession, environmental decay and the rise of Islam only fuels interregional irritation.

GREATER CHINA AND THE MELTDOWN

As the Japanese economy has stalled and the yen has fallen, it has taken the rest of Asia's currencies and economies down with it, exacerbated lingering ethnic, religious and border tensions across littoral Pacific Asia, revealed the weakness of the strong state and exposed the vacuity of the ASEAN way as a method for promoting regional harmony. Yet, Japan's fiscal loss of face has notably facilitated the recuperation of the PRC's international image. China unlike Japan has played 'the politics of the Asian crisis brilliantly.'[39] In June, Jiang Zemin effectively contrasted China's stoic refusal to devalue the yuan with Japan's fiscal and monetary selfishness. This has enabled China to extract political capital from the crisis both by restoring its hitherto frayed relations with the United States and presenting itself as both hero and victim of the currency crisis. Hero because of its monetary rectitude, and victim, because Chinese exports have lost their competitive advantage against the yen-linked tiger economies. With the erosion of Japanese economic leadership and its increasing inability to shape the political destiny of the region,

China is evidently looking to reassert its traditional hegemony in both Northeast and Southeast Asia. This has been recently exemplified by China's criticism of the Indonesian government's handling of the May riots.

However, despite enhancing its international cachet, the Chinese model merely replicates, and on a massive scale, the defects of the late-developing state.[40] Its banking sector sits on a massive amount of bad or non-performing loans, its *soi disant* private sector is effectively run either by regional state collectives or the PLA and is dependent on good links with the party bureaucracy in Beijing. In other words, cronyism, nepotism and corruption are as rife in the People's Republic as they are elsewhere in Southeast Asia. Moreover, only because its currency is not fully convertible has China so far proved impervious to the meltdown. Nevertheless, foreign investment has abandoned the littoral boom towns from Shenzhen to Shanghai and the rate of GDP growth has slowed appreciably since 1997. On the black-market the yuan already trades well below the official rate and Chinese businessmen that can have transferred their assets into foreign denominated currencies. Moreover, if the yen continues to decline against the dollar, China will be unable to sustain its official fiscal virtue. When it devalues, Hong Kong's already fragile peg to the dollar will also be loosened and the economic crisis across Pacific Asia will further intensify .

In other words, what in early 1997 appeared to many regional enthusiasts as the basis for a Pan-Asian regional order premised upon communitarian values and modified by bureaucratically determined, but market-oriented, economic goals, increasingly resembles a ramshackle collection of states characterised only by high debt, bureaucratic mismanagement and a systemic inability to adopt meaningful market-oriented reforms. Pacific Asia is consequently destined to remain a zone of worrying uncertainty dependent on the US security presence and access to the US domestic market. The only relief in this remorselessly gloomy picture is that the traumatic end to the miracle of 30 years growth has also terminated a regional arms race that had notably escalated between 1990-97 despite the public avowal of confidence building measures, harmony and consensus. Significantly, regional arms expenditure, which had soared throughout the decade, came to a dramatic halt in the second half of 1997.[41] Thailand lost its deposit on 18 F18 Hornets it had ordered from the US and cannot afford to keep the aircraft it has in the air for more than two hours per pilot per month. Meanwhile, Malaysia has deferred payment on the attack helicopters it ordered from South Africa. With the collapse of both double digit growth and what one regional commentator euphemistically termed a regional exercise in benchmarking, [42] what remains are a series of weak, fractious and overloaded states with varying, but limited, political and economic capacity to engineer recovery sometime in the next century. Indeed, we can perhaps generate two interesting conclusions from the events in Pacific Asia in the last decade. First, the continuing importance of the state to the process of globalisation. Significantly, it is those states with the most flexible and efficient bureaucracies, Singapore and Taiwan, that have most effectively weathered the storm. Second, the manner in which issues of political economy are ineluctably woven into security problems in the era of globalisation. The most salient feature of the financial crisis is the manner in which it has reawakened dormant nationalisms and ethnic and religious tensions that have rendered regional political and economic arrangements impotent.

Notes

1. R. Higgott, "Shared Response to the Market Shocks?", *The World Today* January 1998, p.6.
2. C. Johnson "Political Institutions and Economic performance: The Government-Business Relationship in Japan, South Korea and Taiwan," in F.C. Deyo (ed), *The Political Economy of the New Asian Industrialism,* Ithaca: Cornell University Press, 1987, ch.4.
3. The report featured Indonesia, South Korea, Malaysia, Taiwan, Thailand, Hong Kong and Singapore. See The World Bank, *The East Asian Miracle: A World Bank Policy Research Report* Oxford: Oxford University Press, 1993, and the various country reports *Lessons of East Asia,* Washington: World Bank, 1993.
4. Endaka means strong yen.
5. *Australian Financial Review,* 10 August 1998.
6. Since Courtis wrote his piece in August 1998, two big Japanese banks, the Long Term Credit Bank and the Nippon Credit Bank, have both gone into government receivership.
7. M. Wolf, "Let Lenders Beware," *Financial Times,* 9 December 1998.
8. M. Wolf, "Threats of Depression," *Financial Times,* 26 August 1998.
9. *Jakarta Post* 22 June 1998.

[10] *Financial Times,* 7 September 1998.

[11] *Financial Times,* 16 September 1998.

[12] *Straits Times,* 2 July 1998.

[13] Economist Intelligence Unit *Country Report Malaysia and Brunei 2nd Quarter 1998,* London: Economist Intelligence Unit Limited, 1998, p.29.

[14] *Straits Times,* 2 July 1998.

[15] *Asian Wall Street Journal*, 8 July 1998.

[16] *Asian Wall Street Journal*, 4 July 1998.

[17] The Sunday Times Singapore, 19 July 1998.

[18] Economist Intelligence Unit, *Indonesia Country Report Ist Quarter 1998.* London: Economist Limited, 1998, p.27.

[19] Anwar Ibrahim, *Asian Renaissance* Singapore: Times Academic Press. 1996.

[20] See *inter alia* K Mahbubani, "The Pacific Way," *Foreign Affairs,* 74,1, 1995,

[21] N Sopiee, "The New World Order: What Southeast Asia Should strive For." In R Mahmood and T Ramnath (eds), *Southeast Asia: The Way Forward*. Kuala Lumpur: Freidrich Ebert Stiftung, 1992.

[22] *Straits Times,* 12th November 1994.

[23] See R Thakur, "Australia and New Zealand Unequal Partners on the Periphery," in J. Cotton and J.Ravenhill (ed), *Seeking Asian Engagement: Australia in World Affairs 1991-95,* Melbourne: Oxford University Press, p.268.

[24] See author's *Political Development in Pacific Asia,* Cambridge: Polity Press, 1997, p.193.

[25] Thailand, Malaysia, Singapore, the Philippines and Indonesia comprised the initial membership of the Association of South East Asian Nations. Brunei joined in 1984 and Vietnam in 1995.

[26] In this context see *inter alia* M Leifer, *ASEAN and the Security of South East Asia* London: Routledge 1989 and *The ASEAN Regional Forum: Extending ASEAN's Model of Regional Security,* Adelphi Paper 302, Oxford: Oxford University Press 1996.

[27] *Straits Times,* 18 July 1998. See also C. Wibisono, "The Economic Role of the Indonesian Chinese," in L. Suryadinata (ed), *Southeast Asian Chinese and China: The Political Economic Dimension,* (vol 1) Singapore: Times Academic Press, 1995.

[28] See E.T. Gomez, *Political Business: Corporate involvement of Malaysian Political Parties.* Townsville: James Cook University Press, 1994.

[29] L. Suryadinata, *Chinese and Nation Building in Southeast Asiam,* Singapore: Singapore Society of Asian Studies, 1997, p.14.

[30] *ibid*, p.54.

[31] *Straits Times,* 20 July 1998.

[32] *Jakarta Post,* 15 July 1998.

[33] *Financial Times,* 4 August 1998.

[34] *Financial Times,* 21 August.1998.

[35] See inter alia J. Naisbitt, "The World's future is in Asia," in *The Eight Asian Megatrends that are Changing the World,* London: N. Brealey, 1995, pp.252 ff.

[36] *Jakarta Post,* 13 July 1998.

[37] *Financial Times,* 21 August 1998.

[38] *Financial Times,* 19 September 1998.

[39] P Archer, "Weakness is Strength in Policy Scapegoating," *Australian Financial Review,* 10 August 1998.

[40] See N Landy, "China and the Asian Contagion," *Foreign Affairs,* July/August 1998 . Landy notes that "loans due to crony conglomerates may be similar to those in Indonesia." p.80.

[41] A. Acharaya, "An Arms race in Southeast Asia?", in Da Cunha (ed), *op cit.* p.83.

[42] D. Da Cunha, *The Sunday Times,* 19 July, 1998.

10

State Collapse and the United Nations: Universality at Risk?[1]

ALEXANDROS YANNIS

PhD Candidate in International Relations Graduate Institute of International Studies, Geneva

In the post-Cold War period, terms such as state collapse, failed states, disintegrated states, anarchy and chaos are often employed to describe the dramatic implications of protracted internal conflicts. The intensity and the consequences of such conflicts imply an extreme disruption of the political order of a state and raise questions about its very survival and, more importantly, of the survival of large numbers of its population.

There is no authoritative definition of state collapse.[2] The common theme is implosion of effective central governmental authority. Implosion indicates that the source of state collapse is civil strife and internal conflict and distinguishes the phenomenon of state collapse from international war and foreign occupation. However, there are several opinions about the definition and threshold of the collapse of effective government, varying from expansive approaches touching upon a large number of modern states to restrictive definitions referring to a few exceptional circumstances.[3] Some authors are even sceptical about the whole effort of defining the collapse of effective government and the concept of state collapse.[4]

For the purpose of this chapter the collapse of effective government will be defined as a situation that signifies an extreme disruption of the political order of a state manifested by protracted violent conflict and fragmentation of authority in conjunction with a humanitarian disaster. While violent conflict implies the absence of a political agreement, and fragmentation of authority signifies the *de facto* apportionment of the territory among different groups, humanitarian disaster demonstrates the inability of the various authorities to sustain elementary conditions of life and sets the material threshold for the collapse of effective government. Since none of these three elements are the deliberate result of the warring parties, the phenomenon of state collapse is associated with a power struggle over the control of government and not over territory. Conflicts emanating from secessionist wars entail struggle over territory and the establishment of separate governments and thereby they resemble international wars and they should be distinguished from the phenomenon of state collapse. While the most classic case of state collapse in the post-Cold War era is the on-going Somali crisis, several other post-Cold War domestic conflicts can be placed under the category of state collapse.

The international implications of state collapse are well recognised, particularly since the state serves as the primary model of domestic and international public order. In general, state disintegration challenges the protection of fundamental human rights such as life itself and threatens the maintenance of regional and international security.[5] Thus, state collapse engages the basic values and interests of the international system. Given that the maintenance of international peace and security and the respect of human rights are major purposes of the United Nations, the phenomenon of state collapse poses great challenges to the United Nations' aspirations for global governance. In fact, the implications of state collapse for human rights and international security have been the main pre-occupation of the academic and political discourse on the subject.

The debate about state collapse reached its peak at the early stages of the post-Cold War era when the US doctrine of a 'New World Order' and the aspirations of the UN's 'Agenda for Peace' were converging in the support for assertive responses to international challenges emanating from domestic conflicts and particularly the humanitarian crises that were formulated as threats to international peace and security.[6] The 1992-95 international intervention in Somalia plunged the international community headlong into its first encounter with a collapsed state. In fact, the Somalia intervention set a precedent in international politics because it was the first time the UN Security Council authorised the use of military force under Chapter VII of the UN Charter, not as a response to an act of aggression, but as a humanitarian intervention intended to lead, eventually to peace-building operations in the collapsed state.[7] However, the intervention was an ominous failure. In assessing the Somalia intervention the then UN Secretary General Boutros Boutros-Ghali stated that:

> The situation in Somalia will continue to deteriorate until the political will exists among the parties to reach a peaceful solution to their dispute, or until the international community gives itself new instruments to address the phenomenon of a failed state.[8]

The current discourse on state collapse also raises questions about the very survival of states deemed collapsed. In that sense, the phenomenon of state collapse also challenges the conceptual underpinnings of the current international system and particularly the idea of universality as the underlying basis of the United Nations. Professor Clapham in addressing the phenomenon of state collapse from an African perspective stated that the main question that state collapse raises is:

> … about the universal applicability of sovereign statehood as a mechanism for combining a measure of local autonomy with the maintenance of global security.[9]

The objective of this chapter is to examine the impact of the phenomenon of state collapse on the post Second World War international architecture and, particularly on the United Nations' aspiration for the formation of a universal international society, with the aim of tracing its potential implications for international security.

THE EVOLUTION OF THE INTERNATIONAL SYSTEM: UNIVERSALITY DEFINED

In abstract, universality stands for the eligibility of all political communities to be members of the international system. In this sense, the concept of universality reflects an ecumenical and egalitarian perception of the world and depicts the international system as a horizontal and non-hierarchical international society. However, like other abstract notions, universality cannot be defined without considering the competing concepts and the contextual circumstances of its evolution.

Contacts and relations among different political communities and civilisations have been common features of human history from ancient times. Historically, these relations have been crucial elements for the self-identification of various political communities. For instance, the very idea of 'Europe' was developed originally through the intellectual construction of a new civilisation emerging across the older parts of the then known world.[10] However, for a long period of time a holistic perception of the world was missing. A holistic perception of humanity was not articulated until the beginning of European expansionism in the fifteenth and sixteenth century. The concept of universality inevitably evolved not through a bottom-up process of putting together the disparate pieces of the world but parallel to the process of European expansionism.[11] Inevitably, structural characteristics of the modern international system, such as the concept of the nation state, largely reflect the values and ideas as well as the social, political and economic conditions that influenced the development of European history. Professor Brownlie in assessing the impact of European colonisation on the international system argues that:

> ... herein lies the paradox, European ideas of nationhood and self-determination were adopted and resulted, eventually, in a programme of statehood, and not a desire for a simple restoration of the traditional *status quo ante.*[12]

A first observation may be that the idea of universality is confined to the imagery of the world as an international society of states. In fact, the modern international system, which originated in Europe at the end of the religious wars and the Peace of Westphalia of 1648, has evolved as an ever-changing framework of relations formed through the process of interaction between its primary components, the states, as well as through the interaction of states with other factors and conditions of the international environment upon which the international system operates. A major factor contributing to the shaping of the international system has been the process of determination of its own members or, in other words, the process of state creation and extinction. The process of determination of the membership to the international system, and particularly the state creation process, has also been the central issue of the idea of universality. Thus, a second observation may be that the concept of universality is closely associated with the debate about the criteria of statehood and the procedures of state creation in international law and politics.

Originally, the idea of universality reflected the predominant conceptions of the Christian world about itself and the intellectual and practical preoccupations of European rulers towards the rest of the world. During the formation period of the modern international system the concept of natural law, the idea that rights and duties of human beings derive from nature, had been elevated to the centre of the political theory of Christendom providing the ideological basis for the perception of the Christian world as a non-hierarchical and horizontal human society.[13] Influential thinkers of the sixteenth and seventeenth century such as Vitoria, Grotius and Pufendorf advocated the idea of universality, at least with respect to Christian Europe, as the necessary corollary of natural law. During the embryonic stages of the international system this profoundly egalitarian imagery of human societies was generally extended, at least in theory, to all of mankind. For instance, the famous medieval jurist Francisco Vitoria defended the rights of the American Indians against the European advance on the basis of natural law.[14]

At that time a significant part of the world remained largely unexplored and unconquered by the European powers and European expansionism had just started gaining momentum. Thus, with respect to the unknown world the concept of universality was as vague and imprecise as the maps of the early explorers. It was based on the assumption that the rest of the world would share, at least eventually, values and conditions of life with Europe. Professor Brownlie states that 'in the period 1648 to 1750 there were no substantial limitations in the world of ideas beyond the view that the entities within the system should be "organised states".'[15] While this criterion for participation in the international system may have been viewed originally as an elementary condition of all human societies, it eventually evolved to be the criterion of effective government. In turn this was perverted to the criterion of 'civilisation', setting an ambiguous threshold for eligibility to sovereign statehood and providing the ideological basis for the gradual disintegration of the horizontal imagery of the international system. In any case, the early perception of a universal international society existing beyond Europe fell short of reality. Professor Bull states that:

> ... in the period of modern European expansion the doctrine of natural law was proclaimed to defend the rights of Amerindians against Spanish conquerors, of Africans forced into trans-Atlantic slavery, and of aboriginal peoples in many

> parts of the world against dispossession and demoralization by European settlers. But the universal international society of mankind contained in the doctrine of natural law was a merely conceptual or theoretical one.[16]

In practice, European expansionism was advancing largely uninterrupted as power relations dictated the attitude of European states towards the rest of the world. With respect to the known world the concept of universality largely reflected the existing balance of power, as some political communities outside Europe were still effectively resisting European expansionism. Professor Abi-Saab states that:

> The universalist view of the international community also reflected the more or less equal and symmetric structure of legal (and power) relations between the European powers and at least the known peoples of the ancient world: relations which implied that they were considered as possible partners in international relations, i.e., as autonomous, and in a way equal, political communities.[17]

This pragmatic interpretation of the concept of universality sheds light on the causes of the eventual transformation of the international system culminating, in the eighteenth and nineteenth century, in the emergence of a highly hierarchical international society. European expansionism, accelerated by the increasing superiority of European powers in military and technological sophistication, altered significantly the international balance of power and gradually led to the establishment of European control over large parts of the world. The well-known euphemism for the British Empire as 'the Empire on which the sun never sets' encapsulates European aspirations for global hegemony.

Inevitably, the concept of universality was replaced by the more palpable 'theory of circles' that divided international society among 'civilised nations' and other layers of humanity that could not claim equal participation in the international club of 'civilised nations'.[18] Several criteria and labels were employed to describe the different categories of humanity. The most frequent distinction was, perhaps, between those people worth of some degree of respect and those dismissed as 'savages'. Professor Hobsbawm describes this categorisation of humanity in reference to the 'Orient' stating that:

> Western observers, and later conquerors, rulers, settlers and entrepreneurs, looked for a common denominator for populations which were plainly unable to stand up to them, but equally plainly belonged to established, ancient cultures and political entities worthy of respect, or at least serious consideration by eighteenth and nineteenth century standards. They were not, in the current terms, 'savages', or 'barbarians' but belonged in a different category, namely that of 'Orientals', whose characteristics as such accounted, among other things, for their inferiority to the West.[19]

The transformation of the legal system in Europe and the advance during the nineteenth century of positive international law – the idea that rights and duties are based on the consent of states – provided further ideological support for the process of rationalisation of European plans for global hegemony. During this period the crystallisation of the meaning of effective government as a standard of 'civilisation' and the emergence of international recognition as the most authoritative method of ascertaining the birth of a new state (constitutive theory of international recognition) reduced, in practice, the process of state creation to a procedure of membership application to the club of the 'civilised nations'. In 1905 Professor Oppenheim stated that:

> A State to be admitted must, first, be a civilised State which is in constant intercourse with members of the Family of Nations: Such a State must expressly or tacitly consent to be bound for its future international conduct by the rules of International law; and those States which have hitherto formed the Family of Nations must expressly or tacitly consent to the reception of the new member.[20]

Therefore, the criterion of effective government as the threshold of eligibility for statehood and admission to the international system was gradually evolved to arbitrary and selective standards of 'organised political communities', 'capacity to govern' and most commonly the standard of 'civilisation'. However, these standards did not refer to an ideal model of governance but to European models of political, social and economic organisation. The self-perceived superiority of these models was behind their elevation into universal standards of government and civilisation. Inevitably, they were perverted to become instruments of foreign policy with the aim of safeguarding existing power relations and legitimising European control over the rest of the world. This situation resulted in denying for a long period self-government to a considerable part of the world. However, the modern international system remained a purely European club only for a short time. Professor Bull states that:

> Later in the nineteenth century, despite the tightening of Europe's grip on the rest of the world and the tendency to define admission into international society in stricter and more exclusive terms, a small number of powers neither Christian in religion nor European in race or culture entered into the originally European circle of states dealing with one another on a reciprocal basis in diplomacy and international law, and represented at multilateral conferences.[21]

While only European states were present at the Congress of Vienna in 1815, by 1899 at the Hague Conference, the United States and Mexico, the Ottoman Empire as well as China, Japan, Persia and Siam had already joined European states in the international system. In many parts of the world, however, statehood and equal participation in the international system were still denied on the basis that the local population was incapable of effective self-government. Even during the inter-war period the international system remained highly hierarchical. This period witnessed the expansion of the British and French Empires through the mandates system, the completion of the partition of Africa through Italy's absorption of Ethiopia and the emergence of racial regimes in South Africa and Rhodesia.

A decisive break with the past was made at the end of the Second World War when the decline of the political, economic and military dominance of Europe reached its peak, leading to a structural transformation of the modern international system. The creation and evolution of the United Nations system provided the forum for the re-introduction of the idea of universality. First, the adoption of the UN Charter and, particularly the procedures for membership of the Organisation, dispensed with the anachronistic divisions between 'civilised nations' and 'non-civilised nations' and reintroduced the idea of universality through the rubric of 'peace-loving states'. While the idea of 'absolute universality' favouring the adoption of a procedure of 'automatic admission' to the United Nations was not originally accepted, as demonstrated by the establishment of conditions for membership (Art. 4.1 of the UN Charter), admission to the United Nations, with the exception of the political complexities of the Cold War, developed was largely a formality[22]. The question concerning the ability of 'micro-states' to fulfil their obligations under the Charter was the only case in which the criteria for admission were discussed. Despite original disagreement over the issue, the supporters of universality finally prevailed and the question was abandoned resulting in the progressive admission of a number of 'micro-states' into the United Nations.[23]

Second, the incorporation of the principle of self-determination of peoples in the normative structure of the international system that started with the adoption of the UN Charter and was consolidated particularly through the practice of the organs of the UN, provided a new ideological basis for the idea of universality. The massive state creation process that was initiated by decolonisation was based on the principle of self-determination of peoples and, where necessary, even dispensed with considerations of effective government. A prominent example arose out of the Congo crisis in which the ex-Belgian colony was granted independence and membership in the United Nations despite the lack of an effective central government in the country. While authors such as Judge Higgins argued that the Congo's admission to the United Nations was a derogation from 'the fairly distinct pattern of consistent adherence to the requirement of a stable and effective government' others, such as Professor Crawford, argued that the Congo case proved that 'the requirement of "government" is less stringent than has been thought, at least in particular contexts'.[24] The profound impact of the principle of self-determination of peoples on the transformation of the modern international system is encapsulated in the following statement by Professor Lachs:

> Thus statehood and sovereignty constitute today an inseparable link with self-determination and rely upon it as the rock and basic principle from which they derive their real force.[25]

The elevation of the principle of self-determination of peoples into a central idea of international law and politics and the re-introduction of the idea of universality to the aspirations of international society reflect a significant transformation of the conceptual foundations of the international system. In practice, the application of the principle of self-determination in the decolonisation process resulted in a considerable expansion of the membership of the international system. The ideological origin of self-determination of peoples as a political principle expressing the aspirations of ethnic groups for statehood and its eventual legal crystallisation as a principle promoting self-government of non-self-governing territories and opposing foreign occupation of established states has not altered at all the ideological basis of the idea of universality as a concept confined to the image of the international system as an international society of states. Given that today the whole world is apportioned among self-governing states and that the process of state creation is discouraged by the international system mainly through the applications of the principle of territorial integrity of states, the idea of universality would seem to have reached its geographical and historical limits.

The gradual reconsideration, however, of the nature and scope of the principle of self-determination of peoples as a notion applicable also within established states – particularly with respect to racial discrimination but also more recently with regard to the idea of popular sovereignty and democratic governance – poses a new challenge to the idea of universality. These developments point to the limitation of the imagery of the international system as simply a universal international society of states and introduces, instead, the idea of a universal society of peoples. This trend is reinforced by the realisation, on the one hand, that the idea of the existence of an international system composed of ethnically homogenous states has been a historical contradiction, and on the other hand, that states alone cannot describe the complexity and diversity of the ever-changing ethnic configurations of human societies. In particular, the emerging principle of democratic governance poses new challenges to the idea of universality.[26] These developments constitute an attempt to construct a more sophisticated international system bringing the idea of universality closer to the original idea of an international society of peoples. Alternative challenges to the idea of universality as it stands today are also provided by the phenomenon of the decline of the state as the result of the dynamic advance of global capitalism.[27] However, the advent of rampant global capitalism at the moment promises only new hierarchies and divisions between the 'haves' and the 'have-nots', rather than a new model of a universal society of peoples.

From a historical perspective the first two observations indicate that the concept of universality is confined to the image of the international system as an international society of states, whose legitimacy is currently based upon the principle of self-determination of peoples. Universality here has a horizontal character. However, there is also a vertical aspect to the idea of universality. A third and final observation distinguishes the idea of universality from other principles of international society such as notions of unilateralism or other forms of multilateralism that do not amount to universality. In that sense, universality refers to the idea of an inclusive and democratic process of community-building within the international system comprising all modern states; it can be understood as the aspiration of the member states of the international system to develop and establish representative institutions and procedures that can authoritatively articulate and protect the common values and interests of international society. In this sense too, the development of the normative content of international law and the establishment of effective mechanisms for the interpretation, application and enforcement of international law then become central issues in defining the idea of universality. Thus, the third characteristic of the concept of universality is that it represents the aspirations of the international society to develop an international system, which is based upon the principle of the rule of law. Such a conception of a universal international society opposes other models of organisation of the international system and particularly the doctrine of unilateralism that is predicated upon power relations and the 'law of the jungle'.

In sum, universality can be defined by the perception of the international system as a horizontal society of states whose legitimacy is based upon the principle of self-determination of peoples and whose aspiration is the creation of an international community based on the rule of law. Today, the spirit, values and objectives of the idea of universality are personified by the establishment and consolidation of the United Nations. In order to determine the implications of the phenomenon of state collapse for the idea of universality we will first examine the contemporary discourse on state collapse and then the post-Cold War state practice in response to state collapse.

THE CONTEMPORARY DISCOURSE ON STATE COLLAPSE: UNIVERSALITY RECONSIDERED

The contemporary discourse on the phenomenon of state collapse can be summarised in the following three approaches: the realist, the radical and the international society approach.

The Realist Approach

The realist approach perceives state collapse as a manifestation of the failure of certain societies to meet the requirements for responsible self-government. Failure is the result of inherent feebleness and the inability to govern. This is attributed to a combination of cultural and historical factors in conjunction with socio-economic and political conditions. According to the realist approach, state collapse is a phenomenon associated almost exclusively with former colonised states in Africa and Asia. In an article that introduced the debate about the phenomenon of state collapse in the post-Cold War period, Gerald Helman and Steven Ratner argued that:

> The current collapse has its roots in the vast proliferation of nation-states, especially in Africa and Asia, since the end of World War II. When the United Nations Charter was signed in 1945, it had 50 signatories. Since that time, membership has more than tripled, reflecting the momentous transformation of the pre-war colonial world to a globe composed of independent states…The idea, then, that states could fail – that they could be simply unable to function as independent entities – was anathema to the *raison d'être* of decolonisation and offensive to the notion of self-determination.[28]

According to this approach, the phenomenon of state collapse is a continuation of the debate about the viability of the new independent states that emerged during the post Second World War decolonisation process. In fact, in 1964 Professor Freeman argued that:

> … a complete evaluation must impeach the practice of admitting into the Society of Nations primeval entities which have no real claim to international status or the capacity to meet international obligations, and whose primary congeries of contributions consist in replacing norms serving the common interest of mankind by others releasing them from inhibitions upon irresponsible conduct.[29]

More recently Professor Jackson, in assessing the post-independence experience of former colonies, stated that:

> It is clearer today than it was in 1960 that numerous emergent states did not and many still do not, disclose substantial and credible statehood by the empirical criteria of classical positive international law… In the past, however, small and weak states had to survive as best they could by their own efforts and those of whatever allies they were able to enlist in their support. Some survived, some succumbed. International history is in large measure the story of this struggle. This is the traditional reality of the states-system as a power or balance of power system which continues to define the dominant theory of international relations: 'realism'… what has changed is not the empirical conditions of states but the international rules and institutions concerning those conditions.[30]

According to the realist approach, the post Second World War changes in the normative structure of the international system, particularly the emergence of the legal principle of self-determination of peoples, have distorted the well-established natural process of state creation and have resulted in the establishment of states that did not possess a basic criterion of statehood, namely, the capacity to govern. Furthermore, states have been protected from extinction irrespective of their ability to govern and survive on their own. In other words, the phenomenon of state collapse is the result of the post Second World War advent of the 'myth of universality' and the corollary descent of the 'Darwinistic' process of state creation and extinction in the value structure of the international system.

The realist approach argues that state collapse signifies the lack of internal sovereignty, which is, at its lowest common denominator, the capacity of a state to maintain minimum law and order within its territory. Since the phenomenon of state collapse signifies the inability of a state to fulfil the most basic criterion of governance, their very existence is questioned. The realist approach rivals assumptions about the universal character of the international system and the dominant role of the principles of sovereign equality and self-determination of peoples in international relations. Instead, it emphasises the hierarchical nature of the international system and the dominant role of state interests and power relations. Therefore, sovereignty and statehood cannot be the right of all political communities by the mere virtue of the application of the principle of self-determination, but only of those that can also demonstrate their capacity to govern.

The realist approach views the international system as a hierarchical structure composed of successful-responsible states and failed-irresponsible states. In fact, there can be several variations of hierarchical perceptions of the international system that include the phenomenon of state collapse. Some argue that the phenomenon of state collapse is the pre-modern component of an international structure that is also made up of modern (parts of Latin America and Asia) and post-modern (the developed world and particularly Europe) components.[31] Other views hold that the world is divided among wealthy and democratic 'open' societies, a group of 'closed' societies and a collection of failed or enfeebled states that may need to be taken over by the others and turned into trusteeships to mitigate the surging violence they contain.[32] Specific proposals on how to deal with collapsed states vary from re-colonisation, the resurrection of the UN Trusteeship system, placing collapsed state under international administration and other forms of international intervention.[33]

The Radical Approach

The radical approach perceives the phenomenon of state collapse as a manifestation of historical injustices and the prevailing social and economic disparities and inequalities in the world that originate from the objectives and ethics of colonisation as well as from other forms of western domination. They are perpetuated by the modern polices of dependency and exploitation by the rich western states of the poor developing world. Not surprisingly, the radical approach, like the realist approach, associates the phenomenon of state collapse almost exclusively with the former colonised states in Africa and Asia. Professor Grovogui states that:

> The related authoritative discourse considers postcolonial institutional deficiencies to be intrinsic to the constitution of the new states. This means that the organic shortcomings of the former colonies are independent of deliberate preindependence strategies and tactics adopted by the protagonists of decolonisation. This discourse also rejects the contention that the structures of the present international system limit the capacity of African nations to achieve self-determination and full sovereignty. It effectively minimizes the

> stifling effects of the subjection of Third World entities to a global political, cultural, scientific, and technological apparatus that guarantees Western hegemony within a hierarchical international order.[34]

Another aspect of this approach focuses on the disruptive impact of the decolonisation process on the nation-building process and particularly the negative ramifications of the creation of artificial states and borders without regard to the configurations of the indigenous populations. Professor Gordon states that:

> … Africa was decolonised by the colonial powers rather than by Africans. Thus, decolonisation and the creation of post-colonial states were as imposed by the West as colonial domination had been. Newly independent states were not connected to the indigenous communities that were in place before the advent of colonialism, and therefore, the contours of the resulting political entities were based on arbitrarily drawn colonial constructs.[35]

The radical approach views the international system as a western dominated structure based on inequality that needs radical change before the aspirations for universality can come closer to reality. The major value of the international system is justice, which can be upheld through the reaffirmation of the principles of development, as the principle for redistribution of power and wealth, and self-determination and sovereign equality, as defensive principles against foreign domination and exploitation particularly by the major powers. Once a state is created and it is recognised as a member of the international system, the principle of self-determination functions as a shield opposing any outside re-evaluation of the normative criteria of statehood and protecting the state from extinction. Thus, implosion of the political order of a state does not have an impact on statehood.

Since the phenomenon of state collapse is often associated with neo-colonialist policies any form of outside military intervention is viewed with suspicion and is opposed categorically. As Professor Richardson states '… a major question in formulating remedies for a state deemed "failed" is the continuing authority of the sovereign state consent requirement, as compared with the feasibility of the UN or other universal or regional organisation, doing anything at all'.[36] Instead of interventionist policies, the radical approach favours long-term strategies to address the root causes of state collapse.

Proposals vary from radical structural reforms of the present international system, including redistribution of political and economic power, changing colonial borders and moving beyond the model of nation-state and towards indigenous patterns of government, to more traditional policies such as strengthening nation-building schemes and developing international and local mechanisms for conflict prevention.[37]

The International Society Approach

The international society approach perceives the phenomenon of state collapse as the manifestation of the erosion of the domestic political order and the social fabric of states. State collapse is viewed neither as the result of an incapacity for self-government and irresponsible behaviour nor as the direct corollary of the abusive colonial rule and prevailing inequalities in the world. Thus, it is not linked directly with the phenomenon of decolonisation. It is rather associated with the inability of states to cope with the destabilising impact of the imperceptible process of change in the power structure. This includes values as well as functions and conditions of the domestic and international political order that have been exacerbated by post-Cold War geopolitical changes. Factors of change in the domestic and international political order include the declining authority of the state, the dynamic emergence of other sources of domestic and international power, and the increasing political, economic and social interdependence of states and peoples. Other factors of change include the declining influence of universal values and aspirations such as life, freedom, equality, solidarity and tolerance that have dominated the politics of twentieth century societies and which are currently often being sacrificed in front of the altars of neo-liberal principles and cultural relativism that promote respectively egotistic and particularistic values. Professor Hobsbawm encapsulates this *inter-regnum* in the following passage:

> The current turmoil of nationalist conflicts and civil wars is … the response to a double collapse: the collapse of political order as represented by functioning states – any effective state which stands watch against the descent into Hobbesian anarchy – and the crumbling of the old frameworks of social relations over large parts of the world – any framework which stands guard against Durkheimian anomie.[38]

The international society approach views the international system as a non-hierarchical society of interdependent states representing peoples who share basic common values and interests such as human dignity and security as well as social and economic development. Since the state is the primary model of domestic and international order that enables international society to pursue the universal goals of peace, development and happiness, the disintegration of the domestic political order of states challenges the integrity and stability of the international system.

According to this approach, state disintegration results from conflicts generated by the inability of states to absorb the destabilising effects of change. The phenomenon of state collapse signifies an extreme disruption of the political order of the state manifested by the incapacity of the state to govern. However, it is viewed as an intrinsically temporary phenomenon. It is expected that political order will be restored when the conflict is over. The state is sick but not dead. Therefore, respect for the sovereignty of an ailing state should be a fundamental principle guiding international responses to state collapse. However, intrusive international responses are deemed necessary and legitimate due to considerations related both to the interests and values of international society. This approach attempts to reconcile what makes international society feel secure, with what it considers just. Professor Schachter stated that international assistance to collapsed states '... would strengthen mutual respect for each other's sovereignty and thus restrain the excesses so often associated with claims of sovereignty'.[39]

The international society approach encourages both short-term and long-term responses to the phenomenon of state collapse aiming at tackling both the symptoms and the structural elements of collapse. Short-term responses may include assertive action to mitigate the effects of humanitarian disasters and protect peoples trapped in collapsed states. Long-term responses focus on efforts to reinvent a functioning political order. In both cases the consent and involvement of local leaderships and populations as well as the development of normative criteria of international conduct are considered essential. As far as long-term action is concerned, a common theme asserts the need to improve the legitimacy and effectiveness of the state. Abdulkwai Yusuf states that:

> To restore confidence in the state, its institutional framework must be radically reformed so as to enable people to identify themselves with their institutions. The creation of structures at the sub-state level and the establishment of a formal system of distributing power through grass-roots empowerment are clearly necessary. This may require the establishment of state institutions based on a social compact which involves recognition of popular sovereignty and sovereign rights at different tiers of political interaction, be they at the village, community, regional or state levels. Alternative models for promoting popular participation, accountability and a redistribution of political and economic power need to be explored.[40]

According to the international society approach popular sovereignty and good governance, which are structural features of the domestic political order of states, are viewed as major pillars of domestic and international stability. In this sense, the phenomenon of state collapse raises questions that go beyond the traditional perceptions of the international system. It touches upon the neuralgic point of the relations between peoples, states and the international system. The phenomenon of state collapse illustrates the need for the international community to develop answers to address this historically turbulent equation.

These three different approaches can be epitomised by the views they have about the impact of state collapse on statehood and the idea of universality. The realist approach argues that the very existence of the state is at stake. The state is virtually dead and the idea of universality is a dangerous myth. The radical approach does not recognise any impact on statehood. The state is alive but the idea of universality is far from a reality. The international society approach does not recognise a direct impact on statehood, but rather it is concerned with the significant domestic and international implications of state collapse. The state is sick and in need of assistance. The idea of universality is at risk and its meaning is in need of re-appraisal. While the realist approach dismisses the idea of universality as a myth, both the radical and the international society approaches include universality to mean the aspirations of international society. However, while the radical approach perceives universality largely as a characteristic of an international society of states, the international society approach views universality as a wider notion also embracing the idea of 'peoples', albeit mainly through the intermediate role of states. Theory is thus divided over the impact of state collapse on the idea of universality. What do contemporary international politics indicate with regard to the impact of state collapse on the idea of universality?

STATE COLLAPSE AND THE UNITED NATIONS: UNIVERSALITY AT RISK?

State practice, particularly through the actions of various UN organs, demonstrates that the presumption of the continuity of states without an effective government is a well-established principle. Despite the fact that neither the UN Security Council nor the UN General Assembly has addressed these questions openly, state practice, particularly with respect to the example of state collapse in Somalia, is conclusive that collapsed states retain their statehood and membership in the international system.[41] Somalia's membership in the UN and other international or regional organisations whose membership is restricted to states alone has not been challenged after eight years of a clear absence of central government – a prominent indication of the position adopted by the international community that the lack of effective central government does not affect statehood.[42]

Furthermore, the UN Security Council, which repeatedly described the absence of government in Somalia as occurring under 'exceptional circumstances', has clearly assumed through its many resolutions the continuity of the Somali state. The Somalia intervention was based on the powers of the UN Security Council to authorise action for the maintenance of international peace and security and, did not thereby challenge the presumption of the continuity of the Somali state.[43] UNOSOM II's extensive state-building mandate, which included highly intrusive operations such as the reconstruction of the police and judiciary and the establishment of district and regional authorities, was also conceived as a separate peace-building component of the humanitarian intervention, and was never articulated as having any impact on Somalia's statehood.[44] The same can be said about the other classic post-Cold War cases of state collapse in Liberia and Afghanistan.[45]

Therefore, practice indicates that, once established, a state is presumed to continue in existence, and it is assumed that with peace, effective governmental authority will be restored. Professor Crawford states that:

> the presumption – in practice a strong one – is in favour of the continuance, and against extinction, of an established state. Extinction is, thus, within broad limits, not affected by more or less prolonged anarchy within the State.[46]

The well-established presumption of continuity of collapsed states can be attributed to the profound influence of the principle of self-determination of peoples in contemporary international law and politics. The protection of established states through the presumption of continuity of statehood – even in cases of extreme disruption of their political order – reveals the defensive aspect of the principle of self-determination. In this case, the application of self-determination prevents states and peoples from being reduced to *'terra nullius'* and *'territoires sans maîtres'*, which would allow their territory to become eligible for outside occupation. Moreover, it protects the stability of the international system by preventing states from re-opening a Pandora's box of power struggle for the acquisition of new territories. In a world entirely apportioned among states, the extinction of statehood could only have destabilising impact on the international system.[47] An argument in favour of 'decertifying' states ravaged from within by protracted conflicts and humanitarian disasters appears to be self-defeating since such action cannot on its own address the challenges of state collapse or serve any other general interest.

While state practice indicates that the phenomenon of state collapse, in principle, does not affect the continuing aspiration of the United Nations to represent a universal international system of states, can we safely assume that the idea of universality is not threatened by the phenomenon of state collapse? International political developments indicate that an affirmative answer to this question would fail to take note of some imperceptible changes occurring in the international system. These have been shifting the centre of international decision making from the universalist forum of the UN General Assembly to the *sui generis* multilateral forum of the UN Security Council, and more recently, even further away from the United Nations to regional or other multilateral fora and, often to unilateral action. Unilateral action aiming to 'restore law and order and put an end to surging anarchy' appears to be emerging as a legitimate underpinning for international intervention. As a result, the phenomenon of state collapse and the plausible image of anarchy that is associated with it appears to enhance these tendencies for dispensing with the universalist basis of the current architecture of the international system.

Practice indicates a discouraging trend to dispense with the United Nations in developing a consensus about the requirements for collective and legitimate responses to post-Cold War challenges, even with respect to the authorisation of military action.[48] The following list, by no means exhaustive, sends alarming signals about the trend towards a gradual disintegration of the current international political and legal order: the military intervention of member states of ECOWAS in Liberia without prior authorisation by the United Nations; the subsequent military intervention of Nigeria in Sierra Leone; Senegal's military intervention in Guinea-Bissau; the successive military operations of Ethiopia inside Somalia; the constant military actions of Turkey inside the Kurdish areas of Iraq; the recent decision of NATO member states to undertake military action in Kosovo without prior approval by the UN Security Council; Iran's unilateral deliberations to intervene militarily in the conflict in Afghanistan; the recent US attacks against 'stateless terrorism' in Afghanistan and Sudan; and South Africa's intervention in Lesotho under the pretext of 'restoring law and order and putting an end to anarchy'. All these appear to reflect a growing feeling of reluctance among members of the international system with respect, in general, to the necessity of involving the United Nations in international policy and decision making and, more specifically, with regard to the necessity of involving the United Nations in the development of an international consensus on how to respond to post-Cold War challenges.[49]

Collapsed states, because of the humanitarian and security challenges they present to the international community, appear to provide the most fertile ground for morally legitimising unilateral action. It is not a mere coincidence, as the above mentioned cases illustrate, that the word 'anarchy' often precedes deliberations about intrusive military action. Self-interpreted threats to international security and humanitarian values by individual or groups of states threaten to re-emerge as the basis for legitimising international intervention. This situation risks leading to the erosion of the conceptual foundations of the modern international system, including the hard core of the principles of sovereign equality and self-determination of peoples. Inevitably, the idea of universality is also at risk.

These trends are exacerbated by the incapacity of the United Nations to develop and implement comprehensive responses to the phenomenon of state collapse. This can be attributed partly to the lack of political commitment on the part of its member states to devise international regimes in response to state collapse, partly because of their reluctance to develop normative criteria and procedures to guide international action, and partly because of the absence of adequate institutions and resources to lead and sustain international involvement in collapsed states. Improvisation, *ad hoc* solutions, spasmodic reactions and humanitarian assistance tend to be the substitutes for political activity and political commitment. In consequence, unilateral action appears to be the preferred choice when perceived state interests are at stake.

However, the frequent re-occurrence and persistence of state collapse, the endemic fragility of state institutions in some parts of the world, and the persistant destabilisation of the world's domestic political systems in the aftermath of the Cold War suggest that the phenomenon of state collapse is likely to continue to pose a major challenge to the requirements for global governance in the twenty-first century. Developing concepts and instruments to respond to the phenomenon of state collapse may facilitate the international community's endeavours to tackle the implications of state collapse and to safeguard the integrity of the international system. However, it is worth underlining here that the recent upsurge of unilateral responses to the phenomenon of state collapse is simply another manifestation of a deeper trend that favours the dismantlement of the universalist basis of the post Second World War order. Instead, these trends are promoting the introduction of new hierarchies. The following comment made by Professor Abi-Saab in the mid- 1980s not only proves to be diachronic, but it appears to have gained additional momentum from the most recent international developments:

> At this juncture, it is difficult to predict the outcome of this latest phase of struggle between universalism and unilateralism. But, it all goes to show that in the dialectical relation between law and power, the civilizing role of law cannot make too much headway over the extent of community feeling obtaining in society.[50]

Notes

[1] This chapter is based on research conducted whilst the author was Visiting Scholar at the School of International and Public Affairs of Columbia University as the 1997-98 Albert Gallatin Fellow in International Affairs. He would like to thank Professor Oscar Schachter for his valuable and inspiring guidance.

[2] The post-Cold War terms 'failed states' and 'state collapse' are used interchangeably in the vocabulary of international relations. The term 'failed states' has been repeatedly endorsed by authoritative figures of international politics such as the previous UN Secretary General, Boutros Boutros-Ghali and the present US Secretary of State, Madeleine Albright. However, the term 'failed states' appears to imply a value judgement suggesting that there are specific standards of success to which all states should aspire rather than minimum standards of effective government. In fact, the term 'failed states', is the offspring of a specific international climate – the euphoria of the post-Cold War assertive multilateralism – and reflects specific perceptions of the international system – a hierarchical structure sustained by an authoritative collective security system. Thus, the more descriptive and dispassionate term 'state collapse' should be preferred. See also von Hippel, Karin, 'The Proliferation of Collapsed States in the Post-Cold War World', *Brassey's Defence Yearbook*, p.194 (1997).

[3] Zartman, William, 'Introduction: Posing the Problem of State Collapse', *Collapsed States: The Disintegration and Restoration of Legitimate Authority*, I.W. Zartman (ed.), Lynne Rienner Publishers, p.5 (1995), and Mazrui, Ali, 'African State as a Political Refugee: Institutional Collapse and Human Displacement', *International Journal of Refugee Law* 21, p.23 (1995).

[4] Richardson, Henry, 'Failed States, Self-Determination, and Preventive Diplomacy: Colonialist Nostalgia and Democratic Expectations', *Temple International and Comparative Law Journal* 10, p.2 (1996).

[5] Professor S. Lyons and Samatar state that 'political disintegration generates instability and threatens neighbouring states through refugee flows, the stimulation of illegal trade in weapons and other contraband, and because the communities imperilled by state collapse often cross borders and can appeal to neighbouring groups for involvement. Because the international system of order is based on states, forces inimical to order move into the empty spaces where states no longer exist. Drug traffickers, money launderers, extremist political movements and terrorist groups move into the vacuum ...', Lyons, Terence and Samatar, Ahmed, *Somalia: State Collapse, Multilateral Intervention and Strategies for Political Reconstruction*, p.3, The Brookings Institution, Washington DC, (1995).

[6] Clarke, Walter and Herbst, Jeffrey, 'Somalia: Lessons from a Humanitarian Intervention', *Current* (382), 1996, pp.10-11. See also the *Note of the President of*

the UN Security Council on a meeting held for the first time in the history of the UN at the level of Heads of State and Government in New York on 31 January 1992 to discuss 'the responsibility of the Security Council in the Maintenance of International Peace and Security' in the post-Cold War era, S/23500.

[7] von Hippel, Karin and Yannis, Alexandros 'The European Response to State Collapse in Somalia', *European Approaches to Crisis Management*, K. E. Joergensen (ed.) Kluwer International Press, p.65 (1997).

[8] *The United Nations and Somalia (1992-1996)*, p.89, The United Nations Blue Books Series, Volume VIII, Department of Public Information of the United Nations, New York (1996).

[9] Clapham, Christopher, *Africa and the International System: The Politics of State Survival*, p.267, Cambridge University Press (1997).

[10] Professor Davies states that 'indeed, one of several possible etymologies [of the word 'Europa' in the ancient Greek mythology] contrasts Asia, 'the land of the Sunrise', with Europa, 'the land of the Sunset'. The Hellenes came to use 'Europa' as a name for their territory to the west of the Aegean as distinct from the older lands in Asia Minor. At the dawn of European history, the known world lay to the east. The unknown waited in the west, in destinations still to be discovered', Davies, Norman, *Europe: A History*, p.xvii, Oxford University Press, New York (1996).

[11] Abi-Saab, Georges, 'Cours Général de Droit International Public, *Collected Courses of the Hague Academy of International Law* 207(VII), pp.49-58 (1987).

[12] Brownlie, Ian, 'The Expansion of International Society: The Consequences for the Law of Nations', *The Expansion of International Society,* H. Bull and A. Watson (eds.), Clarendon Press, Oxford, p.364 (1988).

[13] Bull, Hedley, 'The Emergence of a Universal International Society', *The Expansion of International Society*, H. Bull and A. Watson (eds.), Clarendon Press, Oxford, pp.119-120 (1988).

[14] Vitoria, Francisco, *On the Indians*, (first published in 1557), J.P. Bare (Trs.), Carnegie Institute, Washington DC (1917).

[15] Brownlie, I. 'The Expansion of International Society: The Consequences for the Law of Nations', pp.358-359.

[16] Bull, H. 'The Emergence of Universal International Society', p.120.

[17] Abi-Saab, G. 'International Law and the International Community: The Long Road to Universality', *Essays in Honour of Wang Tieya*, R. Macdonald (ed.), Martinus Nijhoff Publishers, pp.34-35 (1993).

[18] Abi-Saab, 'Cours Général de Droit International Public', pp.55-56.

[19] Hobsbawm, Eric, *On History*, pp.217-218, New Press, New York (1997).

[20] Oppenheim, Lawrence, *International Law*, p.32, Longman's Green, London (1905).

[21] Bull, H. 'The Emergence of Universal International Society', pp.122-123.

[22] Cot, Jean Pierre and Pellet, Alain (eds.), *La Charte des Nations Unies: Commentaire*

article par article, pp.167-172, Economica, Paris (1991).

[23] *ibid,* p.172.

[24] Crawford, James, 'The Criteria of Statehood in International Law', *British Yearbook of International Law* 48, p.117 (1976-77).

[25] Lachs, Manfred, 'The development and general trends of international law in our time', *Collected Courses of the Hague Academy of International Law* 169, p.54 (1979).

[26] See T. Frank, 'The Emerging Right to Democratic Governance', *American Journal of International Law* 86, pp.46-91 (1992), and W.M. Reisman, 'Sovereignty and Human Rights in Contemporary International Law', (editorial comment), *American Journal of International Law* 84, pp.867-877 (1990).

[27] See Schachter, Oscar, 'The Decline of the Nation-State and its Implications for International Law', *Columbia Journal of Transnational Law* 36 (7), pp.7-23 (1997).

[28] Helman, Gerald and Ratner, Steven, 'Saving Failed States', *Foreign Policy* 89, p.3 (Winter 1992-93).

[29] A. Freeman, 'Professor McDougal's Law and Minimum World Public Order', *American Journal of International Law* 58, p.712 (1964).

[30] R. Jackson, *Quasi-States: Sovereignty, International Relations and the Third World*, Cambridge, Cambridge University Press, pp.22-23 (1990).

[31] R. Cooper 'The Post-Modern State and the World Order', *Demos* (1997).

[32] See B. Buzan and G. Segal, *Anticipating the Future: Twenty Millennia of Human Progress*, London, Simon & Schuster, p.384 (1998).

[33] See Helman, Gerald and Ratner, Steven, 'Saving Failed States', pp.12-20, Mazrui Ali, 'The Bondage of Boundaries: Why Africa's Maps Will Be Redrawn', *The Economist*, 11 September 1993, Pfaff, William, 'A New Colonialism? Europe Must Go Back into Africa', *Foreign Affairs* 74 (1), pp.2-6 (1995), Krauthammer, Ch., 'Trusteeship for Somalia; An Old-Colonial-Idea Whose Time Has Come Again', *Washington Post*, 9 October 1992, p.A27, Johnson, Paul, 'Colonialism's Back – And not a Moment too Soon', *New York Times*, 8 April 1993, p.F22.

[34] Grovogui S. N., *Sovereign, Quasi Sovereign and Africans: Peace and Self-Determination in International Law*, pp.179-180, Minneapolis, London, University of Minnesota Press, (1996).

[35] Gordon, Ruth, 'Saving Failed States: Sometimes a Neo-colonialist Notion', *American University Journal of International Law and Policy* 12(6), pp.920-921 (1997).

[36] Richardson, Henry, 'Failed States, Self-Determination, and Preventive Diplomacy: Colonialist Nostalgia and Democratic Expectations', p.9.

[37] See Gordon, Ruth, 'Saving Failed States: Sometimes a Neo-colonialist Notion' pp.971-974, and Herbst Jeffrey, 'Responding to State Failure in Africa', *International*

Security 21(3), p.120 (Winter 1996-1997).

[38] Hobsbawm, Eric, *On History*, p.264, New York, The New Press, (1997).

[39] Schachter, Oscar, 'Sovereignty – Then and Now', *Essays in Honour of Wang Tieya*, R. St. J. Macdonald (ed.), Martinus Nijhoff Publishers, p.688 (1993).

[40] Yusuf, Abdulqawi, 'Reflections on the Fragility of State Institutions in Africa', *African Yearbook of International Law* 2, p.8 (1994). See also Zartman, William, 'Putting things back together', *Collapsed States: The Disintegration and Restoration of Legitimate Authority*, Zartman I.W. (ed.), Boulder, Lynne Rienner Publishers, pp.267-271 (1995).

[41] See *The United Nations and Somalia: 1992-1996*, The United Nations Blue Books Series, Vol. VIII, Department of Public Information of the United Nations, New York, 1996, p.516.

[42] Yannis, Alexandros, 'State Collapse and Prospects for Political Reconstruction and Democratic Governance in Somalia,' *African Yearbook of International Law* (5), p.28-30, (1997).

[43] See the *UN Security Council Resolution 794* of 3 December 1992.

[44] See the *UN Security Council Resolution 814* of 26 March 1993 and the *UN Secretary General Report on the situation in Somalia* of 3 March 1993.

[45] The response of the international community to the Liberian crisis, which was originally devised and implemented under the auspices of the Economic Community of West African States (ECOWAS), eventually endorsed by the United Nations, was based on the assumption that there was not only no functioning government, but also on the presumption of continuity of Liberia's statehood, see *Regional Peace-Keeping and International Enforcement: The Liberia Crisis*, Cambridge International Documents Series, Vol.6, Cambridge, Grotius, 1994. On Afghanistan see the UN Secretary Report of 14 November 1997 on the *Situation in Afghanistan and Its Implications for International Peace and Security*, S/1997/894.

[46] J. Crawford, James, *The Creation of States in International Law*, p.417, Clarendon Press, Oxford (1979), see also Marek, K., *Identity and Continuity of States in Public International Law*, p.548, Librairie Droz, Geneva (1968).

[47] Ruiz Fabri, Hélène, 'Genèse et Disparition de l'Etat à l'Époque Contemporaine', *Annuaire Francais de Droit International* 38, p.154 (1992).

[48] The December 1998 air attacks on Iraq by US-UK forces illustrates the discussion over this.

[49] Righter, Rosemary, *Utopia Lost: The United Nations and World Order*, p.6, The Twentieth Century Fund Press, New York, (1995).

[50] Abi Saab, Geoges, 'The Role of International Law in the Peace Strategy of the Charter', *Universality in Jeopardy?*, United Nations Department of Public Information, New York, p.49 (1987).

11
Corporations and Conflict
Firing in the Line, in the Firing Line or Lining in the Fire ?[1]

NICK HARVEY

Independent consultant specialising in conflict analysis and strategic planning for corporations, government and non-governmental organisations in high-risk environments

INTRODUCTION

The following quotes might help to set the scene:

> Executives working abroad are increasingly being targeted by kidnappers.[2]

> Shadow of slave labour: western oil companies are laying a pipeline through Burma – with the help of slave labour, say critics of the ruling military regime.[3]

> Terrorism against oil companies in the country (Colombia) can increase their operating costs by between 2% and 10% … Oil industry analysts estimate that oil companies lost revenue of more than $50 million in 1997 alone in Colombia as a result of terrorism.[4]

> Nigerian warriors seek spiritual aid as oil discovery provokes land disputes … Increasingly, villagers commanded by chiefs keen to reap compensation from oil companies for environmental degradation of the region's mangrove creeks are vandalising installations.[5]

In recent years, a number of corporations have expanded their core activities away from the relatively stable market environments of Europe and the US to the more complex and risk-prone emerging markets. This is particularly true for extractive activities, oil exploration and production and the utility sector, which are increasingly exploring opportunities in Latin America, Africa, the Balkans, the Caucasus and Central Asia. Although a number of corporations have gained experience of working in these volatile markets over time, as in the oil sector in Nigeria, for example, for many these are new territories. This expansion has been spurred on by deregulation and privatisation programmes that have been at the core of multilateral and bilateral aid programmes of the post-Cold War era.

These are potentially lucrative new markets and, despite recent downswings in confidence for investment in new emerging markets due to Asian, Russian and Latin American financial crises, there has been a steady growth of interest and investment. Naturally there is a flip side. Although deregulation has been rapid, the transitional process has frequently been problematic in many countries where interest groups have competed for political and economic authority. Based on patronage systems and underpinned by links to the informal economy, these interests, or forces, present considerable risks for foreign investments. Weak legal protection and enforcement, fragile finance systems and a history of economic 'command' models add further uncertainties to investments and growth.

Many corporations have found themselves entwined in an environment of conflict. Examples include:

- the mining sector in Sierra Leone, Angola, the Democratic Republic of Congo and Liberia;
- the oil exploration and production sector in Nigeria, Colombia, Myanmar, Angola, the Republic of Congo, the Caucasus, Afghanistan, Algeria, Sudan and Albania;
- utilities in Chechnya and Indonesia.

Within these environments, corporations find themselves under increasing scrutiny regarding how they secure and protect their interests. Pressure groups have largely succeeded in bringing environmental concerns within the standard operating practices of business. They are now focusing their attention on the human rights records of corporations. The expansion and development of international communications means that corporations can no longer act with impunity or behind fully closed doors. In other words, nowadays there is 'no hiding place'.[6] The damage to corporate images ensuing from their exposure to being linked with human rights violations is beginning to have its impact on corporate culture and strategy. It is also coming at a time when there is a wider questioning of the role that business plays in society. As one leading management analyst has commented:

> Organisations have a responsibility to try to find an approach to basic social problems which fits their competence and which, indeed, makes the social problem into an opportunity for the organisation.[7]

Many social problems are highly acute in volatile emerging markets, and they also tend to be politically loaded even to the point of being explosive. In many marginal areas, where public services or international assistance is lacking, corporations are in danger of becoming a target of competing leaderships, who see them as a source of ready finance or as a tool for political manipulation or gain. Mitigating these new risks is a key challenge facing the global business community.

This is an area, which although of high concern to the business community, has received limited attention in terms of research. This is beginning to change, though slowly. On the one hand, much of the work on corporate citizenship has focused on non-volatile environments. On the other, research work on conflicts has tended to focus on peacekeeping, humanitarian responses, conflict resolution and post-war reconstruction efforts. There is a need to explore further the lessons and experiences that can be exchanged between those in pinstripes, blue helmets and the moral fibre which has inspired non-governmental organisations.[8] They are all facing common sets of problems in similar or the same environments.

An area related to this, which is also receiving increased attention, is the opportunity (and indeed risks) that such environments present to other private sector operators. Of particular interest are the growing market opportunities generated for military and security companies who can offer military, logistical and security services for governments, peacekeeping operations and humanitarian responses. These will be referred to where necessary, but do not form the primary focus here.[9]

This chapter will explore the new challenges being faced by the corporate sector in volatile environments. Key questions to be addressed are:

- what are the risks faced by corporations operating in the emerging post-Cold War political and economic environment?
- what new approaches can be adopted for addressing these?

NEW OPPORTUNITIES AND NEW RISKS IN A CHANGING BUSINESS ENVIRONMENT

The world is becoming riskier for a number of reasons:

- markets are becoming global and bringing companies into contact with unfamiliar cultures;
- the values of individuals and societies are changing;
- companies are being required to disclose more and more about themselves – in turn creating a demand for new types of data;
- companies are being held accountable for what they do in a far broader sense than previously.[10]

The end of the Cold War has accelerated trends toward a globalised economy. Structural adjustment and reform programmes now dominate the policy agendas of the so-called second and third world nations of Eastern Europe, Asia, Africa and Latin America. The transition from highly regulated and centrally planned economies to more liberal economic structures will undoubtedly improve long-term prospects for economic growth worldwide. Already this process is creating a plethora of new opportunities for the business community. However, transition is rarely a smooth process, often introducing new political and social tensions that can impact on the profitability of foreign direct investment opportunities.

TRANSITIONAL ECONOMIES: THE GROWTH OF 'COWBOY' CAPITALISM

The transition toward liberal economic structures has created a new set of political formations closely tied to the expansion of grey and parallel economies. This association is the defining characteristic of many newly deregulated political economies, and has led to the first major challenge to be faced in their transition – namely, so-called 'cowboy capitalism'.

Although the actual process of economic deregulation has been rapid, it has not been accompanied by a similar expansion in political liberalism or regulation. Democratisation has often been resisted on the premise that such reforms would promote instability through the flaming of ethnic nationalism (as in Nigeria, for example).

The reality in most transitional countries is that patronage and client systems form the basis of political and economic authority, whether it is in the rise of Mafia-style criminal organisations in Eastern Europe and the newly independent states, or in the rise of militarised ethno-nationalist political organisations in Africa, Asia and the Balkans. By their nature, the new economies within these states operate most effectively beyond the law, and thus have planted within them the seeds of insecurity, often leading to open conflict.

Within this environment, the power and authority of the state has been increasingly reduced. In many areas, the state no longer has the ability to enforce the law or to protect newly privatised property or commercial activities. As a result the opportunities for extortion and the demand for private security has grown. In such extra-legal environments, political and economic organisations have harnessed a burgeoning culture of violence toward enforcing their claims.

What this translates into is a situation in which some actors will seek to instigate or to perpetuate violence and conflict for their own economic and political gain. Conflict can provide the vehicle for economic growth by providing an arena in which they can act with impunity, see overleaf for some examples. As David Keen states:

> ... war has increasingly become the continuation of economics by other means. War is not simply a breakdown in a particular system, but a way of creating an alternative system of profit, power, even protection ... conflict can create war economies, often in regions controlled by rebels or warlords and linked to international trading networks; members of armed gangs can benefit from looting; and regimes can use violence to deflect opposition, reward supporters or maintain their access to resources. Under these circumstances, ending civil wars becomes difficult. Winning may not be desirable: the point of war may be precisely the legitimacy which it confers on actions that in peacetime would be punishable as crimes.[11]

Economic Benefits arising from Conflict[12]

- *Pillage.* Pillaging has long been used to supplement or replace soldiers' wages. In modern times, it has taken place in the Central African Republic in 1996, Zaire, the Democratic Republic of Congo (DROC) since independence in 1960 and parts of Eastern Europe after the collapse of communism. Although plundering has often been seen as the work of reckless individuals, it may also be a group activity organised on a considerable scale, as with the whole-scale looting of villages by Bosnian Serbs during the 1992-95 war.

- *Protection money*. Warlords, security personnel or Mafia-type bosses may offer 'protection' from violence in return for payment. This may take place in wartime or in peace. Examples include paramilitaries in Northern Ireland, particularly the Irish Republican Army (IRA), and regional warlords in Liberia and Somalia. Iraqi prison guards have allowed inmates to escape in return for payment from relatives. Protection money may also be demanded from companies: from the early 1980s, Mozambique's rebel *Resistência Nacional Moçambicana* (Renamo) movement obtained regular payments from a subsidiary of the UK conglomerate Lonrho for 'protecting' the Beira oil pipeline.
- *Trade*. Controlling or monopolising trade has been an important factor in civil wars in Africa, Asia and Latin America, where 'forced markets', rather than market forces, may dictate the distribution of resources. War may cause price movements profitable to some, and may make it easier to threaten or constrain trading rivals. Officials may profit by allowing government restrictions on war time trading to be breached; conflict may make it easier for warlords to avoid paying government taxes. One profitable aspect of trade may be procuring arms, which frequently involves kickbacks for local officials.
- *Labour exploitation*. Threatening individuals or groups in ways that force them to work cheaply or for free.
- *Land*. A conflict may depopulate large areas, allowing new groups to claim land, water and mineral resources.
- *Stealing aid supplies*. Violence causes suffering, and may prompt foreign relief aid. It may also secure access to that aid once it arrives, for combatants.
- *Benefits for the military*. Economically, the military may do better when conflict necessitates a sizeable standing army or justifies them a role in government. Benefits may also include higher salaries or a seat on the board of a private company.

THE DECLINE IN INTERNATIONAL INTERVENTION

The actual allocation of aid has often been influenced by the strategic interests

> of donors. Although donor behaviour differs, total bilateral aid has favoured former colonies and political allies more than open economies or democracies … As a result, much bilateral aid has gone to countries with poor management … The end of the Cold War reduces the pressure to provide aid to strategic allies. In a few highly distorted economies (Myanmar, Nigeria, Zaire) aid declined dramatically in the early 1990s.[13]

In many of the more marginal parts of the world, where most new opportunities for extractive industries are found, the international communities' interest in developmental aid, co-operation and political support tends to be rather limited. This trend is likely to grow in the future. Corporations operating in these regions are in danger of being perceived as a replacement for inter-governmental co-operation. In the vacuum left behind, corporate investors face the risk of being manipulated as the key source of ready finance or as political actors by competing leaderships.

In addition, the expectations and perceptions of different social groups can be harnessed to the political and economic interests of these leaderships. Such developments, if contrary to the economic and political interests of national regimes with whom investing companies must engage, can spark conflict. How corporations deal with such competing interests will determine the level of security risk to which they are exposed.

RISE OF THE 'SHOW ME' SOCIETY IN WESTERN DEMOCRACIES

At the same time, corporations are coming under increasing scrutiny as regards the manner in which they operate whether at home or abroad. Pressure groups are shifting the boundaries of corporate citizenship. Traditional health, safety and environmental requirements are being broadened to cover human rights, corruption, social development and conflict. Corporations can no longer rely solely on the heavy hand of government militia or private security forces to secure their investments and protect assets and personnel. Exposure of their direct or indirect engagement in repressive or corrupt practices will lead to a poor international reputation, legal action and the potential for consumer boycotts. This carries the danger of adding increased risk to their performance and shareholder value, while at the same time fuelling local animosities and the danger of increased risks in terms of the targeting of investments.

Corporations have invested and continue to invest in programmes that are loosely described as community development initiatives. In reality, they tend to be piecemeal projects undertaken by governmental or non-governmental agencies for enhancing public relations, cooling community animosity or buying political support. Many of these initiatives have been based on 'transfer of technology' approaches, which have poor sustainability records.

NEW APPROACHES TO NEW RISKS

> Hundreds of people have been killed along the Nigerian coast, tens of thousands have been forced from their homes, and oil production – crucial to the country's economy – has been cut by a quarter by an escalation of unrest which shows the signs of civil war. The conflict began a month ago between impoverished tribes angered by the exploitation of oil in their areas. This week drilling rigs and oil terminals operated by Shell and Chevron were seized. The military regime has been left with a dilemma: should it obey the traditional impulse to crack down, thus risking international condemnation, or tolerate the growing secessionist ambitions of the country's fourth largest tribe, the Ijaw.[14]

The same dilemma is faced by the oil companies operating in conflict areas. As the preceding sections have illustrated, these new, emerging markets pose large challenges to the corporate world. Some face greater problems than others. The companies that have been operating in these environments for some time have set precedents for relations with government, local communities and the military. These may fuel tensions in the future. Others move into areas where precedents have already been set, making new approaches to address these risks more difficult.

For some, the level of their investment in infrastructural development is small, so allowing a speedy retreat if the situation deteriorates. For others, infrastructural investment is large, and hence they have longer-term interests. This remains the core, unless, as in the case of the oil sector, they are operating offshore, where direct threats are reduced.

Some companies see these new markets as their main strategic focus, where competition is high in the more secure and stable markets. These may be the key areas in which they can gain a competitive lead. This is particularly the case for smaller corporations, such as the UK oil independents. For these corporations, the need to introduce innovative measures to minimise their risks is greater than for the large corporate giants, who can either afford to write off investments if the going gets too difficult, or pay for large-scale security systems.

There have been examples of corporations that have been driven to address these issues as a result of being exposed by the media or pressure groups for being linked to human rights violations or for reportedly backing the heavy hand of paramilitary operations. Their first step has been to translate these concerns into new corporate policy detailing their principles on human rights, corruption and contributions to society. The question that remains is that of how these policies can be translated into practice from headquarter-level policy to on-the-ground action. Also, will these business leaders[15] be joined by other corporations so that there are more heads above the parapet?

A single corporation operating alone in a particular area could develop and implement its own strategy for dealing with ethical and security risks. Such a situation is rare. Consortia members, other corporations operating nearby and sub-contractors (such as pipeline builders, up- and down-stream operators and security firms) are increasingly engaged in new energy and mining operations. This poses difficulties for a single company trying to take on and address what may be seen by others as peripheral activities. More responsible action will have to deal with the precedents already set and the behaviour of others, which could continually undermine new approaches. In the Azeri oil blocks alone, there are around seven consortia, which collectively amount to around 22 oil companies, though not all are operators. Each will have a number of companies contracted to support oil extracting, transport and security activities. In many of these environments, competition for concessions may be won more from what is offered on the table, or more likely under it, than a package structured by transparency and ethical conduct.

MANAGING RISK

One opportunity that may exist for corporations is to take a more proactive stance in their management of risk, by breaking down traditional concepts and approaches to security, community and public relations. Instead of treating these as separate and exclusive spheres of policy and operations, opportunities may exist for their integration. While maintaining essential protective security functions, innovative approaches could be explored that enhance community relations, promote sustainable development, support commercial interests and by doing so minimise security risks.

Traditional approaches to risk management often result in pigeonholing. Risks are classified and treated separately and opportunities for synergy missed. For example, international relations style political appreciations and military-style threat assessments are used to judge risks to the physical security of potential or actual foreign investments. Assessment of economic structures and performance contribute toward an analysis of risks to profitability, while assessments of government proactivism and visible social ills are seen as components of ethical risk through exposure to negative publicity.

Yet in the real world, the boundaries between risks to profitability, physical security and ethical proprietary are not so neatly defined. The security of an investment is dependent on a broad range of factors that spill over into the political, economic and social milieu. Key issues in understanding security risk include:

- economic legitimacy: the level of economic activity that is attributable to domestically or internationally proscribed 'pariah' businesses, and therefore operating outside the law. These would include the extraction, cultivation, manufacture and/or trade in: proscribed narcotics/chemicals/minerals, products derived from endangered species or habitat, fissile material and certain arms transfers, banditry, piracy and extortion, sanctions busting and/or transhipping contraband goods (including economic migrants), pornography and prostitution and so on;
- the rule of law: that is, the degree to which constitutional integrity and judicial independence are respected, the scale of political internment and other human and civil rights violations are good indicators;
- politicisation of the armed forces and/or the militarisation of various political-economic groupings. To what degree has the law of the jungle replaced the rule of law?
- civic competence: namely, how effective is the implementation of legislation? The capacity and integrity of key civil service functions such as the police, customs and excise service and social services are important factors, as is the regulation of the banking and finance sector;
- stakeholder buy-in. How effective and equitable (i.e. non-sectarian) is

economic trickle down? Stability is more likely where economic growth is reflected in improvements in key social problems, such as alleviation of poverty, across all sectors of society (through improvements in terms and conditions of employment, health status, education/employment opportunities and so on).

Clearly all these factors are interdependent, and thus a multidimensional yet integrated approach to security is more likely to yield results. The question is: what measures can be taken by corporations to minimise their impact?

DEFINING LIMITS TO ENGAGEMENT

It would be imprudent for, say, an oil company to become the champion of social, economic and political reform in a host country, or a kind of 'pariah' tsar for the new century. They may not last very long, as they are likely to be somewhat uncompetitive. What is perhaps more prudent is to assess the ways in which they can become engaged with host governments, local communities and the wider international community to mutually support each other's interests in a positive and lasting way. This requires developing a vision of how a corporation perceives the long-term development of the host country or region and the role they can play in shaping this. Do they want to be blessed with the reputation of having supported the development of something resembling the Delta region in Nigeria, or a more secure and flourishing environment? Clearly they are not the dictators of this, but they can and do have some influence over it.

A starting point is to explore the range of primary and subsidiary risks for the short and medium term that each corporation is exposed to, through an in-depth understanding of the dynamics of the relevant political economy. Longer-term risks can be identified through clusters of root causes which, if left unchecked, could interact to exacerbate existing problems or create new uncertainties. From here it would be possible to look at a set of short, medium and long term options that a corporation could use to minimise risk. These could come together as a set of overlapping and coordinated measures for improving security and actively reducing risk.

This process would include assessing core business activities as well as those of a more external nature. This includes issues such as:

- the political and regulatory environment;
- the effectiveness, capabilities and capacities of public services;
- criminality;
- the relative approach of consortia members and other corporate entities operating in the same or similar areas;
- the strategies and programmes of external political, donor and military organisations;
- the potential for a conflict of interests with operations in neighbouring states;
- inter- and intra-government relations;
- stakeholder relations;
- competition and contracting;
- staff employment;
- security systems;
- transparency;
- environmental impact and compensation mechanisms;
- underlying social problems;
- the potential for partnerships;
- the potential for conflict.

It is from these that the relative strengths, weaknesses, opportunities and threats of options in any given situation can be examined for their translation into policy.

PARTNERSHIP OPTIONS

> Foreign oil companies developing the biggest off-shore project in the Caspian Sea region are seeking ways to speed up the remittance of revenues to Azerbaijan, amid concerns that a cash shortage could undermine the country's stability ... but it could be some years before the Baku government saw any sizeable revenues from the project. That is because the production sharing agreement signed by the AIOC and Baku in 1994 allowed the companies to recover their costs first.[16]

The above quotation illustrates the range of different factors that could potentially impinge on an investment. While corporations need to maintain their profit motive and perform their key functions, they need to be aware of the implications that these can bring. As Peter Drucker notes:

> It is, however, irresponsible of an organisation to accept, let alone pursue,

> responsibilities that would seriously impede its capacity to perform its main tasks and mission. And where it has no competence it has no responsibility.[17]

Although some may see this as an illegitimate defence, it opens up the wider question of how the corporate sector inter-links and integrates itself with the wider international community operating in a particular country. In this particular case, the question that follows is the extent to which a contractual agreement between a consortium and a government fits in with or is supported by the programmes and strategies of organisations like the World Bank, the International Monetary Fund and the European Bank for Reconstruction and Development. One of the problems faced in answering this, lies in the co-ordination of the targeting and strategy of donors, many of whom have competing interests. If corporations can provide the means to stimulate revenue earnings and employment, can the donor community provide the necessary support or pressure on governments to help channel these into longer-term growth and stability?

A number of initiatives have been developed to explore opportunities for greater partnership between the corporate sector and the donor world, such as the World Bank's 'Business Partners for Development' programme. The World Bank also has a political risk assurance facility for underwriting transfer restrictions, expropriation, breach of contract and war disturbance through its Multilateral Investment Guarantee Agency (MIGA). This can provide an important safety net for stimulating investments in risk prone or post-conflict environments. These are just a few examples, but are there further opportunities for dialogue, co-operation or even partnership? As Kofi Annan has stated:

> The impact of the private sector is of growing importance. It would be timely to develop means of consultation between the United Nations and the business community.[18]

At the local level, opportunities exist for corporations to form alliances with international or local non-governmental organisations (NGOs) to develop and implement community development initiatives. Such alliances offer the opportunity for corporations to engage with organisations with the requisite expertise and competence to deliver programmes to address key social problems, which at the same time reduce security risks. These programmes could involve the direct implementation by the partner organisation with the host community or in supporting the capacity of local government to deliver key public services. One of the problems facing corporations is that tax receipts paid are not translated into public services on the ground. Some countries have developed policies for ensuring that a percentage of revenue earnings are returned to the investment zone for public service provisions, many have not. As a result, corporations are being double taxed, one tranche for the government and another to garner some credibility with host communities.

A number of partnerships have been explored in countries such as the Democratic Republic of Congo, Angola, Pakistan, Afghanistan and Colombia. There are concerns on the part of many NGOs that partnerships could jeopardise their reputation if principles were manipulated or broken. On the other hand, some NGOs see the corporate sector as a ready means of finance, given the diminishing coffers of donors.

FUTURE DIRECTIONS OF CONFLICT

Many commentators are talking about the impacts of globalisation, the changing nature of the nation state, and the rise in internal conflicts in the post-Cold War order. Another dynamic that is being envisaged by researchers and aid agencies, is the likelihood of a shift from conflict largely within rural settings to more in urban-based environments. Attention should continue to be given to the new directions in which conflicts may develop. If these predictions occur, then many more corporations will have to take heed of their role in these settings than the current mix of oil and mining corporations that principally operate in rural areas.

CONCLUSION

To achieve sustainable growth, global corporations need to reassess how they approach and manage risk in the post-Cold War business environment. While providing new opportunities, many newly deregulated emerging markets pose many challenges both at home and abroad. Corporations need to assess what level of risk they are prepared to take in these potentially lucrative markets. These need to be looked at in terms of risk to infrastructure and personnel at one level and the risks to their corporate image on another. The latter is becoming more imperative as it can damage a corporation's customer base. Some corporations have already discovered this to their cost.

The problem for business leaders who are prepared to bring changes to corporate culture is that of building a consensus. How do they get the support of others to ensure fair play in the tendering, exploratory and operational phases? Their bid for more ethical and transparent practices runs the danger of being non-competitive in an unethical and purposefully non-transparent environment. Opportunities need to be explored for supporting these business leaders in the wider international community, notably by the international donors.

These problems are certainly not going to resolve themselves. Nor are the growing trends of violence, criminalisation and conflict that are becoming increasingly ingrained as new forms of profit, power and protection are extended and consolidated. It is only through exploring new ways in which to promote dialogue and build partnerships between donors, corporations, security organisations, NGOs and the diplomatic community, together with host governments that a more conducive environment for investment, economic growth and partnership will be installed. This will also need to be set in a regulatory environment to ensure observance. In the real world there are few high-risk, emerging markets that have strong constitutional and legal safeguards. The World Bank is currently advocating that international assistance should be conditional on good governance, but it is difficult for corporations to impose similar restrictions on their investment decisions. They may miss out on lucrative opportunities in non-compliant states.

Even analysts in the City are being advised to take heed:

> No longer are E&P (exploration and production) shares seen as merely oil price plays or pure punts on wild cat success. Increasingly the value in the sector will be derived through more complex businesses, many of which are in murky emerging markets. These often depend less on exploration success than on political and commercial relations that defy conventional valuation.[19]

Notes

[1] Parts of this chapter were developed from a paper prepared by James Fennell and the author.

[2] Vanessa Houlder, *Financial Times*, 25 June 1998.

[3] Sandy Barron, *Irish Times*, 4 April 1998

[4] Stavros, R *Energy and Power Risk Management*, September 1998.

[5] Alex Duval Smith, *The Guardian,* 8 October 1998

[6] Control Risk Group, *No hiding place – Business and the politics of pressure.* Control Risk Group, London (1997).

[7] Drucker, Peter, *Post-capitalist society*, Butterworth Heinemann (1993).

[8] A number of initiatives and programmes have been set up for exploring dialogue and experience-sharing between these actors. For example: Corporate Citizenship – An Action Research Conference, University of Warwick 15-16 July 1998; Mitchell, John (Ed.) *Companies in a World of Conflict: NGOs, Sanctions and Corporate Responsibility; Papers from a workshop organised in Oslo by the Royal Institute of International Affairs;* RIIA / Earthscan, London (1998); The Prince of Wales Business Leaders Forum *Dialogues Series on Human Rights* (1998).

[9] For specific studies on military and security companies, see: Shearer, David *Private Armies and Military Intervention*, Adelphi Paper 316, International Institute for Strategic Studies (1998*);* Isenberg, David (1997) *Soldiers of Fortune Ltd.: A Profile of Today's Private Sector Corporate Mercenary Firms*. Centre for Defense Information Monograph, Massachusetts, USA; O'Brien, Kevin *Private Military Companies – Time for Inclusion in the Official Debate?* Paper presented at the conference on 'European Led Military Operations in Support of Humanitarian Missions' London 5-6 November (1998).

[10] This quote is taken from an article by Jim Kelly in the *Financial Times* (4 June 1998) reviewing Elkington, John, *Cannibals with forks – the Triple Bottom Line of 21st century business*, Capstone (1997).

[11] Keen, David, *The Economic Functions of Violence in Civil Wars*, p.11, Adelphi Paper 320. International Institute for Strategic Studies (1998)

[12] *ibid*, p.15-17

[13] World Bank (1998), *Assessing Aid: Overview. Aid Effectiveness Research.* (Internet).

[14] Alex Duval Smith, *The Guardian* 16 October 1998.

[15] Notably Shell International, British Petroleum and Rio Tinto.

[16] *Financial Times,* 13 May 1998.

[17] Drucker, Peter, *Post-capitalist society* (1993).

[18] Excerpt from speech made by Kofi Annan, UN Secretary-General.

[19] Robert Corzine, *Financial Times*. 15 September 1998.

12

The Media and Complex Humanitarian Emergencies

GORDON ADAM

There is little doubt that the media can have a profound effect on complex emergencies. Television and radio stations are normally a priority target of any fighting – either to destroy them so they cannot be used by the opposition, or to capture them so as to make use of the media's power to reach people. The difficulty has always been to define its impact, and to measure it. In some cases it is all too clear: the mass manipulation of the German population by Joseph Goebbels, Minister of Propaganda, during the Nazi era; the incitement to genocide by Radio Milles Collines in Rwanda in 1994, and the radio and TV output in much of former Yugoslavia during the Bosnian war. It is generally accepted that these media interventions had the impact of intensifying the conflict. On the other hand, in the case of the television pictures of slain American servicemen being dragged through the streets of Mogadishu in 1993, the impact took the form of a political response – the rapid withdrawal of American forces from Somalia.

But normally the impact of TV and radio broadcasts is not so clear cut, and can be highly unpredictable. Nick Gowing has argued that television news is not as influential on policy makers as many assume it to be, and that TV pictures of, for instance, starving refugees, is often followed by public commitments to 'the appearance of action by way of palliative humanitarian operations' as a substitute to substantive political action aimed at tackling the root causes of the conflict. [1]

At the same time, the power of the international media – particularly radio and television – is being increasingly harnessed by the warring parties in pursuit of their goals. Liberian warlords showed sophisticated media management in 1996 when they appealed through the foreign correspondents to external donors against an aid boycott imposed by relief agencies on the ground. The boycott had been an attempt by the agencies to stop the warlords plundering the aid convoys, but the pictures of starving Liberian children caused a sufficient public outcry in the West for the donor agencies to put pressure on the agencies in Liberia to lift the boycott. The warlords had won, and the international media had been taken for a ride.[2] In another study on the fighting in the Great Lakes Region,[3] Nick Gowing came to the conclusion that 'even modest sub-regional forces from small, supposedly badly-resourced nations and factions have learned and assimilated much of the latest thinking of information warfare, information control and information manipulation'. As a result, he concludes, 'both the humanitarian community and the media were deceived comprehensively' about the hidden military campaign that was unfolding in Zaire.

The role of the electronic mass media in complex emergencies is multi-faceted: the examples above concern the impact of the fast-changing international news media on unfolding events in the field and on the media consumers in the North, and by extension, on policy-making. This is a big area in itself and one which is attracting increasing interest from scholars. But what I would like to focus on here is the potential for the media to do the opposite of the examples above – that is, to *support the efforts* of the humanitarian aid agencies in complex emergencies, even to the extent of helping with peace-building efforts. International agencies such as UNESCO, UNDP and the World Bank are increasingly interested in the notion that, if handled appropriately, the mass media could make a very positive impact on complex emergencies. When the media has been used in this role, these efforts have largely been isolated with little attempt to learn from experience of others. However, these examples have pointed the way to a potentially fruitful synergy between the communications skills of the media practitioners and the people-centred approaches pioneered by humanitarian aid agencies. This chapter will analyse some of these experiences and draw some tentative conclusions for future guidance.

BACKGROUND

Today, more people in the world are liable to experience conflict than at any time in the past: during this century, an estimated 110 million have died, and at present there are about 20 million refugees and 50 million displaced people in the world. Many of these people are excluded from the global revolution in communications. Half the world's population has never made a phone call,[4] and the growth of FM radio stations is concentrated in population centres. People in more remote areas have to make do with increasingly badly funded state broadcasters, as much victims of structural adjustment as of other financial constraints. These are the people who are most likely to suffer from hunger, health problems and lack of schooling. Often they are in areas of complex emergencies, such as Afghanistan, Somalia, Liberia, Rwanda, Burundi and southern Sudan.

These are also the people that aid organisations and donors such as the British Department for International Development (DfID) are increasingly targeting with their poverty focus programmes. But generally they are the most difficult to reach, because of distance, poor roads and other links, or because of security concerns. They do often possess, however, a vital piece of equipment that could be their lifeline – a radio. Radios are cheap and portable, and they do not require mains electricity, so they tend to survive in conflict zones when other mass media such as newspapers and televisions fail. BBC audience research shows that in Somalia, Rwanda and Liberia, for instance, listenership to the BBC World Service is high. Conflicts in fact generate listeners, as the Gulf War showed.[5] The most recent statistic comes from a large scale United Nations survey in Afghanistan, which showed that no fewer than 50% of the population regularly listen to the BBC Pashto and Persian language services.[6] This, in a country which has been in a state of war for 20 years and which has one of the smallest per capita incomes in the world.

THEORETICAL FRAMEWORK

There is accumulating evidence to support the argument that well targeted media interventions can make a positive contribution to the livelihoods of listeners living in complex emergency areas. Robert Manoff from New York University's Center for War, Peace and News Media sees a potential peace-building role for news broadcasters in conflict areas in the following terms. Journalism can:

- counter misconceptions and rumours, humanise the 'enemy';
- build confidence amongst warring parties;
- build consensus;
- allow for face saving;
- facilitate communication between conflicting parties;
- provide an outlet for emotional expression;
- analyse the conflict;
- educate on the process of resolution;
- propose options and solutions to the conflict;
- influence the balance of power in a conflict.[7]

In theory, the journalist has the ability to tackle many of these objectives. He/she has access to the warring parties, is not aligned to either side, has a responsibility to report impartially, and has the power to reach a mass audience on both sides. In practice, the journalist may be denied access to the policy makers, be threatened, perceived as being biased and may have real difficulties in understanding what is going on in the confusion which usually surrounds complex emergencies.

On the other hand, the Manoff model does allow for the media *enabling communication* as well as *providing information.* Communication has been defined as 'a process by which we make sense out of events … information has meaning to the individual only to the extent that it can be interpreted, understood, and applied to that individual according to his or her own circumstances'.[8] Information of course does not necessarily lead to improved knowledge. Much information in the media is slanted, partial, not relevant or just plain wrong. But in sensitive hands, the media can be used to promote genuine communication, which can help lead to social change.

The media – particularly radio – could contribute to peace in complex emergencies, as Robert Manoff envisages. It could also contribute to a Culture of Peace through a much broader range of programming which addresses the relevant everyday concerns of the target audience in conflict areas and attempts to compensate for the lack of basic services in health and education. The challenge here is to *enable communication* so that the radio acts as a catalyst to help with peoples' understanding of issues such as hygiene and nutrition, or awareness of land-mines or peace-building, and then allows radio listeners to discuss the issues which, through subsequent peer group pressure, may lead to behavioural change. Behavioural change, or social change, is the ultimate aim of this form of broadcasting. Success is not measured by the number of people listening or watching a programme on war trauma or tracing missing people: it is measured, for instance, by whether people's attitudes toward those suffering from trauma have been changed, or whether they wrote and sent off a letter to the International Red Cross with details of their missing family member. It is heightened awareness and action which counts, not just the ability to absorb information.

The implications of this approach is that the strictly impartial journalistic approach of reporting facts gives way to producing programmes with a very definite editorial objective, whether it be to reduce diarrhoea in children through promoting better hygiene, reducing land-mines casualties, or promoting peace-building solutions to conflict. This approach has been termed 'desired outcomes' broadcasting.

Ongoing work by several organisations[9] is attempting to define the criteria which are most likely to lead to effective 'desired outcomes' media interventions in the field of health communications. Many of the same criteria would apply to working in complex emergencies. In addition to the traditional journalistic imperatives of getting the facts right and presenting them in an understandable way, the following additional criteria have been identified as a precondition to an effective media intervention:

- focusing on promoting informed dialogue and choice through more public discussion; more accurate information in those discussions; supporting people making their action choices;
- effectively 'framing' an issue to position the issue of concern in relation to the major matters of concern for the relevant population;
- working in partnership with local organisations with the necessary technical knowledge and understanding of the target area;
- supporting local 'ownership' – the target audience needs to be consulted about the programme style and content;
- placing substantial resources into evaluation to ensure media intervention is on track;
- working for sustainability – the achievement of objectives will lead to long-term change, and the resource base provides a long-term basis for action.

In areas of complex emergency there are often constraints: for instance, security concerns may curtail evaluation activities. There may be serious difficulties in delivering health supplies, which could undermine a planned series of programmes on the importance of immunising children. One of the quickest ways of denting a radio or TV station's credibility is to broadcast information which calls for action which cannot be carried out.

Many problems can nevertheless be avoided if partnerships are formed with the relevant aid organisations. Often, this requires a leap of faith: broadcasters are widely seen as news driven, whose sole objective is to acquire a 'story' - the more sensational the better – and broadcast it with little regard to the consequences in terms of the impact on listeners or viewers. Aid organisations are often regarded by journalists as secretive – afraid to speak openly because of fear of being misquoted. Often, journalists and aid workers work best together in a public information role, the latter providing access to areas of humanitarian crisis, so that the journalists can file television reports which will increase public interest in the emergency but also raise the profile of the organisation concerned amongst its donors back home. In the case of 'desired outcomes' broadcasting, there has to be mutual trust between aid workers, conflict resolvers and broadcasters that they are all working for the same ends, namely, to improve the lives of people in the midst of complex emergencies living in very difficult circumstances.

In the following section, I present a number of case studies in which media interventions have been attempted in complex emergencies, with varying results, and discuss some of the issues which each throws up in the context of this theoretical framework.

THE BBC AFGHAN EDUCATION DRAMA 'NEW HOME NEW LIFE'

The BBC Afghan Education Drama project started life in 1993: the aim was to use radio to broadcast entertaining, relevant and educational programming to the Afghan people in their own languages as a means of compensating for the widespread destruction of the country's health and education infrastructure. The BBC was widely listened to and trusted for its news coverage of the war against the Soviet occupation forces in the 1980s. The educational vehicle chosen was a radio soap opera, broadcast three times weekly in both languages, and called *New Home New Life.* The story was of two communities surviving during a time of war, and storylines ranged from child health to drug addiction, from problems associated with arranged marriages to relations between the community and aid agencies, from handling the symptoms of war trauma to local conflict resolution. Its success with listeners was immediate, and it was clear from the BBC monitoring reports that a whole new audience was tuning in – namely, women. What is more, there was encouraging evidence that men and women were learning and remembering significant health and other information which formed part of the soap opera storylines:

- what should lactating mothers with TB do when feeding their children? Correct answers rose from 30% to 84% within four months of the broadcast, remaining at 68% nearly two years later;
- regular taking of TB medicine: correct answers: 60% to 92% to 90% over the same period;
- best protection against malaria: correct answers: 64% to 93% to 88%;
- benefits of vaccination: correct answers: 23% to 83% to 91%.

This provided evidence that key messages were getting through and that people were remembering them remarkably well. Unlike many surveys in other countries, the BBC team could be almost certain that the knowledge came from *New Home New Life,* as there was no other source of mass health education. But there is no evidence in this sample that knowledge was translated into preventative action. And there is certainly no evidence of the most elusive connection of all – that a mass media health education campaign led to an actual impact on mortality/morbidity rates.

This evidence is hard to come by in any country, especially in a complex emergency where collecting such data is difficult and very expensive. However, one remarkable survey from 1997 by the research organisation CIET International, into mines awareness amongst the general population of Afghanistan, provides compelling evidence that *New Home New Life* has an impact not just on people's understanding of high risk behaviours which could lead to mine accidents, but on the incidence of injury and death. According to the survey, listeners of *New Home New Life* and other BBC programmes on mines awareness were only *half as likely* to be involved in mine explosions than non-listeners. Furthermore, people who attended mines awareness courses were found to be more liable to tamper with mines or unexploded ordinance, incurring a serious risk of injury. This was substantially offset if those people also listened to the BBC, where the dangers of touching 'strange objects' has been a consistently recurring theme in *New Home New Life*. The survey sample was huge – a total of 60,000 people were surveyed altogether, which increases confidence in the validity of the findings.[10]

So what is it about *New Home New Life* which has led to this impact? There are a number of factors: first that the BBC in Afghanistan is widely listened to and trusted, and that there are few other credible information sources. Second, the programmes are entertaining and they contain useful and relevant information – the stories are created by talented Afghan writers situated in the region. The storylines are vetted by Afghan and expatriate staff members of aid organisations to make sure they are technically accurate and the advice they give is useful. And listeners' views are routinely canvassed and their ideas for future storylines are regularly presented to the scriptwriters and the production team. Also, Afghans have a strong oral/aural culture to which radio broadcasting is well suited. Storytelling is popular, and people have excellent memories for what they hear.

In one respect, the CIET survey results are surprising. Fewer than 4% of respondents said they had discussed what they had heard on the dangers of mines with anyone. Typically, the stimulation of discussion, followed by peer pressure, are regarded as key stages in the behaviour change process. However, anthropological research on *New Home New Life* has shown that the programme does stimulate discussion, particularly on issues that are thought to affect the family.[11] The research also points strongly to the fact that the drama characters are viewed by listeners as being almost part of the family – they do not distinguish between fiction and reality. An extreme example of this was when one of the most popular characters in the soap was killed in the course of a feud. There was an outcry from the listeners, with one group of tribesmen even going so far as holding a prayer service in the mosque for the character's departed soul!

This is a significant indicator of the extent to which the audience has assumed 'ownership' of *New Home New Life* and of the educational material it conveys. Information 'ownership' is a key criterion identified by the *Communications Initiative* for effective programming, along with promoting dialogue, forming partnerships, framing the issue and investing in evaluation. Partnerships have been the basis for one of the project's other successes, the joint mobilisation with UNICEF, the World Health Organisation and a number of NGOs of the three mass immunisation weeks. Radio, particularly the BBC, played a key role in explaining the need for immunisation and in appealing for a ceasefire. On all three occasions, the ceasefires were almost 100% respected – the only such occasions in almost 20 years of war.[12]

Only on moving towards sustainability does the BBC Afghan Education Project fall short of the *Communications Initiative* criteria. Ideally, the programme should have been made by an indigenous broadcasting company working towards financial self- sufficiency, and be able to play a significant role in strengthening civil society. Despite being based in neighbouring Pakistan, the BBC Afghan Education Project is Afghan managed with a virtually all Afghan/ Pakistani staff who are potentially the nucleus of an Afghan educational broadcasting service of the future. All too often in complex emergencies, aid interventions have little prospect of becoming self-sustaining until some semblance of normality returns to the country. However, the entire project remains impressive value for money – costing approximately 7p per head of population reached per year.

FORMER YUGOSLAVIA: MEDIA REFORM IN AN ETHNICALLY DIVIDED SOCIETY

The difficulty facing the international community trying to rebuild the peace in former Yugoslavia is that the media has been widely used as an instrument of war, and has been strongly ethno-centric in terms of staffing and output. This section will consider two contrasting approaches to media reform in Bosnia and Macedonia.

Bosnia

In Bosnia, the international community is the effective power in the land, under powers accorded to the Office of the High Representative (OHR). There is the opportunity, therefore, for the international community to have a decisive influence in rebuilding Bosniac media so that it is non-communal, credible and entertaining. The problem of how to handle the recalcitrant local media has all but been ignored in the text of the Dayton Accords which brought the war to an end in 1995. The strategy of the OHR following the Dayton Accords was to support as many alternative radio and TV stations as possible with a view to diluting the impact of the big ethno-centric state broadcasters. The Organisation for Security and Co-operation in Europe (OSCE) charged with holding free elections in Bosnia also decided to sponsor the formation of an independent radio network (FERN), while the OHR established an independent TV service called the Open Broadcasting Network (OBN). Both of these were intended to appeal to the three until recently warring communities, the Muslims, Croats and Serbs. The aid organisations – the UN, the EU and the bilateral funders also funded a number of local radio and TV stations.

The overall objective was to establish a pluralistic media. But the initial lack of emphasis on programming and journalistic skills meant that programming on the smaller local stations was generally poor. They were no challenge to the big state broadcasters, whose programming continued to be partisan and at times (in the case of Republica Serpska TV SRT) poisonous propaganda. Ultimately, NATO troops had to take over SRT transmitters, and allow the OHR to broadcast its own news programme each evening for one hour. And after months of unsuccessful attempts to get Muslim, Croat and Serb journalists to work together, the OBN was only put on the air after an expatriate manager was appointed and the OHR had over-ridden local laws in order to secure the necessary broadcasting frequencies.[13]

What are the lessons to be learned from this experience? The first is that it was a serious omission not to spell out the responsibilities and powers of the international community over the local media in the Dayton Accords, particularly when it was well known that the media had played such a negative role in the war. This was not clarified until two years later, at a NATO summit in May 1997.[14] Second, it is invariably a mistake to throw money at broadcasters in complex emergencies and then walk away, expecting standards to improve. Follow-up advice, training and brainstorming on programme ideas is required. A third problem is related to ownership: amongst the general public, it is ownership of the information that is important. Listeners and viewers are often far more discerning than broadcasters believe, and they are prepared to give credit for a balanced report or an entertaining programme wherever it originates. So the well-intentioned effort by the OHR to make local journalists take responsibility for OBN was probably misconceived, and valuable time was wasted in trying to implement it. Any TV station under OHR supervision will carry weight – after all the High Representative is the most powerful authority in the land. A similar situation arose in Cambodia in 1993, when the United Nations administration supervising the elections set up Radio UNTAC. The station was a popular success and in the subsequent elections, there was a 90% turnout despite Khmer Rouge attempts to enforce a polls boycott. Radio UNTAC was credited with much of this success, despite its non-Cambodian management and editorial policy.

The fourth lesson is the emphasis placed by the international community on news programming. 'Hate' broadcasts cannot, and have not, been tolerated. But despite the presence of a BBC journalism school in Sarajevo, straight, accurate reporting will take many years to achieve in Bosnia. An alternative approach, which is familiar to western audiences, and which is being tried in places such as South Africa, Afghanistan (see p.214), Burundi and Liberia to help build peace, is educational drama – popular programming with a topical theme which is humorous, entertaining and appeals to a wide audience.

There was one attempt to produce a home-grown topical TV soap in the Bosnian Muslim enclave of Gorazde: despite its amateurism it became essential viewing in the valley before it stopped after a year in 1997. Despite the efforts of a leading Bosnian journalist and one of the country's best scriptwriters who produced a pilot script of the TV soap, it was never produced by OBN. It sought to explore topical issues and the recent past through the eyes of a typical Bosnian family; if it had been well done, it could have filled a gap in the market and would have had significant influence.

It is difficult to escape the conclusion that a number of errors could have been avoided had the media strategists started by finding out what the media consumers wanted to listen to and watch, what their aspirations were, and what their most pressing problems were in the post war period. Yet it took two years for the first social research of this kind to be commissioned, with USAID and the World Bank in the lead. The results of this research indicated a preference for entertainment – something they lacked in the difficult task of rebuilding their lives after the war.[15] One fundamental principle of effective media targeting, that is, to know your audience, has been learned late in the Bosnian experience. One possibility would be for the OSCE and other international agencies' monitoring teams to check on programme quality as well as inflammatory broadcasts. This is an essential step in producing effective 'desired outcomes' programming.

The fifth lesson is to set realistic objectives: making allowances for entrenched Bosnian attitudes is critical when it comes to choosing what the key messages should be in an information campaign. The fundamental difficulty with the principal messages which the international community wants put across – the benefits of non-ethnic democracy, the safe return of refugees and the extradition of war criminals for example – is that they are all highly contentious and essentially undeliverable in a society which still has many scores to settle, and would be doing so if there were not 35,000 foreign troops in the way. These messages are also all too easily perceived as being a foreign agenda force-fed on to a reluctant population as part of a pro-social propaganda campaign. Media campaigns on these 'macro-themes' have, therefore, been doomed from the start.

On the other hand, the OSCE public information campaigns on policies such as a change in vehicle licence plates have been undertaken by professional TV advertisement producers and show both imagination and humour. A difficulty is that there is not a systematic means of measuring viewer appreciation of these efforts (focus groups for instance) so there is little feedback on where these campaigns succeed and where they could be improved in the future.

The most impressive examples of media use for peace-building objectives in Bosnia are programmes where there is a combination of creative flair and the ability to set realistic objectives on 'desired outcomes'. *Fresh* is a forty-minute weekly programme produced by a Bosnian film director under the auspices of Internews, a US based media organisation which is committed to using media to bridge ideological, ethnic and political divides. The *Fresh* approach is to use the media to 'de-contaminate' the minds of viewers, many of whom, the director believes, have been influenced by 'hate' media over the war years. He uses film of ordinary people in an attempt to tackle misconceptions that have grown up including the demonisation of 'the enemy'. Shared problems could lead to shared solutions. Incidents in the lives of Serbian, Bosnian and Croat pigeon fanciers, gravediggers and peasant farmers are compared in film reports. However, the recent USAID commissioned survey shows that while *Fresh* is one of OBN's most popular programmes, it has yet to break through the barrier of mistrust and become popular viewing in Croat and Serb areas.[16]

A separate Internews initiative was to broadcast the international war crimes tribunal from The Hague, on television in both Serbo-Croat and English. The objective was to 'show Bosnians that justice can be done [and] ... help provide catharsis and thus prevent many thousands of acts of vengeance being carried out'. Whether or not this succeeded is not known, as again there was no systematic monitoring of audience reactions. The English summary was an attempt to pressurise the international community in Bosnia to take the initiative in hunting down Radovan Karadzic and General Ratko Mladic, both indicted war criminals. One indication that the broadcasts have had an impact was the scheduling of contemporary movies by Republica Serpska Television to clash with the coverage of the tribunal. Another was the OHR belief that the coverage had made Karadzic 'nervous'.[17]

Radio EFM is largely run by Sarajevo university students for their peers, financed and editorially supervised by expatriate radio journalists employed by the United Nations. Its emphasis is quality news reporting, but the entertainment vehicle is a strong selection of contemporary chart music. Local music is also played. Speech programming includes news talks shows, student shows on issues such as AIDS, use of drugs, pollution, tolerance between ethnic groups, 'blind date' shows, and music competitions. The philosophy of the station is to emphasise straight reporting and features of direct relevance to the target listeners (students) rather than a 'hard sell' for specific behaviours. A major new venture is the start of a similar station in Banja Luka at the request of the President of Republika Serpska. This will have a powerful former UN transmitter, and will have their own as well as some shared programming including phone-ins and competitions with the Sarajevo station. The emphasis will be on building contacts between the young listeners of both stations, based on a belief that the younger Bosnian generation have less ideological baggage than their elders and that they are more open to opportunities for building bridges between former enemies.

Macedonia

Unlike Bosnia, where a lot of aid money was invested in attempts to diversify the media, in Macedonia it has been western media organisations which have taken the initiative on a small scale, beginning with attempts to influence attitudes within the print media which have been split into Albanian, Macedonian and Turkish speaking groups. The two American based organisations involved, *Search for Common Ground,* and *The Center for War, Peace and the News Media (CWPNM)* at New York University, believed that by reforming the attitudes and working practices of key journalists, they could help address the problem of local Albanian, Macedonian and Turkish language newspapers socially constructing their own view of the common reality, often with any conflict material being presented in an exaggerated or inflammatory manner.[18] Traditionally, the different ethnic groups in Macedonia have been fed an ethnically slanted version of the news.

To tackle this, CWPNM held a training workshop in November 1994 for 15 Macedonian journalists on 'Journalism and Social Responsibility: the Role of the Media in Inter-Ethnic relations'. This was followed in March 1995 by a workshop for newspaper editors, and then in June by an experiment: four journalists from three ethnic newspapers (Macedonian, Albanian and Turkish) formed an inter-ethnic reporting team to collaborate in a reporting project on '*How we Survive*': stories focused on an entrepreneur, a woman and a youth making ends meet in the midst of economic sanctions. Under the guidance of an experienced *Los Angeles Times* feature writer, the group learned to work together, to interview ordinary people rather than accept the official view on the issue and to find new angles on the story which had been closed to them because of the ethnic divide. Field trips were organised into regions inhabited by the different ethnic groups and the journalists learned to interview people from other ethnic groups for the first time. They discovered that there were winners and losers from all three communities. The stories were published in three newspapers, one in each language, and two of the newspapers and several of the journalists decided to continue the collaboration by investigating Macedonia's drugs trade.

While concluding that the project had been very successful, an independent evaluation also noted that the three newspapers were all owned by one company and had small circulations (maximum:

20,000), so the fruits of the project would only reach a relatively small part of the population.[19] But the CWPNM director sees the Macedonia project as a pilot for future activities along the same lines in the former Yugoslavia and the former Soviet Union. The project ties in with CWPNM's philosophy of requiring local journalists to 'buy into' a re-evaluation of their roles in areas of conflict.[20]

PRO-SOCIAL PROPAGANDA

The most common use of the media in complex emergencies, especially if it is supporting an international peacekeeping force, is producing programmes in the category of *pro-social propaganda.* What differentiates this from most other programming examined in this chapter is not so much its subject matter, as its difference of style and approach. Propaganda – even if it is well-intentioned – is perceived to be the product of a 'handed down' agenda – as in the case of encouraging refugees to return and other 'macro' messages previously cited in the case of Bosnia. *Social education* broadcasting, on the other hand, gains legitimacy from the extent to which it reflects the aspirations of the target media consumers, and the extent to which the listeners and viewers are involved in constructing the agenda, and giving feedback to the broadcasts. This is one reason why *New Home New Life* in Afghanistan is so successful – its listeners believe the programme's subject matter reflects their own concerns and that they have some role in deciding the agenda.

Two contrasting examples of pro-social propaganda, are good illustrations of the difficulties with this approach:

The American PsyOps (Psychological Operations) Radio Rajo (Somalia 1993), suffered from the twin misfortunes of not being heard throughout much of Somalia for most of the time the American forces were on the ground as part of UNITAF, and broadcasting a strong signal only at the point where the reputation of American troops was so low, and the information about UNITAF's impartiality perceived to be so far from reality, that the radio station had severe credibility problems. According to the PsyOps' own account of Radio Rajo, one of the few successes was a campaign to discourage children from carrying imitation handguns which apparently resulted in the number of such incidents 'eventually decreasing'.[21]

But the programming was generally bland – largely consisting of 'news' culled from the associated Rajo Newspaper and reportedly lacking any spark that might have led people to listen for entertainment. According to a senior US military commander 'a regular exchange of information, ideas and opinions between UNITAF, the NGOs and the Somali people is essential to the peace and rehabilitation process'. However, Radio Rajo represented 'top down' imposed agenda broadcasting at its most extreme, operating from the heavily fortified US Embassy compound; this was a one-way communication process from what many Somalis saw as being an increasingly alien force, with virtually no exchange of ideas and opinions which might have helped Radio Rajo radio become an influential voice in Somalia at a time of uncertainty and crisis.[22]

US PsyOps had a happier experience in Haiti in 1994-95. In the months preceding the return to power of President Aristide, they targeted the Haitian public with airdrops of over eight million leaflets and over 900 hours of broadcasting. The messages came from President Aristide, President Clinton and range of Haitian opinion-shapers and international specialists, preparing the people for a transition to democracy and peace.

When the military arrived, the broadcasts switched to messages aimed at reducing violence between the public and the *de facto* regime, and in disarming the public. The US force was faced with Haitian public suspicion about foreign, and in particular, US forces. But there was also the risk that Haitians might see the US as being primarily responsible for delivering peace. To counteract these dangers the PsyOps team tried to communicate the message that 'we are here to help you help yourself'. It did this by promoting the humanitarian relief and civil action programmes that were being undertaken, including a voluntary scheme whereby US soldiers could 'adopt a school or orphanage' and assist in practical re-building or decorating work. The consensus was that this PsyOps campaign was highly professional. By using cultural specialists and French/Creole speaking personnel, PsyOps produced easily accessible messages that appealed to the target audience.

Whilst the work was professionally carried out, and succeeded in the onerous task of securing military and civilian UN mission agreement to key messages, it is much harder to evaluate the peace-building impact because of simultaneous messages from other significant players. It was inherently non-sustainable, with some radio and TV stations receiving almost half of their income from

US purchases of airtime for their messages. The campaign did succeed in that not a single American soldier was killed, but critics suggest that the information campaign aimed at encouraging respect for law and order and inspiring confidence in justice was undermined by US opposition to investigations into major human rights abuses. This, they said, was an example of a 'growing gap between propaganda and reality'.[23]

CONCLUSIONS

Information is power, and communication is the process of providing people with this power of knowledge so that they can make informed decisions about improving their lives. If the media is to be used to this end in complex emergencies, it is clear that careful planning has to be involved. The attempt to harness the media in Bosnia suffered largely because of this lack of planning.

On one level, the planning involves an approach that is close to advertising:

- agree on what you want to 'sell' to the public;
- know who your audiences are so you can target them effectively;
- be sure your product is potentially 'sellable' to the target group.

At another level, for ideas to take root and to become the basis for changed attitudes and behaviour, there is a real need to establish a two way communication process with the target audience, so they feel part of the process. That way, the information conveyed is much more likely to gain acceptance, as it will be relevant and timely. The lack of this dialogue is at the heart of why pro-social propaganda programmes are rarely successful. In respect of understanding people's needs, the skills of partners in the health or conflict resolution fields are of real value – they have the experience which media practitioners often lack. Building partnerships is at the heart of any media strategy in a complex emergency – the problems are so diverse that overcoming them requires a wide variety of expertise.

Afghanistan is a case of a complex emergency where the creative use of the mass media has delivered results where conventional aid efforts have failed. Fewer people are being injured by mines, not as a result of training courses, but through listening to a radio soap opera. Vital health and other social messages are being conveyed, and people are listening because the programme brings humour and drama into their otherwise drab lives. Fun will also be a major element in a project about to begin: daily radio programmes will be used as a means of teaching numeracy, science and basic life skills to Afghan boys and girls. There are virtually no schools in Afghanistan, just as there are few health facilities. The problems of delivering 'bulk aid' to a country at war, with poor communications and a widely dispersed population, are enormous. What is needed is a greater emphasis on 'smart aid', knowledge to allow people to help themselves. If this can work in Afghanistan, it is surely worth giving 'smart aid' a higher priority in complex emergencies elsewhere.

Notes

1 Gowing, Nick, *Media Coverage: Help or Hindrance in Conflict Prevention?* Carnegie Corporation (New York) 1997.

2 Bolton, Samantha, contribution to *Weapons of War, Tools of Peace III*, International Centre for Humanitarian Reporting, Geneva, May 1998.

3 Gowing, Nick, conference paper for *Dispatches from Disaster Zones,* London, May 1998.

4 *Telecomunications Briefing Paper,* Panos, London (1997).

5 *International Broadcasting and Audience Research Reports* (various), BBC World Service, Bush House, London.

6 CIET International, *Afghanistan: the 1997 National Mine Awareness Evaluation,* report to the United Nations Office Co-ordinating Humanitarian Assistance (Islamabad).

7 Manoff, Robert, *Presentation to conference on the Media and Peacebuilding organised by the Voice of America* (September 1997).

8 Mayo, John, *The Third Channel, Broadening Learning Horizons,* UNICEF unpublished report (1993).

9 Feek, Warren, *Communications Initiative,* Website: http://www. comminit. com.

10 CIET International, *Afghanistan: the 1997 National Mine Awareness Evaluation* pp.44-45.

11 Skuse, Andrew: unpublished doctoral research , University College, London (1995 –97).

12 BBC Afghan Education Drama Project, *Reports to Donors* (1995-97).

13 Maclay, David, article in *Prospect,* November 1997, pp.30-33.

14 *ibid* p.33.

[15] Final Report, *Audience Share & Reaction to OBN Programming*, USAID, Sarajevo (1998).

[16] *Audience Share and Reaction to OBN programming,* p22 (1998).

[17] Randal, Jonathan 'War Crimes Tribunal Beamed Live to Bosnia', *Washington Post*, 1 June 1996.

[18] Lumsden, Malvern, *Peacebuilding in Macedonia: the role of Search for Common Ground*, International Peace Research Institute (PRIO) Oslo. (1995).

[19] Lumsden, Malvern, (1995).

[20] Manoff, Robert cited in Adam, Gordon and Thamotheram, Raj, *The Media's Role in Conflict*, unpublished report for the Overseas Development Administration, pp 21-22 (1995).

[21] Psychological Operations in support of Operation Restore Hope, US Army, Fort Bragg 1993.

[22] Adam, Gordon *et al. The Media's Role in Conflict,* p.34 (1995).

[23] Adam, Gordon *et al op cit.* pp 42-43, quoting *PSYOP Support to Operation Hold Democracy: A Psychological Victory.*

ARMS CONTROL

13

Arms Control at the Millennium – Reflections on the Record of the Twentieth Century and Prospects for the Twenty-first.

KEN ALDRED

Director, Council for Arms Control King's College London

Reflecting on the position 'at the turn of the century' necessitates looking at the failures and achievements of the past 100 years and considering the prospects for the period ahead. As it is easier, and more productive, to read history books than a crystal ball, the first part will essentially be long and the second brief. Was arms control, under whatever title, an issue at the start of an extremely bloody twentieth century, and what effect did it have? On reflection, the failures in controlling arms outweigh the successes, although there are some grounds for believing that things might have been worse had the attempts not been made.

SETTING THE SCENE FOR THE TWENTIETH CENTURY

Treaties and conventions are much more likely to be achieved when there is a degree of goodwill shown by the negotiating parties, although they are usually between states which are at least potentially adversaries. The public declarations of participants rarely represent the actual position held, the hidden agenda usually being quite different. There is little need to negotiate on arms control between allies, although situations do change and today's friend can become tomorrow's enemy. Treaties are unlikely to achieve their objectives when they are imposed, the 1919 Treaty of Versailles being a classic twentieth century illustration of this principle.

In the latter part of the nineteenth century there was growing concern being expressed about the potential for death and devastation likely to be caused by the armed might of the, by then, highly industrialised European countries. Statements were made about the waste of material and human resources being diverted from useful ends to unproductive armaments. At the initiative of the Emperor of Russia, the Hague Peace Conferences of 1899 and 1907 were convened with the declared intention of getting rid of these excessive armaments. Although the states agreed to a resolution declaring that restrictions on military expenditure was desirable, almost all of them continued to increase their military expenditures. However, there were attempts made to establish laws of war and to restrict the use of some specified weapons. The efforts made to control weapons like dumdum bullets and asphyxiating gases were nevertheless soon shown to be ineffective during the First World War. That war showed the horrors of modern inter-state warfare and demonstrated how little restraint agreements like the Hague Convention imposed while such conflict was in process.

The 1919 Treaty of Versailles imposed disarmament on the defeated Germans, with its army limited to 100,000 men, its navy reduced to minimal numbers with submarines and naval air forces forbidden. But, compliance was avoided to a large extent because the supervision of the treaty was ineffective and there was no will, or perhaps ability, to enforce its terms; and resentment from the imposition fermented feelings in Germany which helped lead to further conflict in the 1930s. The treaty also encompassed the Covenant of the League of Nations which called for all the states to reduce their armaments 'to the lowest point consistent with national safety and the enforcement of common action of international obligations'. Members of the League were for the first time, in theory, to have their freedom to build up arms put under international supervision dependent on the circumstances of the state. In 1924 the League started to publish figures of the armaments held and the strength of the forces of individual states, together with statistics on spending on arms and data on international transfers. The latter was an early endeavour to place controls on the arms trade, although there had been the 1890 Brussels act forbidding the sale of arms to Africa and the 1919 St Germain convention which endeavoured to forbid arms trading without government-issued export licences. The Convention never came into force because the United States refused to ratify.

The 1925 Geneva Protocol brought another attempt to prohibit the use of chemical and, this time, biological weapons. The 1928 Kellogg-Briand Pact for the Renunciation of War went much further by setting out to take away the right of states to wage aggressive warfare, and this was signed by 63 countries. It led to the 1932 Disarmament Conference in which over 60 states were asked to refrain from increasing their armaments for one year. This conference had participation from non-governmental organisations with their representatives being able to attend and present petitions. Special commissions, sub-commissions and committees of the conference were set up to examine systems of collective security; limitations on armed forces including air, naval and land armaments; control of arms manufacture and trade; supervision of agreements reached and moral disarmament. In 1922 in Washington, and 1930 and 1935 in London, treaties were agreed to limit the size of the naval forces of the major powers.

There were many other international fora in the first half of the twentieth century, but the ones outlined above illustrate that war cannot be prevented by such agreements and that there are limits to the effectiveness of declarations of good intent. For example, although chemical and biological weapons were contained for military reasons, the Second World War showed the limits to the effectiveness of such agreements. The end of that war brought about the formation of the United Nations, which in its Charter differed from the convention of the League of Nations by placing less emphasis on disarmament and more on establishing a system for regulating armaments. This clearly reflected a change in attitude from the belief that the First World War had been caused by the levels of arms to the even stronger feeling that the Second World War had been caused by the failure of the democracies to be strong enough to resist, or more particularly to deter, aggression. The end of the Second World War, its conclusion being signalled by the United States dropping the first atomic bombs on Hiroshima and Nagasaki, launched the nuclear age with its devastating potential for the destruction of cities and eventually the globe itself. Mutually Assured Destruction (MAD) meant just that, and it epitomised the fears of many over what the ever-increasing power of armaments could bring. 1945 also heralded the start of the Cold War, the rising of East-West tensions between erstwhile allies, the superpower stand-off and an era of arms control negotiations.

ARMS CONTROL AND DISARMAMENT

What do we mean by arms control, and how does it differ from disarmament? The failure by some to differentiate between the two has led them to a disillusionment in arms control because it has not achieved their hopes of getting rid of, say, nuclear weapons in their entirety.

Disarmament is frequently the objective of dreamers who believe that the absence of weapons is an automatic guarantee of peace. It has thus been rejected by realists as a 'tragic illusion'. Others are more prepared to link the concepts of arms control and disarmament, anticipating that success in the former would automatically lead to the ultimate goal of universal disarmament. But the dividing line between the two has to be that disarmament can only be achieved through the removal of weapons whereas arms control addresses the causes of conflict, endeavours to bring stability and understanding and to encompass intentions as well as capabilities. It may well also achieve reductions.

Arms control includes agreements between two or more powers, especially actual or potential adversaries, to regulate the quantity, capability, location and state of readiness of some or all of their weapons of a particular type. It can also include limits on manpower and defensive measures, the Anti-Ballistic Missile (ABM) agreement being notable in the latter category. No agreement is really likely to be successful unless it is possible to verify[1] its implementation and, in most cases, unless it is linked to confidence-building measures between its signatories. When it is achieved, the implementation of arms control should make the world a safer place, but it is vital to assess whether it still has the potential of doing so in an environment of such rapid social, political, technological and military change.

To pursue the Utopian idea of the dreamers that a world where all states are without weapons is to assume such a dramatic change in the behaviour of human beings that it beggars belief. It also underestimates the dangers of reducing weapons to a point where the risk of war would in fact be increased. However, a world where there are adequate controls on the armaments possessed by countries and ways of ensuring compliance to the undertakings and commitments entered into must be more secure than a world without such controls.

NUCLEAR WEAPONS IN THE COLD WAR YEARS

This section examines nuclear weapons and explores why they cause so much concern, and looks at the long-term prospects for their elimination. It assesses the legacy left by the Cold War period, with its nearly half a century of tension and nuclear arms build-up, showing that throughout those years proposals for the control of these weapons were being formulated and discussed. Nuclear weapons added a new dimension to arms control, they had been invented and used, and the awesome nature of these weapons increased the need for agreement but added greatly to the difficulties for its achievement. The potentially devastating implications of the failure of treaties or their implementation made verification essential, yet the tensions of the Cold War made such checks impossible to achieve. In 1945 the United States was the sole nuclear power and would, undoubtedly, have liked to keep it that way. In November the following year the US proposed to the UN General Assembly a plan for the elimination of all nuclear weapons. In this proposal, the Baruch Plan named after Bernard Baruch, one of its authors, the United States would dismantle its weapons and make its civil nuclear know-how available to other countries. A new agency, the International Atomic Development Authority would supervise the disposal of weapons and assist in the development of civil nuclear programmes. The UN General Assembly adopted the plan but the Soviet Union and its 'allies' rejected it on the grounds that it gave the United States an advantage because it called for a monitoring and supervision agency to stop further research, and the US had the knowledge of how to make and use weapons and the Soviet Union did not. In 1949 the Soviet Union tested its own atomic bombs and in 1954 an H-bomb. Britain (1952), France (1960), and China (1964) subsequently became nuclear capable. As the so-called 'Nuclear Club' expanded and the prospects for a world without nuclear weapons receded, so there was greater concern that more and more countries would develop nuclear weapons and the chances of their use, whether intentionally or accidentally, increase.

With the road to disarmament blocked, attention switched increasingly to arms limitation and control. In 1953, Dwight Eisenhower, President of the United States, put forward a suggestion for curbing the proliferation of nuclear weapons to other countries. His scheme, dubbed the 'Atoms for Peace' plan and containing elements of the Baruch Plan, offered to transfer nuclear technology for peaceful uses from the existing nuclear powers to countries which promised not to develop nuclear weapons of their own. 1958 saw the opening, at Eisenhower's initiative, supported by Harold Macmillan (the British Prime Minister) and Nikita Khruschev (the Soviet leader), of the first series of tripartite negotiations for a comprehensive ban on nuclear tests. The Cuban Missile Crisis of 1962 took tensions between the United States and the Soviet Union to fever pitch. Shocked and sobered by this near-miss, the leaders of both superpowers agreed to take steps to improve communications and reduce the risk of it happening again. In 1963 a direct 'hot line' was installed connecting the American President and the Soviet leader. In the same year the United States, the Soviet Union and the United Kingdom signed the Partial Test Ban Treaty (PTBT) banning the testing of nuclear weapons above ground or under water; only allowing underground tests. For the first time the existing nuclear powers (with the exception of France) accepted formally-agreed limitations on their nuclear activities. The same three countries made further efforts to negotiate a complete ban on all tests in talks which lasted from 1977 to 1980.

The two superpowers and the UK also co-operated in drafting, and gaining acceptance for, the globally-applicable nuclear Non-Proliferation Treaty (NPT), which was signed in 1968 and came into effect in 1970. This incorporated the basic deal between the nuclear 'haves' and 'have-nots' which President Eisenhower had proposed back in 1953. The non-nuclear states insisted that the nuclear powers promise to pursue negotiations for nuclear disarmament 'in good faith'; their alleged failure to do so has been a source of controversy ever since. Nevertheless more countries have signed the NPT (for 25 years it was subject to periodic renewal and was renewed indefinitely in 1995 with 174 countries as signatories at that time) than any other international arms control agreement, and it has been seen as at least a partial success. There are now 186 state parties to the treaty, some of which have been hesitant about supporting the continuation of the NPT in its existing form, arguing that it will always be one-sided unless the existing nuclear powers show a greater commitment to disarming themselves. Although there have been extensive reductions in the US and Soviet/Russian arsenals through the Intermediate-Range Nuclear forces (INF) and the Strategic Arms Reduction Treaties (START), as well as by unilateral actions, there are still contradictions in the positions of the declared nuclear weapon states. Also there is the difficulty of the threshold states, India, Pakistan and Israel which are nuclear capable but can only join the NPT as non-weapon states as the NPT 'division' is based on the position in January 1968. Following their 1998 nuclear tests, India and Pakistan are under pressure to adhere to the NPT in that capacity, but India has stood rigidly to its position that it would only do so if there is a time-bound framework for complete nuclear disarmament; and Pakistan is unlikely to join unless India does. At the time of its indefinite renewal in 1995 the NPT Review and Extension Conference set up a framework for non-proliferation and disarmament by agreeing 'Principles and Objectives' for future developments. It was also agreed that there should be a four-week review conference in the year 2000, with Preparatory Committee meetings (PrepComs) to consider ways of ensuring the full implementation of the treaty and to set up the procedures for the review conference. The only non-signatories to the NPT are Cuba and Brazil plus the three Threshold States.

The establishment of Nuclear-Weapon-Free Zones (NWFZ) is allowed for under the terms of the NPT by which any group of states has the right to conclude a regional treaty under which a NWFZ is agreed. Countries within such a zone would be less likely to consider the acquisition of nuclear weapons in light of their confidence that their potential enemies in the region do not already have them and are committed not to change this. In addition to forbidding the acquisition of nuclear weapons the treaties concluded so far also proscribe their presence in the area in question. In 1975 the United Nations agreed principles for the setting up of NWFZs and these allowed for the obligations of such zones to be assumed not only by large groups of states or entire continents or regions, but also by smaller groupings or even a sole state. It decreed that participation must be voluntary and that the initiative should come from within the zone, and that once agreed, the zone would remain free of nuclear weapons, and that there would be an effective verification system to ensure that it does so. Like the NPT itself, the arrangement should include provisions to promote the scientific, technological and economic development of the area through co-operation on the civil use of nuclear energy. The 1967 Treaty of Tlatelolco provides for a NWFZ in Latin America and the Caribbean; the 1985 Treaty of Rarotonga covers the South Pacific; the Treaty of Pelindaba covers Africa and there are prospects for others to follow in South-East Asia; Central Asia; and Central and Eastern Europe. Ukraine and Belarus have called for a zone to be established in the latter area but the present uncertainty about the effects of NATO enlargement make this a contentious issue.

The successful negotiation of these early agreements showed that arms control, if not disarmament, was possible when all the parties concerned could agree that they had a shared interest at stake. During the 1970s a series of agreements dealing with strategic nuclear arms were negotiated in the Strategic Arms Limitation Talks (SALT) which had started between the US and the USSR in 1969. SALT was based on the premise that East-West war would not break out if each side knew that it had enough firepower to threaten, convincingly, to destroy the other even if it was attacked first. Each superpower promised not to deploy strategic weapons above agreed limits and not to deploy defensive systems, under the terms of the Anti-Ballistic Missile (ABM) agreement which might impair the other's ability to threaten destructive retaliation for any attack. These talks were suspended in 1983.

The years 1979-83 were bleak times for East-West arms limitation and control. The build-up of Soviet SS20 INF, with ranges of between 500 and 5,500 km, coincided with the Soviet invasion of Afghanistan and the West's 1979 twin-track decision to deploy its own intermediate-range Cruise and Pershing II weapons while negotiating for the removal of the SS20s. By the mid-1980s the situation had changed dramatically with the Soviet government, under the new enlightened and reform-minded leadership of Mikhail Gorbachev, agreeing to permit what was called 'intrusive verification' of military activity on its soil, allowing outside inspectors to check that the activity was non-threatening in nature, and that it was in accordance with the details provided in the advance notification. This represented a real breakthrough, as previous Soviet governments had always refused to accept this kind of inspection. Gorbachev's agreement to allow it in 1986, together with the many changes he was making within the Soviet Union, seemed to many to open the door to agreements with the US and its allies in other areas too, thus marking the beginning of the end for the Cold War. In the following year the United States and the Soviet Union agreed to eliminate all their intermediate-range nuclear weapons and the INF Treaty was signed by Mr Gorbachev and American President

Ronald Reagan in Washington DC in December 1987 and it included provisions for intrusive verification of the missile destruction process on both sides.

Although the INF agreement led to the elimination of missiles carrying only some 4% of the superpowers' then total number of nuclear warheads, it was the first time agreement had been reached on a measure of actual nuclear disarmament. START, which had started in 1985 but made little progress, received new impetus.

THE END OF THE COLD WAR

The fall of the Berlin Wall in November 1989 increased the feeling that there would be a new age of peace and goodwill between countries which would lead to the creation of what President Bush described as a 'New World Order'. In Western Europe and the United States people began to question the level of expenditure on arms and the military now that the Cold War enemy had gone. Arms control and disarmament offered the prospect of saving money on defence and having it spent on education and health, the so-called 'peace dividend'. However, the invasion of Kuwait by Iraq in 1990 showed that by no means all governments were ready to renounce the use of military force in order to get what they wanted. Civil wars between different ethnic or religious groups were on the increase; the most prominent examples being in Bosnia and Somalia. At the end of 1991 the Soviet Union had broken up into 15 separate states, some of which had disputes within their own borders, with their neighbours, or with Russia, causing many areas of tension.

MEANS OF ACHIEVING ARMS CONTROL AFTER THE COLD WAR

It became clear that arms control had not outlived its usefulness, with new means of control being developed and used during the 1990s. Whereas during the Cold War arms control was carried on mainly via grand formal negotiations, often lasting a long time and involving many countries, since 1989 a variety of methods have been used. Arms control, limitation and disarmament are being conducted by:

Dictation – where a country's arms capability is controlled or dismantled by other countries. Iraq has been subject to this since its defeat in the Gulf War in 1991, with the peace agreement allowing the United Nations to oversee the dismantling of military and industrial facilities which could be used to make nuclear, chemical or biological weapons. In Bosnia, during 1995 and 1996, the UN effectively forced the warring groups to accept peace agreements by a combination of diplomatic persuasion, the denial of arms by military means and the use of NATO air strikes.

Denial – when a group of countries, or the international community as a whole acting through the UN, agree not to allow the export of military equipment or potential weapon production technology to countries which pose a threat to international peace and security. Iraq, Libya and Serbia are countries which have been, or are, the targets of UN arms embargoes.

Direct Dealings – when leading countries, most often the United States, bypass international deliberations and take it upon themselves to come to arrangements directly with 'problem' countries. This happened during 1994 when the Americans reached agreement to provide the government of North Korea, suspected of developing a secret nuclear weapons capability, with advanced technology for nuclear power plants from the US, South Korea and Japan in exchange for North Korea agreeing to freeze the development, and allowing international inspection, of its nuclear facilities. Similar direct diplomacy involving the US with Russia and three other former Soviet states, produced an agreement, also in 1994, whereby Ukraine, Belarus and Kazakhstan agreed to give up the nuclear warheads which had been based on their territory when the Soviet Union fell apart, in exchange for economic assistance and security assurances from the US and the West.

Unilateral Action and Reciprocation – when one country or group decides to reduce or get rid of weapons stockpiles, without waiting for a formal agreement to be signed, in the expectation that others will respond. In September 1991, President Bush announced that all American short-range nuclear weapons then deployed outside US territory would be returned to the United States for storage or destruction. He did this without waiting for the Soviet Union to do the same in the expectation that it would respond with a similar announcement of its own, which it did.

Formal Negotiation and Agreement – the traditional kind of arms control as practised during the Cold War, which, although other methods have been developed and used increasingly in recent years, is by no means redundant. Formal international negotiations have continued on a range of weapons and issues. The main negotiating body is the Conference on Disarmament in Geneva, where some 60 governments are now represented. International pressure was applied to India and Pakistan by the application of sanctions following the carrying out of nuclear tests by those two countries in 1998.

POST-COLD WAR NUCLEAR WEAPON AGREEMENTS

The control and reduction in the numbers of nuclear weapons has continued to form an important part of the overall international arms control and disarmament agenda. The US and Russia have continued the Strategic Arms Reduction Talks, signing START I on 31 July 1991, and START II on 3 January 1993. START II which will leave each side with 3,000-3,500 long-range nuclear weapons; down from over 12,000 each at the height of the Cold War, has yet to enter into force. It was ratified by the US in 1996, but the Russian *Duma* has not yet done so. The *Duma's* approval may be helped by agreements reached in 1997 to provide for an extension period for the implementation to 31 December 2007 and a joint statement to the effect that once START II enters into force, negotiations should begin on START III to further reduce numbers to 2,000 - 2,500 on each side by the same date and increase transparency measures which would make it more difficult to reverse the reductions.

The Comprehensive Test Ban Treaty (CTBT) bans all nuclear tests or any other nuclear explosion anywhere in the world and establishes a global monitoring system to enforce and verify adherence to the treaty and to detect violations of its terms. It is a major step in the upkeep of the NPT.[2] Opened for signature in 1996, 152 countries had signed the treaty by early February 1999. The UK and France were the first two nuclear weapon states to ratify the treaty, doing so simultaneously in April 1998 which at that time brought the number of ratifications to 13, and it will enter into force 180 days after being ratified by 44 named countries. Of these 44, 15 have ratified and all except India, Pakistan and North Korea have signed. Working on an annual budget (1998) of $54.8 million, a Preparatory Commission for the Comprehensive Test Ban Treaty Organisation (CBTBOPrepCom) has been established in Vienna. The technicalities of monitoring and verification are clearly vital and are being covered elsewhere in this publication,[3] along with the question of a Fissile Material Cut-off Treaty.

The decision in 1995 to continue the NPT indefinitely was a major achievement since it increased the pressures on the nuclear weapon states to do even more not only to lower their existing capabilities but also to find ways of reducing their reliance on nuclear weapons and fulfilling their commitment to work towards the elimination of these weapons. This objective is complicated by the position of the three Threshold States, India, Pakistan and Israel, which are all nuclear capable but not signatories to the NPT.

The need for movement towards the elimination of nuclear weapons was emphasised by the Canberra Commission, set up by Paul Keating the then Australian Prime Minister in late 1995, in the report it presented to the UN General Assembly on 30 September 1996. Made up of senior military and political figures from around the world the commission found that nuclear weapons are a source of instability; that their possession by some nations encouraged other states to work towards becoming nuclear capable; and that it is not credible to believe that the present situation can be maintained.

CONTRADICTIONS IN THE CONTINUATION OF THE NPT

As an illustration of the above assertion by the Canberra Commission, the contradiction of the present situation is best summed up in a remark reputedly made by former German Chancellor Kurt Georg Kiesinger that the NPT 'is like a bunch of notorious drunks inviting everyone else to sign the pledge'.

The United Kingdom position was outlined as follows in the 1998 Strategic Defence Review 'The Government wishes to see a safer world in which there is no place for nuclear weapons ... Nevertheless, while large nuclear arsenals and risks of proliferation remain, our minimum deterrent remains a necessary element of our security.'

Russia, with the second largest armoury, is in many ways more reliant now on its nuclear weapons than it was during the Cold War with its massive conventional superiority having been diminished through the implementation of the CFE Treaty and the country's sheer economic decline. The Commander-in-Chief of the Russian Strategic Missile Force, Colonel General Yakovlev, speaking on 6 June 1998 acknowledged that the post-Cold War environment will eventually bring about review of the role of nuclear weapons. But as he told a Russian journalist, 'For Russia, the strategic nuclear force is, and will possibly remain for quite some time, the main and probably the only instrument of the state capable of warding off major military threats'.

The 1998 Chinese White Paper on National Defence emphasised that 'China is a responsible big country and a firm force safeguarding world peace and stability.' However, in spite of many paragraphs given over to China's disarmament efforts and the need for a nuclear free world, it also states 'China has persistently exercised great restraint in the development of nuclear weapons and its nuclear arsenal has been very limited. It has developed nuclear weapons for self-defence, not as a threat to other countries'.

These three statements illustrate the main contradiction – that no country has said, or seems likely to say, that they have developed or are developing a nuclear capability in order to dominate the world, or to destroy their potential enemies. It is always for self-defence and as a deterrent against the other guy – the bad guy – who is threatening them. This is why nuclear weapons are so much a political weapon – both in their use as deterrents and by giving status to their possessors. The United States is the world's only remaining superpower and hegemon. It carries the frequently self-imposed burden of trying to keep the world in order, and believes that different rules apply to its needs. In spite of the large reductions made through the START process and other unilateral measures it seems inconceivable that the US will get rid of its nuclear weapons while there are any left elsewhere.

TO THE CRYSTAL BALL

This chapter has tried, within the confines of a short overview, to summarise the attempts made during the twentieth century to achieve some measure of arms control, especially weapons of mass destruction, and to explore the failures and successes of that process. It would be a brave, and foolish, commentator who would say that there has been true success and that arms have been controlled, but it would be very defeatist and cynical to suggest that nothing has been achieved. Alongside arms control comes confidence-building, not discussed in this paper but nevertheless vital to international security, and the combination of the two should take great credit for the ending of the Cold War. In other words, arms control could undoubtedly have achieved more, but without it the present situation could have been very much worse.

Thus, a decade after the fall of the Soviet bloc, although it looks likely that the twenty-first century will start in a turbulent way, it seems unlikely that there will be a major world war in the foreseeable future. However, the absence of such a war does not mean that the new century will arrive in the peaceful glow of the 'New World Order' which President Bush spoke of when the Cold War ended.

Searching the crystal ball is not like going into the Internet, there are no guidelines, search engines or home pages. Signs for the future must be taken from the current situation and that poses more questions than answers. Fortunately this scribe is only looking at arms control requirements and prospects and not trying to predict anything wider.

Control of weapons of mass destruction remains vital for global security, and it seems to many people that there is currently an environment in which the global community has the opportunity to get rid of nuclear weapons or, if that really is not possible, to find better ways of controlling them for all time. If total nuclear disarmament could be achieved would it make the world safer and more peaceful? Or, merely a safer place in which to fight a 'conventional' war? Yet, can the present system of 'those who have' and 'those who do not have'; and those who have but are not officially recognised as having (the threshold states) continue indefinitely? Would the removal of nuclear weapons increase the dangers of chemical and biological weapons acquisition? Would it seem more acceptable, or sensible to some, to use these if there were no chance of a nuclear response? Yet, could a nuclear response ever be justified as retaliation for the use of chemical or biological weapons? If the declared nuclear weapon states do not move towards the elimination of their capability will some, or all, of the non-weapon states decide that the NPT should be abandoned and develop their own? If that happens how many states will be nuclear capable by, say, 2020?

Will the conventions to control chemical and biological weapons work? Will they stop the development, manufacture and use of these de-stabilising and inhumane weapons? Will the example of Iraq be used to ensure that UN inspectors have access to countries suspected of violations of the conventions?

How can the whole range of other weapons be contained and by what agreements? Will the example of the CFE Treaty be used on other regions to specify the limits on weapon holdings by individual countries, or was that agreement merely possible through the particular conditions of the Cold War? Will controls on the arms trade be able to stop potential aggressors, and violators of human rights and freedoms, getting the armaments they need?

It is impossible to conclude with answers to the above questions, but a few predictions seem possible. The NPT will hold for some time to come, with the two main nuclear weapon states making more substantial reductions by following the START process, leading to pressure on the UK, France and China to join in later negotiations. The threshold states will also be called upon to be more open and to reduce or eliminate their holdings. The Comprehensive Test Ban Treaty will hold and this will assist in the upkeep of the NPT. There will be more nuclear-weapon-free-zones and these will help to develop regional security structures. The nuclear weapon states will come under increasing pressure to implement de-alerting and other measures to reduce or eliminate the chances of accident or mishap.

There will be greater efforts made to control the arms trade with the current UN Register being developed further and more controls on the supply of weapons to unstable and aggressive regimes, or those which are seen to be violating human rights. There will be calls for greater openness both in the trade of arms and the holdings and intentions of states.

The trend of intra-state rather than inter-state conflicts seems likely to continue, thus making it necessary to find more ways of controlling supplies of light weapons and small arms. The de-commissioning of weapons after conflicts is also likely to grow in importance. The need for international coalitions for all aspects of peacekeeping and conflict resolution will increase and this will bring demands for new ways to do the job effectively.[4] The United Nations will be under great pressure to co-ordinate international actions and the position of the United States in world affairs, both within the UN framework and as the remaining superpower will be open to question.

Notes

1 See Chapter 14, p.262.

2 *ibid.*

3 *ibid.*

4 See Complex Emergencies section, p.119.

14

UK Nuclear Weapons Policy after the SDR

MALCOLM CHALMERS

Department of Peace Studies, University of Bradford

INTRODUCTION

In the 1980s, despite widespread public opposition, the British government gave an increasingly prominent role to nuclear weapons in its defence policy. A new strategic system (*Trident* D5) was ordered that would involve a massive increase in capability compared with the *Polaris* system it was due to replace. The government also agreed to the stationing of US ground-launched cruise missiles on British soil as part of a NATO-wide programme. Domestic opposition to these policies, reflected in some of the largest popular protests of the post-war period, only increased the determination of the Thatcher government to press ahead.

During the 1990s, by contrast, the Major government sought a more consensual approach to nuclear policy, adopting many of the proposals for partial denuclearisation that were being made by opposition parties. Aided by the progress in US/Soviet arms control, American nuclear bases at Greenham Common and Holy Loch were closed, with only a token arsenal of US free-fall bombs remaining in stores at Lakenheath.[1] The government also ordered a series of unilateral reductions in Britain's own nuclear forces that would, taken together, leave it with the smallest arsenal of the five recognised nuclear powers. The tactical nuclear roles of the Army and the Royal Navy's surface ships were abandoned altogether. The government sought to answer criticism of *Trident* by announcing in 1993 that 'each submarine will deploy no more than 96 warheads, and could carry significantly fewer', and that the total explosive power carried on each *Trident* submarine would not be much changed from *Polaris*.[2] Perhaps most significantly, it announced that the Royal Air Force's WE-177 free-fall bombs, several hundred of which were in service in the late 1980s, would be withdrawn from service altogether, leaving Britain as the only nuclear power to rely on a single delivery system.[3]

THE SDR

When the Labour Party came to power in May 1997, it ordered a thorough re-evaluation of Britain's nuclear policy as part of its Strategic Defence Review (SDR). This review, the results of which were announced in July 1998, took the process of force reductions, begun under the Conservatives, further in several respects. First, the total arsenal of 'operationally available warheads' is being reduced to 'less than 200', compared with 'less than 300' planned by the previous government. As a result, the total number of operationally available warheads will be reduced to only half the level at the end of the Cold War (when Britain's nuclear force comprised *Chevaline* warheads on *Polaris* missiles as well as 'several hundred' WE-177 free-fall bombs).[4] Second, as a result of the new strategic environment, only one *Trident* submarine will now be on patrol at any time. Third, the number of warheads deployed on each submarine is to be limited to 48: higher than the 32 deployed on *Polaris/Chevaline*, but a reduction from the 60 warheads deployed by the previous Conservative government.[5]

In a marked departure from previous practice, the new government has also been significantly more open about Britain's nuclear programme. As well as revealing more information on the size and cost of the nuclear arsenal, it has become the first nuclear weapon state to declare the total size of its stocks of fissile materials held outside international safeguards. These comprise 7.6 tonnes of plutonium, 21.9 tonnes of highly enriched uranium, and 15,000 tonnes of other forms of uranium. The government has also announced that it will begin a process of declassification and historical accounting 'with the aim of producing by Spring 2000 an initial report of defence fissile material production since the start of Britain's defence nuclear programme in the 1940s.'[6] In addition, national capabilities to verify the reduction and elimination of nuclear weapons are to be developed, drawing on specialist skills at the Aldermaston Atomic Weapons Establish-ment:

> The aim is to ensure that, when the time comes for the inclusion of British nuclear weapons in multilateral negotiations, we will have a significant national capability to contribute to the verification process.[7]

Taken together, these measures constitute an important shift in UK nuclear weapons policy.[8] The reductions in force size and readiness go significantly further than those envisaged by the previous government. Perhaps even more significantly, the SDR reflects a marked shift in declaratory policy, with repeated references to the goal of the 'elimination' of nuclear weapons.

This chapter therefore discusses ways in which the British government could promote more progress towards this goal on a multilateral level. It suggests that the UK should promote the formation of a Five-Power Nuclear Forum that would explore ways in which the recognised nuclear weapon states can discharge their shared responsibility, under the Non-Proliferation Treaty (NPT), to pursue nuclear disarmament in good faith. Initially, the most fruitful areas for discussion in such a forum would probably be the establishment of transparency regimes in relation to stocks of both unsafeguarded fissile material and warheads. In the medium term, it could also be used to discuss how the smaller nuclear powers could play a part in multilateral force reductions once the US and Russia have concluded a START III agreement.

WORKING WITH FRANCE

Since 1990, France's nuclear posture has undergone a reorientation similar in many respects to that in the UK. After a doubling in the size of its nuclear arsenal during the 1980s, France has become increasingly willing to take part in international discussions on arms control and non-proliferation. It has joined the NPT, and its production of fissile material for military purposes has ended. Like the UK, it has also made a series of unilateral reductions in the size and composition of its nuclear arsenal. The *Hades* tactical ballistic missile was dismantled in 1997, and the last S3-D strategic land-based missiles were withdrawn from service in 1998. The strategic missile submarine (SSBN) fleet has been reduced from six to four, and the size of the nuclear arsenal reduced by 20-25%.[9] The nuclear equipment budget has fallen from FFr32 billion in 1990 to FFr16 billion for 1998: reducing its share of the total French defence budget from 17% to 10%.[10]

As a result of these measures, together with those made by the UK, the two European nuclear powers can justifiably claim to have made a significant contribution to the nuclear disarmament process since the end of the Cold War. Given the relatively small size of their arsenals, Britain and France could have adopted a 'wait and see' approach, delaying disarmament steps until the US and Russia had reduced their own arsenals more sharply. Instead, responding to the marked improvement in their strategic environment, both powers have pressed ahead with reductions in force levels.

Yet, while both countries have pressed ahead with unilateral disarmament steps, they have remained reluctant to suggest ways in which their forces might be involved directly in disarmament negotiations. On the one hand, they have emphasised the need for substantially more progress in the START talks between the US and Russia before the smaller nuclear powers can be expected to join. On the other hand, after strong resistance from the UK, and a final set of tests by France, both powers have signed up to the Comprehensive Test Ban Treaty (CTBT). Both countries are also strong supporters of a Fissile Material Cut-Off Treaty (FMCT). While very welcome, however, both these latter measures are more effective as non-proliferation measures (capping the programmes of India, Pakistan and other potential new nuclear weapon states) than as contributions to the disarmament of the recognised nuclear weapon states. As a result, many non-nuclear NPT signatory states are actively questioning whether support for these proposals, by itself, adequately fulfils the responsibility of all five nuclear weapon states to pursue nuclear disarmament in good faith. The slow progress of START has added to the general sense of dissatisfaction with the nuclear weapon states.

With left-of-centre governments now in office in both Britain and France, there are some signs of a more constructive approach to multilateral disarmament. Britain and France were the first nuclear weapon states to ratify the CTBT, doing so together on 6 April 1998. They remain the only nuclear weapons state to have done so. Moreover, shortly after the publication of the SDR, the British government indicated that it was considering how best to take forward the multilateral disarmament agenda:

> We are actively considering how best to follow up internationally the initiatives on nuclear disarmament set out in the Strategic Defence Review. We would not rule out the possibility that a forum of all the Nuclear Weapon States could make a constructive contribution to the process of nuclear disarmament.[11]

TRANSPARENCY REGIMES

The establishment of such a forum would be a welcome step forward. If the nuclear weapon states were to avoid raising unjustified expectations for action, however, it would be important to ensure that a clear agenda of initial subjects for discussion could be agreed at an early stage. One of the most promising areas in which progress might be feasible in such a forum might be in relation to transparency measures. Greater transparency is a necessary condition for progress in many aspects of the nuclear disarmament agenda. It can help the nuclear weapon states assure each other that they are each committed to restraint and reduction, increasing the demonstration effect from unilateral reductions and increasing the political costs of unilateral increases. By allowing for the introduction of verification of nuclear capabilities, it can, over time, increase mutual confidence that states are not concealing additional capabilities. As a consequence, it can help create conditions in which further arms control can be implemented more effectively. Transparency need not wait for disarmament. Rather it can be seen as a necessary, although not sufficient, precondition for it.

Perhaps the area in which there is the strongest case for the development of five-power transparency measures is in relation to stocks of fissile material held outside international safeguards. The Conference on Disarmament has now established a committee that will negotiate a ban on the production of fissile materials. But there remain profound disagreements over how far such a ban should also involve constraints on existing stocks of fissile material, with many non-nuclear weapon states emphasising the need to see a fissile cut-off as part of a process of nuclear disarmament.

The new British government may be sympathetic to such concerns. In September 1996, the Labour Party proposed that:

> the nuclear weapons states should declare their existing inventories of plutonium and highly enriched uranium, and open to inspection their nuclear production facilities.[12]

Labour followed up this commitment once in office. In the SDR, Britain became the first nuclear weapon state to announce the size of its stock of fissile material held outside international safeguards. It also described the proposed FMCO as 'an essential step towards global elimination of nuclear weapons',[13] thus rejecting the suggestion that such a treaty would only be concerned with preventing further proliferation.

Rather than seeking to tackle the issue of stocks within the FMCT regime itself, however, there may be a stronger case for examining the issue within a forum the membership which is confined to the five recognised nuclear weapon states. The use of such a forum would avoid the difficulties involved in discussing the stockpiles of the three nuclear weapon states that remain outside the NPT (India, Israel and Pakistan). It would also allow the development of intrusive verification regimes which, if extended to non-nuclear states, might risk transferring sensitive nuclear weapons-related information. In order to contribute to general confidence in the progress being made in reducing stockpiles, moreover, regular summary declarations of stockpiles could be provided to the non-nuclear weapon states.

A verifiable fissile stockpile transparency regime could make a major contribution to the process of nuclear disarmament, laying the foundation for future reductions (both unilateral and multilateral) and making it progressively more difficult for any of the five powers to retain hidden stockpiles. It would not include fissile stockpiles held by non-signatories of the NPT. If any of these states are allowed to obtain a status similar to that of NPT nuclear weapon states at some future date, however, they would be obliged to accept membership of the transparency regime as a condition of doing so. Membership of the 'nuclear club' is too commonly seen as involving rights without obligations. The creation of an additional obligation that would be borne only by members of that club would be an important step towards redressing this imbalance.

A similar transparency regime could be envisaged in relation to stocks of nuclear warheads. During bilateral discussions with Russia in the Joint Working Group on Safeguards, Transparency and Irreversibility, the US proposed a nuclear warhead transparency regime involving the regular exchange of information on stockpiles of warheads and fissile material, together with intrusive reciprocal monitoring and inspection arrangements.[14] Although these discussions were broken off by Russia in 1995, US initiatives along these lines are likely to re-emerge once START III negotiations begin. Even if such measures are sidelined in order to achieve a quick agreement to reduce US and Russian arsenals to around 2,000 START-accountable warheads each, they are likely to be a central concern of subsequent negotiations. As the number of deployed strategic warheads is reduced, the relative importance of other forces (such as strategic warheads held in reserve and tactical nuclear weapons) is increasing. Further reductions in strategic arsenals is therefore likely to depend on agreement on a parallel dismantlement and transparency regime for weapons that are currently not START-accountable.

Although the first steps towards such a regime are probably best left to bilateral US/Russian discussions, Britain and France should make clear their willingness, in principle, to take part in negotiations to expand a bilateral transparency agreement to include all five nuclear weapon states. While the expansion of START itself to include Britain, France and China will have to await much steeper reductions in US and Russian arsenals than are currently envisaged, no such constraint is required for a five-power regime that only involves transparency. At the same time, while such a regime would involve no formal restraints on the size of arsenals, it would help to encourage the already developing competition between the smaller nuclear powers to show that they can manage with fewer nuclear arsenals than their counterparts, while helping to expose unjustified claims of restraint.

Critics of such a proposal would argue that there is little chance of persuading either China or Russia to support it. A similar counsel of despair has been heard in the early stages of most new arms control initiatives. Yet recent experience suggests, for example in relation to bans on landmines and chemical weapons, that sustained lobbying can achieve remarkable progress in bringing about change in international norms. Given the strength of the international desire for further progress on nuclear disarmament, moreover, this may be an issue to which key non-nuclear states – such as Japan and Germany – will be willing to devote a high political priority.

Even if proposals for increased nuclear transparency do not

immediately gain support from China and Russia, however, the Western nuclear powers could gain considerable political credit by pushing for such ideas themselves. Not least, Britain and France could enhance the acceptability of their approach with their EU partners, many of which still see the two countries as insufficiently committed to taking the nuclear disarmament process forwards.

At the same time as pressing for a multilateral transparency agreement, Britain and France could also explore possibilities for further increasing nuclear openness on a unilateral basis. It would not be appropriate to agree to a verifiable regime without the agreement of the other nuclear powers. But the two countries should consider doing more to reveal details of their fissile material programmes, as well as their warhead stockpiles. In parallel with such steps, the two governments should also invest in co-operative development of the verification capabilities that will be necessary for taking the disarmament process forwards. Such co-operation should be well-publicised, helping to assure non-nuclear states that the nuclear powers take their responsibilities under Article V of the NPT seriously.

This combination of proposals for five-power action and unilateral measures would not minimise the many problems ahead, both technical and political. Nor would it specify in advance the exact nature of the final goal (other states may not share the UK's commitment to 'elimination'). But it would do much to assure other states that the three Western nuclear powers are now strongly committed to rapid progress in this area. It would thus provide a solid and united front, including both nuclear and non-nuclear states, that could bring pressure to bear on Russia and China to follow suit. Over time, it would aim to create circumstances in which it will be as difficult for Russia and China to reject increased nuclear transparency as it was for China and France to ignore the international consensus against testing in 1995 and 1996.

START IV AND THE SMALL NUCLEAR POWERS

Over the next decade, the main focus of negotiated nuclear reductions will remain the bilateral US / Russia START talks. These talks have now been stalled for several years by the refusal of the Russian *Duma* to ratify the START II treaty. Yet there is now a growing expectation that ratification may be imminent, not least because of the growing realisation in Russia that it cannot afford to maintain its strategic arsenal at current levels. If START II ratification does take place, a START III agreement could follow quickly, committing both countries to reduce their strategic arsenals to 2,000 warheads each by 2007.

Pressure for disarmament by the two nuclear superpowers will not end with the conclusion of START III. As early as 2003 or 2004, therefore, the US and Russia could be engaged in START IV negotiations aimed at cutting their arsenals well below START III levels: perhaps to 1,000 warheads or so each. Such talks will have particular urgency for Russia, which may be finding it increasingly difficult to finance even START III force levels.

As the US and Russia contemplate reductions to 1,000 warheads each, however, the position of other nuclear powers will become increasingly relevant to their discussions. Russia may voice concern over the possibility of the other four nuclear powers combining against it. Perhaps even more seriously, both the US and Russia may become increasingly concerned at the threat to their political status of agreeing force ceilings that might, at some future date, be exceeded by a third power. Neither country is likely to accept a START IV agreement that allowed an unconstrained China to become the world's largest nuclear power. Both countries might also want some reassurance that the combined arsenals of France and Britain (currently around 600) would not exceed their own. Cold War strategic arms control was built on the twin principles of parity (between the two superpowers) and superiority (over all others). Even if sound on technical grounds, a START IV agreement that did not sustain these two principles would be very difficult to sell to the legislatures of either of the two Cold War superpowers.

It is difficult to envisage all five powers agreeing binding limits on their forces as part of START IV, not least because it would be difficult for the smaller nuclear powers to accept an agreement that enshrined their inferior status permanently in treaty form. The issue of limits on the forces of all five powers could be tackled when the possibility of reducing US and Russian arsenals to the level of Britain and France (that is, 200-400 warheads each) is being seriously discussed. Until then, however, a five-power transparency regime – in place prior to START IV talks – could play an important role in assuaging US and Russian concerns without placing binding ceilings on European and Chinese forces. The smaller nuclear powers could use such a regime to demonstrate that they were restraining their forces at low levels, perhaps accompanying these declarations with unilateral commitments not to increase their arsenals.

REDEFINING MINIMUM DETERRENCE

Over the next decade, parallel START IV and five-power transparency regime agreements could bring about a situation in which all five recognised nuclear powers have reduced their arsenals to levels of 1,000 warheads or less. Debate is then likely to turn to whether other countries can move towards 'minimum deterrent' postures similar to those already adopted by the UK and France: less than 400 warheads in total, only a fraction of which are on alert at any one time.

In considering the possibility of all five nuclear weapon states adopting such postures, however, 'minimum deterrence' cannot simply be defined in terms of the total stockpile of warheads, or even the number of warheads that are deployed. Allowance also has to be made for the estimated rate of attrition by enemy countermeasures, including anti-submarine warfare, anti-ballistic missile defences and anti-aircraft defences. The more exposed that countries feel themselves to be to such measures, other things being equal, the larger and more diversified a 'minimum deterrent' force they are likely to believe they require.

Yet defining the minimum level of force required for deterrence purposes involves political as well as military-technical calculations. In particular, it rests on an assessment of the level of damage with which a potential opponent would have to be threatened in order to deter it from whatever actions (including nuclear aggression) need to be deterred. Current calculations on levels of unacceptable damage still appear to be derived from the experience of early Cold War rivalry with the Soviet Union. During this period, on the basis of the bitter experience of the Second World War, it was assumed that totalitarian powers might be prepared to sacrifice a large part of their own societies in pursuit of the greater goal of world domination. Yet this world-ideological struggle is now at an end. Limited clashes between Western powers and others (possibly including Russia and China) remain a possibility. But, even if nuclear deterrence might still play a role in such conflicts, it can do so at much lower levels of threatened destruction than in the struggle for world domination that lay at the heart of the Cold War. Minimum deterrence might even be consistent with zero arsenals, since the knowledge that nuclear weapons could be rebuilt might be enough in itself to encourage the peaceful resolution, or limitation, of disputes.[15]

Progress towards minimum deterrence at low levels will also have to involve consideration of whether nuclear weapons could be used in response to the use of other Weapons of Mass Destruction (WMD) in regional conflicts by smaller powers (for example in a future Gulf War). This scenario is now often used in discussion of possible levels of minimum deterrence. In concentrating on the possible deterrent utility of nuclear threats in such circumstances, however, analysts tend to ignore the profoundly damaging consequences for global security that breaching the 53-year taboo on nuclear use would involve. Rather than going down the road of relying on nuclear first use in such scenarios, therefore, the major powers should continue to explore ways of minimising the role of nuclear weapons. In particular, the three Western nuclear powers should make clear their determination to overthrow, by conventional means, any regime that uses WMD in a regional conflict.[16]

REPLACING *TRIDENT*

Some of the most heated controversy over Britain's nuclear force in the past, for example in the late 1950s and early 1980s has been precipitated by modernisation decisions. Future British governments are therefore likely to want to postpone any decision on a possible *Trident* replacement for as long as possible. This determination is likely to be increased by the possible financial costs involved. UK defence spending has already fallen sharply since 1990, and is due to fall by a further 4% in real terms over the next three years as a result of the SDR. Unless a profound deterioration in Britain's strategic environment takes place, this trend of gentle decline seems likely to continue into the next century: generating further pressure for economies in military commitments and capabilities.

To some extent, Britain's nuclear force is protected from these pressures by its relatively low cost. Capital expenditure on the *Trident* programme is almost complete, with 91% of the total cost having been incurred by February 1998. The annual direct operating costs of the *Trident* force over its 30-year lifetime still amount to £280 million, and a further £410 million is currently being spent annually on the nuclear warhead programme.[17] Even if some additional allowance is made for indirect costs, the nuclear force is unlikely to account for much more than 5% of the total UK defence budget during the next decade.

If a future government were to replace *Trident* with a system of similar or greater sophistication, however, it could place considerable strain on the defence budget. The capital cost of the *Trident* programme has amounted to £12.5 billion at 1997/98 economic conditions,[18] with annual spending on the programme peaking at more than £1 billion a year (in today's prices) in the late 1980s and early 1990s. If a *Trident* replacement were to cost a comparable amount, it would require a considerable, and very unpopular, diversion of resources from other areas of the budget.

The cost of a *Trident* replacement is not of immediate concern. The first three submarines have just been deployed (starting in December 1994), and the government appears to be assuming a planned life of 30 years. If this assumption is correct, the government will not need to make a firm decision on the form that replacement should take, if any, until around 2010-2015, although preparatory studies might have to be ordered during 2007-2010.[19] If the planned life of a key element (the warhead, missile or boat) is reduced to 25 years, however, preparatory studies on replacement options might have to begin sooner.

The nature of the replacement debate, when it comes, is likely to be strongly influenced by progress in global disarmament. It is unlikely that any of today's other small nuclear powers (China, France, India, Pakistan and Israel) will have given up their capabilities unilaterally by 2010. It is also possible that other small nuclear powers (North Korea, Iraq, Iran?) may have emerged. In these circumstances, the possibility of the UK unilaterally renouncing its nuclear force is unlikely to be any more acceptable politically than it is at present. If recent trends towards an improved strategic environment in Europe continue, however, *Trident* could be replaced by a smaller and less expensive force than at present. Even if the possibility of conflict with Russia is still a factor in force planning, the continuing decline in Russian counter-measure capability may still allow the UK to reduce the resources it devotes to ensuring force survivability. If nuclear weapons are to be retained solely as a balance to the forces of other small nuclear powers, however, the levels of readiness required could be very low indeed. The ability to deploy nuclear weapons within a few days or weeks would be retained, but the requirement to maintain a force of ships, aircraft or missiles dedicated solely to the nuclear role could be abandoned.

The conditions may not exist for such measures when the time comes for *Trident* replacement. By raising the possibility of alternative options for replacement, however, one can see that the British government has a particular financial and political stake in making rapid progress in global disarmament over the next decade.

CONCLUSION

With *Trident* deployed, and serious discussion of its replacement still a decade or so away, the British government could choose to put the nuclear issue on the 'back burner', concentrating the energies of its politicians and officials on more pressing concerns. This would be a serious mistake. Britain now has an opportunity to use the momentum created by the SDR to press for new nuclear initiatives, including the creation of a new five-power transparency regime covering both warheads and fissile material. The government's stated aim is 'to take forward the process of nuclear disarmament to ensure that our security in future can be secured without nuclear weapons'.[20] Whether that objective can be attained before decision time for *Trident* replacement may depend, in part, on the government's willingness to pursue an activist approach to nuclear disarmament over the next five years.

Notes

1. Peter Almond, 'NATO Tactical Nuclear Weapons: Going, Going, Gone?', *Disarmament Diplomacy,* 12, January 1997, p.9.
2. Malcolm Rifkind, Defence Secretary, *UK Defence Strategy: A Continuing Role for Nuclear Weapons?,* speech to Centre for Defence Studies, 16 November 1993.
3. Implementation of this commitment was completed in August 1998. Ministry of Defence, 'All WE177 nuclear bombs dismantled by the end of August 1998', Press Release 200/98, July 30, 1998. 'Deterrence, Arms Control and Proliferation', Supporting Essay Five, in *The Strategic Defence Review*, July 1998, p.5-2 (henceforth, *Strategic Defence Review*.)
4. *Strategic Defence Review*, p.5-2. Figures for 'operationally available warheads' exclude 'missile warheads held as a necessary processing margin or for technical surveillance purposes.'
5. According to a government statement subsequent to the Review announcement,

the first *Trident* submarine, HMS *Vanguard*, first deployed on patrol with slightly fewer than 60 warheads, prior to *Trident* will also be assuming a sub-strategic role. The other two *Trident* submarines currently in service are typically deployed on patrol with 60 warheads. The process of removing 12 warheads from each of these boats will be completed by the end of 1998. The implementation of the Review will not require the decommissioning of any warheads, but will lead to changes in planned future production and refurbishment. George Robertson MP, *House of Commons Written Answer*, 16 July 1998.

[6] *Strategic Defence Review*, pp.5-10.

[7] *Strategic Defence Review*, pp.5-11.

[8] For a more detailed analysis of the nuclear review, see Malcolm Chalmers, 'Bombs Away? Britain and Nuclear Weapons under New Labour', mimeo, 1999.

[9] Camille Grand, *'A French Nuclear Exception?'*, Occasional Paper No. 38, The Henry L. Stimson Center, January 1998.

[10] Jacques Fontanel and Jean-Paul Hebert, 'The end of the 'French Grandeur Policy'', *Defence and Peace Economics*, 8, 1997, p.40; statement by Ambassador Joelle Bourgois, 27 April 1998, quoted in *Disarmament Diplomacy*, May 1998, p.31.

[11] Baroness Symons, Minister of State in the Foreign Office, *Parliamentary Written Answer*, 30 July 1998.

[12] Labour Party, *A Fresh Start for Britain: Labour's Strategy for Britain in the Modern World*, September 1996, p.14.

[13] *Strategic Defence Review*, pp.5-10.

[14] Shannon Kile, 'Nuclear arms control' in *SIPRI Yearbook 1998*, Oxford University Press, 1998, 417.

[15] For an interesting contribution to this debate, see Michael Mazarr, 'Virtual Nuclear Arsenals', *Survival*, Autumn 1995, pp.7-26.

[16] For further discussion, see Malcolm Chalmers, *British Nuclear Weapons Policy: The Next Steps*, International Security Information Service, May 1997.

[17] *Strategic Defence Review*, pp.5-6 to 5-7. In addition to these recurrent costs, the capital cost of the *Trident* programme has amounted to £12.5 billion at 1997/8 economic conditions.

[18] *ibid.*

[19] Assuming a thirty-year service life for each boat, one boat can be kept at sea at all times until either the second boat is retired in 2025 or the third boat in 2027 (these boats first entered service in 1995 and 1997 respectively). Fourteen years elapsed between the initial UK/US agreement to buy *Trident* C4 missiles in 1980 and *Trident* entering into service in 1994. Assuming a similar lead-time for *Trident's* replacement, this implies that a decision on the form that it should take would be made between 2010 and 2015.

[20] *Strategic Defence Review*, pp.5-6.

15

CTBT Verification: No Longer Just Testing

TREVOR FINDLAY[1]

Executive Director, Verification Research, Training and Infromation Centre (VERTIC)

INTRODUCTION

A treaty banning nuclear tests in all environments for all time has been the Holy Grail of arms controllers since the 1960s. When the Comprehensive Nuclear-Test-Ban Treaty (CTBT) was finally concluded in late 1996, with all five declared nuclear weapon states as early signatories, it was regarded as a triumph of diplomacy, an overdue codification of a long-emerging norm against nuclear testing and a watershed event in the history of nuclear weapons. As of 29 October 1998, 151 states had signed the treaty and 21 had ratified.[2] But the story does not end there. There are at least three challenges confronting the treaty. First, it has an unusually demanding entry-into-force provision which may stop it entering into force for years – despite having the overwhelming support of the international community. Second, the treaty envisages the establishment of a substantial verification and compliance regime that is dependent on a high degree of international co-operation and the synergistic operation of several complex monitoring technologies and techniques. Finally, the unexpected nuclear tests by India and Pakistan in May 1998, as well as heightening the CTBT's saliency, have called into question both its verifiability and its relevance to today's most serious cases of nuclear proliferation. While this chapter will focus on verification and compliance issues facing the CTBT, it will touch on all three challenges.

THE COMPREHENSIVE NUCLEAR-TEST-BAN TREATY

Negotiations on the CTBT formally began in January 1994 in the Conference on Disarmament (CD) in Geneva, the single multilateral arms control and disarmament negotiating forum in the United Nations system. Preparatory discussions had begun years before, particularly with regard to the verification of the treaty by seismic means. The negotiations also drew on previous attempts to negotiate a trilateral CTBT by the United Kingdom, the United States and the Soviet Union between the 1960s and 1980s. By the end of 1996, after intensive bargaining and last-minute concessions by key states in the CD, most notably the nuclear weapon states (China, France, Russia, the UK and US), the draft treaty commanded clear majority support. Only India opposed the text outright. Since consensus is required for the CD to transmit a treaty to the UN General Assembly in New York for its approval and opening for signature, it appeared that the CTBT was stymied. However Australia staged a procedural coup by tabling an identical version of the treaty, sponsored by 127 member states, which was adopted by the assembly on 10 September 1996. The treaty was opened for signature at UN headquarters on 24 September, when 71 states signed it, including the five declared nuclear weapon states.

The treaty is 'comprehensive' in banning all nuclear test explosions in all environments – underground, under water and in the atmosphere. It bans not just nuclear weapon tests, but so-called 'peaceful nuclear explosions', the use of nuclear explosives for civil engineering purposes like the diversion of rivers or creation of underground storage cavities.[3] The treaty does not define a nuclear explosion, a decision borne of tortuous but ultimately fruitless attempts by international lawyers, diplomats and nuclear scientists to arrive at a satisfactory, agreed definition. However, the negotiating record indicates a common understanding, at least on the part of the nuclear weapon states, that the treaty bans any explosion which produces a chain-reaction, however small. So-called 'sub-critical' nuclear tests, in which some atoms undergo fission, are not banned.[4] The treaty also does not ban computer simulations of nuclear tests. Such decisions have important implications for the verifiability of the treaty, since they narrow the range of activities to be monitored and the facilities to be inspected. Finally, the treaty does not ban preparations to test, partly because it was found to be difficult to define 'preparations', but also because most states parties will also be parties to the nuclear Non-Proliferation Treaty (NPT), which bans the acquisition of nuclear devices by non-nuclear weapon states and subjects them to an increasingly stringent nuclear safeguards verification regime.[5]

In order to help implement the treaty, the establishment of a Comprehensive Nuclear- Test-Ban Treaty Organisation (CTBTO) is envisaged, located in Vienna, Austria. It will comprise three organs. A Conference of States Parties will oversee the treaty's implementation and the activities of the other two organs and review compliance with the treaty's provisions. The Executive Council, with 51 states parties as members, will be the principal decision-making body and be responsible for supervising the activities of the Technical Secretariat, the third organ. The Secretariat, headed by a Director-General, will assist states parties in implementing the treaty and will carry out verification and other functions.

Pending entry into force of the treaty, a Preparatory Commission for the CTBTO, or PrepCom, has been operating since being established by a meeting of signatory states in November 1996. It is charged with establishing the global verification regime and preparing for entry into force. It comprises two bodies: a plenary composed of all states signatories and a Provisional Technical Secretariat (PTS). The Executive Secretary of the PrepCom and head of the PTS is Wolfgang Hoffmann of Germany, appointed in March 1997. The PrepCom also has two subsidiary bodies: Working Group A on administrative and budgetary matters and Working Group B on verification issues, as well as an Advisory Group on financial, budgetary and associated administrative issues. The antecedent organs of the future CTBTO are thus in place. The expectation is that they and their personnel will simply transmogrify into the CTBTO on entry into force of the treaty.

The treaty's most unusual and controversial feature is its entry-into-force provisions. Article XIV of the treaty provides that it enter into force 180 days after the 44 states listed in its Annex 2 have ratified it, 'but in no case earlier than two years after its opening for signature'. The list comprises the states believed most likely to have the capability to conduct a nuclear test explosion. It includes all the states that formally participated in the 1996 session of the CD, when the treaty was being negotiated, and all those listed by the International Atomic Energy Agency (IAEA) in 1995 as having nuclear research reactors and in 1996 as having nuclear power reactors. While designed to ensure that all states essential to the success of the CTBT become states parties before it enters into force, this provision paradoxically gives the power of veto over entry-into-force to India, the sworn enemy of the treaty, to lukewarm states like Pakistan and North Korea, and to signatories like Israel which are unlikely to ratify soon. Unlike many international agreements, where those states favouring the measure proceed collectively, on the grounds that it offers them net benefits even without universality (and in the expectation that universality may eventually be achieved anyway), the CTBT demands an inclusivity that may yet prove self-defeating. This situation was given added piquancy in May 1998 by the spectacle of India and Pakistan snubbing their noses at the international community by conducting multiple nuclear tests.

THE VERIFICATION SYSTEM

Historically, debate about the merits or otherwise of a comprehensive ban on nuclear testing has largely turned on the verifiability of such a ban. Decades have been spent arguing about the level of detection possible, most concern being expressed about small underground nuclear tests, especially those below one kiloton.[6] On several occasions negotiations over a ban on underground tests broke down over the question of verification. In the most recent bout of negotiations that produced the current treaty, it was apparent that once the nuclear weapon states conceded that they could live without nuclear testing the next big obstacle was verification. The treaty therefore contains an elaborate verification regime which, although lacking the scale of that of the Chemical Weapons Convention (CWC), is global, intrusive, technically complex and backed by a standing international organisation.

It was also planned to be relatively cheap, the original estimate being only $80 million for annual running costs. Concerned about the rising costs of international organisations, the United States, the United Kingdom and others set strict design parameters on the verification system. This had wider implications for verification than simply keeping costs in check, since China, India and others feared that unless a more robust multilateral monitoring system were created there would be increased need for on-site inspections and increased reliance on the so-called National Technical Means (NTM) of the most technologically advanced states.[7] 'National Technical Means' is an arms control euphemism, sometimes used only to refer to national satellite monitoring capabilities, but in effect meaning any legal means by which states collect information on each others' activities.

Article IV of the treaty and a lengthy protocol detail the verification regime to be established upon entry into force. It comprises:

- an International Monitoring System (IMS), including an International Data Centre (IDC), in Vienna;
- consultation and clarification mechanisms;
- on-site inspection (OSI); and
- confidence-building measures (CBMs).

Verification activities are to be based on 'objective information', limited to the subject matter of the treaty and carried out with 'full respect for the sovereignty of States Parties and in the least intrusive manner possible consistent with the effective and timely accomplishment of their objectives'. Expressed herein is the classic verification dilemma: intrusiveness versus effectiveness. As in the case of the Chemical Weapons Convention (CWC), each state party will have the right to take measures to protect sensitive installations and prevent disclosure of confidential information not related to the treaty. However, in return, states are obliged not to interfere with elements of the verification regime, including NTM. For its part, the CTBTO will be required to take all necessary measures to protect the confidentiality of information related to civil and military activities and facilities obtained during the verification process.

All states parties are obliged both to refrain from abusing the right of verification and actively co-operating in it by establishing a National Authority to deal with CTBT matters. Each National Authority will establish the necessary facilities and communication systems to allow it to participate in the international verification system; provide data obtained from national stations that are part of the system; participate in consultation and clarification processes; permit on-site inspections OSI when necessary; and facilitate CBMs. An important political demand of the developing countries – that they be treated as equals in the verification process no matter how poor, technologically backward or irrelevant to the central purposes of the treaty – is enshrined in the treaty. It provides that all states parties, 'irrespective of their technical and financial capabilities, shall enjoy the equal right of verification and assume the equal obligation to accept verification'. While this will result in redundancies and added expense, it was seen as crucial in maintaining broad international support for the treaty.

The three key technical means of verification will be seismic, radionuclide and infrasound/hydroacoustic. A number of other promising detection technologies were not included in the verification regime on the grounds of cost, political sensitivity or uncertainty as to their efficacy. The treaty therefore provides for continuing improvement of the regime and examination of the potential of additional monitoring techniques such as electromagnetic pulse or satellite monitoring. The PrepCom is already pursuing such issues with the establishment of a committee to examine the possibilities.

The International Monitoring System (IMS)

The purpose of the IMS is to detect and identify nuclear explosions prohibited by the treaty. It will include 50 primary and 120 auxiliary seismological stations equipped to detect seismic activity and distinguish between natural events such as earthquakes and nuclear explosions. The IMS will also include 80 radionuclide stations designed to detect and identify radioactive particles released into the atmosphere during a nuclear explosion, including 40 which can detect relevant noble gases such as argon-37, xenon-133 and krypton-85. These stations will be supported by 16 laboratories to analyse the samples detected. Finally, 60 infrasound and 11 hydroacoustic stations will be established to detect the sound of a nuclear explosion in the atmosphere or under water, respectively.

Scattered world-wide, the various monitoring stations will transmit a continuous stream of data to the International Data Centre (IDC). The only exceptions are the auxiliary seismic stations, which will only transmit data on request. The IDC will produce integrated lists of all signals detected by the IMS, possibly up to 200,000 annually, as well as standard event lists and bulletins. It will also produce so-called 'screened event bulletins' that filter out events that appear to be non-nuclear. Both raw and processed data will be available to all states parties, although in practice only a handful will bother to do their own processing and only one, the United States, is likely to have the capacity or incentive to process all of it nationally.

A critical principle of the CTBT is that the IDC's provision of this information to states will be 'without prejudice to final judgements with regard to the nature of any event, which shall remain the responsibility of States Parties'.[8] As the capacity of the Technical Secretariat and IDC grows, however, it will be interesting to see how they finesse the fine line between providing an analysis of what may or may not be a nuclear event and reaching a judgement about such an event. Ultimately this may not matter, since a leaked judgement by the Secretariat would soon find its way into the hands of a state party, which could then raise the suspected violation in the Executive Council.

Consultation and Clarification Mechanisms

States parties are encouraged by the treaty to attempt to revolve, either among themselves, or through the CTBTO, concerns about possible non-compliance, including ambiguous events, before resorting to a request for on-site inspection or other action. Strict deadlines are set for an accused state to respond to a request for clarification, either from a state party or from the Executive Council (48 hours), and for the Executive Council to respond to a state party's request for assistance in obtaining clarification (24 hours). This is meant to preclude procrastination by a suspected treaty violator. If the requesting state is dissatisfied with the response, it may request a meeting of the Executive Council at which action under Article V of the treaty, 'Measures to redress a situation and to ensure compliance, including sanctions', may be decided.

On-Site Inspection (OSI)

Any state party has the right to seek an on-site inspection on the territory or in any other place under the jurisdiction or control of any other state party to determine whether a nuclear test has been conducted. An inspection term would be expected to collect evidence such as air and soil samples and measurements of earth and groundwater displacements. Additionally or alternatively, it may involve overflights of suspected test sites by aircraft or helicopters. An OSI request may be based on information collected by the IMS or, more controversially, 'any relevant technical information' obtained by NTM 'in a manner consistent with generally recognised principles of international law', or on a combination thereof.[9]

Here the deadlines are much tighter. The Director-General must communicate the request to the named state party within six hours and to the Executive Council and all other states parties within 24 hours. The Executive Council is enjoined to take a decision within 96 hours of receiving the request. A decision to approve an OSI must be made by at least 30 affirmative votes out of 51. This so-called 'green light' provision is in contrast to the CWC, in which the 'red light' provision requires a three-quarter majority of votes to stop an OSI proceeding.[10] A separate decision is, however, required by the Executive Council, for an OSI team to conduct drilling, the most likely means of detecting radioactivity caused by an underground nuclear test.

Any OSI must be restricted to an area not exceeding 1,000 square kilometres, with no linear distance greater than 50 kilometres in any direction. As for the speed of the inspection itself, the team must arrive at the point of entry to the receiving state no later than six days following the request for an OSI. The inspected state is obliged to cooperate fully with the OSI, but does have the right to take necessary measures to protect its national security interests and prevent disclosure of confidential information not related to the purpose of the inspection. Nonetheless the inspected state is obliged to provide access to suspect sites, including 'physical access of the inspection team and the inspection equipment to, and the conduct of inspection activities within, the inspection area'. This pedantic wording may well have been inspired by the difficulties experienced by the UN Special Commission (UNSCOM) in conducting OSIs in Iraq. The treaty also contains provisions to avoid 'frivolous or abusive' OSI requests. OSIs cannot be used to confirm suspicions that a state party is preparing to test but only that it has tested.

The treaty's OSI provisions represent a delicate balance between the need for rapid and intrusive access by international inspectors to a suspect nuclear test-site, before evidence has disappeared or been deliberately removed or obscured, and the sensitivity of states about their perceived national security requirements. The OSI provisions, in the view of some, represent more of a deterrent that may never actually be used, than a verification measure of practical import.[11] Once a clandestine test has been conducted it is unlikely that the offending state, unless it were supremely confident of its ability to hide its activities, would permit access to a test-site. Such a refusal would be tantamount to an admission of guilt and is likely to be treated as such. Even if an OSI is agreed, it would not necessarily provide compelling evidence of a violation. As Eric Arnett notes, '... such evidence would not always resolve lingering uncertainties or be compelling to a sceptical audience'.[12]

Hence the emphasis in the treaty is on remote monitoring. A combination of seismic monitoring, atmospheric detection for radioactive venting and satellite monitoring (by National Technical Means) to detect test-site activity and changes in the Earth's surface—especially cratering—after underground tests, is most likely to be the foundation of proof of a violation.

Confidence-Building Measures (CBMs)

The treaty specifies confidence-building measures to reduce the likelihood that verification data may be misinterpreted and to assist the IMS in calibrating seismic stations. The most important CBM involves voluntarily notifying the Technical Secretariat of any single chemical explosion of 300 tonnes or more of TNT-equivalent.

PROGRESS IN IMPLEMENTATION TO DATE

The rudiments of the future CTBTO are now established at the Vienna International Centre, where a number of other UN agencies in Vienna are based. The Provisional Technical Secretariat (PTS) opened on 17 March 1997 with a staff of nine. Its task during its first year was to establish its capacity to organise and operate a treaty verification system. As of October 1998, less than 18 months after its inauguration, the PTS was, according to Executive Secretary Hoffmann, 'fully operational'. It currently has an international staff of 150 from 55 different countries. Encouragingly, in establishing itself the Secretariat has drawn on the experience of both the IAEA and Organisation for the Prohibition of Chemical Weapons (OPCW) in the Hague. A Joint Consultative Group on PrepCom/IAEA Co-operation has been established.

The verification system itself is, however, far from operational and will take years to achieve full operability. All potential IMS participating stations need to be surveyed and most will need upgrading before the PTS can certify them for participation. As an indication of the size of the task, by September 1998 the PTS had been authorised by the PrepCom to initiate work at 79 stations in 29 countries.

The most important element of the verification system, the seismic monitoring network, is also the most advanced. It will be based on an existing trial network gradually established by the CD's Group of Scientific Experts (GSE) since 1976, the operational characteristics of which are well known. 64% of the primary seismic stations for the future network are currently functional, but only 27% of the secondary. Filling gaps in the global coverage, especially in the southern hemisphere, will take time. Some new seismic arrays (comprising several seismic stations) will require years to build and render operational. The seismic network will receive the largest capital investment, about $15.6 million over the next two years.[13]

As for the radionuclide stations, some are already operating and may be certified at the beginning of 1999. At the end of September 1998, eight site surveys had been conducted and 13 others were under way. Procurement and installation of equipment for about 10 stations had been initiated. While 16 radionuclide laboratories are required, the PTS is able to cooperate with the IAEA, which is co-located with it in the Vienna International Centre. The Agency is developing radionuclide sampling skills for its strengthened nuclear safeguards programme and operates its own laboratory.

Of the 11 hydroacoustic stations required for the network, six will be hydrophones, which have three microphones on each end of a 100-kilometre fibre-optic underwater cable. These will be used mostly in the southern hemisphere, which has a larger oceanic area. Although quite effective in their detection capabilities, they are also expensive, costing around $400,000 each. At the end of September 1998, four site surveys had been done or were under way, of which three had been accepted by early October. Procurement of equipment for two of the stations has been initiated.

Infrasound is currently the least developed of the International Monitoring System (IMS) technologies. At the end of September 1998, six site surveys had been conducted and 13 were under way. For both radionuclide and infrasound stations it is advantageous that the PTS develop them in regional clusters. This makes it easier to test their ability to identify event locations and is more cost effective.

The International Data Centre (IDC), inaugurated in Vienna in January 1998, is not yet fully functional but reliant on a prototype established in Arlington, Virginia. By May 1998, 63 stations were reporting to the Vienna IDC via Arlington in real-time using a new high-speed communications link.[14] The system will ultimately use a global satellite network to provide real-time communications between the IDC, participating stations and states parties. The PTS has signed a 10-year contract worth $70 million with an international partnership firm, Hughes Olivetti Telecom (HOT) Ltd, which over the next 10 years will design, install and operate a global network of very small aperture terminals (VSATs) at each IMS station.

Most of the stations are in remote locations exposed to extreme temperatures and severe weather. The network will be required to provide effective error-free transport of up to 11.4 gigabytes of data daily within five seconds of detecting and processing signals from events. It will also be required to operate 99.5% of the time over 365 days a year and be capable of functioning in temperatures between minus 40 and 60°C and during wind speeds of up to 100 kilometres an hour.[15] By April 1999 it is expected that 30 monitoring stations will be connected by VSAT to the IDC. The IDC itself is not expected to be fully operational until 2000.

The PTS appears conscious that in order for the global system to work properly, a great deal of training will need to be provided to countries currently lacking skilled personnel. Four introductory training programmes on the operation of the IMS have been conducted, one for Latin America in Argentina, one for Africa in South Africa, one for Asia-Pacific in Japan and a fourth, for Central Asia in Kazakhstan.[16] The first technical training programme for states hosting stations was held in Vienna in October 1998.

The preparations for developing an on-site inspection capability are proceeding slowly since the work is essentially innovative. The Secretariat is currently preparing on-site inspection manuals and lists of necessary equipment and organising training courses for inspectors. The first training course, involving PTS staff and 72 national authority personnel from 37 countries, will take place in December 1998.

One legal problem that has arisen is over the requirement for states hosting monitoring stations to sign ‘facility agreements’ with the PrepCom. These agreements regulate the issuing of multiple-entry visas for PTS staff, their privileges and immunities and tax and customs exemptions. During 1998 several states indicated they would impose taxes on PrepCom staff, equipment and services. This could raise the PrepCom budget by several million dollars. It also means that some states were effectively giving other states tax breaks as well as disadvantaging competitive bids by some companies depending on where they were based. A key reason behind the problem is the contested legal status of the PrepCom prior to entry into force of the treaty. As a result of this difficulty no facility agreements had been signed as of September 1998. Exchanges of letters have been undertaken as a temporary measure to permit scheduled work to proceed. While most states seem willing to find a solution, this issue has absorbed valuable Secretariat time and attention.

The PrepCom's budget for 1998 was $58.4 million. Over 96% of the contributions for 1997 and over 55% for 1998 had been paid by September 1998,[17] quite an encouraging result, especially given the Asian economic crisis and economic difficulties elsewhere. The cost of the CTBTO is likely to rise for the next couple of years but then decline as capital investment is completed. While some states are pressing for zero budget growth, as is the case in other international organisations, others such as the United Kingdom are arguing that proper funding for the verification system in preparation for entry-into-force is a good investment in future security.

Altogether, in view of the innovatory nature of the organi-sation being established and the global reach of its coverage, progress has to date been impressive, if not spectacular. Whether it will be ready in time for entry into force as the treaty requires depends largely on events outside the PrepCom's control—such as the rate of ratification by existing signatories and, ultimately, signature and ratification by the three 'holdouts', India, Pakistan and North Korea.

THE IMPACT OF THE MAY 1998 INDIAN AND PAKISTANI NUCLEAR TESTS

In May 1998, in the most intensive bout of nuclear testing since 1991, India and Pakistan between them detonated what they claimed were up to 11 underground nuclear tests. To date these are the only nuclear tests conducted since the CTBT was negotiated.

India began with purportedly three virtually simultaneous underground tests on 11 May and a further two on 13 May. The first three were announced by the Indian government, after the event, as comprising a fission device (an 'atomic' bomb, fuelled by plutonium, of the Hiroshima variety), a thermonuclear device (a so-called hydrogen or H-bomb) and a 'low-yield' device. It was later reported that the thermonuclear device was in fact a technically less sophisticated 'boosted' fission device using tritium fuses to increase the yield of the explosion. All were conducted in the Pokharan Range in the northwest state of Rajasthan, where India's first test was carried out 24 years ago.

On 28 May Pakistan matched India's 'accomplishment' by detonating a reported five virtually simultaneous tests, followed by one more (originally believed to have been two) on 30 May. This purportedly brought Pakistan's total to six, the same as India if its May 1974 test is included. All of the Pakistani tests were reported to be fission devices using highly-enriched uranium (U-235) and were conducted at its test site in the Chagai Hills in southwest Pakistan.

Apart from the serious implications of the tests for peace and security on the Indian subcontinent and the wider ramifications for international security, especially arms control and disarmament, the tests raised troubling questions about verification. In particular, did the tests demonstrate the failure of seismic and other means for remotely detecting and identifying nuclear explosions? If so, as some in the US Congress suggested at the time, is a CTBT unverifiable?

Did Verification Fail?

While there would appear to be a prima facie case that the current monitoring systems under-performed in detecting and identifying the tests, the conclusion that a CTBT is therefore unverifiable is simplistic.[18]

In the first place, the 11 May series by India and both series by Pakistan (although not all of the individual explosions) were successfully detected and the location and approximate size identified, and probably would have been even if an attempt had been made to conduct them clandestinely. The monitoring system, even in its nascent form, did, to that extent, work.[19]

Identification of the source of the events – whether a nuclear test or an earthquake – was more difficult. Based on so-called mb:Ms data (the relative size of two seismic wave types, which helps distinguish nuclear tests from earthquakes) and compared with a dataset of earthquakes in the western United States and underground nuclear explosions at the Nevada Test Site, the 11 May event was clearly in the explosion population. In other datasets it was close to the separation between earthquake and explosion populations and was therefore ambiguous. This highlights the need for local calibration of both natural and man-made events in the Indian subcontinent.

Detection of separate signals for the purportedly simultaneous multiple explosions was more problematic than identification of the source.[20] However, while under a CTBT it might be useful to know how many clandestine explosions had been conducted simultaneously in order to determine the magnitude of a treaty violation, in effect such information is irrelevant to the fact of a violation having occurred. Any explosion, regardless of its size or characteristics, would constitute a violation.

In contrast to the Indian tests of 11 May and the two Pakistani rounds, the performance of the seismic monitoring system in the case of the 'low-yield' Indian test series of 13 May was initially troubling. No seismic data has been reported for these events. Official Indian reports put the yields of the two explosions at 0.5 kt and 0.3 kt and the site(s) as being 'in a sand-dune' (a rather unusual location if venting of radioactivity is to be avoided). A fully-contained explosion of the announced yields in soft rock should have a magnitude of around three, yet be detectable by the most powerful stations, such as seismic arrays. There was thus possibly some attenuation of the seismic signal because of the sandy nature of the test site.[21]

It has long been known that the seismic monitoring network for a CTBT would have difficulty detecting events below 1 kt because the constant movement of the earth's crust makes it difficult to distinguish very small nuclear tests from small earthquakes. It has been assumed, however, that a newly proliferant country testing a nuclear weapon for the first time would not be technically proficient enough to confidently detonate devices at such low yields. India had 24 years to perfect the technology of nuclear devices after its 1974 test, while Pakistan had also been working on its nuclear weapon technology for decades and reportedly obtained blueprints from China.

There are now widespread doubts about the claimed number and character of both the Indian and Pakistani tests. According to a study by seismologist Terry Wallace of the University of Arizona, seismic data reveals that their size and number were exaggerated by a factor of four.[22] The research suggests that two of the five tests announced by India may never have occurred, while only two of Pakistan's were real nuclear explosions. The performance of the seismic network would be vindicated if it turns out that the problematic events were not nuclear and therefore could not have been expected to have been detected and identified even in the best of circumstances.

A second and equally important reason why the Indian and Pakistani tests should not be seen as a demonstration of the failure of the IMS is that it is still in its infancy. Although the first four releases of applications software from the Arlington prototype to the Vienna IDC took place in early May, the system was not quite ready to undertake real-time analysis of the Indian tests. It later analysed and archived data from the 11 May event. The IDC did, however, receive and process data in real-time for Pakistan's tests from 27 primary and 23 secondary seismic stations.

Since a monitoring system the size and sophistication of that planned for the CTBT has never been created before, its synergistic capabilities remain unknown. While this is of concern to the verifiers, it should also give pause to potential violators of a CTBT. In any event the capabilities of the IMS when fully operational is bound to be greater than the current fragmented, undeveloped system. Under a fully operational CTBT, moreover, a state party would be subject to challenge on-site inspections if suspicious events occur.

A third reason why the Indian and Pakistani nuclear detonations were not a good test of the system is that, once the first Indian series had alerted the world to the possibility of further events, the tests were expected and all detection systems, including so-called National Technical Means (NTM), were on high alert. US satellites detected the Pakistanis pouring concrete into their test shafts to seal them prior to detonation. Even the Indian first series were not a perfect test of the system's ability to detect and identify secret tests, since the Indians made no attempt to conceal the fact that they had been conducted and, moreover, announced them.

A fourth reason why the verification system cannot be said to have failed is that neither India nor Pakistan, as non-signatories, has undertaken any legal obligation not to test nuclear weapons underground and neither has contributed to the IMS, in particular by providing seismic stations. If India and Pakistan sign the CTBT they will be expected to contribute geophysical calibration data to permit better detection and identification of seismic events on the Indian subcontinent. But in that case they would probably not attempt to violate the treaty.

The Failure of National Technical Means

The most surprising verification failure in the whole episode was not that of the nascent international monitoring system, but that of NTM. In particular the United States' NTM, including its intelligence services, failed to detect Indian preparations for the first Indian test series. By contrast, in December 1995 US agencies did succeed in detecting test preparations, and the Rao government was warned off from proceeding. But Indian preparations to test have been so longwinded – boreholes were dug in the 1980s – and the decision to test so long in coming, that intelligence agencies were apparently lulled into complacency. This is a phenomenon dangerous for national and international verification systems alike. In addition, Indian scientists reportedly calculated windows of opportunity when American KH-12 satellites would not be over the Indian test-site, permitting final preparations for the tests to go undetected. By the time the satellites did detect the preparations the tests had been conducted. Under a fully-operational CTBT regime, however, satellite imagery would be crucial in providing grounds for a challenge on-site inspection after a suspected event.

THE FUTURE

For verification, the major lessons of the Indian tests are: to bring the CTBT into force and establish the international monitoring system as soon as possible; to give the system as powerful a capability as feasible; and to build in procedures to avoid complacency. Naturally the best outcome would be if both India and Pakistan were to sign and ratify the CTBT. Ironically this day may have come closer because of the tests. Political pressure, economic sanctions and the sheer isolation that India and Pakistan have experienced in international fora since May 1998 appear to have taken their toll. Both countries announced at the 1998 session of the UN General Assembly their willingness to sign the CTBT under certain conditions. Pakistan, under crippling economic pressures, is likely to move first. The spotlight will then fall on India, North Korea and signatories which have not yet ratified, like Israel.

The treaty provides that if it has not entered into force three years after being opened for signature on 24 September 1996, a conference may be convened at the request of a majority of states parties to consider what measures might be taken. The earliest this conference could be convened would thus be September 1999. It is however not clear what steps such a conference could take, other than exhortation, since coercing a state into becoming a party to an international agreement short of their defeat in war would be unconscionable.

For the proper operation of the verification system, entry into force is highly desirable, but late entry into force is not disastrous. Development and refinement of the verification system can proceed unhindered providing the United States ratifies and contributes its large assessed financial contribution, technical expertise and powerful monitoring stations and provided other states with large land masses, favourable geographic locations and seismological capabilities, such as Australia, Brazil, China, Norway, Russia, Sweden and the United Kingdom, also contribute. Global coverage can be achieved without the hold-out states. Moreover, even if the treaty has not entered into force and the compliance provisions are not operative, any evidence provided by the IMS indicating non-compliance will be brought to world attention by one state party or other. If proven, that state is likely to incur condemnation, penalties and sanctions comparable to that provided for in the treaty. Ultimately, however, it is in the long-term interests of arms control and international law generally for the CTBT to enter into force as soon as possible and for a fully operational verification and compliance system to be an integral part of that much-heralded event.

Notes

1 Research for this paper was in part funded by the John Merck Fund of Chicago.

2 Information from CTBTO website, http://www.ctbto.org

3 For a detailed account of the history of peaceful nuclear explosions see Findlay,

Trevor, *Nuclear Dynamite: The Peaceful Nuclear Explosions Fiasco*, Brassey's Australia, Sydney, 1990.

[4] Arnett, Eric, 'The Comprehensive Nuclear Test-Ban Treaty' in *SIPRI Yearbook 1997: Armaments, Disarmament and International Security*, Oxford University Press, Oxford, 1997, p.406.

[5] For arguments about the pros and cons of including an explicit ban on preparations to test in the CTBT see Arnett, Eric, 'The proscription on preparing to test: Consequences for verification' in Arnett, Eric (ed.), *Implementing the Comprehensive Test Ban: New Aspects of Definition, Organisation and Verification*, SIPRI Research Report no. 8, Oxford University Press, Oxford, 1994, pp.48-64.

[6] The yield of nuclear test explosions is expressed in kilotons, the equivalent of 1,000 tons of conventional explosive (TNT).

[7] Arnett, *op.cit.,* p.406.

[8] Protocol to the Comprehensive Nuclear-Test-Ban Treaty, Part 1 (F), para. 18.

[9] Comprehensive Nuclear-Test-Ban Treaty, Article V (D), para. 37.

[10] Convention on the Prohibition of the Development, Production, Stockpiling, and Use of Chemical Weapons and on their Destruction, Article IX, para. 17.

[11] Fetter, S., *Towards a Comprehensive Test Ban*, Ballinger, Cambridge, Mass., 1988, pp.132-136.

[12] Arnett, E., 'The complementary roles of national, private and multinational means of verification' in Arnett, Eric (ed.), *Implementing the Comprehensive Test Ban: New Aspects of Definition, Organisation and Verification*, SIPRI Research Report no. 8, Oxford University Press, Oxford, 1994, p.83.

[13] Preparatory Commission for the Comprehensive Nuclear-Test-Ban Treaty, Provisional Secretariat, Vienna, Press Release, PI/PTS/Ann.2, 23 Sept. 1998, p.1.

[14] Preparatory Commission for the Comprehensive Nuclear-Test-Ban Treaty, Provisional Secretariat, Vienna, Press Release, PI/PTS/Ann.2, 23 Sept. 1998, p.2.

[15] Preparatory Commission for the Comprehensive Nuclear-Test-Ban Treaty, Provisional Secretariat, Vienna, Press Release, PI/GCI/1, 7 Sept. 1998, p.1.

[16] Preparatory Commission for the Comprehensive Nuclear-Test-Ban Treaty, Provisional Secretariat, Vienna, Press Release, PI/PR/12, 19 March, 1998, p.1.

[17] Preparatory Commission for the Comprehensive Nuclear-Test-Ban Treaty, Provisional Secretariat, Vienna, Press Release, PI/PTS/Ann.2, 23 Sept. 1998, p.2.

[18] The following section draws on analysis by seismologist Dr Roger Clark, Lecturer in Geophysics at the University of Leeds. For further analysis see Suzanna van Moyland and Roger Clark, 'The Paper Trail', *Bulletin of the Atomic Scientists*, July/August 1998, pp.26-29.

[19] For the first Indian series – crucial because it was totally unexpected –seismic data were quickly available from the US-based Incorporated Research Institutions for

Seismology (IRIS) global network. The data showed a single event, originally estimated at magnitude 4.7, equating to a yield of some 20 kilotons (kt) of TNT, with an uncertainty factor of around 2. The waveform of the event (as depicted on seismographs) was simple and not obviously derived from multiple sources, such as the double explosions conducted by the Soviet Union in the 1970s. Eight days after the event the US Geological Survey, using more reliable seismic data from 125 stations, estimated that the 11 May explosions were: conducted at 10:13:42.0 Greenwich Mean Time (GMT) at a latitude of 27.102N and longitude 71.857E with depth constrained at zero kilometres, and with a body-wave magnitude of 5.2 and surface-wave magnitude of 3.6. The estimated seismic location was 12 km from the actual location. The new magnitudes suggested a combined yield of 30-60 kt, consistent with the announced total yield of 56 kt.

20 Simultaneous explosions at the separation of the explosions cited in media reports (about 1 km) would give seismic signals separated by at most some 0.2 seconds or so. Since this is much less than the dominant period (around 1 second) of each seismic signal, the combined signal would not obviously appear as two explosions since they would overlap. A careful analysis of waveform data could perhaps detect the subtle variation in the signals, and thus the multiple sources of the 11 May event, given sufficiently dense coverage by seismic stations. However, this is by no means guaranteed.

21 Seifs (linear sand dunes), in which the devices were reportedly buried, can reach 150 metres or more in height.

22 Wallace, Terry C., 'The May 1998 India and Pakistan Nuclear Tests', *Research Letters*, Seismological Society of America, vol. 69, no. 5, Sept./Oct. 1998, pp.386-393.

16
Fissile Material Cut-Off

STEPHEN PULLINGER

Director, International Security Information Service ISIS

INTRODUCTION

Achieving an end to the production of fissile material for nuclear weapons purposes is a key priority for arms controllers today. Because fissile materials (plutonium and highly-enriched uranium (HEU)) are the basic ingredients of such weapons, controlling their production and availability will be a crucial component of international efforts to bring about disarmament. Once all production is subject to international scrutiny and all stockpiles are safeguarded it could pave the way for the eventual global elimination of nuclear weapons themselves.

At this stage, however, the realistic near-term ambitions are less grandiose. Reaching an agreement to halt the production of any more material for weapons, codified in a Fissile Material Cut-off Treaty (FMCT), would be a start. This, more limited, approach is the one favoured by the Nuclear Weapon States (NWS). Others, amongst the Non-Nuclear Weapon States (NNWS), support a more wide-ranging treaty that would tackle existing stockpiles of material as well as future production. This chapter examines the background to this debate and offers an analysis of the prospects for international agreement on a FMCT.

HISTORICAL BACKGROUND

Calls for an end to the production of fissile material for bomb-making date back to just after the Second World War, when the idea was set out in the Baruch Plan. Since that time the issue has re-surfaced periodically.[1] India proposed a universal, non-discriminatory convention in 1954. Two years later, when President Eisenhower proposed a cut-off it was rejected by Khrushchev as an attempt to make permanent US quantitative superiority over the USSR. In 1989, the roles were reversed when US President Bush, resisting his Soviet counterpart's more radical approach to nuclear disarmament, spurned President Gorbachev's offer.

Only when President Clinton reversed US policy in September 1993 in a speech to the United Nations (UN) did the two superpowers enjoy a common position of support for a cut-off. Two months later a consensus was finally achieved at the United Nations General Assembly (UNGA) when members called for the negotiation of a 'non-discriminatory, multilateral and internationally effectively verifiable treaty banning the production of fissile material for nuclear weapons or other explosive devices'.[2] The key to reaching consensus had been dropping any consideration of 'stockpiles' from the resolution. As previously, the terms continued to allow production for civilian uses and non-explosive military purposes such as naval propulsion.

This enabled the issue to be put on the agenda of the Conference on Disarmament (CD) in Geneva (the leading international multilateral negotiating forum for arms control and disarmament). Yet because of major disagreements among the participant states it was to be a further 18 months before a negotiating mandate was eventually agreed, and not until August 1998 that consensus was achieved on the convening of an *ad hoc* committee to begin to negotiate the ban.

LINKAGE WITH THE NPT

A fissile cut-off was afforded additional import and impetus at the conclusion of the Review and Extension Conference of the Nuclear Non-Proliferation Treaty (NPT) in 1995. Here, the states parties, in accordance with their obligations under Article VI of the treaty, made a series of political commitments to pursue and accomplish further measures of arms control and disarmament. These goals, set out in the 'Principles and Objectives for Nuclear Non-Proliferation and Disarmament', placed the negotiation of a Comprehensive Test Ban Treaty (CTBT) as the top priority for NPT parties. Second on the list was 'the immediate commencement and early conclusion of a fissile material cut-off convention'. The third element of the 'principles package' was 'the determined pursuit... of systematic and progressive efforts to reduce nuclear weapons globally, with the ultimate goal of eliminating those weapons'.

If the CTBT was intended to tackle the qualitative development of nuclear weapons, the cut-off is aimed at halting the quantitative expansion of such weapons by choking off their most crucial ingredients. With the successful conclusion of the CTBT at the end of 1996, therefore, the subsequent focus of nuclear arms controllers has been the fissile cut-off. Indeed, it was largely because the NWS made these renewed political commitments to additional measures of nuclear arms control and disarmament that many of the NNWS acceded to the NPT's indefinite extension (at one stage there had been considerable minority support for a more finite or rolling extension of the treaty).

One of the main tensions between the nuclear 'haves' and 'have-nots' within the NPT is the discriminatory obligations placed upon the two camps. Whereas the NWS are permitted to manufacture fissile material for their weapons programmes outside the treaty's inspection regime, the NNWS are obliged to allow intrusive inspection of their civil nuclear facilities by the International Atomic Energy Agency (IAEA) (in accordance with the safeguards provisions mandated in Article III of the treaty). Essentially, it is the IAEA's job to ensure there is no diversion of fissile materials for weapons purposes.

A Fissile Material Cut-off Treaty (FMCT) would require the nuclear production facilities of the NWS to be brought under some form of international control to ensure that production of materials for weapons purposes has ceased and that no civil products are being diverted for such purposes. Hence, such an agreement would at least begin to address this fundamental discrimination between NWS and NNWS and thereby hopefully defuse some of the simmering resentment of the NNWS towards the in-built inequities of the NPT.

THE POSITIONS OF THE NUCLEAR WEAPON STATES

The United States halted production of fissile material for its nuclear weapons programme many years ago (highly-enriched uranium (HEU) in 1964 and plutonium in 1988). In 1989, Russia announced a cessation of HEU production for weapons purposes and in 1994 made a similar declaration for plutonium. Russia does still produce some weapons-grade plutonium resulting from a small number of reprocessing reactors (the purpose of which is to heat nearby cities). But under an agreement with the US, signed in 1994, it has agreed to shut down these reactors by 2000 and to allow the US to verify that the plutonium produced in the interim is not being used for weapons purposes.

Both the US and Russia now have enormous surpluses of fissile materials arising from the significant reductions each has made in their nuclear arsenals (under the Strategic Arms Reduction Treaties (START), Intermediate-range Nuclear Forces (INF) Treaty and from unilateral decisions). Re-cycling of materials from old and dismantled weapons has permitted the manufacture of new weapons without a resumption of the production of fissile materials.

Following the US/Russia summit in September 1998, Presidents Clinton and Yeltsin signed a 'Joint Statement of Principles for Management and Disposition of Plutonium Designated as No Longer Required for Defense Purposes'. This includes a commitment for both countries to develop methods and technologies for transparency measures including appropriate verification measures.[3] The two countries have already each identified approximately 50 tonnes of plutonium to be addressed by a future agreement stemming from this joint statement.

The UK announced at the 1995 NPT Review and Extension Conference that it no longer produced enriched uranium or plutonium for its nuclear weapons programme. Clearly, the UK concluded that it had produced and could re-cycle sufficient fissile materials to sustain its *Trident* nuclear weapon programme as well as to fuel its nuclear submarine fleet. The dismantlement of 'several hundred' WE-177 nuclear bombs more than made up for the additional warheads required for *Trident* compared to its predecessor *Polaris/Chevaline* (whereas the UK possessed over 400 operational warheads in the 1970s – the vast majority of which were believed to be of yields about 200 kt, by 1995 the Conservative government planned for fewer than 300 warheads for *Trident* – believed to be about 100 kt each). The number of nuclear-powered, hunter-killer submarines (SSNs) was also cut (from 16 to 12) under 'Options for Change' in the early 1990s.

Traditionally, Britain's regulatory policies on fissile materials have been clearly divided between civil and military. Whereas all activities and holdings in the former were transparent and open to international verification, all those in the latter were classified and not subject to international verification.[4]

THE STRATEGIC DEFENCE REVIEW AND UK POLICY

One of the first decisions of the new Labour government (elected in May 1997) was to implement a full-scale strategic review of Britain's defence posture. Despite Labour's *a priori* sworn intention to retain a nuclear weapons capability with *Trident*, the review was mandated to subject other aspects of nuclear policy to a thorough re-appraisal.

The Strategic Defence Review (SDR), published in July 1998, announced further restrictions on the total number of operational nuclear warheads for *Trident* that Britain intends to maintain (fewer than 200), along with a further cut in the number of SSNs from 12 to 10. It also reiterated Britain's commitment to the negotiation of a FMCT, describing it as 'an essential step towards global elimination of nuclear weapons'.[5]

As part of that commitment to the control of fissile material the government announced that it would become the first NWS to declare the total size of its stocks of nuclear materials held outside international safeguards. These comprise 7.6 tonnes of plutonium, 21.9 tonnes of HEU and 15,000 tonnes of other forms of uranium. It also announced that because much of this stock was no longer required for defence purposes Britain would place under EURATOM safeguards (and therefore liable to IAEA inspection) 4.4 tonnes of plutonium, including 0.3 tonnes of weapons-grade plutonium, and over 9,000 tonnes of non-highly enriched uranium.

In order to allow a recycling of material from dismantled weapons to naval propulsion, however, the British government decided to retain all stocks of HEU outside safeguards. HMG did not feel able 'at this stage' to disaggregate further the material totals provided. Another change involved the placing of the re-processing of spent fuel from defence reactors at Chapelcross under safeguards, thereby bringing all future reprocessing and enrichment in Britain under such control (although the government reserved the right to resume such activities outside safeguards pending the conclusion of a FMCT). In further recognition that global nuclear weapons elimination will eventually require all fissile material produced outside safeguards to be accounted for, the government announced its intention to begin a process of declassification and historical accounting.

These welcome initiatives constitute important confidence-building measures in the context of the FMCT negotiations. We wait to see whether the other NWS respond to these British initiatives with reciprocal action of their own. The development of greater transparency in relation to the production and whereabouts of nuclear materials will play a crucial role in the nuclear reduction process.

France declared a cessation of HEU and plutonium production in 1996. Its nuclear forces have also been reduced as a result of recent policy changes. There will now be four rather than six SSBNs carrying 96 warheads each. France's 18 surface-to-surface missiles and 30 short-range mobile missiles were due to be dismantled by the end of 1998. It also announced, in April 1998, the closure and dismantlement of its military enrichment and reprocessing facilities, although, like the UK, France intends to retain its large commercial reprocessing facilities.

Although China has not made any public statement to this effect[6] it too is believed to have stopped production of fissile materials for nuclear weapons purposes, and has supported the 'earliest possible achievement' of a FMCT. Presumably, this is an indication that China now has sufficient materials to sustain any nuclear modernisation plans from existing stockpiles and re-cycling capacity.

The other 180 signatories to the NPT are already obliged not to produce fissile material for weapons purposes and are subject to full-scope safeguards to ensure their compliance. The three key non-signatories – India, Pakistan and Israel – are not, of course, subject to the treaty's controls.

DIFFERENT PERSPECTIVES ON A FISSILE CUT-OFF

Broadly speaking there are two approaches to the fissile cut-off issue. First, there are those who are primarily interested in it as a non-proliferation measure. These comprise the acknowledged nuclear weapons states, along with Israel and India, which are keen to restrict the scope of the treaty to future production. Second, there are those who want to use it to further nuclear disarmament. This grouping insists that the negotiations must include consideration of existing stockpiles too.[7]

Essentially, the NWS want to preserve the status quo whilst trying to prevent accumulation in other countries, namely the threshold states (India, Pakistan and Israel). They maintain that it is valuable to codify and thereby help cement their own present cessation of production into a verifiable treaty.

Those states that spearheaded CD pressure for a wider negotiating remit – principally Algeria, Egypt, Iran and Pakistan – argued that any agreement on future production alone would be practically meaningless given that most if not all NWS had already ceased such production in any case. For ideological and regional security reasons Algeria, Egypt and Iran especially want to ensure that Israel's fissile stocks should be taken into account. Israel's extant, though undeclared nuclear weapons capability, is of widespread concern to its Arab neighbours who fear that a simple cut-off treaty would not only leave such capability untouched but also confer it with a degree of legitimacy.

Before eventually acceding to the final negotiating mandate at the CD, India introduced an additional spoiling tactic by insisting that a cut-off treaty could only be negotiated in the context of a timebound framework for complete nuclear disarmament. This insistence, guaranteed to be categorically rejected by the acknowledged NWS, served to deflect attention away from India's own reluctance to consider stockpiles. India's subsequent change of position and acceptance of the mandate may have been influenced partly by the international opprobrium generated by its nuclear tests. Perhaps now keener to demonstrate its disarmament credentials, India has also indicated, albeit in rather ambiguous language, a preparedness to sign the CTBT.

The positions adopted by both India and Pakistan at the CD are bound to be pivotal to the success or otherwise of the fissile cut-off negotiations. It should not be underestimated how aggrieved India felt at the treatment it received during the talks to secure the CTBT: treatment that merely reinforced the strength of the grudge it harbours against what it perceives to be the discriminatory nature of the NPT. It will not want to endure a similar fate in the FMCT negotiations.

Nevertheless, India could find itself in an awkward position. If the FMCT is confined to future production India can be expected to refuse to allow its stockpile to be capped at a far lower level than that of China. If, on the other hand, the treaty seeks reductions in stocks, India is unlikely to agree to its perceived nuclear superiority over Pakistan being whittled away. It may take some comfort from the reduced likelihood of it being isolated over a cut-off (as it became over the CTBT), because it shares with the NWS and Israel an unwillingness to discuss stocks, and shares with the other threshold states a reluctance to be drawn into the NPT via the 'backdoor' of a fissile cut-off. Its presence in the talks, however, still runs the risk that India will be squeezed by both sides and once again be portrayed as the villain of the piece if progress stalls.

Despite its constant challenges to India, Pakistan actually tends to mimic its neighbour in much of its approach to nuclear weapons policy and disarmament. When India conducted nuclear tests Pakistan followed suit, and if India signs the CTBT Pakistan has said it will too. As the junior partner in any South Asian arms race, Pakistan not only wants India's bomb-making production stopped but also its large plutonium reserves cut to a level more akin to its own, much smaller, stocks of HEU. It cannot be expected to favour a cut-off that simply freezes its rival's advantage.

Israel did not block the necessary consensus at the CD to prevent the establishment of the *ad hoc* committee, chiefly because of strong diplomatic pressure from Washington, but it clearly has strong reservations about where the talks might lead. Israel is not prepared to see its nuclear 'insurance policy' devalued through a cut-off treaty. As its entire nuclear posture is deliberately shrouded in ambiguity, Israel will find it very difficult to concede foreign inspection of its production facilities, let alone to bring its existing stocks of fissile material under international supervision. One possible way around this problem, assuming that Israel now has sufficient stocks of weapons-grade material, might be to close down the Dimona production facility rather than allow on-site inspection. Future non-production could be verified from space.[8] Israel's 'bottom line' remains that it will not abandon its nuclear capability outside of a general Middle East settlement that embraces all weapons of mass destruction and which deals satisfactorily with its regional security concerns. Its stance during the cut-off negotiations can be expected to reflect that position.

Given the strong disagreements amongst CD member states, it required all of the impressive diplomatic skills of Ambassador Shannon (the Canadian Chairman) to break the impasse and obtain a consensus for a negotiating mandate (one that mirrored the UNGA resolution referred to earlier). The breakthrough came about because Shannon accompanied the mandate with an assurance that discussion of other issues, including the scope of the treaty, could be discussed in the committee. Nevertheless, he gave no commitment that anything other than future production would be included in any final treaty. This is a classic diplomatic compromise aimed at getting the show on the road. In reality, it simply defers the disagreements to recur once the negotiations begin in earnest.

THE SCOPE OF A FMCT?

Prior to a negotiating mandate being agreed, when the CD was deadlocked, the US and a number of arms control analysts considered the possibility of achieving a cut-off limited to the five permanent members of the UN Security Council (P5). This would have been relatively straightforward to accomplish because it would simply have cemented current practice. Obviously, this was just about the minimum one could have expected of a cut-off treaty, and even other NWS were not keen. France and the UK rejected:

> ... the practical notion of an interim cut-off agreement solely among the nuclear weapon powers ... the primary benefit of a fissban is to put the threshold states under full safeguards.[9]

It is true that the impact of a FMCT would be greatest if it could include those who are currently outside the NPT, especially the threshold states. All of these states are believed to have military nuclear programmes and some or all of them may have already weaponised their capabilities. India and Pakistan's underground tests of 1998 were a telling reminder of these states' nuclear weapons potential.

If a FMCT were to embrace these states it could have a significant non-proliferation benefit. Stopping their production of bomb-making materials would contribute to international and regional security. For the first time, unsafeguarded military nuclear programmes, namely, those lying outside the remit of the NPT and IAEA, would be brought under some form of international control. However, there is a danger that a regime that merely verified a cessation of further production – whilst ignoring current stockpiles of unsafeguarded materials in non-NPT states – might serve to confer some unwanted legitimacy to those weapons-usable stocks.

On the other hand, if a treaty did address stockpiles, and there is every indication that this will be resisted strongly by a number of parties to the talks, various definitional problems would arise. Would stockpiles only cover materials that were surplus to requirements or include all materials, including those within actual weapons, for example? And if agreement could be reached on that score what would then happen to those stocks? Would they simply be placed under safeguards or be subject to phased reduction (disarmament through fissile withdrawal)? Undoubtedly, a FMCT that deals with stockpiles will not only be a much more difficult treaty to achieve politically but also be a far more complex one.

VERIFICATION OF A FMCT

Obviously, the nature of the verification regime associated with the implementation of a FMCT will depend on the scope of any eventual treaty. But even if that scope is confined to a ban on future production it will require the production of all civilian material in NWS currently not under safeguards, as well as military production of fissile materials, being placed under safeguards. Otherwise, civilian material could be declared as earlier production and diverted into military use, for example.[10]

As mentioned earlier, the obligation of not diverting nuclear materials for weapons purposes is already being imposed on the NNWS by the IAEA. There has been some debate as to whether the NWS need to be subject to the same degree of inspection. The logic here being that for those who already possess nuclear weapons the significance of a small diversion of materials from civil to military use is of little concern. Yet, for the NWS to enjoy a more relaxed verification regime would merely add to the sense of discriminatory treatment that many NNWS already feel within the non-proliferation regime. Moreover, the negotiating mandate clearly calls for a 'non-discriminatory' treaty.

Nevertheless, establishing verification systems in facilities that have not been designed to receive them is certain to be a costly exercise. Russia has already indicated an unwillingness to accept a new set of arms control expenses. One can also imagine the US Congress blanching at extra costs associated with accepting more intrusions upon its nuclear weapons programme. Conversely, it must be doubtful whether the NWS themselves will be prepared to accept less strict verification of threshold states' production facilities than are applied to NNWS.

This has led some analysts to conclude that if we want an effective and non-discriminatory treaty we will need universal full-scope safeguards.[11] The cost of a universal system based on existing verification procedures is about three times the present expenditure and the number of inspectors will have to increase too. Some will argue that this will merely exacerbate the problems already associated with wasting time and energy inspecting facilities where there is no suggestion of suspicious activity. Indeed, the thrust of the '93 + 2' process was precisely intended to change the emphasis away from inspecting declared facilities to finding and inspecting any undeclared ones.

OTHER RISKS NOT COVERED BY A FMCT

One very real and urgent challenge to global security centres on how we can bring enormous quantities of unsafeguarded bomb-making material under international supervision. The situation in Russia and the former Soviet Republics is particularly grave. Thousands of nuclear weapons are spread across a vast geographical area, some parts of which lack the control mechanisms to ensure their safety, and thousands more nuclear warheads are either being dismantled or are due for dismantlement. Records of nuclear material holdings are often inadequate and incomplete. The potential for error – for materials to go missing – is worryingly high. In addition, the presence of powerful criminal gangs, the incentives for impoverished nuclear scientists to sell their skills to the highest bidder, and a black market for the components of nuclear bomb programmes combine to create a very considerable proliferation risk.

Dangers are also associated with the availability of sensitive nuclear materials and the perception of a growing threat of terrorists seeking to acquire the means to develop a crude nuclear device. This has put more focus on the security of civil nuclear production. France, the UK, Russia and Japan are all generating large amounts of plutonium through their reprocessing activities. Although intended for use in the nuclear fuel cycle, as the Rand Corporation observes, these activities:

> ...will involve transfers between holding points including transfers to other countries. It is from these ... points that nations or subnational groups might divert or seize some of the material.[12]

IMPLEMENTING THE NPT

A concomitant of a successful FMCT must be the continued and effective maintenance of the NPT. The treaty prohibits 180 of its state parties from developing nuclear weapons. Yet the discovery of an extensive and advanced clandestine nuclear weapons programme in Iraq (a NNWS party to the NPT), demonstrates that the prohibitions under the treaty need to be vigorously upheld. Iraq had evaded IAEA inspection mainly by establishing entirely undeclared facilities. Inspections of declared facilities had allowed Iraq to present clean hands to the world, thus creating an entirely false sense of security.

Hence, the IAEA has to be given the teeth and resources to adequately implement the terms of the NPT. The '93 + 2' process, undertaken by the IAEA in 1993, was specifically intended to improve the international inspectorate's ability to detect undeclared, proscribed activities through improvements to safeguard procedures. However, India and Israel, and perhaps the P5 and Pakistan too, can be expected to mount strong resistance to allowing the IAEA powers to investigate their undeclared facilities.

CONCLUSION – PROSPECTS FOR A TREATY?

A combination of the seeming intractability of a number of the issues involved in the negotiations, a lack of goodwill amongst the participants and the need for consensus may render a successful outcome extremely difficult to obtain at the CD.

The CTBT proved difficult enough to conclude and that was a negotiation in which the differences between the various parties were far less significant than those relating to a FMCT. The CTBT also enjoyed a high political and media profile and as such was an arms control measure which could be highlighted in the international headlines and hence used in applying pressure to those dragging their feet in the talks. Almost universal revulsion against French testing in the Pacific proved to be a powerful catalyst for advance in the negotiations towards a better treaty. It is difficult to imagine an equivalent spur to the FMCT if negotiations become bogged down in procedural and substantive wrangling. With the cut-off there is far less political impetus behind the negotiations. The issue has a lower profile partly because the production and accumulation of materials (which also occur in civil programmes) do not capture the imagination in the same way that nuclear explosions do.

We should not forget that despite its eventual negotiation, the CTBT has yet to enter into force because of the clause that insists as a pre-requisite that 44 named states with nuclear capabilities ratify the treaty. India's refusal to do so (and Pakistan's consequent following of suit) has left the CTBT in limbo for the present. It takes no great leap of imagination to envisage a similar vetoing of entry into force occurring with a FMCT, and that India may not be the only party giving consideration to exercising that option. The chances of the treaty not stipulating a particular number of named states becoming parties before entry into force would seem to be low, given the insistence of the NWS that the FMCT must cap the ambitions of the non-NPT states.

In light of the NNWS' demand for more than a confirmation of something that has already happened, they can be expected to use negotiations to push for wider nuclear disarmament – something the NWS will resist. For their part, the NWS are unwilling to invest a significant amount of diplomatic energy and financial resources in a treaty which does not include the threshold states. In turn, the threshold states will not accept being drawn into the NPT's discriminatory regime by default. Such a combination of factors suggests that the prospects for a FMCT are poor.

Currently, there is a real chance that protracted negotiations will slowly become mired in bickering and dispute, ending in frustration and failure. This could lead to bitter recriminations surfacing vocally at the 2000 NPT Review Conference, leaving the achievement of a CTBT but a distant memory. In order for this damaging outcome to be avoided probably requires the NNWS to accept the value of a limited FMCT but for the NWS to keep stockpiles on the agenda.

Notes

1. Berkhout, Frans, 'Should Britain Support a Fissile Cut-Off?, *Special ISIS Briefing*, August 1994.
2. Resolution 48/75 of 16 December 1993 – adopted without a vote.
3. Statement on Behalf of the Russian Federation, the United States and the IAEA, IAEA Press Release PR 98/18, 22 September. Cited in *Disarmament Diplomacy*, Journal of the Acronym Institute, No.30, September 1998, p.34.

[4] Walker, Prof. William, 'Britain's Policies on Fissile Materials: The Next Steps', *Special ISIS Report No.2*, July 1997, pp.28-29.

[5] *The Strategic Defence Review, Supporting Essays*, Essay 5, (HMSO, 1998) p.10.

[6] China is believed to have informed Washington privately that it has ceased production, according to *Arms Control Today*, Vol.25, No.8, October 1995.

[7] For a more detailed analysis of the negotiating positions adopted by the various participant states at the CD see the Reports published by the Acronym Institute, London. Available at *http://www.gn.apc.org/acronym*.

[8] *Arms Control Today*, *op. cit*., p.7.

[9] Johnson, Rebecca, 'Little Orphan Fissban', *Bulletin of Atomic Scientists*, May-June 1997, p.4.

[10] Schaper, Annette, A Treaty on the Cutoff of Fissile Material for Nuclear Weapons – What to Cover? How to Verify?, *PRIF Reports*, No.48, July 1997, p.30.

[11] *ibid.* p.50

[12] Chow, Brian, G., *et al*., 'The Proposed Fissile-Material Production Cutoff: Next Steps', RAND 1995, *http://www.rand.org/publications/MR/MR586.1.html.*

17

Strengthening the Biological and Toxin Weapons Convention through Negotiation of a Verification Protocol: Will the Present Opportunity be Seized?

MALCOLM DANDO

Professor of International Security, Department of Peace Studies, University of Bradford

INTRODUCTION

It is now more widely understood that biological weapons present a major danger to international society: they can have a lethality equivalent to nuclear weapons; they are relatively cheap and easy to produce; and their proliferation is constrained only by the weak Biological and Toxin Weapons Convention (BTWC) which lacks effective verification provisions for ensuring that the 141 State Parties are living up to their obligations.

Now, almost a decade after the 1991 Gulf War, the United Nations was again in disarray in 1998 over what should be done to ensure that Iraq was complying with the undertakings it accepted after its defeat – in particular, to demonstrate that it no longer has an offensive biological weapons programme. Many people despair of bringing UNSCOM's mission to a successful conclusion and accept that Iraq will probably eventually get sanctions lifted without meeting its obligations even in the wake of the UK-US airstrikes of December 1998. Since Iraq could have had UN sanctions lifted at any time over the last seven years by revealing the truth about its weapons programmes, failure to complete the UNSCOM mission would inevitably put ideas in the minds of other possible proliferators about the potential value of biological weapons and the possibility of defying the international community.

Over the same period of time since the 1991 war, however, a much more constructive and hopeful (but much less well known) process has also been underway. This process could soon lead to the strengthening of the BTWC through the agreement of an effective Verification Protocol (VP) which could play a major part in future efforts to prevent the proliferation of biological weapons. It is crucial to strengthen the BTWC *now*, not just because of political processes that could favour proliferation of biological weapons, but also because the revolution in biotechnology, and its technological application in industry, seem bound to spread advanced capabilities rapidly around the world. Modern biotechnology will surely underpin a major world industry in the early decades of the next century.

This contribution concentrates on giving an overview of the current multilateral negotiations in Geneva, between states parties to the BTWC, which are devoted to achieving a Verification Protocol. The central point is that agreement is possible, but a great deal more political will and public support will be necessary to achieve success in the next few years.

THE 1991 THIRD REVIEW CONFERENCE OF THE BTWC AND THE VEREX PROCESS

The experience of the 1991 Gulf War, with the possibility that Iraq might have deployed biological weapons, had a salutory effect. As General Colin Powell testified in 1993:

> The one that scares me to death, perhaps even more so than tactical nuclear weapons, and the one we have the least capability against is biological weapons ... that's where we really have to do the best possible job we can in our nonproliferation efforts ...[1]

This perception, in part, led the participants in the Third Five-Year Review Conference of the BTWC in 1991 to attempt to enhance the confidence-building measures (annual data exchanges) they had agreed in 1986 and, more importantly, to initiate a process of analysing whether the convention could, from a scientific and technical viewpoint, be verified.

In this process, which became known as VEREX, government experts met in four sessions during 1992 and 1993 in order to evaluate a series of 21 potential verification measures, both singly and, to some extent, in combination. For example, the Rapporteur for 'Declarations' stated:

> Declarations were considered to be a major off-site measure from which national profiles or patterns of biological activity could be assessed against other sources of information[2]

The VEREX report was considered at a Special Conference of States Parties in 1994 which then mandated the presently-operating Ad Hoc Group (AHG) of government officials to take forward the process of developing a verification system for the BTWC.

THE 1994 SPECIAL CONFERENCE AND AD HOC GROUP

The Final Declaration of the 1994 Special Conference noted the complexity of the issues involved in constructing a verification system for the Convention:

> The Conference...recognized that the complex nature of the issues pertaining to the strengthening of the Biological Weapons Convention underlined the need for a gradual approach towards the establishment of a coherent regime to enhance the effectiveness and improve compliance with the Convention ...[3]

The Conference, nevertheless, decided to establish an Ad Hoc Group open to all States Parties and stated:

> The objective of this Ad Hoc Group shall be to consider appropriate measures, including possible verification measures, and draft proposals to strengthen the Convention, to be included, as appropriate, in a legally binding instrument, to be submitted for the consideration of the States Parties ...

In this context the Ad Hoc Group was asked to consider:

- definitions of terms and objective criteria;
- the incorporation of existing and further enhanced confidence-building measures;
- a system of measures to promote compliance with the Convention, including, as appropriate, measures identified, examined and evaluated in the VEREX Report;

- specific measures designed to ensure effective and full implementation of Article X [of the Convention – on international co-operation].

The mandate further noted that:

> This regime would include, *inter alia*, potential verification measures, as well as agreed procedures and mechanisms for their efficient implementation *and measures for the investigation of alleged use*. [emphasis added]

Measures were also needed to be designed to protect commercial proprietary and national security information and not to have a negative impact on scientific work or international co-operation and development.

Table 1: Meetings of the Ad Hoc Group

YEAR	SESSION	DATES	NEGOTIATING PERIOD
1995	I (Procedural)	4 – 6/1	-
	II	10 – 21/7	2 weeks
	III	27/11 – 8/12	2 weeks
1996	IV	15 – 26/7	2 weeks
	V	16 – 27/9	2 weeks
1997	VI	3 – 21/3	3 weeks
	VII	14/7 – 1/8	3 weeks
	VIII	15/9 – 3/10	3 weeks
1998	IX	5 – 23/1	3 weeks
	X	9 – 13/3	1 week
	XI	22/6 – 10/7	3 weeks
	XII	14/9 – 9/10	4 weeks
1999	XIII	4 – 22/1	3 weeks
(Agreed)	XIV	29/3 – 9/4	2 weeks
	XV	28/6 – 23/7	4 weeks
	XVI	13/9 – 8/10	4 weeks
	XVII	22/11 – 10/12	2 weeks

The Ad Hoc Group has held 12 sessions to date and has another five sessions agreed and scheduled for 1999 (Table 1). Two points are immediately obvious from the foregoing record. First, although there has been a steady increase in the amount of time the international community has devoted to negotiating the Verification Protocol, strengthening of the Biological Weapons Convention has not been given the same attention in the 1990s as what were perceived to be higher priority issues like the Chemical Weapons Convention or nuclear testing and non-proliferation. Second, substantial and rapid progress will need to be made during 1999 before the Review Conference of the Nuclear Non-Proliferation Treaty in 2000 inevitably again begins to take priority.

Table 2: Participation in the meetings of the Ad Hoc Group

Session	Participation		Nos. of Working Papers
	States Parties	Signatory States*	(submitted by States Parties)
I	51	-	1
II	52	1	21**
III	52	1	30
IV	51	2	27
V	51	3	12
VI	51	2	28
VII	54	2	36
VIII	58	3	25
IX	54	3	22
X	49	3	6
XI	50	2	16
XII	57	3	24

* Signatory states have signed but, unlike States Parties, not ratified the BTWC.
** Different numbering sequence

Nevertheless, it is clear from the numbers of states parties participating in the meetings and the large numbers of Working Papers being produced (Table 2) that a serious and substantial negotiation is underway. Moreover, despite the prominence of two of the Depositary States (the UK and Russia) and one state of the Non-Aligned Movement (South Africa) in the production of Working Papers for the Ad Hoc Group, it is also clear that a wide range of

States are making contributions (Table 3).

Table 3: Working Papers produced by various States Parties*

Country	No. of Working Papers
South Africa	57
United Kingdom	41
Russian Federation	20
Japan	11
Canada, France, USA	10 each
Cuba	9
Brazil	8
Netherlands, Sweden	7 each
Australia, Iran	6 each
Argentina, Austria, China, Czech Republic, Germany, Indonesia, Italy, South Korea, New Zealand, Switzerland, Turkey, Ukraine	5 or fewer each

* As nearly all State Working Papers are produced by single states, and most of the rest by two states acting together, the very small number of multiple-authored State Working Papers are not included here.

The multilateral nature of the process is also reflected in the Friends of the Chairs (FOCs) appointed at various stages of the negotiations to assist the Chairman, Ambassador Tibor Tóth of Hungary, with particular aspects of the negotiations.[4] In the initial stage, discussions at Ad Hoc Group sessions were summarised by four FOCs on:

- definitions of terms and objective criteria (Dr Ali A Mohammadi of Iran);
- confidence-building and transparency measures (the Chairman of the Ad Hoc Group);
- measures to promote compliance (Stephen Pattison of the United Kingdom);
- measures related to Article X (Ambassador Jorge Berguño of Chile).

The FOCs remained unchanged through the Fifth Session of the Ad Hoc Group in the autumn of 1996.

The Ad Hoc Group reported to the Fourth Five-Year Review Conference of the BTWC in late 1996. The Review Conference, in its Final Declaration, noted that:

> The Conference welcomes the decision of the Ad Hoc Group, in order to fulfil its mandate, to intensify its work with a view to completing it as soon as possible before the commencement of the Fifth Review Conference [in 2001] ... The Conference encourages the Ad Hoc Group to review its method of work and to move to a negotiating format in order to fulfil its mandate.[5]

This added urgency was manifest by the time of the Seventh Session of the Ad Hoc Group in the summer of 1997 when the list of FOCs was expanded to:

- definitions of terms and objective criteria (Dr Ali A Mohammadi of Iran);
- measures to promote compliance (Sir Michael Weston of the UK);
- investigations Annex (Mr. Peter Gosen of South Africa);
- confidence-building and transparency measures (the Chairman of the Ad Hoc Group);
- measures related to Article X (Carlos S. Duarte of Brazil); and
- legal issues (John Campbell of Australia).[6]

The list of FOCs has continued to be expanded so that at the Twelfth Session[7] nine Friends of the Chair were operating (Table 4).

Table 4: Friends of the Chair at the Twelfth Session of the Ad Hoc Group*

- definitions of Terms and Objective Criteria (Ali A. Mohammadi of Iran)
- measures to Promote Compliance (Richard Tauwhare of the United Kingdom).
- investigations Annex (Peter Gosen of South Africa).
- measures Related to Article X (Carlos S. Duarte of Brazil).
- legal Issues (Ambassador John Campbell of Australia).
- confidentiality Issues (Ambassador Dr. Günther Seibert of Germany).
- national Implementation and Assistance (Ajit Kumar of India).
- seat of the Organisation (Ambassador Akira Hayashi of Japan).
- preamble (Malik Azhar Ellahi of Pakistan).

* From [7]

The shift to a negotiating format requested by the Fourth Review Conference of the Convention was manifested in the production of a first draft 'Rolling Text of a Protocol to the Convention' by the Chairman at the Seventh Session.[8] This reflected, in a structured manner, the progress that the Ad Hoc Group had made up to the end of the Sixth Session, and it is this document which has been the subject of continued development in subsequent sessions.

THE BTWC VERIFICATION PROTOCOL

In mid-1998 one experienced commentator argued that the Rolling Text now has all of the necessary elements in place.[9] These elements are set out in Table 5. It should be noted that the central compliance-monitoring measures will need to be complemented by measures to control transfers of biological agents, toxins and equipment, measures to enact national legislation, and proper implementation of Article X of the Convention, on international co-operation. All these measures will be required in a regime if it is to be satisfactory to the diverse states parties and therefore likely to attract wide-ranging support.

Table 5: A Verification Protocol for the BTWC*

Compliance Monitoring

a. Mandatory Declarations of those facilities and activities of most relevance to the Convention.
b. Non-Challenge Visits, both focused and random, to declared facilities.
c. Compliance Concern Investigations, both facility and field.

Article III Measures (Non-Transfer)

a. Guidelines for transfer of biological agents, toxins and equipment.
b. Requirement for annual declarations by States Parties.
c. Provisions for investigations of concerns that a transfer has occurred in breach of Article III of the Convention.

Article IV Measures (National Implementation)

a. Requirements for States Parties to enact penal legislation to implement the prohibition of any activity prohibited under the Convention.
b. Requirement for States Parties to set up a National Authority to implement the Protocol.
c. Requirements for States Parties to report to the BTWC Organisation on the national laws, regulations, administrative and other national measures that it has taken to implement Article IV of the Convention.

Article X Measures (Cooperation for Peaceful Purposes)

a. Measures to facilitate the harmonisation of national, regional and international safety rules for pathogens involving both the collection of data and the inspection of facilities.

b. Measures to assist countries to adopt internationally harmonised standards for GMP[Good Manufacturing Practice] of pharmaceutical products and to establish national inspectorates to carry out regular inspections of pharmaceutical manufacturers.

* From [9]

The central compliance measures – declarations, non-challenge visits (both focused and random) to declared facilities, and compliance concern investigations (both facility and field) – have also to be seen as an integrated set that will only be effective in combination. As Douglas J MacEachin (former Deputy Director for Intelligence of the US Central Intelligence Agency) has argued recently:

> Absent a regime for subjecting legitimate activities to a high degree of transparency, the best way for a violator to carry out a covert programme would be to bury it – piggy-back it – inside a legitimate programme...[10]

However, when the regime is in place, if a potential violator's declared facilities – those that pose the greatest risk of non-compliant activity – are subject to mandatory non-challenge visits, then the violator is always at risk of discovery in using a declared site for prohibited activities. To move the non-compliant activity to an undeclared site, however, means that all signs of the activity, not just its illegal purpose, have to be concealed because any undeclared site will be potentially subject to challenge (compliance concern) inspection. Knowledge of a site's illegal use could come from the national intelligence activities of other states, from a defector or by other means. This point about non-challenge visits is an important one because the powerful pharmaceutical industry in the United States has voiced strong opposition to the idea of such visits to its facilities.[11] Clearly, if the issue cannot be satisfactorily resolved, the eventual Verification Protocol could face major difficulties in its ratification process in the United States. This is one of a number of problems that will have to be overcome if a successful agreement is to be reached in the period prior to the 2001 Fifth Review Conference. These difficulties will be reviewed after a consideration of the structure of the Protocol itself.

The report of the Twelfth Session of the Ad Hoc Group is a massive two-part Document.[12] Part I consists of a brief Procedural Report and then an annex (I) which contains the 304 pages of the current 'Rolling Text'. This text has a Preamble, 23 Articles, seven Annexes and four Appendices as set out in Table 6. It will be seen that if the Verification Protocol is agreed, it will have many of the attributes of the recently implemented, modern, Chemical Weapons Convention. For example, there will be provision for sanctions against non-compliance (Protocol Article V) and for national legislation to implement the Protocol properly (Protocol Article X). However, the fact that even the titles of some of the Articles are in brackets (Protocol Articles II, VII, IX), as well as some of the titles of the Annexes (B, C) and Appendices (A, B, D), suggests that a great deal of disagreement, both technical and political, remains to be resolved in the negotiations.

Table 6: Structure of the Verification Protocol*

Preamble	
Article I	General Provisions
Article II	[Definitions]
Article III	Compliance Measures
Article IV	Confidentiality Provisions
Article V	Measures to Redress a Situation and Ensure Compliance
Article VI	Assistance and Protection Against Biological and Toxin Weapons
Article VII	[Scientific and Technological Exchange for Peaceful Purposes] [Implementation Assistance] and Technical Cooperation
Article VIII	Confidence-Building Measures
Article IX	[The Organisation] [and Implementation Arrangements]
Article X	National Implementation Measures
Article XI	Relationship of the Protocol to the BWC and Other International Agreements
Article XII	Settlement of Disputes
Article XIII	Review of the Protocol
Article XIV	Amendments

Article XV	Duration and Withdrawal
Article XVI	Status of the Annexes and Appendices
Article XVII	Signature, XVIII Ratification, XIX Accession, XX Entry into Force, XXI Reservations, XXII Depositary(ies), XXIII Authentic Texts.

Annexes

A. Declarations
B. [Visits]
C. [Measures to Strengthen the Implementation of Article III]
D. Investigations
E. Confidentiality Provisions
F. Scientific and Technological Exchange for Peaceful Purposes and Technical Cooperation
G. Confidence-Building Measures

Appendices

A. [Information to be Provided in Declarations of Past Biological and Toxins Offensive and/or Defensive Research and Development Programmes]
B. [Information to be Provided in Declarations of [Biological] Defence Programmes [Against Biological Weapons]]
C. Information to be Provided in Declarations of Facilities
D. [List of Approved Investigation/Visit Equipment]

* From [12]

As an example of these difficulties, it should be noted that Article VII of the Protocol will implement the requirements of Article X of the Convention (on co-operation). These requirements, as we have seen, were specifically written into the mandate of the Ad Hoc Group in 1994 by the Special Conference. At the end of the Ninth Session of the Ad Hoc Group in January 1998 the title of Article VII read thus: Article VII Scientific and Technological Exchange for Peaceful Purposes and Technical Cooperation. At the end of the Tenth Session of the Ad Hoc Group in March 1998, however, this has been changed to: Article VII [Scientific and Technological Exchange for Peaceful Purposes] [Implementation Assistance] and Technical Cooperation. As one commentator noted, these and other associated changes:

> are seriously retrograde steps as they unnecessarily cast doubts on the intention of the Ad Hoc Group to address the element of its mandate requiring it...to consider 'specific measures designed to ensure effective and full implementation of Article X'...[13]

Not surprisingly, the developing states of the Non-Aligned Movement, who consider this aspect of the Protocol essential, reacted very strongly to the changes and noted that substantive progress in reaching an agreement required an appropriate balance between the various elements of the Protocol.

Table 7: Friends of the Chair Papers, October 1998*

Title	Reference
Proposals for further consideration by the Friend of the Chair on the Investigations Annex	BWC/AD HOC GROUP/FOC/1
Proposals for further consideration by the Friend of the Chair on Measures to Promote Compliance	BWC/AD HOC GROUP/FOC/2
Proposals for further consideration by the Friend of the Chair on Confidentiality	BWC/AD HOC GROUP/FOC/3
Proposals for further consideration by the Chairman on Organisation/ Implementational Arrangements	BWC/AD HOC GROUP/FOC/4
Proposals for further consideration by the Friend of the Chair on Legal Issues	BWC/AD HOC GROUP/FOC/5

TITLE	REFERENCE
Proposals for further consideration by the Friend of the Chair on Measures Related to Article X	BWC/AD HOC GROUP/FOC/6
Proposals for further consideration by the Friend of the Chair on Measures to Promote Compliance	BWC/AD HOC GROUP/FOC/7

* From [12]

Despite such differences, there were clear signs at the end of the Twelfth Session in late 1998 that progress was possible. A series of papers occupying 154 pages of Part II of the report of the session included seven entitled 'Proposals for further consideration...' by Friends of the Chair (Table 7). Whilst not replacing the official rolling text, these papers clearly attempted to reduce the number of square brackets and suggest alternative formulations which provide a cleaner text for further development. An example of this can be seen in the 'Proposals for further consideration by the Friend of the Chair on Measures to Promote Compliance', in BWC/AD HOC GROUP/FOC/2, where the probable eventual structure of Article III in regard to declarations, visits and consultation, clarification and co-operation is evident from the headings and sub-headings proposed (Table 8). Analysis of these *triggers* for declarations strongly suggests that they have been carefully crafted to include only those facilities of most relevance to the Convention and that very limited numbers of industrial facilities will be required to make declarations.[14] Furthermore, the information required in declarations (BWC/AD HOC GROUP/FOC/7) is unlikely to place an undue burden on an industry which is well accustomed to stringent regulation for civil purposes.

Table 8: Headings and sub-headings proposed for Article III elements in BWC/AD HOC GROUP/FOC/2*

D. Declarations

I. Submission of Declarations

Initial Declarations

(A) Past Offensive and/or Defensive Programmes

[(B) National Legislation and Regulations...]
(C) Current Defensive Programmes
(D) Vaccine Production Facilities
(E) Maximum Biological Containment/Biosafety Level 4 Facilities
(F) High Biological Containment/Biosafety Level 3 (BL3) Facilities
(G) Work with Listed Agents and/or Toxins
[(H) Other Production Facilities]
[(I) Other Facilities...]
[(J) Transfers...]
[(K) Declarations on the Implementation of Article X of the Convention...] [Notifications]
[(L) Outbreaks of disease]

II. Follow-Up After Submission of Declarations
[(A) [Random visits]...]
[(B) Clarification Procedures...]
[(C) [Voluntary Request Visits]]
E. Consultation, Clarification and Cooperation

* From [12]

PROGNOSIS

In terms of straight technical issues it might therefore appear possible for the Ad Hoc Group to come to an agreement during the negotiating sessions scheduled for 1999. However, there are political problems as well as technical issues that will need to be resolved. In late 1997 the Chairman of the Ad Hoc Group, Ambassador Tóth, argued that there were four clusters of significant problems that had to be resolved:

> One cluster concerns on-site visits and investigations and another what kind of declarations there should be. A further set of issues relates to definitions, lists and criteria and a fourth set addressing Article X [of the Convention] (scientific and technical cooperation) and Article III (non-transfer measures)...[15]

Whilst powerful commercial interests, as noted, have continuing concerns about the potential loss of commercial proprietary information, the negotiators seem to have taken great care to avoid interference with legitimate industry. It seems likely that concerns will subside as industry gets to grips with the detail of the Verification

Protocol text and realises that few industrial sites will be subject to declaration, and thus to visits, and that the possibility of a credible challenge inspection being mounted against an industrial site in a major state with a properly regulated industry is very small.

Ambassador Tóth pointed out that the problem with definitions, lists and so on, is that they might come to be viewed as defining what the Convention prohibits instead of what the Protocol is being designed to implement. The Convention itself, in Article I, has an all-embracing General Purpose Criterion embodied in the undertaking that each state party will:

> never in any circumstances...develop, produce, stockpile or otherwise acquire or retain:
>
> 1. Microbial or other biological agents, or toxins whatever their origin or method of production, of types and in quantities that have no justification for prophylactic, protective or other peaceful purposes...

Clearly, the prohibition applies not just, for example, to natural pathogens known in 1972 when the Convention was signed, but to genetically engineered organisms that might be manufactured in an offensive biological weapons programme today or in the future. Ambassador Tóth suggested that a pragmatic solution to this problem is possible if those who strongly favour increasing definition of what is prohibited accept that the increased definition be clearly embedded in the Protocol, thus leaving the General Purpose Criterion of the Convention itself unaltered. Such an accommodation is not yet completely realised in the Rolling Text.

As noted, the developing countries are greatly concerned that the increased technological co-operation referred to in Article X of the Convention is properly recognised in the Protocol. Many countries from the developed world, however, believe that they have a serious obligation to control exports of goods under Article III of the Convention which states:

> Each State Party to this Convention undertakes not to transfer to any recipient whatsover, directly or indirectly, and not in any way to assist, encourage, or induce any State, group of States or international organisations to manufacture or otherwise acquire any of the agents, toxins, weapons, equipment or means of delivery specified in Article I of the Convention.

Moreover, following their individual difficulties with export controls relating to weapons of mass destruction in the 1980s, numerous states began to co-ordinate their export controls, first for chemical weapons and then also for biological weapons, within the Australia Group. This caused problems in the later stages of the negotiation of the Chemical Weapons Convention and the issue was set aside rather than resolved then. Whilst the situation in the Ad Hoc Group is not one of total opposition and stalemate on this issue, the disjunction between the requirements of Articles III and X of the Convention will not be easily bridged by the negotiators. It seems probable that this very politicised issue will have to be resolved very late in the final endgame of the negotiations.

Despite such problems and differences, many countries have made clear statements of support for a rapid conclusion to the negotiations. For example, John Holum, Director of the US Arms Control and Disarmament Agency, strongly endorsed the work of the Ad Hoc Group in a presentation to the negotiators during the Twelfth Session.[16] Nevertheless, it has to be accepted that the negotiations may not be completed in 1999. If they are not, it seems likely that proliferation of biological weapons could again drop down the international agenda. The Nuclear Non-Proliferation Treaty Review Conference in 2000 is certain to occupy an increasing amount of the arms control community's time and attention. Then, also, imminent presidential elections are likely to dominate political considerations in Russia and America, two of the Depositary States of the Biological and Toxin Weapons Convention.

In that situation, it is not impossible to envisage an incomplete Verification Protocol at the time of the Fifth Review Conference of the BTWC in 2001. If that is the case, it has to be asked when a protocol *will* eventually come into force and what, by then, will be the technological and military operational situation in regard to biological weapons. Will the goalposts have moved and, rather than having to prevent a potentially usable range of weapons systems from becoming firmly embedded in a few states' military forces, will we be faced with the problem of trying to halt, and roll back, a steadily escalating new armament process in many countries? The historical record of the past 100 years suggests that advances in the understanding of pathogens have been consistently applied in offensive biological warfare programmes in a series of major states.[17] Current and future technological developments are likely to facilitate a wide range of uses of more specific and effective weapons systems, for example genetically engineered, antibiotic-resistant biological weapons agents, unless we put in place a strong regulatory regime.[18]

Notes

1. Spertzel, R. O. *et al.* (1994) *Biological Weapons Proliferation: Technical Report*, US Army Medical Research Institute for Infectious Diseases, Fort Detrick, Maryland.
2. United Nations (1993) *Declarations (Rapporteur: Ms A. Duncan)*, BWC/CONF.III/VEREX/WP.156, reproduced in BWC/CONF.III/VEREX/9, pp.166-173 Geneva, 24 September.
3. United Nations (1994) *Final Report,* Special Conference of the States Parties to the Convention on the Prohibition of the Development, Production and Stockpiling of Bacteriological (Biological) and Toxin Weapons and on their Destruction, BWC/SPCONF/1, Geneva, 19-30 September.
4. United Nations (1995) *Second Session*. Procedural Report of the Ad Hoc Group of the States Parties to the Convention on the Prohibition of the Development, Production and Stockpiling of Bacteriological (Biological) and Toxin Weapons and on their Destruction, BWC/AD HOC GROUP/28. Geneva, 10-21 July.
5. United Nations (1996) *Final Document.* Fourth Review Conference of the States Parties to the Convention on the Prohibition of the Development, Production and Stockpiling of Bacteriological (Biological) and Toxin Weapons and on their Destruction, BWC/CONF.IV/9, Geneva, 25 November-6 December.
6. United Nations (1997) *Seventh Session*. Procedural Report of the Ad Hoc Group of the States Parties to the Convention on the Prohibition of the Development, Production and Stockpiling of Bacteriological (Biological) and Toxin Weapons and on their Destruction, BWC/AD HOC GROUP/36, Geneva, 14 July-1 August.
7. United Nations (1998) *Twelfth Session*. Procedural Report of the Ad Hoc Group of the States Parties to the Convention on the Prohibition of the Development, Production and Stockpiling of Bacteriological (Biological) and Toxin Weapons and on their Destruction, BWC/AD HOC GROUP/43 (Part 1), Geneva, 14 September-9 October.
8. United Nations (1997) *Rolling Text of a Protocol to the Convention on the Prohibition of the Development, Production and Stockpiling of Bacteriological (Biological) and Toxin Weapons and on their Destruction*, BWC/AD HOC GROUP/35, Geneva, 9 June.
9. Pearson, G. S. (1998) *The Protocol to Strengthen the BTWC: An Integrated Regime*, paper presented at the CBW Protection Symposium, Stockholm, 10 May.
10. MacEachin, D. J. (1998) 'Routine and challenge: Two pillars of verification'. *The CBW Conventions Bulletin*, **39**, 1-3.
11. PhRMA (1998) *Summary of PhRMA's position on a Compliance Protocol to the*

Biological Weapons Convention, paper presented at the Twelfth Session of the AHG, Geneva, September.

12. United Nations (1998) *Twelfth Session*. Procedural Report of the Ad Hoc Group of the States Parties to the Convention on the Prohibition of the Development, Production and Stockpiling of Bacteriological (Biological) and Toxin Weapons and on their Destruction, BWC/AD HOC GROUP/43 (Parts 1 and II), Geneva, 14 September-9 October.
13. Pearson, G. S. (1998) *The Strengthened BTWC Protocol: An Integrated Regime*, Briefing Paper No. 10, Department of Peace Studies, University of Bradford. Available on the worldwidewebsite (http://www.brad.ac.uk/acad/sbtwc).
14. Dando, M. R. (1998) *The Strengthened BTWC Protocol: Implications for the Biotechnology and Pharmaceutical Industry*, Briefing Paper No. 17, Department of Peace Studies, University of Bradford. Available on the worldwidewebsite (http://www.brad.ac.uk/acad/sbtwc).
15. Tóth, T. (1997) 'A window of opportunity for the BWC Ad Hoc Group'. *The CBW Conventions Bulletin,* **37**, 1-5.
16. Holum, J. D. (1998) *Statement to the Biological Weapons Convention Ad Hoc Group Session XII*, Mission of the United States of America, Geneve, 6 October.
17. Dando, M. R. (1998) 'The impact of the development of modern biology and medicine on the evolution of offensive biological warfare programmes in the 20th century.' *Defense Analysis,* in press.
18. Cohen, W. S. (1997) *Proliferation: Threat and Response* (Technical Annex). Office of the Secretary of Defense, Washington, D.C.

* Work supported by an Airey Neave Fellowship for study of the negotiations of the Biological and Toxin Weapons Convention Verification Protocol.

SECURITY SECTOR REFORM

18
The Security Sector and Civil Society: The Unfolding Debate

CHRIS SMITH

North-South Programme Centre for Defence, Studies Kings College London

INTRODUCTION

Across the international community of states, national security forces are undergoing transformation. On the one hand, they are facing new roles and missions; large- and medium-scale wars are increasingly a phenomenon of the past. Also, technological change is proving to be an important driver. In the United States, there is a growing feeling that the scope now exists to exploit the full potential of the capabilities afforded by 'smart' weapons and information technology; the so-called 'revolution in military affairs'.[1]

On the other, at the lower end of the military capability spectrum, in pursuit of good governance, aid dependent countries are coming under intense pressure from bilateral and multilateral donors to reform security institutions in the same way as other organs of government. In pursuit of transparency, accountability, accessibility and coherence – the essential hallmarks of a strong civil society – it is now considered imperative that security policy-making is brought under more sustainable, democratic control. A separate but nevertheless important development is the growing desire by military and political leaderships to take part in collective missions overseas, especially peace support operations. In many cases, ranging from Bulgaria, to Argentina, to South Africa, military institutions appear willing to solicit external help and advice in achieving these goals, though confidence in the sincerity of the requests for help differ from country to country and from one observer to another; many NGOs take the position that military institutions are beyond reform. Also, given the changing nature of security concerns and bearing in mind the scope of the good governance agenda, it is also appropriate to include the police and internal security forces in this process, though we currently lack a holistic framework which can be applied. Much the same can be said for the judiciary.

The rate of progress and the attainment of successful reform will influence significantly how OECD countries think about individual, developing countries. It will influence future aid decisions, both directly and indirectly. It will also dictate access to advanced military technology and modern weapons systems. Genuine reform will increase a country's international standing, whereas cosmetic reform will raise serious concerns over the abiding power of the military in society and uneven civil-military relations.

The aim of this chapter is to understand how and which institutions are addressing security sector reform and the type of dynamics which might develop in the future.

DEVELOPMENT, INTERNATIONAL INSTITUTIONS AND THE MILITARY

One of the most interesting developments in recent years is the growing inclination on the part of international aid organisations and donor governments to factor in the behaviour of security and military institutions when assessing their relations with former Warsaw Pact nations and developing countries. Indeed, this is a trend which in some cases has preceded, albeit marginally, the end of the Cold War. However, this has not always been the case.

During the Cold War, armed forces on both sides of the divide were treated as special cases. In the West, a strong culture of secrecy pervaded NATO institutions, at least up until the 1980s when unprecedented public pressure spurred on by a genuine, collective fear of nuclear policies and postures, forced governments to offer greater transparency and public debate. These trends were not replicated within the Warsaw Pact, nor in the Third World.

Within the developing world, the state and military institutions used political affiliations to acquire military aid. The onset of the Cold War coincided roughly with the collapse of colonial empires and the onset of independence in most parts of Asia, Africa and the Middle East – indeed, some revisionist historians see the entry of the United States into the war as conditional upon a dismantling of empire once the war ended, to provide equal, open access to foreign markets.[2] Fundamental to the policy of containment, the United States attempted to draw together a series of interlocking treaties – NATO, CENTO, SEATO – to ensure a massive response, if and when the Soviet Union embarked upon its programme of global expansion, not least in the direction of warm-water ports, or so it was generally believed in the US. The Soviets retaliated by attempting to break down the weakest links in the chain and, also, by looking beyond the front-line to make links with left-leaning, emerging independent states – Cuba being the most extreme example. During this long, drawn out geo-political competition, billions of dollars of military aid flowed from north to south as both the superpowers and the former colonial powers pursued influence and advantage amongst the vulnerable states in the Third World.

During this fascinating chapter of the Cold War, developments occurred which afforded military institutions special access to military equipment, resources and power, especially the extension of superpower political competition to the Third World. The combination of Cold War politics and the need of weak governments to defend a tenuous monopoly of force at home and to handle conflicts emerging from disputed border claims, allowed the armed forces to manoeuvre themselves into an extremely privileged position; strong on the one hand and indispensable on the other, the more so in countries where political legitimacy was weak. What this meant in practice was a deepening sense of autonomy, which grew even more robust as the importance of the military links between north and south grew stronger. The superpowers and the former colonial powers became fiercely protective of and unduly tolerant towards the negative aspects of military practices, from Chile to Indonesia. In practice, this meant that human and civil rights abuses carried out by the military and claims for excessive shares of government spending on defence went largely unnoticed. In addition, some political sociologists sought to define, commend and advocate the role of the military in development.[3]

The end of the Cold War is usually used as the benchmark for change but, in reality, reform trends were in progress well before the fall of the Berlin Wall. The major opportunity for a more critical appraisal of the security forces in the Third World came with the financial debt crisis of the 1980s, although the political and intellectual groundwork was achieved even earlier. Few now remember President Carter's genuine efforts to curb the arms sales to countries which refused to respect human rights and the direct impact this had on US arms sales to Latin America, restrictions which have only recently been lifted or weakened.[4] Through the late-1970s and early-1980s efforts were made by dependency theorists to link excessive armament to underdevelopment and, conversely, disarmament to development.[5]

Up until the early-1980s, international financial institutions and bilateral donors seemed, from the outside, to remain largely oblivious to the importance of high military expenditure and profligate defence procurement when considering what might be done to alleviate chronic underdevelopment. (However, enterprising archival research may yet upturn memoranda and position papers which indicate signs of a growing impatience and concern.) The international debt crisis and the response of international finance organisations, notably the IMF and the World Bank, combined to make a mockery of economic sovereignty in the poorest and most indebted states; this time around, the defence sector was seen as a viable area from which to make significant contributions to cuts in government expenditure. Thus, the IMF denied Peru the latitude to purchase the *Mirage* 2000 from France and Jordan's plans to procure the *Tornado* from the UK were similarly abandoned soon after the arrival of an IMF crisis team. The World Bank surreptitiously placed itself in direct control of the Ugandan defence budget when the economy hit rock bottom in the late-1980s and early-1990s and, to a lesser extent, Argentina suffered a similar fate.[6] The worm, it seems, was turning and international finance organisations were beginning to grow tired of inappropriate military spenders and poorly-managed security sectors.

The fall of the Berlin Wall offered further impetus. International finance organisations needed no more than the chink of political light offered by the eradication of superpower competition to pursue further the perceived need to prune defence budgets and bring the security sector into line. In addition, the end of the Cold War straddled two overlapping generations of conditionality. The first was primarily economic, though few could miss the political overtones. The conditions set by the Bretton Woods establishments during the 1980s focused upon the reform of economic policy. However, they also carried heavy and discernible political baggage aimed at reducing the role of the state in favour of the workings of the market, using structural adjustment as a blunt and heavy tool. By the late-1980s, the weight of criticism levelled against structural adjustment, which hinged upon its negative impact upon the poor, led to the development of 'second generation conditionality'. Here, the focus was on governance – the pursuit of democracy and participation and verifiable respect for human, political and civil rights, which is where it largely remains.

Consequently, the political and intellectual ground became less cluttered. Far fewer obstacles remained in the way of a more direct attack upon all things military in the Third World – military expenditure as a percentage of GDP, inappropriate arms imports, attitudes towards weapons of mass destruction, the role of the military in and responsibility for human and civil rights abuses. The Development Assistance Committee of the OECD was perhaps the most proactive, stating unequivocally in 1993:

> DAC members recognise the importance of peace and security for development. When military expenditure is excessive, it can result in conflict and repression, contribute to instability in the region and divert scarce resources away from development needs. DAC members emphasise the importance of establishing and maintaining the primacy of the role of civilians in political and economic affairs and the significance they attach to avoiding or reducing excessive military expenditure.[7]

Although many governments now recognise that the development process can be profoundly affected by the security sector, it has only recently become apparent where the development sector might make a difference. One of the most important consequences of the end of the Cold War was on the collapse of bipolarity as the primary form of organisation for the international order. This in turn led to a major transformation of the strategic landscape, which had a profound effect upon the Third World. For a complex mix of reasons, the end of the Cold War placed extreme, additional pressure upon state formation when Third World leaders found that they could no longer rely upon the borrowing and aid resources generated by Cold War rivalry. Many states proved too weak to sustain the pressure, which in many cases came swiftly on the heels of structural adjustment programmes. What happened next is a remarkable and complex story of transition from post-colonial to post-modern state building witnessing the emergence of political projects in the South which no longer need to establish territorial, bureaucratic or consent-based political authority.[8]

Weak and collapsing states set the scene for complex political emergencies, involving not just high levels of violent, intra-state conflict but also humanitarian disasters, such as mass human displacement and migration, starvation and the brutal reversal of previously achieved development. Understanding how to respond effectively to complex emergencies remains a hotly debated subject. However, what is clear is that organisations primarily responsible for development have been forced to prioritise humanitarian concerns and responses, a move further compounded by a spate of humanitarian disasters unrelated to conflict, Nicaragua, Honduras and Bangladesh being the most recent examples. As a result, the development community has arrived at the coalface of conflict, meeting in the process human rights organisations and, tellingly, military institutions involved in peace support operations.

The result has been a revolution in relations between development and the military. Just as development agencies have been forced to respond to complex emergencies, the military have also been forced to think about and plan in more detail, doctrines which govern and direct operations other than war as the need to respond to internal wars and their consequences increases, especially in Africa. The result, though still ongoing, has been to make peacekeeping doctrine less of an additional task, weakly attached to existing warfighting doctrine and more a freestanding, holistic doctrine in its own right.[9]

The dynamics which underpin the fusion of military and developmental perspectives are outlined in Figure one.

Yet another opportunity has presented itself to the development community, now that some previously failed states have begun the process of reconstruction. The good governance agenda is central to visions of state reconstruction and those responsible for defining the reconstruction agenda, as well as footing the bill, have opted to address the roles and missions of the armed forces and civil-military relations as being central to the overall process. For several decades the military have spurned the development community and vice versa. This should never have been the case – in many instances the interests of both are inter-linked. Now, institutional links have been established and the military-development circle is closing.

Figure One

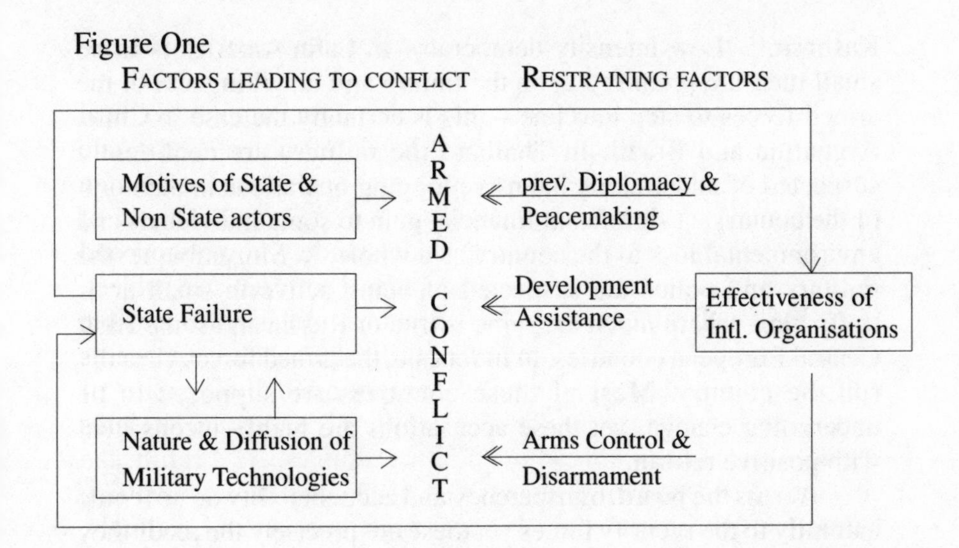

Consequently, security sector reform is rapidly becoming a major item on the development agenda. This has coincided with similar dynamics within other sectors of government, not just in the UK. Amongst OECD countries, there is a growing desire to encourage wherever possible security sector reform, to ensure that the size and cost of the armed forces relate to perceived roles, missions and threat perceptions and to ensure where possible that the armed forces are disconnected from potential sources of intra-state conflict, the abuse of rights and the opponents of transparency and accountability. In the UK, security sector reform is implied, albeit broadly, under the rubric of preventive diplomacy (FCO) and defence diplomacy (MoD).

Although the trend towards the democratisation of control of the security forces is unmistakable, there is resistance nevertheless. Military and police personnel are liable to resent what they perceive to be the interference of civilians and outsiders in the evaluation of their professional conduct, all the more so if the outsiders are western NGOs. Police intelligence in South Africa, for example, attempted to influence constitutional change even after the 1994 election.[10] Members of the Pakistan military are suspected of maintaining undue politico-religious ambitions and the military-intelligence nexus is largely responsible for arming and training the Taliban, as well as facilitating the movement of weapons and combatants into

Kashmir.[11] 'Low-intensity democracy' in Latin America is in no small measure premised upon the failure and unwillingness of the armed forces to step into line – this is certainly the case in Chile, Argentina and Brazil. In Thailand the military are confidently suspected of undertaking intensive logging operations in the north of the country, at significant financial gain to some individuals and environmental loss to the country as a whole. In Mozambique, the military and police are suspected of being active in small arms trafficking, where much the same is true of Russia and some East/Central European countries. In Indonesia, the armed forces virtually run the country. Most of these countries are supposed to be undergoing change, yet these accusations are highly inconsistent with positive reform.

Across the board, transparency and accountability do not come naturally to the security forces yet these are precisely the roads they must travel if the richer, post-military aid donors are to keep faith. In developing countries especially, military institutions are detached and superior and largely of the belief that they are above the norms and values which shape civil society. There is, therefore, a special case to be made regarding the need to monitor the reform of security institutions very carefully. In this context, it is unfortunate that the communities responsible for the evaluation of good governance programmes may not have much experience in dealing with and, therefore, of understanding the sometimes arcane workings of the security forces. For development NGOs and international organisations, for example, interaction with the security forces is comparatively recent and political-cultural barriers remain very strong; as the two communities move closer together, the NGOs are appearing as the more conservative and resistant force.

In countries where reform programmes proceed apace, there is a growing recognition that the security forces cannot undertake reform programmes in isolation. If the key tenets of good governance do not come naturally to the security forces, then individual members of those forces must be taught new codes and practices, such as the responsibility of the individual during operations and the international norms and standards which govern human rights. Over the past five years, a wide range of countries have requested the help of defence, human rights and governance experts from the West to contribute to their training programmes.

Unfortunately, it is not always the clear that the security forces are completely sincere in their overtures to western institutions. Possibly, training and education programmes are used as a smokescreen but this is not always evident at the outset. Obversely, if it suits their purposes, western governments may use such programmes as implicit evidence of reform, which might then be used to render the sale of certain types of defence equipment less controversial.

These observations beg questions of fundamental importance. When a foreign government appeals to a western democracy for guidance and help over the course of the reform process, what are the criteria to judge the sincerity of the request and the value of responding? Equally important, who should be responsible for the inevitable judgement call? For example, an MoD might have its own agenda and for diametrically opposed reasons, so might the NGO community, especially single-issue pressure groups.

If the reform process proceeds apace, then donors will be forced to make a series of ethical and political choices about the individuals and the institutions with whom and with which they are prepared to work. In some cases, interaction and contact may be highly controversial, yet the links should not be kept secret, unless there are exceptionally strong reasons for doing so; the exercise should be visible and public otherwise an important part of the process will be either lost or downgraded, namely that of persuading a potentially doubtful public and bringing the NGO community onside. One of the most difficult professional tasks in this emerging area will be the need to work with individuals and institutions who and which might not initially share donor government's strength of commitment to the political ideals which underpin the programmes upon which they will be encouraged to embark. Now that opportunities are arising to undertake such programmes it is important to maintain a forward momentum.

SECURITY SECTOR REFORM: AN EVOLVING AGENDA

Security sector reform nudges ever closer to the international agenda as the 'like-minded' post-military aid donors follow the lead which appears to have been set by the UK, questions will be asked as to what might be expected from the process and how success and failure might usefully be evaluated. The following section suggests what donors might realistically come to expect from the process.

At the outset, however, it is important to point out that the donor countries are firmly bound by current trends against the use of conditionality, the first generation of which was widely considered to have been too blunt an instrument. Economic conditionality – the 'first generation' described above – largely turned on the structural adjustment programmes introduced by the World Bank in the 1980s and the willingness of bilateral donors to support the process. Basically, structural adjustment entailed imposing a series of policy changes on developing countries to increase exports and slow the rate of growth for imports, while still maintaining a high rate of economic activity overall. The policy changes were those favoured by the neo-liberal development counter-revolution which held sway at that time: the avoidance of over-valued exchange rates; rates of interest which reflect the market forces of supply and demand; shrinkage of the public sector; deregulation of markets; the setting of agricultural prices which are 'properly remunerative' to cultivators; the dismantling of direct controls over trade and investment; the equalisation of domestic and imported energy prices and the reform of energy taxation.[12] In the absence of robust welfare structures, many of the perceived distortions were in fact surrogate welfare operations, though many also played a dual role in keeping vote banks robust.

Within the circles of development studies which opposed the neo-liberal revolution there was immense consternation over the harsh and unforgiving overtones inherent in development policy's new look, hence the pleas to work towards a process which included adjustment but with a human face. As a result, however, the very act of conditionality became linked to not just harshness but also hypocrisy – the United States steadfastly refused to undertake any form of structural adjustment in the first half of the 1990s, despite a massive budget deficit and declining export competitiveness – a clear case of do as we say, not as we do.[13]

Second generation conditionality was understandably more sensitive to the leverage issue, in part because of the criticism afforded the neo-liberals, partly because this generation was controlled much more by bilateral, liberal donors and partly because of the nature of the goal, which sat uneasily with the 'arm twisting' of the past. Now, as the second generation moves into adolescence, overt conditionality is very much out of favour. Developing countries, sensing the uneasiness amongst liberals have been quick to press their case against conditionality, especially amongst the more liberal donors. As a result, it is somewhat unlikely that aid donors will resort to conditionality when addressing security sector reform issues, not least because there is little that they can do directly which would disadvantage the military, rather than the civilian poor or civil society as a whole. Equivocation over conditionality has, nevertheless, come at a difficult time as, arguably, attempts to move the military in certain unfamiliar directions would certainly benefit from extra leverage.

Security sector reform will differ according to state strength and weakness, as well as the extant regional tensions which drive external threat perception at any given time. Donors have recently become more sensitive to external and internal security needs and may also become flexible on cultural issues, such as the perceived need on the part of most African states for a presidential guard.

As a part of the good governance project, transparency and accountability are likely to be the corner stones of security sector reform. This will turn upon the ability of the legislature to control the military as an institution. For example, the Public Accounts Committee in Ghana has recently bemoaned the reluctance of the military to offer the committee decent accounts. Donor recipients will be encouraged to take steps to ensure that the military is made fully accountable for expenditures on, for example, living conditions and overseas visits – the military in Pakistan and Bangladesh are renowned for ensuring that extravagant comfort levels in the cantonments are a first charge on the defence budget. Donors will also be keen to see a minimal or non-existent role for the military in politics and an end to military involvement in economic ventures, as has become almost *de rigeur* in China.

Another major area of investigation will be military expenditure overall. The main donors, many of whom are themselves low military spenders will be keen to ensure that military expenditure does not diminish the government's capacity to fund civil sector projects (infrastructure projects, agricultural research, health and welfare), thereby crowding out programmes which then require donor support.[14] Effectively, this amounts to donors subsidising defence programmes. Japan and Germany have already made this an explicit requirement. Initially, the World Bank toyed with the idea of a formula which would set an upper limit to the GDP which could be expended on the military before penalties were applied – 7% was the generally agreed figure. However, in the case of South Asia, this would give Pakistan very little room for manoeuvre at the current rate of expenditure of 5.6% of GDP. Conversely, India would enjoy considerable flexibility given that it spends a mere 2.5% of GDP on defence. [15] Yet, India traditionally enjoys a 3:1 conventional superiority over Pakistan. Given the long-standing development tenet that no two developing countries are the same, a formula approach is, thankfully, unlikely to take root.

A third area of concern will be arms procurement, though this will most certainly be complicated by donor arms export aspirations, especially where large aid donors are also active players on the international arms export market – Britain, Germany and Sweden spring quickly to mind. This will need especially nimble footwork at a time when defence and development ministries are moving towards a uniquely healthy symbiotic relationship. Nevertheless, there are perceived opportunities here to cut out 'inappropriate' procurement and defence deals which are tainted with corruption. In the 1980s, India spent $2 billion on the *Mirage* 2000, a single-engined fighter-bomber which the Indian Air Force appeared not to want because of the problems associated with bird strikes. Unfortunately, these types of 'big ticket deals' are precisely those which major arms producers need to tie down on a regular basis to ensure the continuity of their own production lines. How donor governments resolve this contradiction will be one of the most interesting, and difficult, debates of the future.

Without doubt, much will be made of human rights and the problem of unacceptable behaviour during internal operations. Here, the donors are likely to encourage comprehensive education programmes, to ensure that military officers are fully aware and informed of international norms and standards of, not just human rights, but the culpability of individuals in operations. ICRC already run such programmes, in Indonesia for example. Here, the problem of verification will loom large. To an extent, the larger human rights organisations will most certainly be involved. However, smaller, single-issue groups will also demand their say. As in the case of allegations of British *Hawk* fighters being used in counter-insurgency operations in Indonesia, watertight evidence has proved hard to come by, which may worry donors a lot more than the more vocal NGOs thus giving rise to the potential for considerable friction. The donors will also need to take care not to place themselves in a position whereby the NGOs acquire a veto, with or without verifiable evidence.

Weak, collapsing and failed states provide a separate set of problems. During periods of extreme weakness the donors will strive to ensure that the military adheres to best practice and is kept under tight control. The problems associated with military activities when states begin to fail are numerous and include the sale of state-owned weapons – Russia being the most worrying contemporary example – and the development and execution of political programmes. The maintenance of discipline will be a key factor.

Peace support operations also require the support and assistance of the local armed forces, where they exist – almost by definition a collapsed state implies the collapse of the security sector as well. Also, many countries which provide troops for peace support operations are themselves major aid recipients, such as Ghana and Bangladesh. The problems which have beset some peace support operations, such as the involvement of peacekeeping troops in racketeering, could prompt a reaction on the part of donors.

Finally, during the period of reconstruction, it is now widely accepted that the security forces, including the police, will require special attention, not least because the state cannot be seen to be reconstituted until a monopoly of force has been acquired. These issues pose some interesting moral and political dilemmas, such as whether or not war lords should be fully recognised as political actors and drawn into the process of reconstruction, especially when there are implications for human rights and crimes against humanity. The reconstruction of Liberia, Afghanistan and Somalia cannot be contemplated without the involvement of those who share in the oligopolisation of force.

CONCLUSIONS

Whether or not and to what extent security sector reform programmes will meet with success remains to be seen. On the one hand, the military are notorious for their conservative views. Those who have enjoyed a long-standing immunity from public scrutiny will not take kindly to the sharp light of transparency and accountability, especially if the professional standing, creature comforts and personal bank balances of military élites stand to be adversely affected, and when it becomes clear that a refusal to co-operate may not bring with it a direct cost. Also, the problem of who decides will endure. Who is best placed to decide the appropriate fit between threat perception and military requirement? To what extent will pressure from the donors bring the donors themselves into conflict with the legislation that governs their activities? What happens when the inability to maintain territorial defence is blamed upon donor pressure to limit defence expenditure and procurement?

On the other hand, the picture might not be so bleak. There is some evidence that the military in some countries may be developing proactive programmes to promote education and best practice. There are plenty of examples of senior military officers from Third World and former Warsaw Pact countries approaching western governments for assistance focused upon education and reform. The origins of these initiatives are unknown in most cases. Are they the result of a gentle push or enlightened self-interest? Also, and of paramount importance, it is not yet known whether these initiatives are seen by the military as cushions to procrastinate and avoid making fundamental changes by giving the appearance of seeking the very changes they really wish to avoid – a handful of in-country training programmes to be followed by business as usual. An associated problem concerns the ethical and political problems posed by the need to reform security forces which have in the past been guilty of severe abuses. Where should donors draw the line, with whom should they work and whom should they ignore as beyond reform? What happens when they make a mistake?

In addition, the security sector reform process will be assisted by the changing role of the military on a global level. On the one hand, the role of the armed forces has become defined in a large number of cases by the onset of complex emergencies and the increasing number of peace support operations underway at any given time. On the other, security threats closer to home have changed dramatically. More than ever, nation states feel less threatened by invasion. Traditional wars, such as those which raged throughout the Middle East and South Asia in the 1960s and 1970s, are less frequent in occurrence and number than at any time since the end of the Second World War – a trend which will hopefully be maintained. Obversely, however, new threats to security and stability, often termed 'soft security' problems have emerged; terrorism, migration, arms trafficking and smuggling, for example. The nature of soft security threats has forced the armed forces to work more closely with national police forces, as witnessed by the links between the South African police and armed forces on border security controls. Terrorists, for example, almost invariably support their operations through criminal activities such as drug trafficking and robbing banks. As the proliferation of illegal weapons proceeds apace, the gap between arms and firearms control is diminishing.

National police forces have not been immune from the purview of the international community. There is concern over the propensity of certain governments to allow their policemen to engage in repressive and heavy-handed policing to achieve domestic stability. The persecution of street children by the Latin American police is a particularly appalling example, while the Russian police have become infamous for exceptionally deep-seated levels of corruption. There is strong pressure on some governments to adopt more benign community policing methods and aid has on occasions been made available to assist transition. Concern over the export of equipment and technology designed primarily for torture and repression is increasing and the international community is currently thinking through ways of choking off these flows.

The changing nature of security threats suggests that, in the future, the police and the national security forces in many countries will merge closer together and, over time, the institutional gap between the two may become almost invisible. This will occur on the international as well as the national stage, the significant though precisely defined supervisory role of the International Police Task Force in Bosnia being a case in point, though the long-term utility of the task force is debatable. Overall, however, this is to be welcomed and the armed forces should be encouraged by their political masters to shake off roles and missions which have become anachronistic and irrelevant, especially those which consume a high level of resources.

All this amounts to a considerable number of new opportunities for those in search of security sector reform. If major wars are to occur less frequently and in fewer parts of the world, then the strength of the argument for appropriate procurement increases. If the procurement budget can be made to shrink, then military expenditure overall can be decreased. Greater involvement by aid-dependent countries in peace support operations can be used to offset military expenditure, thus strengthening the prospects for durable – and resilient – development programmes.

Notes

[1] For a comprehensive analysis of this potential and its implications see Freedman, L., 'The Revolution in Strategic Affairs', *Adelphi Paper No.318*, (April 1998).

[2] Gardner, L.C., LaFeber, W.F. and McCormick, T.J., *Creation of the American Empire: US Diplomatic History,* Rand McNally and Company, 1973.

[3] There is a vast literature on the role of the military in development. For a critical review, see, Kaldor, M., 'The Military in Third World Development', in, Graham, M., Jolly, R. and C.Smith, (Eds.), *Disarmament and World Development*, (Pergamon, London, 1985), pp.71-102.

[4] For a review of these policy debates see Pierre, A., *The Global Politics of Arms Sales*, (Princeton University Press, Princeton, 1982), especially pp.232-249, and, Klare, M.T., *American Arms Supermarket*, (University of Texas Press, Austin, 1984).

[5] On the former see Kaldor, M. and A. Eide, *The World Military Order: The Impact of Military Technologies on the Third World*, (Macmillan, London, 1979), and, Deger, S. and R. West, (Eds.), *Defence, Security and* Development, (Frances Pinter, London, 1987). On the latter, Graham, M., Jolly, R. and C.Smith, *op cit*, which also contains a useful, annotated bibliography, and, United Nations, *Disarmament and Development: Report of the Group of Experts on the Economic and Social Consequences of the Arms Race*, (Department of Economic and Social Affairs, ST/ECA/174, New York, 1992).

[6] This view is based upon confidential information made available to the author but corroborated to an extent in Stevens, M, and S. Gnanaselvam, 'The World Bank and Governance', *IDS Bulletin,* Vol 26, No 2, (April 1995), p.102, when they state 'where a government has already made up its mind to reduce military expenditure, the Bank may assist the country articulate a budgetary framework within which the scaling down of military programmes can occur. Argentina and Uganda are two countries where such help has been given.'

[7] *DAC Orientations on Participatory Development and Good Governance*, OCDE/GD(93)191, OECD, Paris, 1993, para 53.

[8] Duffield, M., 'Post-modern Conflict: Warlords, Post-adjustment States and Private Protection', *Civil Wars*, Vol 1, No 1, (Spring 1998), pp.65-102.

[9] See, for example, the UK version, also one of the most progressive, 'Peace Support Operations', *Joint Warfare Publication 3-50*, (PJHQ, Northwood, Middlesex, undated).

[10] Police intelligence attempted, unsuccessfully, to retain the guilty until proven innocent presumption in the firearms trafficking act, arguing that it would make their task more difficult.

[11] Gupta, S. and R. Pathak, 'Exporting Terror', *India Today*, Vol XIX, No 9, (15 May 1994), pp.24-45.

[12] Toye, J., *Dilemmas of Development: Reflections on the Counter-Revolution in Development Theory and Policy*, (Basil Blackwell, Oxford, 1987), p.156.

[13] *ibid*, p.158.

[14] Stevens, M, and S. Gnanaselvam, *op cit*, p.102.

[15] SIPRI, *op cit*, Table 6A.4, p.230.

19

The Politics of Security Sector Reform in West Africa

ABIODUN ALAO

African Security Programme Centre for Defence Studies,
Kings College London

INTRODUCTION

The post-Cold War security situation in West Africa has attracted considerable interest, reaching its peak with the publication of Richard Kaplan's now controversial piece, 'The Coming Anarchy' in 1994.[1] While the article can be criticised for some preconceived and sometimes simplistic conclusions, its main thesis that the security situation in West Africa deserves a closer look can hardly be faulted. Since the end of the Cold War, a number of major problems have brought the region to international attention. These include the collapse of the central government in Liberia, the failed democratic transition and subsequent establishment of a dictatorship in Nigeria, ethnic conflict in northern Ghana, civil war in Sierra Leone, political instability in Guinea Bissau, questionable democracy in the Gambia, secessionist agitation in Senegal, weapons proliferation in Mali and a host of other examples. Indeed, by the middle of the 1990s, the region may be said to have replaced southern Africa as Africa's main theatre of conflict.

The aim of this chapter is to consider one of the neglected aspects of the region's security complexities. This is the emerging discussion on security sector reform. The intention here is to situate the topic within the framework that has traditionally governed domestic security in most West African states, and to investigate, in the process, the factors impeding the establishment and consolidation of viable security sector reform. The chapter is conceived against two important backgrounds. First, is the importance of security issues to a sub-region that exhibits the serious problems identified above, while the second is the recognition of the role that security sector reform has come to play in post-Cold War security dispensations, especially for countries who have to claim to be engaged in it (even if under false pretensions) in order to appease international donors.

The chapter is divided into six short sections. The first provides a panoramic survey of the security situation in West Africa, looking specifically at the role of the region's militaries, whose traditional primacy is central to the whole debate of security sector reform. The second focuses on the actual content of security sector reform in post Cold-War West Africa. The third looks at the manifestation (or the lack of it) of security sector reform in war-torn states, while the fourth and fifth sections respectively investigate security sector reform in democratic and autocratic states of the region. The sixth section concludes by looking at the future of security sector reform in West Africa.

WEST AFRICAN MILITARY IN THE POST COLD-WAR ERA: A NEW FACE IN THE NEW PHASE?

Perhaps the most important characteristic of the military in West Africa is their involvement in politics. Indeed, with the exception of Côte d'Ivoire and Senegal, all states in the region have witnessed one form of military of intervention or other since their independence. So predominant has been the influence of the military in politics that they are regarded in many countries as being the only substitute to 'erring' ruling political parties. Even though they always consider themselves as 'corrective' and often promise to leave once they complete their 'sanitisation mission' they often hold on to power for a long time, only to be overthrown by another 'corrective' military regime. The result is a vicious circle of military rule.

Two factors determine the role of the military within the discussion of security sector reform. The first is the largely 'military' perception of security during the Cold War era, while the second is the effective grip of the military on the political affairs of most of these states. Each of these has left considerable consequences. For example, the 'militarised' concept of security relegated other indices of security that could have guaranteed better standards of socio-economic life and good governance to the background. Such neglected aspects include economic security, environmental security, and so on. The military's grip on political affairs, resulted in a situation where, whether in or out of government, the military remained a powerful force whose interests had to be considered in any proposed reforms. It also led to the militarisation of the psyche of the people, and civilian élites. Even those held in high esteem for their credibility, eventually mortgaged their consciences to assist the military in perpetuating an assault on democracy. But perhaps worse than this is that there emerged in most of the states in question a blurred distinction between the roles of the police and the armed forces, with the latter usurping the role of the police in the provision of domestic security.

Some developments, which unfolded in the late-1980s and early-1990s, impressed upon the military the need to reduce their grip on political power and to concede to reform in the security sector. Two of these developments are worth noting. The first was the demystification of the military that came with the end of the Cold War, exemplified in the sub-region by Charles Taylor's rebellion against the Doe government in Liberia. In this case, a civilian warlord led a successful rebellion that removed a military turned-civilian leader. This success encouraged civilians in other countries to challenge the military and demand from it accountability in its management of state affairs. The second development was the global call for democratic governance that followed the end of the Cold War. This made military dictatorship no longer quite so tolerable, and many donor agencies increasingly tied aid and assistance to democratic and security reform.

The overall outcome was that, by the beginning of the 1990s, most military governments in the region had realised that their days were numbered, and that a strategy must be put in place to ensure that while they continued to dictate the pace of any security sector reforms, they must appear on the surface as conceding to democratic reform. The modified strategy came in two forms. In some states, incumbent military governments metamorphosed themselves into civilian regimes. Such states include Ghana, Burkina Faso, Liberia, Guinea, and Chad. In others, the military handed over the visible reins of government to elected civilians, with the implicit acceptance by the latter that the interests of the military would continue to be protected.

THE CONTENT OF SECURITY SECTOR REFORM IN POST-COLD WAR WEST AFRICA

Just as the end of the Cold War brought out the need to rethink the nature of global security, so it also dictated the need for states to reconsider the structure of their domestic security. Although in many places in West Africa the phrase 'security sector reform' is not really being used, what it entails has been a cause for concern across the countries in the region for at least two reasons. First, since the end of the Cold War, the international community has made reform paramount to disbursing aid and loans to most of the region's states. As economic stresses have made them particularly vulnerable, most of these countries are willing to take steps towards satisfying the donor community in order to obtain aid. Second, the collapse of Liberia, and the near collapse of Sierra Leone, showed many countries in the region that existing security structures could not meet the post-Cold War challenges, and so they saw the need to instigate change themselves before circumstances forced less palatable changes on them.

Put crudely, states in West Africa saw the whole debate on security sector reform as entailing a process through which the management of national security was made to meet a set of standards. These standards include the process through which security decisions are made and how they are implemented. Within this broad spectrum are issues like democracy and good governance, a proper definition of the role of the armed forces, the role of the judiciary, the police and a proper evaluation of what constitutes national security problems and external threats.

In virtually all the countries in the region, there was no clear articulation of all these issues during the Cold War, and the consequence was that the security of the inhabitants of the countries was sublimated within regime security, and state survival became the survival of the regime in power. While the legal constitutions of each state the countries may in theory separate powers between the executive, the legislature and the judiciary, government practice was a different story. The military became the instrument of oppression of those it was meant to protect. An excess of counter-vailing tensions led to the collapse of some of the states, while a host of others were badly affected. The remainder of this chapter provides a situation report on the degrees of commitment and success that has attended reforms.

SECURITY SECTOR REFORM IN 'FAILED' AND 'WOUNDED' STATES

While not investigating the whole debate on the usage of the term 'failed states'; this chapter has taken the term to refer to states in which the central authorities have collapsed. Similarly, 'wounded' states are taken here to refer to societies, in which the central government is still intact, but which have been seriously affected by bitter civil conflicts. In the West African sub-region, two countries – Liberia and Sierra Leone – fall under this category.

In Liberia and Sierra Leone, the state of security sector reform is inter-mingled with the entire post-war reconstruction process, and the politics governing it has been the same as that underlining the civil conflicts in both countries. The expectation has been that post-war reconstruction efforts would give both nations the opportunity to restructure their states, incorporating security sector reform within this, in order to learn from the failures of the past to design the challenges of the future. In both countries, the primary objective has been to create new national security forces that would command respect and acceptability to the population. This has inevitably required that soldiers be recruited from a broad social base that would address the ethnic and social divergences of both countries. It would also entail providing them with a professional training that would inculcate in them the need to respect the rule of law and accept the primacy of civilian control. Other issues include the consolidation of democracy, the independence of the judiciary and the retraining of the police.

The reality, however, has been different, and the local ingredients that coloured the civil conflict have re-emerged to play a role in the politics of security sector reform. In Liberia, for example, there were many factions defeated in the war which have not been effectively disarmed and demobilised. Second, the election was won by a presidential candidate who was the leader of one of the warring factions. Third, the elected government rejected the pre-election agreement, which assigned to ECOMOG, the regional peacekeeping force, the task of re-organising the security forces. Finally, there are fears on the part of the leaders of the other warring factions that former fighters of the incumbent President's warring faction would dominate the new national army.[2]

The state of security sector reforms in Liberia is still very weak, as the new leadership has not shown any convincing determination to reform the military. While it has been convenient to put the blame on post-war economic difficulties, there are obviously aspects of reform that could be undertaken even within the government's slender budget. To a large extent, the new government still looks at issues and takes decisions within the framework of the divisions of the civil war. The ability of the police to handle domestic security has not been effective while the judiciary is still not independent. The police and the security forces, too, have been linked to the mysterious deaths and disappearances of known critics of the government. Although after the war, President Taylor gave the impression that he wanted to include all former rivals in new government structures, this has not materialised, and forms of behaviour which paralleled the divisions of the past still remain intact.

The situation in Sierra Leone is equally complex. Although there was a crude semblance of order in most parts of the country, by late 1998, there were still a number of complications associated with security sector reform. Perhaps the most important of these is the fact that the country, at least at the time of writing, still had not got a national army. With the complicity of the national army in the military coup of 1997, and their subsequent alliance with the rebel movement that has been fighting successive governments since 1991, the Kabbah government, on its return, decided to create a new national army. Presently, ECOMOG is still providing security for the country, and the regional force is also charged with the creation of a new national army.

Since Kabbah's return, his government has been trying to create a blue-print for how the security sector could be reformed. In a way, the government has been torn between the conflicting tendencies of wanting to satisfy the donors that have been assisting its post-war reconstruction, and of attempting to stage reforms in ways that would make it capable of addressing unexpected crises. This apart, many people in the country felt that Kabbah was weak, and that it was this weakness that accounted, at least in part, for the military take-over of May 1997. Thus, since his return to power, the President has tried to portray a harder image, for example, in the endorsement he gave for the execution of those who overthrew him in 1997.

There have nevertheless been some positive developments in Sierra Leone. Considerable efforts have been made to restructure the police and attune it to its tasks of providing domestic security. Here, the British government and the Commonwealth have been of considerable assistance. The judiciary, too, has been undergoing some reform. It is likely that this will continue, and as Kabbah reasserts his rule, commitments to other areas of security sector reform are likely to intensify. However, the main factor determining the success of security sector reform in the country is the civil conflict which, as of November 1998, was still continuing in some parts of the country.[3]

Other factors that have advanced the pace of reform in Sierra Leone are the efforts being made to restructure the national economy and strengthen an active civil society. Since its return, the Kabbah government has tried to close the loopholes in the Sierra Leonean economy. While inflation at the time Kabbah came back to power was about 95%, the government had, by October 1998, brought it down to less than 40%.[4] Efforts too have been made to control the management of the mining sector, traditionally believed to be the main source of corruption and misappropriation in Sierra Leone.[5]

The nature and extent of security sector reform in 'failed' and 'wounded' societies in West Africa shows at least two glaring characteristics. The first is that the politics of civil conflict still remains a crucial factor in determining the length to which the incumbent governments are willing to go in their reforms. In all cases, governments are willing to regulate the doses of reform to suit their own perception of the prevailing security situation at home and the extent of their grip on power. The second is that the international community is able to have considerable influence in dictating the pace of reform in these countries. This, no doubt, is due to the extent of the latter's reliance on external aid.

SECURITY SECTOR REFORM IN DEMOCRATIC STATES

Democratic states in West Africa can be placed within two broad categories: namely those that have traditionally been democratic and those which have been forced down democratic paths in the post-Cold War era. Those in the second category can be divided into broken down into two: those where the incumbent military government metamorphosed into a civilian government and those where there were transitions towards an elected civilian regime. Although the politics governing the management of security sector reform has varied, they all have a number of things in common. The first is the weakness of the economy of these countries, which makes the implementation of any meaningful security reform difficult. The second is the role of the military which, though not necessarily still in power, is always at the background anxious to safeguard their interests, while the third is the desire of the government in power only to concede to as much reform as is required to remain in office.

Two countries – Senegal and Côte d'Ivoire – have a fairly long democratic tradition. However, this democratic longevity has not translated into strong and well-balanced civil-military relations. Indeed, in recent years, there has been no attempt to undertake any new security sector reforms mainly because there has not been much internal or external pressure on these governments to do so. The democratic credentials they flaunt before donors are often considered as sufficient, or at best, in need of only minor modifications. The danger inherent in this is the tendency to dismiss major error on the part of these governments as an aberration, or to overlook developments which have potentially cataclysmic consequences. Each of these countries also has major security problems with which to contend. This is particularly serious in the case of Senegal, where there is a secessionist agitation in the Casamance region, while Côte d'Ivoire is contending with problems across its borders and the rise in local crime.

In the countries where the military has transformed itself into a civilian government, the most important danger to future security sector reform has emanated from the process of the conversion itself. In virtually all cases, the method has been similar: after the incumbent military government has put in place all the structures that would enable it to win any election, it has then gone ahead to hold elections. The 'advantage of incumbency', usually a euphemism for election rigging, is often employed to ensure victory at the polls. As a result, in most cases, the means through which the elected governments assumed office has made them unsuitable candidates to embark on any credible reform.

The governments in the states under this umbrella are often quick to consider some form of security sector reform upon assuming office. However, the kind of reform they embark on is usually of the kind that would consolidate their hold on power in the transition from military to civilian leadership. The leader exploits his dual constituencies (as a military and civilian) to strike a balance between the groups. He concedes as much to the military as is needed to keep him in power and prevent a military coup, and as much to the civilians as is required to justify their mandate. In balancing the tensions between these two groups, however, it is obvious that more concessions are granted to the military, which, apart from being the leader's original constituency, also retain the power to topple him in a military coup. The outcome in most cases here is that security sector reform goes only as far as measures which would not threaten the military's traditional grip on power.

Some countries have, however, perfected this practice better than others. Ghana, one of the earliest countries to transform its government from military to civilian, seems to have effected the transition in a relatively seamless fashion. In reality, the favourable press that the incumbent President Rawlings seems to be enjoying as one of the faithful implementers of World Bank and IMF reforms has blurred darker aspects of his domestic security policy. However, what seems to have accounted more for the silence on Ghana's security sector reform policies is that the Rawlings government has made a creditable transition through elections from a military to an apparently civilian government. The situation in The Gambia has been more crudely executed, as the incumbent President Yahya Jammeh has done little to disguise his harsh management of domestic security since the transformation of his office to that of a civilian leader. Indeed, as late as November 1998, a number of people were condemned to death accused of an attempted military coup, in a judicial process many considered as constituting a major violation of their human rights.

In countries where civilian regimes are becoming consolidated, security sector reform is being undertaken on a more gradual basis. Pressure groups, largely in the form of non-governmental organisations and university students, continually put pressure on governments to follow the path of good governance and accountability. It is no coincidence that there have been riots across universities in virtually all of these countries, as university students and staff have taken it on themselves to be the guarantors of democratic values.

SECURITY SECTOR REFORM UNDER AUTOCRACY

Only one West African country falls into this category, and that is

Nigeria. The irony, however, is that this country is also the region's most powerful and most important nation. With a population that is almost double that of all other West African states together, and with enormous economic potential, Nigeria has the power to browbeat other states in the region into conformity.

The complexities of security sector reform in Nigeria can be dated back to Babangida's eight years presidency (1985-93), during which civil-military relations deteriorated. The judiciary became far more corrupt, the police had neither the capacity, nor the will to manage domestic security, and corruption pervaded all spheres of Nigerian society. Indeed, by the time Babangida left office, there was virtually no internal security to talk about. Even the national army lost the *esprit de corp* that united it in all its years of administration.

The greatest damage Babangida caused to the creation and sustenance of viable democratic developments in Nigeria was his cancellation of the democratic elections to elect his successor. This nullification, which came without any explanation, resulted in a brief period with an interim president before the military came back to power under Sani Abacha. The most important fall-out from this period was that it prevented the country from having a democratically elected government that could launch it on the path of inclusive national dialogue to discuss its problems.

Whatever hope people had about progress in this direction was lost during the four and half years of Abacha's administration. During this period, autocracy was entrenched in a way that was unprecedented. All sections of the official security network became structurally distorted. The corruption of the judiciary reached epidemic proportions; the regime was known to have unilaterally overthrown decisions made by the court, while judges insisting on judicial independence were rapidly removed from office. The police were further starved of funds and their ability to provide security was worsened by corruption. Indeed, in many parts of the country, soldiers took over the provision of domestic security. The military itself was not spared assaults on its integrity, as spurious allegations of coup plots resulted in the jailing of many top military leaders, including, in fact, Abacha's own deputy. Violation of human rights became the order of the day, reaching its peak in the hanging of writer Ken Saro Wiwa and other environmental activists despite global appeals for clemency.

During Abacha's reign of terror, the struggle to instil good governance was fought by many pro-democracy groups. While a few of these stayed at home to engage directly with the dictator, most operated from outside the country, especially Europe, where they attempted to sensitise the international community about the situation in Nigeria and to campaign for an economic boycott. The activities of some of these pro-democracy groups, however, present another paradox in Nigeria's search for good governance. Some of them had, in the past, taken active roles in the perpetuation of autocracy in the country. Indeed, the struggle for democracy in Nigeria brought together many strange bedfellows.

External concerns for the establishment of a more accountable government in Nigeria and the restructuring of its security sector were weak, uncoordinated and ineffective. The EU and the United States imposed limited military sanctions on Nigeria and the country was suspended from the Commonwealth. All these fell far short of the demands from the pro-democracy forces in the country that an all-encompassing sanctions regime be imposed on the country, including, above all, oil sanctions. The refusal to do this fuelled Abacha's intransigence, since Nigeria's relative economic strength made it possible for him to survive the limited pressures of the international community.

Abacha died in June 1998, and another military regime, headed by Abubakar Abdul Salaam, former Chief of Defence Staff, replaced him. One of the first steps taken by the new leader was to disassociate himself from the brutality and corruption of the Abacha regime. He has also planned a transition to a democratic government by May 1999, with discussion on security sector reform in Nigeria appearing to have to wait until there is a government that enjoys both domestic and international credibility.

There are, however, a number of factors that could frustrate any progress towards good governance in Nigeria. First is the fact that the next civilian government is still going to operate under a constitution that is known to be defective. Second, most of those that have so far shown interest in leading the country belong to the old class that was responsible for the present economic and political deadlock in which Nigeria finds itself. These include retired military officers; former ministers from discredited political and military regimes and a so-called new breed of politicians with no clearly defined political agenda. In short, the past is likely to haunt Nigeria's political future, and almost implicitly, the chances for future reform of the security sector.

CONCLUSION

On the whole, it would appear that there are three factors impeding the establishment of durable security sector reforms in West Africa. The first is the weakness of the economies of most of the states in the region, which erodes the basis on which meaningful reform can stand. The second is the role of the military who still want to hold on to the position of primacy they have held during and since the end of the Cold War, while the third is the perception of many West African governments that reforms are undertaken more to satisfy the international donor community than to put their states on the path of accountability and good governance.

The future of security sector reform in West Africa is difficult to predict. For states recovering from the throes of war, there is an opportunity to start afresh and build on civil-military relations on which enduring democratic traditions could be established. In Liberia, and to an extent, Sierra Leone, this seems not to be the case, as decisions are still being taken in line with the divisions of the past and present.

The situation in states just coming to terms with multi-party democracy is slightly different. Many leaders are willing to engage in reform, provided, of course, that not too much is conceded which would undermine their grip on power. In other words, they do not want to 'reform' themselves out of power for the sake of satisfying external demands for security sector reform. A change of attitude is needed before any benefit can arise from the exercise. Security sector reform should be seen not as a means of satisfying aid agencies to release more funds, but as a process that will institutionalise structures which are strong enough to withstand the challenges of the coming century. Good governance should transcend the periodic holding of elections and accountability. Also required is the participation of broad sections of society in debates about security and the active involvement of civil society in the management of public affairs.

Nigeria, the only country still under autocratic rule in the region faces the greatest challenge in putting in place acceptable security sector reforms, especially safeguards to prevent the military from returning to power. When a new government is installed in 1999, the new regime will need to address these issues as a priority. Subtle efforts now being undertaken to appease the military are unlikely to work. Indeed, it is on the basis of such methods of appeasement that problems are created, and on which they have thrived so often.

Notes

[1] Richard Kaplan, "The Coming Anarchy", *The Atlantic Monthly*, February 1994.

[2] See Amos Sawyer, "Reconstructing Liberia", *Democracy and Development*, Vol. 1 October – December 1998, p 6.

[3] As of 10 November 1998, the rebels and their AFRC allies killed 100 people in Gbedenbu, a situation which worsened into 1999.

[4] Figure quoted by Finance Minister, James Jonah, *Newswave*, October 1998.

[5] A new minister has been appointed for the Ministry of Mines which now works closely with the Finance Ministry and the Presidency.

20

The Armed Services and 'A Policy for People: Problems and Prospects'[1]

CHRISTOPHER DANDEKER

Department of War Studies, King's College London

INTRODUCTION: WHY A POLICY FOR PEOPLE?

For the military the pace of change since 1989 has been extraordinary. In the new strategic context, armed forces in most industrial countries have experienced sharp cuts in the size of their establishments while much of Europe is in the midst of a process of shifting away from mass conscript-based forces. Military personnel have to prepare for a wider variety of missions encompassing peace support operations as well as traditional war fighting. Consequently, states are demanding greater flexibility from their military establishments. This demand can lead to 'overstretch' and deterioration in morale. There can also be difficulties associated with continuing to train in order to fight high-intensity wars while, in fact, the most likely deployments are quite different kinds of peace support operations. Furthermore, as a result of an increased emphasis on various forms of international partnership, national armed forces have to devise ways of making that cooperation effective. This will require policy-makers to address a range of 'inter-operability' issues: these include not only technology and equipment but also socio-cultural problems arising from cooperation between formations of different military cultures working under quite different national personnel policies. Armed forces also have to adapt to a rapidly changing society. A series of economic, social and legal changes offer challenges to the armed forces, as is evident in current debates on ethnic minority representation in the armed services, whether women should be employed in *all* military occupations, and the policy of formally excluding homosexuals from military service.

As a result of this period of domestic and international turbulence, since 1989, the 'people dimension' of the UK's armed services has become a central problem in defence debates. As is evident from the outcome of the Strategic Defence Review (SDR), a range of personnel issues – equal opportunities and 'overstretch' for example – have moved up the political agenda. At RUSI (Royal United Services Institute), on 31 May 1995, Lieutenant General Sir Thomas Boyd-Carpenter argued:

> Service men and women including civilian staff are our most critical asset. Even the most cursory reading of history will tell you that wars are won and lost by the qualities of people, from the inspiration of the leader or commander to the courage, initiative, doggedness and endurance of the force that he commands. Of course, even the highest quality people will fail if ill equipped or supported; but a country or cause will be defeated even more ignominiously if it lacks a unifying ethos of people committed to a common purpose.[2]

General Boyd-Carpenter also pointed out that 'people are not merely a vital asset but an expensive one', with, in 1995, about 28% of budget devoted to service personnel.[3] Given the downward pressures on the defence budget and increased political expectations that defence is seen to provide value for money, service planners are being asked, to provide innovative, cost-effective ways of managing these expensive assets.

The Strategic Defence Review (SDR) places explicit emphasis on the 'Policy for People':

> Past defence reviews have concentrated on strategy and equipment, sometimes with insufficient consideration of people. This Review has given people their proper place at the centre of our plans. [4]

SDR sets out detailed proposals intended to address short-term and long-term personnel problems so as to produce high quality people with 'confidence of their future in defence'.[5] These build on earlier work, [6] but also seek to go further and provide conditions for people relevant for the twenty-first century. The emphasis placed upon the people dimension is both novel and justified.

The following analysis considers some of the key ideas of the

'Policy for People' and the obstacles that need to be overcome for them to succeed. The focus is on three major themes:

- breaking out of the vicious circle[7] of overstretch and undermanning:
- the armed services and the representation of society;
- sustaining civil-military understanding.

Underlying this discussion is a wider concern: whatever priority is given to 'Policy for People' now, there must be uncertainty about whether the funding basis is sufficient to underpin them. If public spending plans overall have to be revised over the next few years, there may be some hard choices to be made between technology programmes and people policies. In many ways, the excellent education and training measures will no doubt be expensive and are not costed in the material available to the public. One must ask, whatever their intrinsic merits, how secure these proposals are.

OVERSTRETCH AND UNDERMANNING: BREAKING OUT OF THE VICIOUS CIRCLE

The core of the services' problems lies in the fact that the country is asking them to 'do more with less', together with persistent difficulties in persuading enough young people to choose a military career, especially in certain specialisations such as the combat arm of the British Army. As SDR notes, the services confront two mutually reinforcing problems: overstretch and undermanning.[8]

Unit overstretch is caused by a mismatch between available personnel numbers and commitments, leading to a reduction in the intervals between tours and thus less time for training, career and self-development as well as family and personal activities.[9] When combined with the effects of undermanning, unit overstretch produces individual overstretch, leading to an early exit of people from the services, i.e. poor retention. It is interesting to note that in recent years service personnel, at least in the Army, have tended to focus their complaints less on general conditions of service, including accommodation, but more on problems arising from overstretch: such are the human costs of doing more with less in leaner forces.[10]

The problem of overstretch is unevenly spread in the services. It is especially pronounced in the area of support and logistics. Accordingly, SDR announced that 'extra logistic and medical units will be formed for all three Services and, as they become fully manned, they will relieve overstretch in some of the most hard pressed areas'.[11] This will, it is admitted, take time. Furthermore, SDR addresses the overall problem of mismatches between commitments and resources. It asks rather less of the Navy in terms of peacetime tasks, while establishing the RAF in terms of the scale of commitments likely to arise. The Army receives an increase in establishment to meet its existing commitments. This increase, once it is fully manned, will create a 'sixth deployable brigade.'[12]

It is difficult to take an overall service view of the problem of overstretch. This is not only because it is more pronounced in some areas rather than others, but also because the effects on the individual service person will depend upon his or her perceptions and aspirations. For example, overstretch can, in fact, be financially rewarding and exhilarating for a young single person, while the same experience can cause stress and discomfort for a junior NCO with a young family. Perceptions of stress and what the services can reasonably be expected to demand of their people are also informed by comparisons made with those who work for civilian organisations.

Undermanning is the second of the key problems facing the services, and SDR admits that both 'have existed for years and are themselves manifestations of deeper problems'.[13] The problem of undermanning is one of a gap between actual and planned strengths; it is one of the causes of overstretch. Personnel in undermanned units have to do more, and especially when on operations have to be reinforced with personnel from other units, from giving them less time for training, family or personal development. The most serious problem arising from undermanning and overstretch is that both can be linked in a mutually reinforcing and vicious circle. Thus, undermanned units produce unit and individual overstretch leading to dissatisfaction with service conditions and poor retention. As dissatisfied service personnel leave, their negative perceptions of service life can exacerbate the difficulties encountered by recruiters. This can lead to the persistence of undermanning and, unless more radical moves are made in connection with commitments and resources, of unit and individual overstretch.

Two questions arise from this discussion. First, while it is admitted that the above difficulties cannot be resolved over the immediate or short term, a question remains. Will the mismatch between available numbers of people and commitments (as in extra logistics and medical units) be resolved to the satisfaction of service personnel, thus leading to satisfactory improvement in morale, retention and recruitment?[14] Second, are the time scales for full manning (RAF 2000, Royal Navy 2002 and the Army around 2004) realistic; and will the conditions be provided to recruit and retain the numbers and quality needed? Here the focus is not on whether the commitment-resource problem has been handled appropriately. Rather the concern is whether, within that framework, sufficient people can be recruited, retained and given attractive enough conditions of service life that their morale will be satisfactory. Indeed, will this morale be high enough so that when they leave, they can inform others that a military career is worth pursuing. In effect, can the 'vicious circle' be converted into a 'virtuous' one?[15]

To address this problem successfully, there is a need to think *strategically* about the different components of personnel policy. The factors associated with recruitment, retention, resettlement and transferability of skills from military to civilian life have to be viewed as elements in an overall approach to producing fully manned, highly motivated (and thus not overstretched) services. It is unhelpful to focus on one dimension of a policy for people without an overall appreciation of the personnel strategy of which it is a part. Rigid compartmentalising of responsibilities in the individual areas can be unhelpful, not least by 'buck passing' when a more integrated approach is likely to produce better results. To illustrate: improvements in the *quality* of recruits can ease the problem of meeting recruitment target numbers, and the costs of the recruitment, selection and training machine by reducing wastage rates. Better retention through re-enlistment or longer initial service, say from a three-year to four-year engagement can make major inroads in recruitment shortages and manning levels (although these will not occur immediately). In the case of the Army, for example, an increase in the initial engagement from three to four years could produce an extra 600 soldiers.[16] Similar results might be realised by allowing personnel to stay in a military career for longer than 22 years.

Focusing overly on one dimension of personnel strategy can produce distorting effects. For example, during the first half of the 1990s, the failure of the Army to resolve its undermanning problem and to manage its retention satisfactorily led to an over-emphasis on recruiting targets as a policy response. Currently, (1998) there is a shift in emphasis to retention as the basis for achieving a fully manned service, although this is in explicit recognition of the dangers of letting the pendulum swing too far, thus leading to a neglect of the issues of recruitment targets and recruit quality.

Overstretch can lead to poor retention, which, in turn, can have a negative effect on the public perception of the worth of military careers and thus recruitment. This negative effect can be reinforced if those who resettle in civilian society have skills and qualifications that are insufficient to make them feel that their military careers have been worthwhile. Managing retention involves ensuring that both partners to what is known as the 'psychological contract' are content.[17] The key point is that the services need to send people out from the military on a *mutually* satisfactory basis. On the one hand, the services need to recoup their training and related investment costs; currently, as with pilots, they lose heavily by the premature exit of expensively trained personnel. On the other hand, personnel who leave should be leaving at a time in their lives that they find acceptable. They need to possess skills and qualifications that will assist them in civilian life. It is also desirable that they be equipped with a positive view of the overall benefits of a military career, one that they will communicate to others in the wider civilian community. SDR is right to emphasise that whether ex-service personnel are content or not will depend on whether they were satisfied with conditions, had an enjoyable career, and left with useful skills and qualifications. This is a key theme in the idea of 'learning forces' and the extension of provision for education and training.[18] A significant issue here is the extent to which service personnel are (and will increasingly be) exercised by *opportunity/cost* considerations. In a society where people are increasingly ambitious for themselves and their families, the services' goal should be to be able to say the following to their personnel: 'Join us and you will not only go on to a reasonable second career, you will be able to move on to a position that is better than that which you would have been in had you not pursued a career in the armed services in the first place'. That is, you did not lose by joining the military. This is, it would appear, the meaning of the commendable point about 'added value' in SDR.[19] The initiatives on learning forces deserve monitoring to see how effective they are in addressing such opportunity/cost considerations. Not the least of the problems will be whether employers' fears about 'credential inflation' and the wider debate about standards in school and mass higher education will undermine any gains.[20]

In addition to providing transferable skills, the services need to create a positive image of service life as a means of both managing retention and having an impact on *recruitment*. This is why SDR is right to stress the importance of looking after the individual and the individual's family. Laudable initiatives include those such as ensuring that with new accommodation, 'in most instances, individuals of all ranks will be provided with a single room'.[21] The same can be said for the recognition that the services need to take 'individual aspirations for family stability into account as far as practicable' when managing postings although operational requirement must be paramount.[22] Other matters connected with looking after the individual such as reform of the disciplinary system not least Courts Martial raise wider issues concerning military culture and civilian society, which are addressed later.

In seeking to provide highly motivated and fully manned forces, the services are naturally concerned to widen their access to the potential recruitment pool. By doing so not only will they meet their manning difficulties; they will also meet their legal and social obligations to be an equal opportunities employer while reinforcing their links between the services and the civilian community. Furthermore, this will also help to reinforce the bonds of civil-military understanding.

THE ARMED SERVICES AND REPRESENTING SOCIETY

In the 'Policy for People' chapter of the Strategic Defence Review emphasis has been placed on the need for the services to represent society.[23] This reflects a broader discussion that has taken place in recent years on the need for the all-volunteer forces to remain in touch with the wider society on which they depend, notwithstanding the development of trends that may have weakened these civil-military bonds. These trends include the following. First, the services are smaller and have a lower social profile in society as a result of downsizing and base closures. Second, since the abolition of conscription in 1963, there has been a profound decline in the number of people who possess a direct understanding of military affairs. Such people include influential opinion leaders, who can play a significant role in the defending of the defence budget and the wider interests of the armed services, and 'gatekeepers' (those who can influence young people in their choice of careers). Third, the purpose of the armed forces is less clear than it was in the era of the Cold War when a direct and palpable military threat to the UK was widely recognised. Consequently, it is rather easier than before for non-military demands on public expenditure, such as health and social welfare to push the armed services further down the order of spending priorities. With defence spending having fallen from 5.4% of GDP in 1985 to 2.8% in 1998, it is at its lowest point since the 1930s.[24] It would take the re-emergence of a major and direct threat to the UK for the current downward trend in defence spending to be reversed. Finally, the armed services have a unique culture because of the requirement to prepare and conduct war and other military operations. Maintaining the legitimacy of the services' 'need to be different' has become more problematic in recent years because of the social and legal changes mentioned in the introduction to this chapter.

In the context of these changes, it is not surprising that there has been a good deal of discussion about the need for the armed services to be broadly 'representative' of the society of which it is a part. The 'Policy for People' chapter includes the statement that:

> We are determined that the Armed Forces should better reflect the ethnic composition of the British population. Currently some 6% of the general population are from ethnic minority backgrounds, but they make up just 1% of the services. This must not continue. We have set a goal of attracting 2% of new recruits this year from ethnic minority communities for each Service. We want that goal to increase by 1% each year so that, eventually, the composition of our Armed Forces reflects that of the population as whole.[25]

John Spellar MP, Under Secretary of State for Defence, discussed this political objective earlier, in 1997, in a speech for the armed forces. He argued that the policy:

> had to change, not only because media coverage of isolated incidents of racial abuse is hugely damaging to the Services reputation, but also because the Armed Forces must be in a position to compete for the best people, regardless of their ethnic origin. There has been much public criticism of the Services, most notably by the Commission for Racial Equality. All three Services have stepped up their efforts to stamp out racial harassment or racist bullying, and have targeted recruiting campaigns at minority groups. It is only right that the Services should

> reflect the ethnic composition of the society that they seek to defend and that means at all levels, especially the officer intake.[26]

The key question arising from all of this is whether the goal of closing the gap with regard to the issue of ethnic minorities, is defensible and achievable? The idea of representativeness can be given at least two rather different interpretations. First, one can refer to a socio-demographic match between military and society. In this context this would involve the military matching the 6% statistical profile in the wider population – a goal achieved through planned targets if not quotas. As Sir Michael Howard has pointed out, this is very much an American value.[27] Second, one might argue that the armed services should subscribe to core societal values such as equality of opportunity, decency, fairness, careers open to all, and advancement in the organisation on merit. Accordingly, the services could feel relatively comfortable about the task of explaining the mismatch between their profile and that of society, but with one proviso. The gap would need to be explained not by a failure to have an effective equality of opportunity programme, but in terms of the propensity of particular groups to select certain kinds of occupations, military or civilian.[28] For reasons that will become clearer later, it is most unlikely that the Services will be able to achieve the goals of representation in the first sense of that concept. Reaching such a goal would require programmes of affirmative action that are illegal in the UK and, perhaps, on the wane in the USA.[29]

Significant progress is achievable so far as the second meaning is concerned. This is evident from recent developments. Within the space of two to three years, the armed services, having been held up as a problem case by such agencies as the Equal Opportunities Commission (EOC) and the Commission for Racial Equality (CRE) is now regarded in a rather different light. For example, the CRE has been impressed with the changes introduced concerning ethnic monitoring, equal opportunities training, and the right of resort to tribunals outside the chain of command.[30] In addition, there have been changes such as the disciplinary code on racial harassment as well as attempts to build effective bridges between the services and ethnic minority communities. It is remarkable to reflect on the fact that in 1996 the CRE had declared war on the MoD and armed services on the matter of racism. By contrast, in November 1998, at the first conference of its kind in the UK, the Chief of the Defence

Staff himself declared war in public on racism in the British armed services. Meanwhile, having championed the cases of pregnant servicewoman in a number of costly to the MoD) disputes, the EOC now uses the services as a case study in how to introduce an equal opportunities policy. The commission highlights the key imperatives of training and monitoring as means of making such polices effective.[31] Interestingly, the rate of complaints has declined probably due to a more effective equal opportunities environment as well as greater trust in the chain of command.

It might be asked why the services should be (as they are) devoting so much attention to the issue of equal opportunities, whether in the context of ethnic minorities or the dimension of gender. In recent discussions, it has become clear that, in this area at least, there is a perceived zero-sum conflict between functional and socio-political imperatives. Some take the view that meeting (so-called politically correct) equal opportunities objectives detracts from operational effectiveness. Such action diverts investment from more worthy objectives such as platforms or other equipment. [32] Also equal opportunities would, perhaps, undermine the traditional cohesion of the military community; that, here was another area where the military rather than being used to defend the country was being used as a 'social experiment' or part of a project to build a new, more inclusive society.

However, commentators have identified a number of reasons why this objective is a desirable one from the point of view of the *operational effectiveness* of the armed services.[33] First of all it can improve access to a wider recruitment pool as the armed services compete with civilian companies for scarce labour both in terms of quantity and quality. In this context one can point to the fact that ethnic minorities, although about 6% of the national population constitute over 19% of the 16-24 year military recruitment pool. In addition, there is the predisposition of some ethnic minority populations to pursue education as a means of improving their labour market positions thus providing the services with a useful additional pool of skilled labour. Second, the armed services would benefit from a diversity of skills and backgrounds that a broader-based entry would produce. With the need for more intelligent and flexible service personnel likely to increase rather than decrease, such diversity is likely to prove an advantage in future years. Third, a military freed from racial discrimination and focused instead on diversity, tolerance and decency would be more operationally effective than one in which racial harassment was permitted.[34] Fourth, the services could benefit from being seen to live up to the ideal of an equal opportunities employer. While this may enhance their standing in ethnic minority communities it is just as important to sustain the legitimacy of the armed services and thus the fount of goodwill amongst the general public. In any case, the legal pressure to conform to this ideal is real enough. While the services have much to gain from recruiting a greater proportion of the ethnic minority communities than they currently do, those communities themselves would also derive some benefit. Lieutenant Colonel Crawford has argued (drawing on the work of Cynthia Enloe[35]) that, if American experience is anything to go by, military service can provide ethnic minority communities with a sense that they are valuable elements of the social and political system. That is to say, they are and feel included not excluded: they develop skills that enhance their socio-economic mobility as well as acquiring a range of leadership skills that can be transferred back to local communities. This would suggest that all three could be seen as facets of a process of citizenship building.

Closing the gap between ethic minority communities and the military will not be easy, although it would be unwise to underplay progress that has been made already on the broader front of equal opportunities. In 1997 it was reported that:

> Although the services continue to recruit from families where the tradition of military service is strong, there has also been a considerable widening of the basis for armed forces and a substantial increase in the number of officers commissioned from the main spectrum of society. The key issue is to ensure that a career in the armed forces is clearly open to people with the right talents and skills, and the opportunity to rise to the top in a meritocratic system.[36]

A good deal of further work is needed to understand the barriers such as they are within ethnic minority communities and within the services. In the former one would want to examine the role of family culture and the differential propensity to see a military career as desirable and to pursue education thus making them attractive to both military and civilian employers. A key problem for the military is establishing effective bridges with ethnic minority communities. This is not just as an aid to recruitment; there are broader issues at stake. One of these is the need to establish the legitimacy of the armed services in these communities. That is to say, they need to establish the idea that the services not only recruit from the diverse population of the UK but also are organisations that command respect from all sections of the population, including those who decide not to select it as a career opportunity.

With regard to the services themselves, the issue of 'institutional racism' needs to be considered. Is racism a feature of individual attitudes or a more deep-rooted phenomenon? Normally, commentators refer to the term when describing deeply ingrained, discriminatory attitudes and beliefs of which people are unaware or only dimly so. Institutional racism is, therefore, a structural phenomenon, rooted in organisational routines and procedures and its culture, or 'the way an organisation does business'. It is the product of a lengthy historical process, one that encompassed not just the services but that of British society as a whole in an imperial context. By the same token, removing institutional racism would require much more than a statement of new policy: a culture change would be required.

The idea of institutional racism can be used to support positive discrimination through the application of quotas to recruitment and promotion. Such a policy can be justified in terms of righting historic wrongs. Thus developing an evaluation of the merits and flaws of the idea of institutional racism necessarily broaches key issues of policy implementation in this area of equal opportunities. For example, both in terms of UK law and the culture of the armed services, quotas are not acceptable and are looked on with disdain.[37] A distinction can be drawn between quotas and targets. The latter could be used effectively as a focus for management action in pursuit of equal opportunities yet remain within the law, (and, it has to be said, widely-held conceptions of natural justice within both the armed services and the civilian community). Thus targets could be used to drive a move to more equal opportunities within the organisation. If they were not met then such targets could be used as a means of focusing attention on what were the barriers preventing their achievement. Such targets could focus managerial attention on whether decisions that had been taken, e.g. on recruitment and promotion had indeed been on the basis of merit with no more or less tacit or hidden mechanisms of discrimination being allowed to operate.

It is evident that successful policies require an effective strategy. Previous research indicates that in implementing organisational change the following are key positive factors: the statement of a vision by the leaders of an organisation, the explicit commitment of leaders to that vision; the effective communication of that vision throughout the various levels of the organisation's hierarchy. Furthermore, the vision must be translated from formal policy documents into action through effective and responsible leadership. The achievement of policy must be made the specific responsibility of each level of authority and leadership at each level focused on this. In addition, the organisation must establish effective training and monitoring systems as well as a system of incentives and penalties for non-compliance with an equal opportunities programme. This means, for example, a zero-tolerance policy on racial harassment and thus the exercise of heavy penalties on those who refuse to comply, together with the ejection of those personnel who decide to 'remain part of the problem rather than part of the solution'.[38] How successful the services will be in implementing change will be a matter of wider public concern, and thus their reputation will be at stake. This leads us to the third theme of the analysis of 'Policy for People': that of civil-military understanding.

THE PROBLEM OF CIVIL-MILITARY UNDERSTANDING

By 'civil-military understanding', I refer to a mutually supportive relationship between the armed services and the civilian community; this is a relationship of communication and perception, trust and legitimacy.

The military needs to communicate to the public a clear idea of the purpose of the armed services. Two particular difficulties arise here. The first concerns strategy and public perceptions. Given the *perceived* decline in major, direct, military threats to the UK, and the apparent priority given to non-war fighting roles such as peacekeeping and military assistance to humanitarian operations, the question may be asked: why should scarce resources continue to be expended on a maintaining a high-intensity war machine? There is some concern that the core warfighting role is being obscured in public perceptions.[39] The public needs to be made more aware of the view that it makes sense to train the armed forces for war fighting and then to train 'down', as it were, in order to cater for the needs of missions in which a more restrained use of force is appropriate. The idea is based on the view that industrial democracies, such as those in western Europe, have to prepare for war even if major interstate wars are the least likely scenarios that they will face in future. It is prudent to prepare for the unlikely because it cannot be discounted entirely (especially if one countenances, for example, the more gloomy predictions about the future conduct of Russia if it were to perceive NATO expansion as a major threat to its security). Furthermore, the capacity to respond to the need for a war-fighting machine cannot be prepared over-night. Such war fighting preparation is required to buttress the conduct of the new age of more 'muscular' peace support operations in which peacekeepers face a much more violent tempo of life than classic peacekeepers are likely to encounter. It is also the case that with a downsized and ever cost-vigilant military, there is little scope for specialised peacekeepers even if such an option made strategic and military sense. Finally, it is a key interest of the UK (both economically and politically) to continue to contribute to international peace and security. This requires a capability of being able to contribute to intervention forces with a range of other partners. While this may, in future, not always include the US, it is critical to continue to maintain the means of being able to participate with US armed forces. This serves as a means of exerting UK influence, and also as a basis for being an attractive partner to other key European powers, through having access to technology and intelligence. All of this points to the need for continued investment in the high technology and high intensity means of war, and to the need to legitimise this activity in the public eye. In this context, the evolution of a European security and defence policy will be significant in highlighting the UK's attempt to balance European and US interests.

In a turbulent world of risks and 'violent peace', the task of building a national consensus on what armed forces the UK needs for its security and defence policy is not made any easier by the decline in the knowledgeability of military affairs in the civilian community – both opinion formers and the general public. Respect for and support of the armed forces is quite robust in the UK, US, France, and the Netherlands.[40] However, support for the current level of funding for defence is less so particularly in face of demands from other areas of public expenditure such as health, education, the environment and public transport. In countries which no longer have conscription, especially the UK and USA, direct experience and appreciation of military affairs has declined markedly over the past 20 years both in the political élite as well as in broader sections of the population. Countries who have abolished or are considering abolishing conscription need to be concerned with this issue. Most people's experience of the military is gained second-hand from the media and the information produced in this way often reflects past rather than current realities of life in the armed forces.

In the UK, there has been a reduction in the number of people with direct military experience.[41] As a consequence of the long-term decline in the size of the military establishment since the end of conscription, there has been a corresponding diminution in the number of military and ex-military personnel in society. In addition, with base closures and rationalisation, the 'footprint' made by the military on society has diminished. This process has been reinforced by the security problems in Northern Ireland since 1968, which have led to the military becoming invisible, until very recently, because of the lack of public display of uniforms.[42] The number of those – especially opinion formers – who can speak knowledgeably about the services, has declined in recent decades.[43] Linkages between the services and MPs are being improved but this has to be part of a broader effort in public relations, and in making more of the role of reserve forces as a means of sustaining civil-military understanding. Whatever operational advantages are to be gained from a more closely integrated regular/reserve mix, there remains a concern that the reduction in the size of the TA and unit amalgamations will leave significant areas of the country having little or no military presence. All this will not provide favourable conditions for sustaining the public profile of the armed forces and the legitimacy of its core war-fighting mission, let alone the legitimacy of regenerating stronger military capability should the need arise in future. The warning times of threats may be shorter than those required to garner public support for action designed to address them.

A key component of civil-military understanding concerns the military's need to be different from civilian society.[44] On the one hand, armed services and their political masters have to respond to the strategic context by building militarily effective organisations. On the other hand, especially in democracies, they have to ensure that the armed services are responsive to the changing society which they defend, that pays for them and without whose support they can do little. Conservatives tend to be suspicious of tempering military culture in order to accommodate changes in wider society even to the extent of arguing that military effectiveness requires a supportive framework of robust conservative values in civilian society. In contrast, liberals tend to expect the armed services to conform to civilian values and underestimate the unique character and demands of military life. Closer examination of the issues, as was evident in the discussion of representation earlier, shows that the most sensible approach lies somewhere between the conservative and liberal positions and that it is misleading to assume that military accommodation to civilian social values must necessarily undermine military effectiveness. The challenge for the personnel strategist is to ensure that a balance is struck between these, sometimes competing, demands. Furthermore, in adjusting to changes in society and international security, the personnel strategist has to take into account the history and traditions of the individual services which are normally critical factors in sustaining their identity, sense of shared purpose and morale.

The functional imperatives of war and military operations ensure that the services stand apart from civilian society. Ensuring that service personnel are prepared to fight involves leadership, management and motivation. For the military the core values of military culture are subordination of the self to the group and the idea of sacrifice: the individual must be willing to subordinate him or herself to the common good – the team and common task. Furthermore, there must be a willingness to sacrifice one's life for the team in peace and war – without this an armed force will risk defeat. Ideally, as a result of leadership and training, these values will be upheld voluntarily as a result of conscience. However, necessary coercion may be required. This is what makes military discipline – an effective structure of command for the giving and receiving of orders – quite different from other organisations in terms of the demands it places upon personnel. The military is unique in the nature and extent of the demands it places upon its personnel. They are obliged to train to kill and to sacrifice self, to participate in a military community where one works, lives and socialises with other service personnel and, when necessary, to respond to a 24-hour commitment with the risk of separation from family at short-notice.

Changes in society are challenging the unique culture of the military. Tensions between the services and civilian community have emerged, especially with a new generation entering the services. As we saw in the discussion of overstretch and undermanning, they adhere to social values focused on the desire to be consulted about organisational decisions, for more choice about career paths within the organisation, and a desire for a less demanding 'social burden' such as time away from family or greater opportunities for a personal life.

In a broader social climate that is much less deferential, it is now up to the military to *prove* that conforming to the changing norms and values of wider society would be likely to damage operational efficiency rather than the burden of proof being on the proponents of change. Authority has to *seen to be* earned and not taken for granted. This trend poses questions for the armed forces with their highly-structured authority relations as for example in recent discussions on whether service personnel ought to have the right to be able to air and represent their grievances in fora that are outside the formal chain of command.[45]

In today's society, a higher value is placed upon individualism and social equality with citizens, attuned to the 'blame and compensation' culture more disposed to enforce their rights in the courts. Previously the Crown together with the MoD and services were exempt from legislation. Although this is no longer the case the policy had been for some years to behave as if the law did apply. In future, exemptions are only likely to be supported if and when it can be demonstrated that the imposition of law would be incompatible with essential training and operations of the military. A case in point would be minimum wage legislation, another the possibility of preventing the employment of soldiers below the age of 18. In a climate that is less deferential, it is now up to the military to prove that conforming to the changing norms and values of wider society would be likely to damage operational efficiency rather than the burden of proof being on the proponents of change. More often than not these issues will have to be addressed in a legal context as a series of rulings and directives will continue to flow not so much from the UK legislature but from such bodies as the EU Commission and European Court. These will concern, in particular, the fields of employment law, health and safety at work and freedom of information.

Finally, significant sections of the young population are less physically fit than before. In a more individualistic society a lower priority is given to values of the community and the subordination of the self to that of the team. Also in a 'post-modern' subjective culture it is more difficult to sustain objective definitions of right and wrong. In order to maintain standards the costs of the training machine are likely to rise in order to bring poorer quality recruits up to the standard required. It is now very difficult to maintain the traditional expectation that military personnel should conform to a code of moral conduct that is more demanding than that expected in civilian life with respect to issues of honesty, integrity, and adultery.

CONCLUSION

As the armed forces adjust to the framework of SDR, the 'Policy for People' will form a critical part of this work. From the above discussion, it is clear that building bridges between the services and all sections of the civilian community is essential for their mutual well-being. The services need to recruit and retain quality people in face of competition from civilian employers. Furthermore they need a supportive and understanding civilian community in order to do their job, which must remain in key respects unique and different from jobs within the society the armed services have a duty to protect. Much is made of the need for the military to explain why they need to be different from wider society. However one might ask whether the services themselves are doing enough to ensure that personnel at all levels understand that the society from which it recruits, and to which it returns its personnel; there is the need for a two-way dialogue here.

In addition, the services face two key, and overlapping, organisational challenges. First, they need to establish the ways in which 'Policy for People' issues can be addressed on a tri-service basis while continuing to recognise the legitimate needs of individual services. This process is being driven not just by cost considerations but the operational need to develop a culture of 'jointery' in the military so as to equip it for joint and coalition activities of various kinds. Second, there is the continuing challenge of European law. A series of rulings and directives will continue to flow less from the UK legislature than from such bodies as the EU Commission and European Court especially in the field of employment law, health and safety at work and freedom of information.

The prospects for the success of 'Policy for People' will depend upon a number of considerations, not least provision of the necessary funds in the defence budget.

As the services move forward they need to continue to consult and garner trust – if the resources required for the 'Policy for People' are not provided then one can expect a slump in morale, while undermanning, and overstretch will not be resolved. This would be a shame given the many sensible and imaginative ideas that the 'Policy for People' contains.

Notes

1 The ideas for this chapter were developed initially in a presentation by the author at a conference on 'The Consequences of the Strategic Defence Review', held at RUSI on September 10, 1998. I am grateful for the comments from those who attended this event as well as to those officers on the staff of the Adjutant General (AG) who took time to discuss personnel issues with me. I would also like to thank Professor David Mason and John Ross who commented on an earlier draft of sections of this paper. Responsibility for the arguments outlined here and any factual errors rest with myself.

2 Lieutenant General the Hon Sir Thomas Boyd-Carpenter, 'Personnel Issues and the Bett Report', *RUSI Journal*, August 1995, 1-5, 1. See also *Independent Review of the Armed Forces' Manpower, Career and Remuneration Structures – Managing People in Tomorrow's Armed Forces, Report to The Secretary of State for Defence,* Chairman, Michael Bett, CBE, London HMSO 1995.

3 *ibid.* He went on to argue that 'even that figure does not represent the totality of our expenditure on people when one considers not merely pay and pensions but also training, quartering, medical services, and a myriad of other activities required to maintain a professional standing Armed Forces'.

4 *Strategic Defence Review*, Cm 3999, July 1998, 36, para 138. Whether Policy for People became much more important during the process of SDR than was envisaged initially is a matter of debate.

5 *ibid.*

6 Namely, the Bett report *op cit.* and *A Personnel Strategy for the Armed Forces,* MOD, February 1997.

7 This formulation of breaking out of a vicious circle is used in *SDR Supporting Essay Nine*, 9-2,3, paras 12-13.

8 See *SDR, Supporting Essay Nine, A Policy for People*, 9-2, paras 9-16.

9 As far as the Army is concerned, in recent years the percentage of their personnel committed to operations has risen significantly during the 1990s and is higher than

the proportion committed during the early 1970s. (from discussions with AG staff.)

[10] Discussions with AG staff. This is not to say that accommodation especially for single personnel continues to be a concern, and *SDR* does address this issue. See later discussion.

[11] *SDR* Supporting Essay Nine, 9-2, para 10.

[12] *ibid.*

[13] *ibid,* 9-2 para.

[14] In this connection, one of the financial battles to be fought is how much of a manpower margin over the establishment is allowable for the services. Too lean an establishment leaves too little margin for flexibility and for comfort.

[15] I borrow this formulation from discussions with officers on the staff at AG.

[16] This point emerged in discussions with AG staff.

[17] The RAF developed the term 'psychological contract' in personnel studies; it is also common in Army personnel circles.

[18] *SDR Supporting Essay Nine*, 9-3-9-4, paras 22-27.

[19] *SDR Supporting Essay Nine*, Policy for People, 9-4, 22.

[20] This issue is discussed in Dandeker and Paton, *The Military and Social Change*, with particular reference to the value of NVQ's.

[21] *ibid*. 9-5, para 29.

[22] *SDR Supporting Essay Nine, Policy for People*, 9-3, 17. Leave and facilities for improved communication with families are also welcome improvements to Service family life.

[23] *Strategic Defence Review*, Cm 3999, July 1998.

[24] See 'The Strategic Defence Review: How Strategic? How Much of a Review'. *London Defence Studies*, 46, Centre for Defence Studies, for Brassey's London, 1998, 3. As the authors of this study observe, military effectiveness cannot simply be extrapolated from such percentages. Much depends upon what manpower systems and technology are purchased with the sums available and how these are put into operation through doctrine and strategy.

[25] *SDR Supporting Essay Nine*, 9-8 41.

[26] The speech was delivered to a British Military Studies Group (BMSG) seminar in October 1997. See *The Future of British Military Cultures* BMSG 1998.

[27] Sir Michael Howard, 'The Armed Forces and the Community', *RUSI Journal*, August 1996, 10.

[28] This point raises difficult and complex issues. Not the least of these is the matter of constrained choice. A proportion of lack of ethnic minority participation in the military is due to the perception that they are not welcome there. Yet one must ask, even if that perception is challenged effectively (say by a policy of zero tolerance on racial harassment) it would be interesting to know more detailed information on the differential propensity of groups (whether ethnic minority or not) to view the

prospect of a military career positively. This point is part of a related study by the author with Professor David Mason of the University of Plymouth.

[29] Crawford points out that the Race Relations Act 1976 permits the provision of help to members of under-represented groups in their efforts to enter certain occupational sectors. Personal communication. Can be in the form of education and training or encouragement through advertising and promotional initiatives. However, the selection process must be clearly on grounds of merit. This issue has also arisen in the context of widening employment opportunities for women in the military, not least debates over whether entry standards (as for female combat pilots) were relaxed for reasons of 'political correctness'. Kamlesh Bahl, in her RSA presentation made specific reference to this provision of the 1976 Act in her suggestion that while quotas were illegal in the UK, specific groups could be targeted in order to assist them in meeting the standard required to be successful in the selection process. Others suggested that something like the Black American Colleges might be used to increase the flow of good quality ethnic minority candidates especially for the officer entry. It was in the officer corps that black role models needed to be established. Others meanwhile suggested that the pattern of educational attainment of blacks and ethnic minorities was not the problem, it was more an issue of making the forces attractive and removing the perception that either in selection of conditions of services, racism meant that such applicants were not welcome. This discussion relates to the target/quota debate, which is addressed later.

[30] On 1 October 1997, service personnel were given the right of appeal to an industrial tribunal (although complaints had first to be referred to the chain of command). It is hoped that this will lessen the chances of the following occurring. In a recent RAF survey, 70% of ethnic minority personnel reported that they had experienced discrimination but the majority had not voiced complaints because they feared that their careers would be damaged or that nothing material would have been done about their grievances. It was reported that ethnic monitoring was 98% effective.

[31] Employment opportunities continue to be extended in all three services. Currently, 70% of posts in the Army are open to women. The figures in the Royal Navy and RAF are 73% and 96% respectively. While the possibility of opening positions in the infantry and armour is under review, it is interesting to note that General Colin Powell argued strongly against any such extension in the US armed services. He claimed that this area was no place for women and that neither government nor public opinion thought it necessary or desirable to require women in combat for the purposes of its defence policy.

[32] Some personnel in the services have taken this view, one that is hardly absent in wider society.

[33] The work of Lt. Col. Stuart Crawford is particularly noteworthy in this connection. The arguments developed here draw on Crawford's work and on a number of

conversations with him over the past two years. See Crawford's 'Racial Integration in the Army – An Historical Perspective', *British Army Review*, 111, December 1995, 24-28. His Defence Fellowship thesis on this subject is, as yet, unpublished and not available to the public.

[34] Speech by General Colin Powell and subsequent discussion at the Equal Opportunities Conference, Royal Society of Arts, November 10, 1998.

[35] See C Enloe, *Ethnic Soldiers: State Security in Divided Societies*, (University of Georgia Press, USA, 1980), Also see, Charles Moskos and John S Butler *All That We Can Be, Black Leadership and Racial Integration the Army Way,* Twentieth Century Fund Book, Basic Books 1996.

[36] John Spellar MP, *Future of British Military Cultures.*

[37] But see earlier discussion of this in note 5.

[38] A phrase used by Powell and others at the conference in connection with the problem of removing racism from the armed services. In so far as gender integration in the UK military has been a success, these wider lessons have been very germane. See C. Dandeker and M.W. Segal, 'Gender Integration in Armed Forces: Recent Policy Developments in the United Kingdom,' *Armed Forces & Society* (Fall 1996):29-47.

[39] Of course, there is a case for not retaining this capability, or that by overly focusing on it one diverts attention from the key tasks of the armed forces for the foreseeable future: peace support and humanitarian relief. In a recent paper for the Fabian society (one which has triggered much social and political debate within and outside the services) Major Eric Joyce has argued that the army no longer needs to prepare for war in time of peace. This is because peacekeeping is the only thing that is likely to occur. Presumably long warning times will allow such a shift in the *modus operandi* of an army at peace.

[40] See B. Boene, W. von Bredow and C Dandeker, 'The Military in Common Risk Societies: Elements of Comparison among Nine countries of West Central and East Europe', in J. Kuhlmann (Ed) *The Military in Common Risk Societies* (forthcoming).

[41] In a recent speech to a BMSG conference a government minister reported that 'over the past 50 years there has been a dramatic reduction in the numbers of personnel in uniform. At the end of the Second World War the Army alone numbered over two and three quarter million. Over the following 15 years until conscription ended in 1960, millions more went through the Forces. In the 20 years prior to 1964 it is estimated that no less than 6.3 million people went through the Forces and therefore 6.3 million families, about 20 million people, had a direct or indirect involvement in military life, almost half the population.

The total number entering the Armed Forces between 1974 and 1994 amounted to no more than 660,000. There is, therefore, roughly 10 percent of the residual military experience in contemporary society compared to even 20/30 years ago.

The natural death rate, plus the reduced size of today's Armed Forces means that this figure will continue to fall. The number of informed people including politicians and opinion-formers in the community, who can speak knowledgeably about and in support of defence and the Armed Forces is therefore reducing rapidly.' See Key note address *The Future of British Military Cultures: Social and Legal Change into the 21st century- Britain in Comparative Perspective.*

[42] In November 1998, the ban on wearing uniform in public at least in mainland UK, while on duty, has been lifted in order to raise the public profile of the armed services.

[43] Similar trends can be found in the US. See the data reported by John Hillen in his 'The Gap Between American Society and its Military: Keep it, Defend It, Manage It', paper delivered to the *Cantigny Conference on Soldiers and Citizens; The Responsibilities of Service in Twenty First Democracies*, Wheaton Il, USA, April 30-May 1 1998. Hillen's sources are *VFW Magazine*, February 1997 p.15 and Marx Shields, 'When Heroes Were Ordinary Men', *The Washington Post*, August 3, 1998, pA21.

[44] See *The Future of British Military Cultures*.

[45] A key part of Major Joyce's argument and the subsequent controversy over his publication.

21

A Future in Stability? ABRI, State Failure and the Paradox of Indonesian Security Sector Reform

JAMES D. KIRAS

PhD candidate, Centre for Security Studies, Department of Politics and Asian Studies, University of Hull

According to classical Javanese literature, a king is replaced by either immediate family or deposed by a challenger, and accounts of the process are 'filled with betrayal, with coup d'états, with deceit, magic ... and horrible cruelty.'[1] The authors of newspaper and economic journals articles on the future of Indonesia recognise this traditional theme and whilst some remain optimistic about Indonesia's future, the majority are pessimistic in tone. Last year, prior to former President Suharto's abdication, a leading weekly journal declared that the unrest in Indonesia was the forebearer of 'Asia's coming explosion'.[2]

Yet almost six months after President Suharto was succeeded by his civilian Minister of Research and Technology, Bacharuddin Jusuf Habibie,[3] there has been renewed rioting and confrontation between demonstrators, looters and elements of the military but surprisingly little bloodshed. Whilst there are a number of troublesome indicators within the country, not the least of which are questions of the competence, permanence and succession of its current leadership, Indonesia possesses a number of unique qualities and institutions that make the country resilient to the stresses that can lead to failure. It is somewhat paradoxical that one of the primary sources of Indonesia's resilience is also the greatest impediment to democratisation and the one most in need of reform: The Armed Forces of the Republic of Indonesia (*Angkatan Bersenjata Republik Indonesia*, or ABRI).

The reason for this tangential entry into the subject of security sector reform in Indonesia, as well as a diversion into a discussion on 'failed states' and problems confronting the state in question, is to place the subject in its proper context. It is relatively easy to prescribe a list of entirely necessary changes and reforms to the Indonesian military; given substantial political, social and economic obstacles within the state, however, the problem arises in attempting to implement them. If there is a moral for this chapter, it is that whilst we in the West would like to see a range of security and human rights reforms implemented in countries like Indonesia, we *must* understand the complete ramifications and specific context of those reforms before we exert premature pressure that could lead to more problematic state collapse.

This chapter is structured in three main sections. First, the concept of the 'failed state' requires investigation as it is the conceptual linchpin for Western responses when reforms have failed in the developing world. Second, using the factors explored in the previous section as a framework, a brief survey of the events in Indonesia in the previous year appears to confirm that the viability of the state in question may be on the verge of failure. Finally, the unique role that ABRI plays in maintaining the resilience of the regime will be examined to understand further what makes some states resilient or less prone to catastrophic collapse, in addition to the problems this creates for reform.

FAILED STATES

The relatively recent phenomenon of 'failed states'[4] is of great interest to the international community, major regional players and neighbouring states for a number of reasons. In many cases, state failure propels the international community or regional organisations into lengthy peacekeeping or humanitarian missions in order to contain the resulting conflicts within the boundaries of the state or to prevent them from expanding into bordering or regional states. To take the example of West Africa, ethnic violence in Liberia has resulted in two separate peacekeeping missions being deployed as well as refugee problems and insurrections in Sierra Leone and Cote d'Ivoire.[5] The costs of such interventions are high and the deployments tend to be lengthy, as a whole host of social, political, economic and military organisations and infrastructures must either be rebuilt or created anew.[6] State meltdown, apparent or anticipated, may also cause investors to panic and further speed along the destabilising process.

Whilst the traits associated with failed states are obvious, such as the complete dissolution of government agencies, and widespread civil disorder and economic collapse, a full understanding of the causal relationships between the underlying elements that set the chain of failure in motion is often only possible in hindsight. In the example of Rwanda, the assassination of President Juvenal Habyarimana lit the pre-existing fuse of the Tutsi insurrection.[7] Most external observers were aware of the friction between the Hutus and Tutsis, and that an insurgent organisation existed, but few foresaw the extreme prejudice between both groups that manifested itself in the eventual massacres. Fewer still recognised just how fragile the Rwandan government really was. It is relatively easy after the fact to outline the linkages that led to the collapse of the Rwandan state, but in the case of Indonesia it is useful to understand the various factors that have until now *prevented* that state from failing.

The factors that can lead to loss of state legitimacy, which in turn leads to state failure, fall into three broad, yet interconnected, categories: economic, social and political. Economic factors that can undermine state legitimacy include the collapse of the national currency, the reliance on and draining of limited non-renewable natural resources for export, the rapid devaluation of the national stock exchange, unsound banking and trading policies and strategies, and the financing of large-scale state or private projects with high interest overseas loans. Social factors leading to state failure include inequitable ethnic and religious representation, historical ethnic grievances or divisions, and polar cultural distinctions. The political factors include the inability to protect or provide basic services for all levels of society, systemic corruption, little or no sense of nation, and an authoritarian or despotic system without options for change or legitimate succession. Many of these factors are interrelated and a combination of them, and not any one in particular, leads to a critical mass of pressures that overwhelm a weak state's atrophied or non-existent institutions. This 'critical mass' can be triggered by a single incident — as in Rwanda — or can take years to overwhelm the fragile state.

INDONESIA: A STATE ON THE BRINK OF FAILURE?

Based on a linear application of the criteria for state failure outlined above, Indonesia was (and continues to be) an authoritarian state that not only had discernible stress fractures, but seemed on the verge of a tectonic shift over the past two years. The executive authority of the state was either unwilling or unable to mobilise the resources to contain the fires which swept through Kalimantan, blanketing its neighbours in a potentially hazardous haze for several months. Maritime piracy in its internal waters remained unchecked, posing a threat to strategic international shipping passing through the Lombok, Sunda and Makassar Straits.[8] The Bre-X scandal affected investor confidence and reflected badly on Indonesia's mining sector. Internal conflicts continued in both Irian Jaya and East Timor, with increasing Western ostracisation and criticism as well as little hope for resolution.[9] The one area in which Indonesia's future continued to look promising was the economic sector, or so it seemed.

In strictly economic terms, the regional currency crisis that started in Thailand hit Indonesia extremely hard. The national currency, the *rupiah*, dropped significantly in value and currency speculators and stock market investors rushed to sell off their shares and currency, leading to a fall in the national stock index and further devaluation.[10] Over a dozen lending institutions without sufficient supporting capital went bankrupt and many loans for state projects, often in stable foreign currencies at high interest rates, pentupled in terms of debt owed due to the currency failure.[11]

The severe devaluation of the *rupiah* and subsequent economic fallout led to outbursts of socio-economic violence based on pre-existing tensions and appeared to confirm impressions that the state was descending into systemic failure.[12] Ethnic violence had mostly targeted businesses owned by ethnic Chinese,[13] who form a minority of the population but hold a majority of its wealth. As the shop owners raised prices to match the drop in the currency, many locals found that they could no longer afford basic staples such as rice. This led to food riots, attacks on shop owners, looting rampages and the flight of many ethnic Chinese and their capital. Currency devaluation and bankruptcy also led to higher unemployment in a country where much of the workforce was already underemployed,[14] further exacerbating social tensions. A more disturbing trend was the appearance of large numbers of economic refugees, who were sailing across the Malacca Straits in search of employment in neighbouring Malaysia.[15]

Domestic social and economic frustration led to unprecedented and relatively outspoken political criticism of both President Suharto, who led the country for some 32 years, and his immediate circle of advisers. Embodied in the acronym 'KKN', popular discontent focused on three attributes associated with the Suharto regime: corruption, cronyism and nepotism. Populist political leaders tapped into this discontent, drawing attention to the relatively low increase in the standard of living, the obvious growing wealth of Suharto's family and friends and the decreasing validity of the political process.[16] Additionally, the leaders of the largest Muslim organisations in the country called for greater legitimisation of Islam as the official religion of the state, whilst students echoed the calls of the political and religious leaders for Suharto to step down.[17] Suharto relented after a number of students were shot by police and widespread rioting broke out in many major urban centres throughout the island chain. Further, there were rumours of a power struggle between generals that almost erupted into a coup and civil war in the streets.[18]

THE SECURITY SECTOR IN INDONESIA: REGIME RESILIENCY AND ABRI'S ROLE

The brief portrait painted above of the bleak economic, social and political conditions in Indonesia over the past two years might give ardent supporters of the 'Coming Anarchy' thesis[19] cause to extend that argument to include Southeast Asia. Given the archipelagic geography of the state, a population of almost 200 million people and numerous ethnic and religious divisions spread out across 13,600 islands,[20] not to mention the stresses on the state discussed previously, one could easily have reached the conclusion that the Indonesian state would immediately collapse.[21] Although still wracked by protests and violence, the state has not failed and some economists and financial forecasters are predicting recovery in as little as three years, even if such optimism is based entirely on assumptions such as a stable currency and a status quo maintenance of economic policy.[22] The question remains as to how the Indonesian state has managed thus far to cope with the stresses that have driven other nations to ruin.

There are four predominant factors which account for Indonesia's relative stability. The first is the state's economic strength, including but not limited to relatively cheap labour costs and abundant natural resources such as oil, gas, timber and precious metals. The second is a comparatively small middle class sector of the population tied to the economic success of the state and with little to gain from political rebellion. The third factor contributing to Indonesia's stability is the speed with which neighbouring countries and the International Monetary Fund (IMF) put together an aid package to sustain the country in the near term, in order to maintain cohesion and buy time for the state to manage its problems. For the purposes of our discussion, however, the most important factor contributing to Indonesia's stability is the fourth, namely the role that ABRI plays in society. By incorporating ABRI in social, political and economic programmes over the past three decades, as well as focusing its efforts on internal threats to security and economic development, the 'New Order'[23] Indonesian state has attained a certain degree of resilience to overcoming the various stresses with which it was and continues to be faced. ABRI is not an armed force in the conventional Western sense of the definition; it challenges the Western definition of civil-military relations and actively participates in most civilian state endeavours.

To grasp the pervasiveness of ABRI's involvement in Indonesian society, it is necessary to understand its guiding philosophy of *dwi fungsi* and its development. Having won independence from the Dutch in 1949, Indonesia's political experiment with parliamentary democracy ended in a number of secessionist rebellions based on ethnic divisions within the country but carried out by regional commanders and their local forces. In addition, Sukarno's flirtation with the superpowers, confrontation with neighbouring states and relations with the domestic communist party played a role in the subsequent coup attempt and corresponding social upheaval and domestic violence in 1965. This convinced a number of senior military leaders, including the newly inaugurated President Suharto, that the regime needed to be strengthened from within.[24] ABRI would be the lead agency to provide not just stability, but through its dual role (*dwi fungsi*) as a socio-political force, also ensure the social, economic and political maturation of the state. *Dwi fungsi* serves another important purpose associated with nation-building and the preservation of the state: by engaging ABRI's leadership in its development and giving them a vested interest in its preservation, Suharto would not just ensure a degree of stability to allow the economic programmes to take root, but also bolster the stability of the presidency.[25]

Dwi fungsi assures that ABRI participates in most aspects of the Indonesian state, but this dispersed activity alone does not guarantee domestic security. The military's preoccupation with civilian activities could be a dangerous diversion in the face of a serious external threat. In the absence of such a credible threat, ABRI's primary focus has been on the internal destabilising impediments to economic development. The spectrum of impediments ranges from 'threats' to 'challenges'; it is broad enough to cover insurgencies, organised criminal activity and the importation of foreign values such as democratisation and human rights.[26] This expansive definition of security is akin to recent Western theoretical expansion of the security agenda to include such aspects as economic and environmental security.[27] ABRI not only views security in generous terms; its leaders also have a liberal view of the resources to be used to guarantee it. The national police, so visible during the most recent violence in Jakarta, were established as a fourth armed service in 1960 ostensibly to expand the state's presence 'down to the village level to maintain public security, order and tranquillity' throughout the archipelago.[28] Civilian participation in the security of the state is not just encouraged, it is expected and legally required in times of crisis.[29] Previous reports have suggested that ABRI employs large numbers of civilian informers to augment its intelligence as well as paramilitary 'demonstrators'. These have been lent further weight both by the publication of documents from East Timor as well as the release of figures of substantial numbers of volunteer 'disciplinarians' deployed in Jakarta to uphold the values of the state.[30]

The first and perhaps most important nation-building role of ABRI under *dwi fungsi* is as proselytiser, as well as enforcer, of the social values of the state. The five fundamental social values, the *Pancasila*, formed the basis of the 1945 Constitution and were enshrined as state policy in 1985. They include one God, humanitarian values, nationalism for the one state, popular sovereignty in a consultative democracy, and social justice.[31] All political and social organisations must subscribe to *Pancasila* and as a result, the state enjoys the ability to revoke their charters for violating any one of the values. ABRI not only conducts indoctrination seminars in the five values and provides training to civilian lecturers through its National Resilience Institute (Lemhanas), it also engages in civil-military action programmes to promote *Pancasila* down to the village level.[32] In addition, to gain public confidence and win 'the hearts and minds' of their own people, some ABRI units have devoted a portion of their training time to nation-building initiatives such as the drilling of wells and the construction of roads and schools.[33] The utility of some initiatives and the methods that certain ABRI units have used to enforce these 'national' values are questionable, but the spreading of the *Pancasila* message in conjunction with the adoption of a single language, Bahasa Indonesian, has created a degree of nationalism amongst the varied social groups of this ethnically and geographically diverse state.

The success ABRI has had in fostering a sense of nation is offset by its activities in commercial enterprises, a nation-building area that remains problematic. Partly through necessity and partly by design, ABRI's commercial activities have reinforced the economic development agenda of the 'New Order' and have alleviated the state from the burden of financial support for a sizeable military structure. As a result, ABRI receives from the state only a portion of its operational and maintenance budget, historically between one-half to one-third of its needs, and its officers and troops engage in a wide range of commercial activities to supplement the core budget and their own income.[34] These activities, which range from partnerships in resource exploitation to retail cooperatives at the individual unit level, are designed to generate income to fill the budgetary shortfall. Officers take business and management courses and develop contacts in the domestic economy. Links are especially numerous with the ethnic Chinese community, 'providing the Chinese with access to business opportunities and protection from a resentful society and the military with funds to supplement their meagre official budgets and to satisfy individual desires.'[35] In addition, ABRI officers are encouraged to 'facilitate' deals, namely, influencing contracts and resolving low-level trade disputes.[36] All of these activities are designed to prepare military officers for post-military careers in the commercial sector and tie their prosperity to that of the state, thereby further contributing to the state's economic development, as well as stabilising the economic sector by preventing unnecessary competition.

The theory of involving the military in the economic arena as a nation-building tool itself is perhaps sound, but in practice it is prone to abuse at all levels. Personnel are given free reign to run their business affairs, with no external supervision, and therefore the businesses are only as successful and honest as the individuals running them.[37] Corruption remains a problem and this was one of the reasons that the police, officially the fourth Indonesian armed service, did not have the respect of the students with whom they came into direct conflict in May 1998, leading indirectly to the sparking of the Jakarta riots. There have been noteworthy examples of gross fraud or inept mismanagement of ABRI-run commercial endeavours, such as the state-owned petroleum company Pertamina and National Logistics Board (Bulog) scandals of 1970. The amount of money siphoned off for personal use has never been revealed, presumably because of subsistence accounting and the embarrassment it would cause the government.[38] Official 'corruption' is accepted as a fact of life within Indonesia and was tolerated by both government and the expanding middle class during the 'New Order' because their individual standard of living and access to services continued to rise.[39]

Also accepted as a fact of life, although under some internal pressure for reform, is ABRI's role in domestic politics, the last of its *dwi fungsi* roles. ABRI founded and supports the state-sponsored majority *Golongan Karya* (Golkar) party that, along with two other predominant political parties, gives the state the trappings of a parliamentary system and therefore a shallow degree of democratic legitimacy. Formerly guaranteed one-fifth of all seats in the parliaments from the district through to the national level, when combined with the seats already occupied by Golkar members, ABRI ensures that presidential legislation is passed and more parochially, matters of defence are raised.[40] Another political role for ABRI is in the filling of civilian government posts. If key positions in other government organs remain empty even after presidential patronage appointments, then retired officers are appointed or ABRI staff seconded to fill them.[41] ABRI's role in domestic politics, however, has been waning for some time due to former President Suharto's strengthening of the civilian Golkar element to offset ABRI and keep it in check.[42]

Whilst suitably impressive when viewed from an organisational perspective, ABRI is not an authoritarian monolith;

it has substantial internal flaws and potentially grievous divisions. In the Byzantine world of Indonesian military politics encouraged by former President Suharto to keep potential rivals occupied, factionalism between nationalist and Muslim elements as well as careerism amongst elements of the officer corps create distrust, competition and unnecessary diversion of resources within ABRI.[43] Degrees of training and unit proficiency vary between units and there is an extent of inter- and intra-service rivalry for patronage, influence and resources. These shortcomings notwithstanding, the depth and breadth of ABRI's involvement in both the civilian and military spheres have provided a bulwark for the state against the substantial pressures of the past year.

SECURITY SECTOR REFORM IN INDONESIA

According to a Western understanding of the role of militaries in society, reforms would be undertaken immediately to divest ABRI of its civilian enterprises and internal defence role, assuming instead the shape of a defence force designed to deter or repel threats to state sovereignty. However desirable that might appear to outsiders, it would be impractical and inadvisable for Indonesia to do so in the near future, especially when both the state and its private sector are struggling to repay billions of dollars in debt. Indonesia simply cannot afford the substantial costs involved in both restructuring and re-equipping its armed forces for external defence, much less buy ABRI out of its substantial commercial concerns. The executive could conceivably order the immediate privatisation of all ABRI, and therefore state-owned, businesses, but such a move would be both political suicide and an invitation to a coup as well as a deeper retrenchment of the authoritarian system in place. To reform the security sector in Indonesia in order to conform to our model of what a security sector should be is to imply the reform of the entire structure of the Indonesian state. Not only is such a task well beyond the state's grasp in the near term and based on a number of questionable assumptions, but it is largely dependent on the personality, influence and popularity of the president.

It is not difficult to criticise ideas for security sector reform in Indonesia as quickly as they can be articulated, but such asides bring us no closer to a practical solution to the issue at hand. There are a number of reforms which can be undertaken, but it is essential to separate them into those that are feasible in the short term and those that will take longer to implement. Included below is a short list of potential reforms:

Near-Term Reforms

- Divesting the police from ABRI and remoulding it as a civilian force, subject to oversight from a civilian body including investigations into corruption and human rights abuses; [44]
- the removal of the ABRI from the domestic political realm, including but not limited to giving up its seats in both the People's Consultative Assembly and the House of People's Representatives; [45]
- the establishment of a non-partisan, civilian advisory board to oversee ABRI's commercial enterprises, creating greater transparency and suggesting methods by which ABRI eventually can be divested of its interests altogether; [46]
- the creation of a consultative group to resolve the security problems in East Timor and Irian Jaya, in exchange for the lifting of embargoes on surplus western military hardware and training to replace ageing equipment and assisting the progressive evolution of ABRI into a credible defensive force.[47]

Longer-Term Reforms

- Review and eventually downscale ABRI's *dwi fungsi* role to the point where civilian agencies and personnel are ultimately responsible for the spreading of *Pancasila*; [48]
- restore civilian confidence in and the legitimacy of the military by conducting an investigation similar to that carried out in South Africa, in order to distance ABRI from its involvement in the excesses of the previous regime; [49]
- downsize ABRI and create instead a more rapid reaction brigade that either could be deployed within the archipelago for territorial defence, in aid of the civil power or as part of a regional/ international peacekeeping initiative; [50]
- in conjunction with downsizing, expand and structure the civilian reserve programme into a credible force that can be mobilised in time of national crisis or in aid of the civil power;
- streamline the defence procurement process to ensure greater interoperability and commonality of systems, rather than relying on the

haphazard procurement of incompatible ones from numerous domestic and foreign suppliers;

- increase sizeably the number of aerial and maritime platforms for the Indonesian Navy and Air Force, to ensure unimpeded access of maritime traffic to sea lanes that pass through Indonesian waters and to protect sovereign maritime resources and territory.[51]

There are two discernable themes in the suggestions listed above but few surprises or radical ideas. The first theme is that ABRI should be scaled down and made more professional and conventional in outlook. The second is that civilian individuals and agencies should eventually relieve ABRI of most, if not all, of its civilian roles. There is an obvious need to retrench ABRI and relieve it of some of its domestic responsibilities, in order to provide for greater individual accountability and responsibility for its actions. Without reform, there is a possibility that individuals or factions within ABRI will seek to justify their role by quietly engineering incidents or crises. There have been allegations to suggest that elements within ABRI, rogue or otherwise, have instigated violence including the so-called 'ninja' attacks of October 1998.[52] By deliberately destabilising the rural areas, popular fear would rise, a crisis would develop and eventually ABRI would be required to provide security and reinforce its role as guardian of the people.

CONCLUSION

Many of the economic, political and social frictions that have combined to rend states apart have been ameliorated to date in Indonesia by foreign aid, promises of future reform as well as ABRI's presence within and role throughout the nation. Although ABRI is a bulwark against the various frictions and strains tearing at the fabric of the state, even the stoutest bulwarks can eventually give way given enough pressure. Whilst analysts and experts can understand the traits that contribute to state failure and identify states exhibiting them, such as Indonesia, even the most erudite observer cannot predetermine with any degree of certainty when, how or even if the event will occur.

The reasons for this inability to divine the collapse of states are due in large part to the complex interactions and interconnectivity between correlates that guide all human and, by extension, state endeavours. With this in mind, the multifaceted role that ABRI plays within Indonesia has been examined here to understand not only the ubiquitous nature of the state security apparatus that has provided a degree of regime resilience through its nation-building activities and presence in a number of other sectors. It has also been to contextualise the difficulties inherent in reforming ABRI to any great extent at any time in the near future. Finally, security sector reforms have been postulated and prioritised not according to their degree of desirability but rather to their degree of *achievability* given the pressures to which the Indonesian state is still subjected.

To restate the paradox of security sector reform in Indonesia from the beginning of this chapter, the very institution that contributes significantly to state stability and legitimacy is the one most in need of reform, yet to undertake substantial reforms could threaten the continued viability of the state itself. Knowing when internally to make reforms, or when Western leaders should press for such reforms, will be *the* critical issues should the Indonesian state remain solvent enough to implement them. A closing quote, from a news report during the height of the most recent street clashes, will doubtless muddy the waters further but will also underscore the complex and seemingly paradoxical nature of Indonesian civil-military relations:

> Students shouted and wept in shock, anger and fear ... 'You are killers! You are dogs!' they shouted ... In the light of small gasoline bombs, demonstrators danced and taunted lines of troops, running forward occasionally to hurl stones and then retreating ... unexpectedly ... a police officer walked into no-man's land outside the university's gate ... and offered a truce. Students poured from the university and embraced the startled riot policemen ... soon the students and policemen were sitting on the ground together in the thin yellow light of the street lamps. They sang the national anthem.[53]

Notes

1. Abel, Ben, 'A Javanese King Talks of His End', *Inside Indonesia* 54, (April-June 1998).
2. 'Asia's Coming Explosion', *The Economist* 346 (8056), p.17 (21 February 1998).
3. East, Colin, 'Who is Dr Habibie?', *Asia-Pacific Defence Reporter* 21 (4/5), pp.7-9 (October-November 1994).
4. Academically, the term 'failed states' has been revised and the term 'complex

emergencies' used instead, presumably to give a less negative connotation. See for example Helman, Gerald and Ratner, Steven, 'Saving Failed States', *Foreign Policy*, (89), pp.3-20 (Winter 1992-93); Munslow, Barry and Brown, Christopher, 'Complex emergencies and institutional complexes', *Contemporary Politics*, 3 (4), pp.307-320 (1997); and, Mackinlay, John and Kent, Randolph, 'A New Approach to Complex Emergencies', *International Peacekeeping*, 4 (4), pp.31-49 (Winter 1997).

5. The first peacekeeping mission was ECOMOG, led by the Economic Community of West African States (ECOWAS); the second was the UN-sponsored United Nations Observer Mission in Liberia (UNOMIL).
6. Whilst the approximate costs of the United Nations Advance Mission in Cambodia (UNAMIC) and the United Nations Transitional Authority in Cambodia (UNTAC), over US$1.5 billion, pales in comparison to the IMF financial bailout package put together for Indonesia (US$43 billion), one can only speculate as to the costs to the international community of an armed intervention, peacemaking and sustained nation building programme into a area of 1.9 million square kilometres (almost eight times the size of the United Kingdom) amongst a population of almost 200 million. Assessments for UNAMIC/UNTAC appear in Schear, James A. 'Riding the Tiger: The United Nations and Cambodia's Struggle for Peace' in Durch, William J. (ed.) *UN Peacekeeping, American Policy and the Uncivil Wars of the 1990s*, p.177, St. Martin's Press, New York (1997).
7. Hunter, Thomas, 'Manportable SAMs: the airline anathema', *Jane's Intelligence Review* 8 (10), p.474 (October 1996).
8. The Indonesian archipelago straddles important sea lanes between Japan and Europe and the Middle East, Japan being dependent for the supply of over three-quarters of its petroleum imports through these routes. In a display of sovereignty over its archipelagic waters, Indonesia has legally, but not physically, closed one or more of the straits on numerous occasions, the most recent of which was in 1988. Although there is little agreement on the impact to regional and global trade should one or more of these 'chokepoints' be rendered unnavigable for an extended period of time, their potential closure has warranted more than one study of the consequences. See Noer, John and Gregory, David, *Chokepoints: Maritime Economic Concerns in Southeast Asia*, National Defense University Press, Washington (1996); and Kenny, Henry, *An Analysis of Possible Threats to Shipping in Key Southeast Asian Sea Lanes*, CNA Occasional Paper, Alexandria, Center for Naval Analyses (February 1996).
9. Peel, Quentin, and Thoenes, Sander, 'Regime tarnished by man-made calamities', *Financial Times*, p.I (24 November 1997); Counsell, Anne, 'Investor confidence has been shaken' *Financial Times*, p.III (24 November 1997); and 1997 IMB piracy statistics for Southeast Asia are included in Binnendijk, Hans, (ed.), *1998 Strategic Assessment: Engaging Power for Peace*, pp.208-209, National Defense University

Press, Washington (1998).

10. Thoenes, Sander, 'Fire and brimstone', *Financial Times*, p.75 (8 October 1997); and Thoenes, Sander, 'Domestic debt crisis mounts in Indonesia', *Financial Times*, p.7 (6 March 1998)
11. 'Once again, Indonesia starts living dangerously', *The Economist* 346 (8056), p.75 (21 February 1998).
12. Resentment of Chinese wealth and their historic role between local islanders and the ruling Dutch colonial administration has fuelled periodic violence at least as far back as 1740. Frederick, William and Worden, Robert (eds.), *Indonesia: A Country Study*, pp.30, 57, 288, Fifth Edition, US Department of the Army, Washington (1993).
13. Ethnic Chinese is the generic term, although there is an Indonesian linguistic differentiation between integrated Chinese (*peranankan*) and those of purely Chinese ancestry (*totok*). Skinner, G. William, 'The Chinese Minority', in McVey, Ruth, (ed.), *Indonesia*, pp.105-106, HRAF Press, New Haven (1963). For a more recent and substantive exploration of the subject, see Coppel, Charles, *Indonesian Chinese in Crisis*, Oxford University Press, Kuala Lumpur (1983).
14. Frederick and Worden, *Indonesia*, p.164.
15. 'Indons seeking jobs in M'sia, boat capsizes', *KITLV Daily Report* (4 March 1998), gopher://oasis.leidenuniv.nl:71/00/kitlv/daily-report/980309.TXT
16. First Suharto and now Habibie are targets for opposition campaigning against KKN. Megawati has singled out corruption in particular as a 'fungus' that 'we must destroy'. 'Sukarno's Daughter Hits a Nerve: Indonesian Opposition Leader Campaigns on Plight of the Poor', *International Herald Tribune*, p.4 (9 October 1998). On Suharto family wealth, see 'Indonesian government says Suharto has $2.6 million in accounts', *Nando Times* (16 November 1998), http://www.nando.net/newsroom/ntn/world/111698/world 34_12099_S1_noframes.html; and Glass, Charles, 'They no longer rule — but they still rule the country,' *The Sunday Telegraph*, p.32 (24 May 1998).
17. Sheridan, Michael, 'Muslims mobilise to oust Suharto', *The Sunday Times*, p.19 (8 March 1998).
18. Sheridan, Michael, 'The day civil war simmered in Indonesia', *The Sunday Times*, p.26 (8 November 1998).
19. 'How scarcity, crime, overpopulation, tribalism, and disease are rapidly destroying the social fabric of our planet'. Kaplan, Robert, 'The Coming Anarchy', *The Atlantic Monthly*, 273 (2), p.44 (February 1994).
20. Figures on the number of islands that comprise the Indonesian archipelago vary from 13,600 to as many as 17,000. I have chosen the figure in Frederick and Worden, *Indonesia*, pp.xxx, 354-356.
21. The 'nightmare' collapse scenario for Indonesia, however improbable, would be if the 'peripheral' islands and territories declared their political and economic

independence from 'central' Java. The population-dense but resource poor Java could then conceivably descend into ethnic factionalism and chaos. A variation of this scenario has and continues to haunt Indonesia's senior leadership over the future of East Timor, as it is believed that if and when a precedent for secession has been set, other territories such as Irian Jaya and Aceh will follow suit and could spur even more dubious secessionist movements (the South Moluccans) into doing the same.

22. Richardson, Michael, 'Prospects of a Recovery Brighten for Indonesia', *International Herald Tribune*, pp.1, 7 (2 November 1998).
23. 'New Order' refers to policies of nation building through economic development during the reign of President Suharto (1967-1998); prior to that, the 'Guided Democracy' (1959-1966) of President Sukarno was characterised by more nationalist policies.
24. Major General Abdul Haris Nasution is widely regarded as the intellectual father of the *dwi fungsi* concept. Crouch, Harold, *The Army and Politics of Indonesia*, Revised edition, pp.24-25, Cornell University Press, Ithaca (1988).
25. A characteristic of Suharto's political management style was an adroit manipulation of groups and individuals who could challenge or overthrow him. Crouch, *The Army and Politics of Indonesia*, pp.39-40; and Lowry, Robert, *The Armed Forces of Indonesia*, pp.135-136, Allen & Unwin, St. Leonards (1996).
26. As a measure of the scope of security challenges identified by Indonesian military leaders, poverty is also identified as a threat to the stability of the regime, as it can lead to unrest and the withdrawal of foreign aid. It should also be noted that communism, long considered by ABRI leaders as the primary threat to the state, is still used a justification for riots and other disturbances. Lowry, Robert, *Indonesian Defence Policy and the Indonesian Armed Forces*, pp.10-11, Canberra Papers on Strategy and Defence No. 99, Strategic and Defence Studies Centre, Canberra (1993).
27. See for example Dupont, Alan, 'New Dimensions of Security', in Roy, Denny, (ed.), *The New Security Agenda in the Asia-Pacific Region*, pp.31-50, St. Martin's Press, New York (1997).
28. The incorporation of the police also served to counterbalance the expanded influence ABRI gained after quelling the PRRI rebellion from 1958-1961. According to the White Paper, the force ratio of police to civilians should be 1:750. Haseman, John, 'Police could separate from Indonesian forces', *Jane's Defence Weekly*, 30 (18), p.15 (4 Nov 1998); and *The Policy of the State Defence and Security of the Republic of Indonesia*, pp.31, 34.
29. Haseman, John, 'Indonesia counts civilian assets in state defence', *Jane's Defence Weekly*, 27 (7), p.12 (19 Feb 1997).
30. Lowry, Robert, 'Indonesia plans its defence', *Asia-Pacific Defence Reporter*, 24

(1), p.8 (December 1997-January 1998).

31. Adiwijoyo, Brigadier General Suwarno, (ed.) *ABRI: Patriot and Soldier*, p.1, Jakarta, ABRI Headquarters (1995).
32. Lowry, *The Armed Forces of Indonesia*, pp.202-203.
33. *The Policy of the State Defence and Security of the Republic of Indonesia*, pp.52-54, Jakarta, Department of Defence and Security (1995).
34. Frederick and Worden, *Indonesia*, pp.298-301; Crouch, *The Army and Politics of Indonesia*, p.274; and Lowry, *The Armed Forces of Indonesia*, p.134.
35. The scope of such activities is extensive. Business ventures range from individuals hiring out equipment for a variety of tasks to ownership of holding companies. Lowry, *The Armed Forces of Indonesia*, pp.134-136; and Frederick and Worden, *Indonesia*, p.300.
36. Lowry, *The Armed Forces of Indonesia*, pp.141-142.
37. Such business activities are tolerated officially 'as long as it was within "acceptable limits"', although the question remains as to whom. Frederick and Worden, *Indonesia*, p.301; and Lowry, *The Armed Forces of Indonesia*, pp.144-145.
38. Crouch, *The Army and Politics of Indonesia*, pp.275-281.
39. Uhlin, Anders, *Indonesia and the 'Third Wave of Democratization': The Indonesian Pro-Democracy Movement in a Changing World*, p.46, St. Martin's Press, New York (1997).
40. Frederick and Worden, *Indonesia*, p.297; and Lowry, *The Armed Forces of Indonesia*, pp.182-183.
41. Lowry, *The Armed Forces of Indonesia*, pp.187-188.
42. Cronin, Patrick, and Ott, Marvin, 'The Indonesian Armed Forces (ABRI): Role, Prospect and Implications', *Strategic Forum*, (126), p.2 (August 1997).
43. Ott and Cronin, 'The Indonesian Armed Forces (ABRI)', p.2.
44. One part of this suggested reform, the removal of the police from the military structure, is already under serious consideration, although which organisation will be responsible for this police is undetermined. Haseman, *Police could separate from Indonesian forces*, p.15.
45. This reform has been suggested and ABRI's Chief of Staff recently declared that initial steps have been taken (the dissolution of the position of Chief of the Socio-Political Division), but the question of when and how ABRI will extract itself fully from politics has yet to be addressed. 'Parliament Convenes Amid Massive Protests', *Pinkerton Weekly Intelligence Summary*, 15 (46), (13 November 1998); and 'To stop polemics on military in parliament, Armed Forces must take initiative', *Kompas Online* (11 November 1998), http://www.kompas.com/kompas-cetak/9811/11/ENGLISH/arme.htm.
46. Lowry, *The Armed Forces of Indonesia*, p.144.
47. The speed with which President Habibie has sought to place the East Timor and

Irian Jaya issues on the agenda is understood to be a tactic to spur further foreign aid. One potential problem is that activists in East Timor are utilising their recent 'freedoms' to increase pressure on the Indonesian government for a referendum, something that neither Habibie or the ABRI leadership has been readily willing to grant. On the restructuring of ABRI along 'defensive' lines and the acquisition of more modern and compatible platforms, well-intentioned yet perhaps misinformed individuals will see this as further contributing to the 'arms race in Asia'. In reality, such acquisitions will contribute to the professionalism of the armed forces and safeguard national sovereignty, but will not compel neighbouring states to purchase with non-existent funds to achieve parity. To highlight ABRI's shortcomings, in an incident in July 1998 the Indonesian Navy was unable to locate or intercept a private vessel illegally fishing in Australian waters that repeatedly rammed a pursuing Australian naval vessel. McKinnon, Michael, 'Warship rammed by Indonesian boat', *The Australian*, (17 July 1998), http://www.theaustralian.com/au/world/4141432.htm; Frei, Matt, 'Rise in tension threatens peace in East Timor', *Sunday Telegraph*, p.35 (8 November 1998); and on suggestions 'to achieve genuine security' in the region, see Friedman, Jordana, 'Asia's Military Budget', *International Herald Tribune*, p.11 (5 November 1998).

48. Students have called for ABRI to relinquish its *dwi fungsi* role. During the period of new freedom in 1994 however 'some journalists may have misread the apparent atmosphere of openness and gone too far in exercising their rights to free speech.' Alatas, Syed Fahid, *Democracy and Authoritarianism in Indonesia and Malaysia: The Rise of the Post-Colonial State*, p.158, St. Martin's Press, New York (1997); 'Starting, Friction Between Pro And Contra Of The MPR Special Session', *Kompas Online* (10 November 1998), http://www.kompas.com/kompas-cetak/9811/10/ENGLISH/kompas.htm.
49. The Truth and Reconciliation Commission (TRC) of South Africa was established to examine abuses by the South African Defence Forces, African National Congress and Inkatha during the Apartheid era. The end result was amnesty for those who sought it and testified before the Commission, but more importantly as the title suggests, led to national reconciliation between former adversaries. For more details see http://www.truth.org.za. On the issue of the importance of legitimacy and civilian perceptions of ABRI, see Haseman, John, 'Credibility Gap,' *Jane's Defence Weekly*, 30 (20), pp.25-27 (18 November 1998); and Mydans, Seth, 'Indonesia's Military Is Losing an Image Battle,' *International Herald Tribune*, pp.1, 7 (16 November 1998).
50. A nascent rapid reaction capability has existed in Indonesia since 1984, although it was recently dealt a severe blow when the order for Russian Mi-8 helicopters was cancelled as a result of the currency crisis. The rapid reaction brigades suggested here would not only be more numerous but have integral support elements and command structure. Huxley, Tim, 'Indonesia's armed forces face up to new threats,'

Jane's Intelligence Review, 9 (1), p.37 (January 1997).

51. Lowry, Robert, 'Questions for Indonesia's ABRI in the democratic era', *Asia-Pacific Defence Reporter*, 24 (5), p.7 (August – September 1998).
52. Uhlin, *Indonesia and the 'Third Wave of Democratization'*, p.51; and Sheridan, Michael, 'Army's ninja killers terrorise Indonesia', *The Sunday Times*, p.23 (23 October 1998).
53. Mydans, Seth, '6 Dead on a Bloody Night in Jakarta,' *International Herald Tribune*, p.4 (14-15 November 1998).